CONIECTANEA BIBLICA • NEW TESTAMENT SERIES 40

To Prof. Hans Dieter Betz.
Best wishes from Lund,
   Runar M Thorsteinsson

CB

CONIECTANEA BIBLICA
NEW TESTAMENT SERIES
40

Present editors:
Birger Olsson (Lund) and Kari Syreeni (Uppsala)

Paul's Interlocutor
in Romans 2

Function and Identity
in the Context of Ancient Epistolography

RUNAR M. THORSTEINSSON

Almqvist & Wiksell International
Stockholm, Sweden

2003

Abstract
Thorsteinsson, Runar M. 2003. Paul's Interlocutor in Romans 2: Function and Identity in the Context of Ancient Epistolography. Coniectanea Biblica. New Testament Series 40. 283 pp. Monograph. Dissertation Lund University. ISBN 91-22-02047-0.

Romans 2 has long been a *crux interpretum*. Among matters of dispute is the function and identity of Paul's interlocutor(s) in the chapter. While scholars agree that the individual addressed in 2:17–29 is a Jew, there is no such consensus with respect to the identity of the person addressed in 2:1–5. On the one hand, the scholarly majority holds that this person is depicted as a Jew and that the same interlocutor is involved throughout the chapter. A weighty minority, on the other hand, argues that the individual addressed in 2:1–5 is a gentile and that there is a shift of interlocutor in 2:17. The former interpretation largely fails to do justice to a linear reading of the letter, whereas the latter appears to neglect the continuous and progressive flow of Paul's discourse in chapter 2. A fresh approach is needed in which these shortcomings are addressed.

This study seeks to allow the larger context and framework of Romans to be of help in assessing the function and identity of Paul's interlocutor(s) in chapter 2. The epistolary structure and setting of Romans is first investigated in order to determine what factors relating to that structure and setting may inform us about the relationship between Paul and the Roman recipients. The identity of the people to whom Paul wrote his letter is then considered. The utilization of interlocutors by Greco-Roman epistolographers is also assessed and compared to Paul's use of a dialogical style in Romans 2–11. In view of these aspects of the larger context and framework of the letter, an attempt is made to ascertain the function and identity of Paul's interlocutor(s) in Romans 2.

It is concluded that Paul wrote Romans to a particular group of people in a specific, contemporaneous situation. The letter's message arose out of the relationship between Paul as an apostle to the gentiles and the Roman audience as subject to this commission of his. Paul wrote the letter exclusively to people of non-Jewish origin. His use of a dialogical style in Romans 2–11 has parallels in other letters from Greco-Roman antiquity, in which fictitious interlocutors normally represent or speak for the letter's recipient(s) and remain the same throughout the discourse. A linear reading of Romans 1–2 strongly suggests that Paul's interlocutor in 2:1–5 is a gentile, and that the address to this very person is resumed in 2:17. Contrary to common opinion, the imaginary individual addressed in 2:17–29 is not a (native) Jew, but a gentile who wants to call himself a Jew. The Roman readers are meant to correlate their own views with the gentile interlocutor's.

Key Words
Bible, New Testament, Paul, Romans, Romans 2, interlocutor, epistolography, Greco-Roman letters, epistolary analysis, epistolary structure, epistolary setting, audience, dialogical style, diatribe, identity, function, gentiles, Jews, proselytes, Judaism, circumcision, Jewish Law, Rome.

© Runar M. Thorsteinsson
Published by Almqvist & Wiksell International, Stockholm
Printed at Studentlitteratur, Lund 2003   ISBN 91-22-02047-0

Preface

"'His letters,' they say, 'are weighty and powerful'" (2 Cor 10:10). Though "absent in body," Paul the apostle has been "present in spirit" (1 Cor 5:3) for little less than twenty centuries through his weighty and powerful letters. This doctoral dissertation is the result of my wrestling with Paul's most fascinating, influential, and yet intricate text—his letter to the Romans.

A number of people have added to the quality of this study and made its publication possible. It is a joy to have the opportunity to express my thanks to them in writing. Above all, I wish to thank my supervisor, Prof. Birger Olsson (now em.), whose experienced scholarship, open-mindedness, and constant encouragement has proved to be invaluable to me during both the preparation and composition of this dissertation. A wholehearted man, he has been a true *Doktorvater*. For that I am deeply grateful.

My sincere thanks go to my colleague Dr. Dieter Mitternacht for kindly reading and commenting on an earlier draft of this thesis. His methodological insight and constructive criticism have enriched the quality of the work considerably. He has also generously helped me with the layout of this book. For all this I am truly thankful.

Thanks are due to the Senior New Testament Seminar at Lund University for useful discussions at various stages of the study. In particular, I wish to thank Prof. Bengt Holmberg, Prof. em. René Kieffer, and Assoc. Prof. Walter Übelacker for their interest in and comments on my work.

I am grateful to Dr. Clarence E. Glad for a number of valuable suggestions, and for improving my English. Needless to say, any mistakes remain my own.

I am indebted to the Centre for Theology and Religious Studies at Lund University for granting me a scholarship during the past four years. Thanks are due to the competent staff at Lund's University Library, and especially librarian Leif Lindin and his team at the Centre for Theology and Religious Studies. I wish to express my thanks also to the editors of the Coniectanea Biblica New Testament Series, Prof. em. Birger Olsson and Prof. Kari Syreeni, for including the present study in the series.

No man is an island and no research is done in isolation from life itself. My closest relatives have helped me in so many ways to make the completion of this work possible. Thanks to you all.

Last but not least I wish to express my deepest gratitude to my wife, Silla, and our two wonderful children, Sigrún Rut and Dagur Hrafn. Though present in body, I have been largely absent "in spirit" as a husband and a father for quite some time. I thank them for their patience during this strenuous period. Without the love and support of my wife and partner-in-life for seventeen years, my wrestling would not have been brought to fruition but remained in my dreams only. As a small token of my thankfulness, I wish to dedicate this book to her.

Lund, October 4, 2003
Runar M. Thorsteinsson

To Silla

Contents

Introduction 1

1. Paul's Interlocutor(s) in Romans 2: The Scholarly Debate . . . 1
2. A Macrostructural, Author-Audience Relational Approach: The Context of Ancient Epistolography 5
3. The Procedure of the Study 10

Chapter One

The Epistolary Structure and Setting of Romans 13

Introduction 13

1. Epistolary Structure in Greco-Roman Antiquity 18
    1.1. Epistolary Opening 19
    1.2. Epistolary Closing 22
    1.3. Epistolary Body 22
2. Epistolary Structure of Paul's Letters: Three, Four, or Five Letter Parts? 24

3. Epistolary Structure of Romans 31
   3.1. Epistolary Opening (1:1–7). 31
      3.1.1. The Superscription (1:1) and the Identification of the Sender 32
      3.1.2. The Opening Extension (1:2–6) and the Εὐαγγέλιον Θεοῦ 34
      3.1.3. The Adscription (1:7a) and the Identification of the Recipients 37
   3.2. Epistolary Body (1:8–15:33) 39
      3.2.1. The Transition To and Beginning of the Body . . 41
      3.2.2. The Παρακαλῶ Sentence in 12:1–2 47
      3.2.3. The Confidence Expression and Visiting Theme in 15:14–29 54
      3.2.4. The Παρακαλῶ Sentence in 15:30–32 and the Closing of the Body (15:33) 58
   3.3. Epistolary Closing (16:1–24) 60
      3.3.1. The Introduction of Phoebe (16:1–2) 61
      3.3.2. Closing Greetings (16:3–16, 21–23). 63
      3.3.3. The Admonition in 16:17–20: A Foreign Text? . . 66
4. Epistolary Setting of Romans 70
   4.1. Classifications of Ancient Letters: Some Problems and Benefits 71
   4.2. Ancient Epistolary Settings and Paul's Letter to the Romans 74
      4.2.1. Fictitious Settings and Paul's Letter 75
      4.2.2. Extended Settings and Paul's Letter 76
      4.2.3. Normative Settings and Paul's Letter 82
Concluding Summary. 84

Chapter Two

The Intended Audience of Romans. 87

Introduction 87

1. Presuppositions in the Study of Paul's Audience: The Composition of "Roman Christianity". 91

    1.1. Romans 14–15 and the Claudian Edict 92

    1.2. Paul's Greetings in Romans 16 98

    1.3. The Distinction between the Composition of "Roman Christianity" and Paul's Intended Audience 99

2. Paul's Intended Audience according to Romans. 100

    2.1. Explicit References to the Letter's Audience 102

        2.1.1. Romans 1:5–7 102

        2.1.2. Romans 1:13–14a, 14b–15 106

        2.1.3. Romans 11:13 109

        2.1.4. Romans 15:15–16 111

    2.2. Implicit References to the Letter's Audience 113

        2.2.1. Jewish Issues and Scriptural References in Romans. 114

        2.2.2. Various Potential References to the Letter's Audience 116

Concluding Summary 121

Chapter Three

The Dialogical Style and Epistolary Interlocutor in Romans 2–11 123

Introduction 123

1. Paul's Letter and the Greco-Roman "Diatribe" 124
    1.1. Basic Characteristics of the "Diatribe" Style 125
    1.2. Identifying the "Diatribal" Interlocutor: The Problem of Distinct Settings 126
2. The Ancient Letter as a "Kind of Written Conversation" . . . 131
3. Epistolary Interlocutors in Greco-Roman Antiquity 134
    3.1. Formal Features of Epistolary Interlocutors 135
    3.2. Function and Identity of Epistolary Interlocutors . . . 140
4. The Epistolary Interlocutor in Romans 2–11: Macrostructural Aspects 145

Concluding Summary 149

Chapter Four

Paul's Interlocutor in Romans 2 151

Introduction 151

1. Continuity in Romans 2 152
    1.1. The Unity and Immediate Context of Romans 2:6–16 . 153

    1.2. Romans 2:17–29 as a Resumption of Paul's Address in
        2:1–5 159
2. The Identity of Paul's Interlocutor in Romans 2 165
    2.1. Paul's Indictment of Gentiles in Romans 1:18–32. . . . 165
        2.1.1. Paul's Indictment as a Characteristic Jewish
            Polemic. 167
        2.1.2. The Gentile Condition 173
    2.2. Paul's Gentile Interlocutor in Romans 2:1–5 177
        2.2.1. The Διό Debate: The Connection between
            Romans 2:1 and 1:18–32. 177
        2.2.2. The Gentile Identity of Paul's Interlocutor in
            Romans 2:1–5 188
        2.2.3. Paul's Gentile Interlocutor and Judgment
            according to Deeds (2:6–16) 194
    2.3. Paul's Gentile Interlocutor in Romans 2:17–29 196
        2.3.1. A Gentile Who Wants to Call Himself a Jew
            (2:17a) 197
        2.3.2. Jewishness vis-à-vis Gentiles (2:17–20) 204
        2.3.3. A Transgressor of the Law (2:21–24) 211
        2.3.4. The Value of Circumcision for the Gentile
            Interlocutor (2:25–29) 221
3. The Function of Paul's Interlocutor in Romans 2 231
4. Implications for the Subsequent Discourse in Romans 234
    4.1. The Meaning of the Verb Προητιασάμεθα in Romans
        3:9 235
    4.2. Function and Identity of Paul's Interlocutor in the
        Subsequent Dialogical Exchanges 236

Conclusions 243

Bibliography 247

1. Primary Sources 247
2. Lexica and Tools 250
3. Secondary Sources 251

Index of Names 277

Introduction

> *The relationship between Paul and the congregation at Rome seems to be other than scholars have assumed, and no simple readjustment of our old notions is likely to bring it into focus. . . . [S]omething in our usual interpretation of Romans is wrong.*[1]

1. Paul's Interlocutor(s) in Romans 2: The Scholarly Debate

As "one of the most puzzling pieces of Pauline writing,"[2] Romans 2 has long stood up to scholarly efforts to explain both its meaning and presence in Paul's letter. Because it does not easily "fit the system,"[3] this "stumblingblock for the Lutheran interpretation of Paul"[4] and "Achilles heel of schemes on Paul and the Law"[5] has repeatedly been set aside in Pauline studies. In his survey of the history of interpretation of the chapter, Klyne R. Snodgrass remarks that "even where this text has been discussed, more time has been spent explaining the text *away* than explaining it."[6] This is

---

[1] Mullins, "Greeting" (1968) 426.
[2] Segal, *Paul* (1990) 258.
[3] See Snodgrass, "Justification" (1986) 72–73.
[4] Watson, *Paul* (1986) 109. Cf. Boyarin, *Jew* (1994) 87: "a stone ignored by the builders of Reformation Paulinism."
[5] Wright, "Law" (1996) 132.
[6] "Justification" (1986) 73 (emphasis his). Snodgrass also notes: "An important criterion by which any explanation of Paul's thought or of Romans can be judged is the question 'What does the explanation do with the pieces that do not fit?' The

the case, for example, in E. P. Sanders' influential work *Paul, the Law, and the Jewish People* in which he treats Romans 2 separately in an appendix, viewing it as a non-Pauline synagogue sermon incompatible with the rest of Paul's thought. "[W]hy is the chapter in Romans at all?" he wonders.[7] Many a commentator on Paul's letter pays no more than obligatory attention to its second chapter which, as Snodgrass complains, "has often been lost in the shuffle as people move quickly from the description of human sin in 1.18 f. to the proclamation of the righteousness of God in 3.21 f."[8] Or, as Stanley K. Stowers puts it, "[c]ommentators are so clear about their destination at 3:9 ('all are sinners in need of Christ') that they tend to fly over chapter 2 quickly and at a high altitude, seeing only the message of 3:9 being worked out."[9] No wonder N. T. Wright calls Romans 2 "the joker in the pack."[10]

The problems encountered in Romans 2 are diverse. Not only does the chapter contain viewpoints which have widely been regarded as incongruous both with other parts of the letter and with "Pauline thought" at large, but the presence of a conversational partner or partners whom Paul addresses directly in the chapter has also given rise to an unsettled scholarly debate. The way in which this or these interlocutors were meant to function for Paul's audience, the relationship between the person addressed in

---

pieces that do not appear to fit are telling criticisms of the inadequacy of our 'systems'. When pieces have been omitted, other components of the 'system' are stretched and overworked, and as a result various problems emerge because the whole 'system' is thrown off balance" (p. 72).

[7] *Paul* (1983) 123–35 (quotation on p. 131). More specifically, Sanders takes 1:18–2:29 to constitute such a sermon. According to him, there are not only "internal inconsistencies within the section" but "chapter 2 cannot be harmonized with any of the diverse things which Paul says about the law elsewhere" (p. 123). Further, there is "no distinctively Pauline imprint in 1:18–2:29, apart from the tag in 2:16. Christians are not in mind, the Christian viewpoint plays no role, and the entire chapter is written from a Jewish perspective" (p. 129). In other words, "in Romans 2 we are dealing with a point of view which at no point reflects specifically Christian thinking" (pp. 131–32).

[8] "Justification" (1986) 72.

[9] *Rereading* (1994) 126.

[10] "Law" (1996) 131.

2:1–5 and the one addressed in 2:17–29, and especially the identity of this or these individuals is currently a matter of dispute. While all facets of Romans 2 are textually interrelated, the present study will mainly be concerned with the function and identity of Paul's interlocutor(s) in the chapter.

Until recently, most readers of Romans have been comfortably content with the centuries old Christian tradition of taking chapter 2 as Paul's cutting critique of Jews and Judaism. C. H. Dodd, for instance, claimed in his comments on Romans 2 some seventy years ago that there is "evidence enough of the terrible degradation of Jewish morals in the period preceding the Destruction of the Temple."[11] Several decades later, Herman Ridderbos spoke of Romans 2:1–3:20 as "the great indictment of Judaism," the section in 2:1–12 being a "telling accusation."[12] Even today, one may come across the view that Romans 2 is "perhaps the most extensive and direct critique of Jews and Judaism in the letters of Paul."[13] However, due to an enriched knowledge of Second Temple Judaism and growing awareness of Paul's own Jewishness as well as greater acknowledgment of his mission being aimed (primarily) at non-Jews, scholars are now gradually beginning to recognize the inadequacy of such readings.

And yet, old perspectives still prevail. Although few would consent to Dodd's unfounded claims about pre-70 C.E. Jewish morality, a number of scholars tend to read Romans 2 through the lens of Jesus' censure of "hypocritical Pharisees" recorded in Christian writings of a later date, which by generalization is then applied to Jews at large. Thus, James D. G. Dunn holds that Paul's interlocutor throughout Romans 2 is "the typical Jew . . . that is, the Jew per se," whose views are largely "applicable to the sort of attitude among the Pharisees already criticized within the Jesus tradition." Paul is attacking "what he sees to be a typically Jewish attitude," viz. that of the pre-Christian Paul himself, "Paul the unconverted Pharisee."[14] Similarly, Wright asserts that "[i]n addressing 'the Jew' [in 2:17]

---

[11] *Romans* (1932) 39.
[12] Cited in Sanders, *Paul* (1983) 124.
[13] Carras, "Romans 2,1–29" (1992) 185.
[14] *Romans* (1988) 1.80, 90–91, 109. See further Ch. 4 sec. 2.2.1 below.

Paul was, of course, talking to his own former self."[15] The image of the "self-righteous Jew"[16] is so fixed that even a prominent scholar such as C. E. B. Cranfield finds it only "natural to assume that Paul is apostrophizing the typical Jew in 2.1ff," considering it "clear" also that Paul is addressing such a "typical Jew" in 2:17–29.[17] But if this has seemed clear to commentators, the question whether the Jewish interlocutor was meant to represent the Jewish nation as a whole or just a portion of it has not. Indeed, how some of Paul's charges against the interlocutor in 2:17–29 could either have applied to Jews at large or to specific Jewish groups or to certain individuals is a well-known point of controversy.

Whereas opinions differ on the representative function of the interlocutor in 2:17–29, all seem to agree that this person is depicted as a Jew. What is disputed is whether or not this "Jew" is already in view in 2:1–5. The scholarly majority holds that, subsequent to the indictment (mainly) of gentiles in 1:18–32, Paul addresses a Jewish interlocutor in 2:1, the identity of whom becomes explicit in 2:17 with the word Ἰουδαῖος.[18] A weighty minority, however, argues that the person addressed in 2:1–5 is not a Jew but a gentile, and that it is first in 2:17 that Paul aims his words at a Jewish interlocutor.[19] The main problem with the former approach is its neglect of reading the text linearly, neither providing any adequate explanation of the logical connection between 2:1 and the foregoing nor offering legitimate reasons for reading the "Jew" of 2:17–29 back into 2:1–5. The latter approach, on the other hand, fails to account for the relationship between the persons addressed in 2:1–5 and 2:17–29, largely overlooking the continuous and progressive flow of the text. Neither approach pays sufficient attention to the wording εἰ δὲ σὺ Ἰουδαῖος ἐπονομάζῃ in 2:17 within its immediate context. I will attempt to meet these flaws in my reading of Romans 2 in this dissertation.

---

[15] "Letter" (2002) 445. Cf. Wilckens, *Römer* (1978) 1.151; McKnight, *Light* (1991) 105, 153 n. 21.
[16] Barrett, *Romans* (1957) 55.
[17] *Romans* (1975) 1.137–38.
[18] So most standard commentaries. The scholarly discussion will be presented in more details in Ch. 4 below.
[19] See esp. Elliott, *Rhetoric* (1990); Stowers, *Rereading* (1994).

But interpretations of Romans 2 are not only entangled by certain presuppositions about Jews and Judaism and polarized approaches to the text. They are further complicated by widespread disagreements about the form and function of Paul's letter as a whole, its occasion and purpose, and its intended audience. Furthermore, although interpreters customarily note that Paul is utilizing the literary technique of the Greco-Roman "diatribe" in chapter 2, few pay much heed to the question what that in effect means for Paul's discourse, for what purposes this technique was used in antiquity, and how it was employed in letters specifically. All these features relate to the function and identity of Paul's interlocutor(s) in Romans 2 and must therefore be attended to. Since the functional aspect has been well treated by others,[20] and because the scholarly debate centers upon the question of identity, it is chiefly the latter that will be under scrutiny in this study.

2. A Macrostructural, Author-Audience Relational Approach: The Context of Ancient Epistolography

In my approach to Romans 2, the letter's larger context and framework are allowed to carry considerable weight. That means that features such as the letter's macrostructure (i.e. the way in which the letter functions as a whole), the letter's original setting, its intended audience, and specific literary traits are taken into account as decisive for determining the function and identity of Paul's interlocutor(s). In other words, the part focused upon is taken to be largely conditioned by the whole,[21] the latter of which per-

---

[20] Esp. Stowers, *Diatribe* (1981). See further Ch. 3 below.
[21] Of course, one has to be conscious of the circular processes inevitably present in readings of ancient texts like Rom. For instance, while the text's parts must be understood in terms of the whole, an understanding of the text as a whole is dependent upon the parts. Such "hermeneutical circles" or, more accurately, "spirals" can never be fully avoided, but it is important to be aware of their potential effect on the course of reading. See further the fine discussion in Dunn, "Exposition" (2003) 153–55. He concludes: "As readers of biblical texts which are also historical texts . . . we need not despair over the hermeneutical circle but can hope to

tains not only to the text itself but also to the historical and literary context within which it was written. This study is therefore a study not only of a single chapter in Romans but of many aspects of the letter as a whole as well.

In general terms, as soon as any given author has chosen a particular literary genre, he or she has created or, more accurately, entered an environment that affects the form, function, and content of the text. This is because "[g]eneric structures are not merely a matter of convention, but exhibit a rationale which allows one to recognize certain elements as appropriate in relation to others."[22] The readers, in turn, recognize the genre concerned and its boundaries, and expect the text's more specific details to be relevant to its larger framework. These expectations heavily influence their understanding of the text's constituent parts. As E. D. Hirsch observes, the readers' "notion of the meaning as a whole grounds and helps determine [their] understanding of details."[23] According to Hirsch, communication between the text's author and readers is made possible by a system of expectations. In order to understand the text as the author wanted it to be understood,[24] the readers must proceed under the same system of ex-

---

find that the reality of a historical-critical, self-critical, community-critical scrutiny of these texts can and does provide a growing appreciation and understanding of why they were written, what they must have conveyed to their first auditors and readers, and how they may still be expected to function today" (p. 155).

[22] Buss, "Principles" (1980) 77. Cf. Reed, *Discourse* (1997) 153: "[S]tructure creates predictability, allowing the reader to recognize the type of discourse being spoken of and, in turn, to use other similar discourses as a schema for interpreting the immediate one."

[23] *Validity* (1967) 72.

[24] With respect to Paul's letter, I agree with Dabourne that "[w]hile authorial intention can be placed low in considering the meaning of literary texts, it is much more important for letters, like Romans, which are direct communication from one person to particular others" (*Purpose* [1999] 80). Her earlier, more general observation that "[t]he author created a text consisting of these words in this order in the process of carrying out a particular purpose" (p. 42) is well to the point for a text like Rom. In his discussion of "the intentional fallacy," Dunn states that "it is neither desirable nor necessary to dispense with the concept of authorial intention, but the realistic goal is the authorial intention *as entextualized*. . . . It is the text as

pectations as the author. This shared generic conception is a structural necessity in communication, viz. "that sense of the whole by means of which an interpreter can correctly understand any part in its determinacy."[25]

In his discussion of the literary environment of New Testament writings, David E. Aune underlines not only this conditioning of the part by the whole but also the social implications inherent in conventional literary genres and constituent forms:

> Literary genres and forms are not simply neutral containers used as convenient ways to package various types of written communication. They are social conventions that provide contextual meaning for the smaller units of language and text they enclose. The original significance that a literary text had for both author and reader is tied to the genre of that text, so that the meaning of the part is dependent upon the meaning of the whole.[26]

"Genre" can be a tricky term, to be sure, not least because of its various applications in scholarly works.[27] Furthermore, as Harry Y. Gamble points

---

embodying that intention, as a communicative act between author and intended readers/auditors, to which attention is to be given" ("Exposition" [2003] 151; emphasis his). As Buss, "Principles" (1980) 76, rightly remarks, "there is an inner or logical connection between what is said and what the speaker seeks to accomplish in a situation presupposed."

[25] *Validity* (1967) 86.

[26] *New Testament* (1987) 13.

[27] While it is not of immediate interest for the present study to engage in the scholarly discussion of the term, the analytical advantage of defining genre in broad terms and making a primary distinction between literary genres and literary forms may be noted. For instance, whereas the NT contains four major literary genres (gospels, acts, letters, and apocalypse), each one of these genres may include variety of literary forms; cf. Doty, *Letters* (1973) 53: "[T]he largest category we take to be the genre, as 'the epistolary genre.' Within the genre are various stylistic traits, characteristic forms, and recurring types." So also Aune, *New Testament* (1987) 13; Pearson and Porter, "Genres" (1997) 134; Reiser, *Sprache* (2001) 92–97. Differently, e.g., Bailey and Vander Broek, *Forms* (1992), who speak simultaneously of, e.g., ancient letters, specific types of letters, the so-called "paraenesis," the Greco-Roman "diatribe," the author's "visit plans," letter openings, salutations, and doxologies, as "literary forms" (see pp. 15–16, 23–26, 28, 38–39, 62–63, 72–75).

out, genre "can only be inferred through literary analysis and comparison of the texts themselves, and even this rarely produces a clean definition." However, Gamble is right in his subsequent assessment:

> Nevertheless, genre is presupposed in the act of writing and in the act of reading, and though they may not correspond absolutely, the aims of writing and reading can meet only if recognizable generic signs are provided either in the text or in the situation where the text is received and read, or both. A sense of the genre of any particular text is essential to its comprehension: the reader must be able to judge what sort of writing is being read.[28]

The epistolary genre constituted a common form of medium in Greco-Roman antiquity, primarily serving as a written communication between two or more individuals who were separated by distance[29] or by social status.[30] Basically, the letter's purpose was to a) make, enhance, or maintain contact, b) to provide information, and c) to make requests or to give instructions or commands.[31] Purposes such as these could easily overlap and each one of them was dependent on the relationship between the sender(s) and recipient(s). The nature of this relationship was cardinal for epistolary communication in general.

When Paul penned his message to the Roman recipients he entered a literary milieu in which certain conventions of structure were regularly followed, and within which formulaic expressions were characteristically employed to convey the message concerned and to give it a proper literary as well as social framework. The way in which conventional epistolary formulas were used was often an expression in itself. Not only could the author's use of such fixed language facilitate the reading and reception of the letter's message but also affect the relationship between the correspondents. Furthermore, employments of epistolary formulas often disclose the nature of

---

[28] *Books* (1995) 38.
[29] Cicero states: "That there are many different categories (*genera*) of letters you are aware. But the most authentic, the purpose in fact for which letter-writing was invented, is to inform the absent of what it is desirable for them to know, whether in our interest or their own" (*Fam.* 48.1). Cf. *Quint. fratr.* 1.37.
[30] As rightly pointed out by Aune, *New Testament* (1987) 158.
[31] Cf. Dahl, "Letter" (1976) 539; White, "Greek Letters" (1988) 95.

this relationship as presupposed by the author. Few literary genres register the relationship between an author and a reader so well as letters normally do. Uses of common epistolary expressions are also informative of the specific setting in which a letter was written,[32] and of the immediate epistolary situation.[33] That setting and situation, in turn, can provide further clues about the connection existing between an author and an audience, as well as the letter's occasion and purpose.

Every component part of Paul's message in Romans is more or less affected by the letter's larger context and framework, and especially by Paul's relationship with his audience. Paul's own identity, as it is presented in Romans, and his choice and use of specific literary forms within the letter are interrelated. To be more specific, Paul's application of certain fixed phrases, whether they were considered obligatory or optional for the epistolary medium, and his preference for certain forms of expression rather than others are all potential indicators of his actual or claimed status vis-à-vis the audience. It is precisely this status which decides both the choice and use of such expressions. The identity of the audience is even more important. No matter if it concerns the letter's form, function, or content, it must con-

---

[32] Epistolary settings in Greco-Roman antiquity were basically of three kinds: 1) normative, 2) extended, and 3) fictitious, differing "according to the degree to which the correspondents and the contexts move from reality to imaginary construct" (Stirewalt, *Studies* [1993] 1–2). Briefly speaking, the first category applies to genuine letters, written to and meant to be read by a particular audience whose identity is explicitly notified in the letter; the second includes those by which the author intends to communicate with a wider audience than those explicitly identified in the letter; the third category pertains to pseudonymous letters with little or no contemporary relevance. See further in Ch. 1 sec. 4.2 below.

[33] While the two are closely related, the term "epistolary situation" is here used somewhat more narrowly than "epistolary setting" (see the previous n.), the former being more historically oriented: "In its widest sense it denotes the entire historical background in which writer and addressee are united. In its strictest sense it denotes the specific problems existing between and uniting the sender and the recipient in a unique and exclusive relationship. The letter is then the specific means through which these specific problems are being dealt with" (Schubert, "Form" [1939] 376).

tinually be kept in mind that Romans is necessarily contingent upon and shaped by the identity of those to whom it was written.

All this is of significance for the reading of Romans 2. The question both of function and identity of the interlocutor(s) in the chapter is largely defined by such broader aspects as the letter's epistolary structure and setting, and the relationship between Paul and his intended audience. These aspects may provide some answers—or at least limit the scope of potential answers—to the questions why and for what purpose Paul chose to address a certain individual or individuals in Romans 2, and who this or these persons were. Hence, before focusing specifically upon chapter 2 in the letter, it is useful, if not requisite, to attend first to some basic features relating to the letter's larger context and framework, which then are allowed to be of help in ascertaining the function and identity of Paul's interlocutor(s) in Romans 2. That is what I intend to do in the present study.

3. The Procedure of the Study

The following study will proceed from the whole to the part.[34] More specifically, within the range of focus specified above, the subject of the study will be gradually narrowed from the larger context and framework of Romans to one of the letter's more particular elements, namely, Paul's interlocutor(s) in chapter 2.

Chapter One deals with the largest category concerned, viz. the epistolary genre and Paul's letter to the Romans within that context. After a survey of epistolary structure in Greco-Roman antiquity (sec. 1), the question whether Paul divided his letters formally into three, four, or five parts is briefly discussed (sec. 2). In section 3, which occupies the bulk of the chap-

---

[34] Although differing in many details, the approach taken here has some basic commonalities with the "top-down" approach recently advocated by some discourse analysts. Cf. esp. Reed's study of Paul's letter to the Philippians (*Discourse* [1997]). Reed observes: "If possible, the analyst is better off identifying the genre of the text before moving to an analysis of its parts, that is, starting from the top and then working downwards" (p. 28).

ter, Romans is analyzed in terms of its epistolary structure, and conventional epistolary expressions investigated with respect specifically to the question what these may inform of the relationship between the letter's sender and recipients. This relationship is also in view in the final main section (sec. 4) where the epistolary setting of Romans is determined and weighed.

Chapter Two focuses upon the question with whom Paul intended to communicate by his letter. The chapter includes two main sections. In section 1 the scholarly discussion is scanned, and certain presuppositions prevailing in studies of Paul's audience, mostly based on external evidence, are confronted. In section 2 the information provided by Romans itself about its audience is brought to light and assessed.

In Chapter Three the scope of inquiry is demarcated to Paul's use of a dialogical style in Romans 2–11, which closely resembles the Greco-Roman "diatribe." The first section presents some basic characteristics of the "diatribe" style and discusses some difficulties involved in identifying "diatribal" interlocutors in lectures and speeches as compared to letters. In section 2 the dialogical nature of the epistolary medium is considered, and in section 3 some of the ways in which interlocutors were employed in Greco-Roman letters are explored, both with regard to form, function, and identity. In that light, and as a prelude to the final chapter, section 4 addresses the question of the macrostructural significance of the dialogical style in Romans 2–11.

Chapter Four constitutes the kernel of this study and the point at which the preceding chapters are aimed, namely, a detailed discussion of Paul's interlocutor(s) in Romans 2. First to be analyzed is the text's coherence and argumentative flow (sec. 1). Section 2 offers a linear reading of Romans 2 in which the identity of Paul's interlocutor(s) is the central issue. While the question of function is not always easily separated from that of identity, and thus also addressed in section 2, section 3 focuses specifically on the functional aspect. The final section (sec. 4) draws attention to some of the implications of the present study on Romans 2 for Paul's discourse in subsequent chapters of the letter.

Each of Chapters One to Four begins with an introduction of the issue under discussion. Concluding summaries are given at the end of Chapters

One to Three, whereas Chapter Four is summarized in the general Conclusions. When necessary, certain key terms will be discussed or defined as they appear.

Chapter One

The Epistolary Structure and Setting of Romans

Introduction

As a surrogate for oral communication the epistolary medium was sometimes likened to an actual conversation between people,[1] and could properly be described as a "written means of keeping oral conversation in motion."[2] Letters were normally—but not always—read aloud in Greco-Roman antiquity,[3] a procedure which may have strengthened the notion of letter reading as a "speech event."[4] This oral character of letters makes many of them open for rhetorical analysis. Indeed, it has been claimed that most, if not all, forms of literature in antiquity were deeply influenced by rhetorical theory and practice.[5] Recent analyses of letters like Paul's in terms of rhetoric, whether ancient or modern, have also yielded many useful results.

---

[1] See further Ch. 3 sec. 2 below.
[2] White, "Documentary" (1981) 91.
[3] See Achtemeier, "*Omne*" (1990) 9–19. His discussion of the practice of reading in antiquity, however, must be corrected by Gilliard, "Silent" (1993). As Gilliard shows, Achtemeier's assertions that "the general—indeed, from all evidence, the exclusive—practice was to read aloud" (p. 15), that "even solitary readers, reading only to themselves, read aloud" (p. 16), and that reading was therefore "oral performance *whenever* it occurred and in whatever circumstances" (p. 17; his italics), do not speak for the evidence.
[4] Keck, "*Pathos*" (2001) 77–87, with respect to Paul's letter to the Romans.
[5] So, e.g., Schneider, "Brief" (1954) 570; Aune, *New Testament* (1987) 158; Kennedy, "Genres" (1997) 43–50.

However, rhetorical analysis of ancient letters should not be pressed too far. Letters were letters and not speeches. There are several signs of correlations between the two modes of communication, especially in matters of style,[6] but the effect of rhetoric on letter writing appears to have pertained to function rather than to form. In other words, while epistolographers may have adapted functional features from rhetorical theory and practice, they did not write their letters according to formal arrangement (*dispositio*)[7] of rhetorical speeches.[8] Exceptions to this are notably rare.[9] As Stanley K. Stowers observes,

> [l]etter writing remained only on the fringes of formal rhetorical education throughout antiquity. It was never integrated into the rhetorical systems and thus

---

[6] See Classen, "Paulus" (1991); idem, *Rhetorical* (2000) 1–28; Porter, "Theoretical" (1993); Stamps, "Rhetorical" (1995) 141–48; Reed, "Epistle" (1997) 182–86, 190-92. For examples and overview of theories of style in classical rhetoric, see Rowe, "Style" (1997). Cf. also Russell, *Criticism* (1981) 129–47. For examples of stylistic features in the Pauline letters as potential parallels to those found in the ancient rhetorical handbooks, see Porter, "Paul" (1997) 576–85.

[7] The Latin term *dispositio* is normally used in scholarly discussions of classical rhetoric. The ancients, however, used several terms for rhetorical arrangement. Most frequently, the Romans used *dispositio*, *compositio*, or *ordo*, corresponding to διάθεσις, οἰκονομία, and τάξις among the Greeks. See Wuellner, "Arrangement" (1997) 51–52.

[8] While the areas of rhetorical argumentation (*inventio*/εὕρεσις) (see Eriksson, *Traditions* [1998] 30–72) and especially style (*elocutio*/λέξις) (see n. 6) can be helpful in analyses of Paul's letters, attempts to analyze them according to rhetorical *dispositio* are methodologically suspect. See esp. Reed, "Epistle" (1997). Cf. also idem, "Using" (1993); idem, *Discourse* (1997) 156–65; Stamps, "Rhetorical" (1995) 147–48; Kern, *Rhetoric* (1998) 30–34; Klauck, *Briefliteratur* (1998) 176–80; Porter, "Epistolographer" (1999) 226–34; Classen, *Rhetorical* (2000) 23–27; Weima, "Epistolary" (2000) 328–29. Similar observations are made, e.g., by du Toit, "Persuasion" (1989) 193–96; Murphy-O'Connor, *Paul* (1995) 77–86; Anderson, *Rhetorical* (1996) 100–109, Müller, *Schluß* (1997) 36–54; Dabourne, *Purpose* (1999) 87–90; Mitternacht, *Forum* (1999) 156–68; Nanos, *Irony* (2002) 323–31, with respect to Paul's letters specifically.

[9] Among possible exceptions are Demosthenes' *Epp.* 1–4; see further Reed, "Epistle" (1997) 186–90; Anderson, *Rhetorical* (1996) 105–8.

does not appear in the standard handbooks. This means there were never any detailed systematic rules for letters, as there were for standard rhetorical forms. The rules for certain types of speeches, however, were adapted for use in corresponding letter types.[10]

The somewhat distinct settings of letters and rhetorical speeches, as well as the basically different communicative mode involved, can partly explain the above fact. Rhetorical speeches were mainly intended for courtrooms and political or public assemblies, involving immediate contact between participants. Letters, on the other hand, served as a means for verbal exchange between individuals or groups of people unable to communicate face to face. Thus, the fourth century C.E. rhetorician, Julius Victor, advised: "[A]void obscurity more assiduously [in letters] than you do in speeches (*oratione*) and conversation (*sermocinando*). For while you can ask someone who is speaking unclearly to elucidate his point, it is altogether impossible in correspondence when the party is absent (*in absentium epistolis non datur*)."[11] Even Demosthenes, "the true model and exemplar of oratory,"[12] pointed up this difference between the presence and absence of the author. In a letter to the Athenian council and assembly, he wrote:

> It is a difficult thing, I know, for advice conveyed by letter (ἐπιστολῆς) to hold its ground, because you Athenians have a way of opposing many suggestions without waiting to understand them. In the case of a speaker (λέγοντι μέν), of course, it is possible to perceive what you want and easy to correct your misap-

---

[10] *Letter* (1986) 34. Cf. on p. 52: "The classification of letter types according to the three species of rhetoric [i.e. judicial, deliberative, and epideictic] only partially works. This is because the letter-writing tradition was essentially independent of rhetoric." Cf. also Malherbe, *Epistolary* (1988) 2: "Epistolary theory in antiquity belonged to the domain of the rhetoricians, but it was not originally part of their theoretical systems. It is absent from the earliest extant rhetorical handbooks, and it only gradually made its way into the genre." A useful summary discussion of the three species of rhetoric (and others) may be found in Kennedy's "Genres" (1997).
[11] *Rhet.* 27.
[12] Pliny, *Ep.* 9.26.8.

prehensions; but the written page (τὸ δὲ βιβλίον) possesses no such aid against those who raise a clamour.[13]

While the use of letters originated in administrative practices—and this is perhaps the clearest example of common settings for letters and rhetorical speeches[14]—the letter was eventually adopted as a common genre also of familial and personal correspondence.[15] Moreover, the fundamental difference between oral and written communication should not be overlooked,[16] even though letters were usually read aloud and frequently likened to actual dialogues. This difference is recognized, for instance, in Demetrius' *De elocutione*, the earliest extant rhetorical work that discusses letter writing.[17] Responding to the view of Artemon, the editor of Aristotle's letters, that "a letter ought to be written in the same manner as a dialogue (διάλογον)," Demetrius urges that the letter "should be a little more studied (ὑποκατεσκευάσθαι) than the dialogue, since the latter reproduces (μιμεῖται) an extemporary utterance (αὐτοσχεδιάζοντα), while the former is committed to writing and is (in a way) sent as a gift." Subsequently, Demetrius notes that it is "absurd to build up periods [in letters], as if you were writing not a let-

---

[13] *Ep.* 1.3; cf. *Ep.* 3.35. Cf. also Seneca, *Ep.* 38.1; Diogenes, *Ep.* 17. Interestingly, according to Paul, he was accused of being a bad speaker (i.e. when present), whereas the letters sent in his absence were considered "weighty and powerful" (2 Cor 10:10).

[14] Cf. Stirewalt, *Studies* (1993) 9.

[15] See White, "Greek Letters" (1988) 85–88; Stirewalt, *Studies* (1993) 4–15.

[16] Cf. Aune, *New Testament* (1987) 159; Stowers, "Typification" (1988) 79. Classen, *Rhetorical* (2000) 7, observes that "[o]bviously, a fundamental difference was felt in antiquity between a speech or even a poem or another type of composition on the one hand and a letter on the other."

[17] The exact date of this work, erroneously ascribed to Demetrius of Phalerum (4th cent. B.C.E.), is uncertain. Most suggestions range from the 3rd cent. B.C.E. to the 1st cent. C.E.; see Thraede, *Grundzüge* (1970) 19–25; Malherbe, *Epistolary* (1988) 2, 17; Anderson, *Rhetorical* (1996) 44–45; Kennedy, "Historical" (1997) 27. Doty believes that Demetrius based his rules for letter writing on earlier authorities, and that his discussion in many ways "summarize[s] the theory of letter writing in Greek and Roman literary circles that prevailed for several centuries" (*Letters* [1973] 9).

ter (ἐπιστολήν) but a speech for the law courts (δίκην)."[18] Cicero, the distinguished rhetorician and epistolographer, observed similarly: "A letter is one thing, a court of law or a public meeting quite another."[19]

Hence, whereas ancient letters and speeches display some functional resemblances, it cannot be taken for granted that a letter writer would have chosen to compose his or her letter according to rhetorical *dispositio*. Neither can it be assumed that any given recipient would have expected a letter to constitute a rhetorical speech. There were certain rules operative for the rhetorician, and there were certain rules operative for the epistolographer, although the latter may have been less fixed, more optional, and thus variously applied. This is not do say that there were no formal similarities between letters and speeches; after all, functional features are not always so easily distinguished from formal ones. But, as Jeffrey T. Reed rightly remarks, "[t]he similarities may be explained by the fact that language is often used pragmatically in different genres to do similar things."[20] Rhetorical analyses and epistolary analyses of ancient letters are by no means mutually exclusive,[21] but the primary contribution of the former is in terms of function.

In short, letters from Greco-Roman antiquity should be taken for what they are, viz. letters, and, *as a point of departure*, they should be analyzed with respect to prevailing *epistolary* practices. Recent research into Paul's letter to the Romans has tended to neglect this requirement.

In this chapter, I will first offer a brief survey of epistolary structure in Greco-Roman antiquity (sec. 1), and then turn to the question whether or not Paul wrote his letters according to regular norms (sec. 2). Subsequently, the epistolary structure of Romans will be determined and conventional epistolary expressions within it analyzed, particularly with a view to the re-

---

[18] *Eloc.* 223–224, 229.
[19] *Fam.* 188.1 (*quid enim simile habet epistula aut iudicio aut contioni?* [a rhetorical question]).
[20] "Epistle" (1997) 182.
[21] A fine discussion of both sides of this ongoing debate may be found in Donfried and Beutler (eds.), *Thessalonians Debate* (2000).

lationship between Paul and his audience (sec. 3). Finally, the epistolary setting in which Romans was penned will be considered (sec. 4).

1. Epistolary Structure in Greco-Roman Antiquity

Ancient letters served multiple functions.[22] Therefore it comes as no surprise that the letters also exhibit considerable formal flexibility. In fact, ancient epistolary theorists showed little interest in setting forth detailed norms for letter writing, but allowed for individual creativity within the larger framework.[23] Thus Demetrius instructs: "There should be a certain degree of freedom in the structure (τῇ συντάξει) of a letter."[24] However, actual practice was evidently more concerned with formal features than were the theorists.[25] The bulk of extant letters from Greco-Roman antiquity[26] betray that the larger framework was generally standardized,[27] consisting of opening, body, and closing.[28]

---

[22] Cf. Pseudo-Demetrius, *Ep. Typ.*; Pseudo-Libanius, *Ep. Char.* See also the list of potential functions in Stowers, *Letter* (1986) 15–16.

[23] Cf. Thraede, *Grundzüge* (1970) 9 n. 17; Malherbe, *Epistolary* (1988) 5; Anderson, *Rhetorical* (1996) 98; Classen, *Rhetorical* (2000) 7.

[24] *Eloc.* 229.

[25] According to Weima, "Epistolary" (2000) 328, this suggests in fact that "the epistolary theorists were not successful in influencing the practice of letter writing." Cf., however, White, *Light* (1986) 190.

[26] It may be noted that the tripartite letter structure was not limited to Greco-Roman letters. Somewhat similar conventions can be seen in the majority of Hebrew (mostly ostraca) and Aramaic letters, though various combinations of formulaic features are found in these letters, especially the Hebrew ones. Although Hebrew "letters" differ from Aramaic letters in many details (possibly because of the material used), they show basic structural similarities. See Fitzmyer, "Aramaic" (1974); Pardee, "Hebrew" (1978); Alexander, "Epistolary" (1984) esp. 588–95; Lindenberger, *Ancient* (1994) 1–9 and passim.

[27] In his still important study of Greek papyrus letters, Exler showed that the basic structure of the papyri remained constant from at least the 3rd cent. B.C.E. to the 3rd cent. C.E. (*Form* [1923] 12). A decade later Roller concluded similarly for Greek letters in general (*Formular* [1933] 55–56). Subsequent research has not

John L. White has suggested that there is a correlation between the tripartite structure of the letter and its basic functions. Whereas the opening and the closing convey the important "keeping-in-touch aspect of letter writing,"[29] the letter's specific occasions tend to be expressed "through stock phrases of the letter's body."[30]

1.1. Epistolary Opening

The opening was the only literary element that was considered obligatory.[31] In Greek letters it usually included the superscription (i.e. the identification of the sender) in the nominative case and the adscription (i.e. the identification of the recipient)[32] in the dative, frequently followed by salutation. Thus, "A (nom.) to B (dat.), greeting (χαίρειν)" was the common way to begin a letter.[33] To this a health wish was often added,[34] sometimes com-

---

shown this to be inaccurate (cf. Koskenniemi, *Studien* [1956] 155; White, *Light* [1986] 194–98).

[28] Whereas "body" is a modern category, traces of the other two can be found among the ancients. Seneca, for instance, tells of an old custom among the Romans to add a health wish to the "opening words of a letter (*primis epistulae verbis*)" (*Ep.* 15.1). More explicitly, Julius Victor claims that "[t]he openings and conclusions of letters (*praefationes ac subscriptiones litterarum*) . . . should be written according to customary practice" (*Rhet.* 27).

[29] Cf. Artemidorus Daldianus' (2nd cent. C.E.) remarks that "speaking the greeting and farewell is the personal part of every letter" (*Onir.* 3.44; cited in Stirewalt, *Studies* [1993] 75).

[30] *Light* (1986) 219. Cf. Reed, "Epistle" (1997) 180.

[31] White, "New Testament" (1984) 1731–32. Cf. Roller, *Formular* (1933) 57.

[32] By using the terms "superscription" and "adscription" for the units in which the sender and recipient (resp.) are identified, I follow several scholars specialized in studies of ancient epistolography and the NT, e.g. Aune, *New Testament* (1987) 163; Schnider and Stenger, *Studien* (1987) 4–25; Reed, *Discourse* (1997) 181–92. These terms are not to be confused with the identical terminology employed within text-criticism.

[33] So Pseudo-Libanius, *Ep. Char.* 51, instructs: "[The letter] should begin as follows: 'So-and-so to So-and-so, greeting' (ὁ δεῖνα τῷ δεῖνι χαίρειν). For thus all the ancients (ἅπαντες οἱ παλαιοί) who were eminent in wisdom and eloquence appear

bined with a prayer.³⁵ The conventional ways of opening a letter were no doubt well known to most ancients, since official letters³⁶ were often posted or inscribed in public places.³⁷ These letters usually opened with the con-

---

to have done." According to White, "New Testament" (1984) 1733–34, this opening formula is found in about two-thirds of the papyri, with a health wish frequently added by the 2nd cent. B.C.E. onward. A number of variants of the basic form exist. The principal alternative formula would be "To B from A," or "To B χαίρειν A." See esp. Exler, *Form* (1923) 23–68. Cf. Meecham, *Light* (1923) 114–16; Reed, *Discourse* (1997) 181–84. For NT examples of the basic form, see Acts 15:23; 23:26; Jas 1:1.

34 The so-called ὑγιαίνειν wish in Greek terms, largely corresponding to the Latin *formula valetudinis*, the main difference being that the former was less stereotyped. The basic form of the ὑγιαίνειν wish was πρὸ μὲν πάντων εὔχομαί σε ὑγιαίνειν ("Above all, I pray that you may be well"), or equivalent expressions. For examples from the papyri, see Exler, *Form* (1923) 107–11, and for discussions, see Roller, *Formular* (1933) 61–63; Koskenniemi, *Studien* (1956) 130–39. The constant Latin form was *Si vales bene est, ego valeo* ("If you are well, it is well; I also am well"); see, e.g., Seneca, *Ep.* 15.1.

35 The so-called προσκύνημα ("act of worship"; LSJ s.v.) formula or phrase, which appears in letters from the 1st cent. C.E. onward. The basic form was τὸ προσκύνημα σου ποιῶ παρὰ τοῖς θεοῖς ("I make your supplication before the gods"), or equivalent expressions, usually in combination with the health wish. See esp. the discussion in Koskenniemi, *Studien* (1956) 139–45. Several examples from the papyri can also be found in Exler, *Form* (1923) 108–10; Meecham, *Light* (1923) 70; Roller, *Formular* (1933) 63–64 (with nn.). See also Aune, *New Testament* (1987) 163–64.

36 Definitions of "official letters" are not entirely uniform in scholarly works. While some want to distinguish between royal/diplomatic letters and other types of official letters (e.g. White, *Light* [1986] 5; Klauck, *Briefliteratur* [1998] 71–73), others do not (e.g. Aune, *New Testament* [1987] 164–65; Stirewalt, *Paul* [2003] 27–28). In this study I refer to official correspondence in broad terms, encompassing such letters as royal, diplomatic, and administrative. One important characteristic of these letters is that the sender writes as an authority or as a duly authorized person to deal with the issue or task in question (cf. Stirewalt, *Studies* [1993] 6).

37 See, e.g., the edict of the prefect of Egypt stating the reasons for the publication of a letter of the emperor Claudius to residents of Alexandria (*CPJ* 2.153 [41 C.E.] [=P.Lond. 6.1912]): "Since the entire population was unable to be present, because of its size, at the reading of the most sacred and beneficent letter to the city, I

ventional "A to B," the order of which does not seem to have been dependent on the social status of correspondents. It was used when superiors wrote to their inferiors and vice versa.[38] On the other hand, an alternative formula in which the recipient was named first ("To B from A") was peculiar to letters from inferiors containing petitions, complaints, or applications.[39] Thus, a specific form of address could sometimes be identified with a specific type of letter. However, as White points out, "the order of names in the opening address is no certain indicator of the correspondents' comparative status. A better index of status . . . is the use of modifying nouns of relation in the address."[40] At any rate, all this indicates that already in the opening address a social relationship was established between the parties involved.[41] In this respect, Richard Bauckham rightly stresses the importance of the opening:

---

considered it necessary to display (ἐκθεῖναι) the letter (publicly)" (trans. White, *Light* [1986] 133). Claudius' letter opens with the "A to B χαίρειν" formula. Cf. 1 Macc 11:37; Josephus, *A.J.* 16.165. See also Welles, *Royal* (1934) xl and passim; Sherk, *Roman* (1969) 11–13, 186–89, 196–97 and passim.

[38] Exler, *Form* (1923) 62.

[39] Exler, *Form* (1923) 23, 60–61, 65–67, 133. The standard salutation was usually omitted in these types of letters; see Aune, *New Testament* (1987) 163.

[40] "Epistolography Group" (1981) 8.

[41] An interesting example where the order of names *does* appear to have been determined by the nature of the epistolary situation may be found in 2 Macc 9 and 11 (embedded letters). In 11:16 Lysias, "the king's guardian and kinsman" (v. 1), opens his letter thus: Λυσίας τῷ πλήθει τῶν Ἰουδαίων χαίρειν. Similarly, a royal letter begins in v. 27 with βασιλεὺς Ἀντίοχος τῇ γερουσίᾳ τῶν Ἰουδαίων καὶ τοῖς ἄλλοις Ἰουδαίοις χαίρειν, and in v. 34 an official letter from Rome opens with Κόιντος Μέμμιος Τίτος Μάνιος πρεσβῦται Ῥωμαίων τῷ δήμῳ τῶν Ἰουδαίων χαίρειν. Thus, all these official letters begin with the usual "A to B" formula. In 9:19–27, on the other hand, is a letter (probably fictitious) written by the king Antiochus (Epiphanes) to "his worthy Jewish citizens." In the letter, written "in the form of a supplication" (ἱκετηρίας τάξιν ἔχουσαν, v. 18), the king is full of regrets because of his former conduct against the Jewish nation. This letter is presented as opening with τοῖς χρηστοῖς Ἰουδαίοις τοῖς πολίταις πολλὰ χαίρειν καὶ ὑγιαίνειν καὶ εὖ πράττειν βασιλεὺς καὶ στρατηγὸς Ἀντίοχος, i.e. "To B . . .

[W]hat makes a letter a letter is not so much the nature of its contents, which can vary enormously, but the fact that the content is directly addressed by one person to another (or, of course, more than one person in either case). Hence the really essential feature of the literary form of the letter is the parties formula in which the sender(s) and the recipient(s) are named or specified in some other way.[42]

1.2. Epistolary Closing

As in the opening of the letter, several conventional phrases are evident in the closing, some of which could also belong to the opening or the body of the letter. Most frequent is the farewell wish, usually expressed by ἔρρωσω ("Be strong!")[43] or εὐτύχει ("Prosper!"), both commonly translated as "Farewell." Other epistolary conventions include, for instance, a health wish (also found in the opening; possibly a part of the body in some cases), a secondary greeting (virtually always with the verb ἀσπάζομαι), and an autograph.[44] Except for the farewell wish, none of these appear to have been essential for closing a letter, and the instances in which all, or even most, of them occur simultaneously are quite rare. This suggests that, rather than being generally bound by use of specific formulas, letter writers "attempted to construct closings that were appropriate to each letter's contents."[45]

1.3. Epistolary Body

Basically, the so-called body of the letter consisted of the portion in which the letter's central message was stated. Compared to the opening and closing, formal analysis of the body has been less successful, simply because the

---

from A," in spite of its royal origin. In other words, the king's humility and humble attitude towards the Jewish nation is already hinted at in the opening formula.

[42] "Pseudo-Apostolic" (1988) 471.
[43] Cf. Acts 15:29; 23:30 (variant reading).
[44] See Gamble, *Textual* (1977) 57–65; Weima, *Endings* (1994) 28–56; Müller, *Schluß* (1997) 56–67. Other common forms are illiteracy formula, dating formula, and postscript.
[45] Weima, *Endings* (1994) 56.

body does normally not contain the amount of stereotyped patterns found in the other parts.[46] This does not mean that the body contained no conventional expressions by means of which the author could lead the audience through the text. On the contrary, it was, for example, quite customary to introduce or close the central section with certain formulaic phrases,[47] which often contain important information about the text's structure and content. Most of these, however, were alternative transitional markers, some of which could be positioned almost anywhere in the letter's body. In this light, Terence Y. Mullins cautions:

> When dealing with epistolary forms, we must not lose sight of their epistolary nature. They were tools for communication between a writer and a specific reader or group of readers. They were not used by a writer as part of a purely literary project. They constitute a social gesture, not a thematic ploy. They show the writer's attitude toward the *audience* to which he is writing, not his attitude toward the *material* he is presenting.[48]

Nonetheless, it is clear that specific formulaic expressions could be, and often were, used in the body of the letter, serving both as a "social gesture" and as an important aid for the audience to recognize the letter's argumentative structure. The more stereotypical and more widely applied, the more potentials for such purposes. Where such expressions were placed within the body ultimately depended on the nature of the letter itself and on the nature of the epistolary situation.

---

[46] See discussion in White, "Epistolography Group" (1981) 9–10.

[47] See, e.g., White, "New Testament" (1984) 1736–38, for examples from the papyri, and ibid., 1742–50, for discussion of these elements in Paul's letters. Several formulaic expressions within the body will be discussed below in connection with the analysis of the epistolary structure of Rom (sec. 3.2).

[48] "Formulas" (1972) 388 (his italics; on potential placements of epistolary formulas, see pp. 386–89).

2. Epistolary Structure of Paul's Letters: Three, Four, or Five Letter Parts?

It is generally agreed that Paul wrote his letters[49] more or less in line with contemporary epistolary practices. His employment of various conventional epistolary formulas suffice to show that Paul as a letter writer stood firmly within the established tradition of Greco-Roman letter writing.[50] It is further clear that Paul added a flavor of his own to each one of his letters, occasionally combining Greco-Roman with more characteristic Jewish expressions, as exemplified by the standard salutation used in all his letters.[51]

---

[49] In this study I will presuppose that Paul composed Rom, 1–2 Cor, Gal, Phil, 1 Thess, and Phlm, i.e. the seven undisputed ones. Other letters in the NT which are generally thought to stand in the "Pauline tradition" will occasionally be referred to for comparison.

[50] For the claim that Paul's practice of letter writing was primarily based on his knowledge of Jewish official letters ("offizielle gemeindeleitende Briefe"), see Taatz, *Frühjüdische* (1991) esp. 110–14. Taatz concludes that since Paul was a rabbinical student in Jerusalem (referring to Acts 22:3), he was familiar with such a tradition of Jewish letter writing and, therefore, consciously adopted it in his correspondence (p. 111). Against Taatz it must be pointed out that even if Paul was familiar with such a tradition, that does not necessarily mean that he adopted it, consciously or not. While Taatz has shown that certain Jewish traditions of letter writing may have been available to Paul, she has not shown by analysis of his letters that he did adopt them—indeed, Taatz fails to provide any analysis of any of Paul's letters to prove her case. Moreover, her partial selection of Jewish official letters as comparative documents seems suspect. Cf. the critique in Reed, *Discourse* (1997) 175–76 n. 93. See also the discussion in Doty, *Letters* (1973) 22–23.

[51] I.e. χάρις [from χαίρειν] ὑμῖν καὶ εἰρήνη [for the Hebrew *shalom*], most frequently followed by ἀπὸ θεοῦ πατρὸς ἡμῶν καὶ κυρίου Ἰησοῦ Χριστοῦ. This form is used in all the canonical Pauline letters, except in 1–2 Tim where χάρις ἔλεος εἰρήνη is used, and in Titus where χάρις εἰρήνη is used (along with ἔλεος in several MSS). On the salutation as a combination of Greco-Roman and Jewish conventions, see esp. Reed, *Discourse* (1997) 192–97. Reed notes that the salutation is "perhaps the most clear case of [Paul's] modification of epistolary traditions" (p. 196). See also Koskenniemi, *Studien* (1956) 162; Doty, *Letters* (1973) 22, 29–30; Stowers, *Letter* (1986) 21; Aune, *New Testament* (1987) 184–85. On the Pauline

This flavor of Paul's has led a number of scholars to believe that Paul was so much of an innovator in letter writing that he deviated from the standard tripartite structure by adding one or two formally distinct letter parts of his own.[52] At first sight, this difference may perhaps seem trivial. It will be noticed, however, that the nature of the basic structure has a considerable bearing on the understanding of the letter concerned. It affects not only connections between the letter's parts but also the function of each part within the whole.

In his important study of Paul as a letter writer, William G. Doty insisted that Paul followed the Greco-Roman pattern in general, but that he "developed certain subunits and expanded others," so that the basic outline of "the Pauline way of writing letters" consisted of the following five parts: 1) opening, 2) thanksgiving or blessing, 3) body, 4) paraenesis, and 5) closing.[53] In Doty's view, Paul developed or expanded ordinary epistolary thanksgivings and the so-called paraenesis with the result that these became formally identifiable units within his letters.

To begin with the latter, it is stunning in light of Doty's division that "paraenesis"[54] is merely found in three out of Paul's seven letters. According to Doty, it is found in Romans, Galatians, and First Thessalonians; it is

---

salutation as a Jewish form in the strictest sense, see Taatz, *Frühjüdische* (1991) 112. Cf. Berger, "Apostelbrief" (1974) 191–207; Schnider and Stenger, *Studien* (1987) 25–41. According to White, "Mission" (1993) 150, Paul's salutation would be the "religious equivalent" to the common health wish.

[52] On Paul as an eminent innovator in letter writing, see, e.g., Dunn, *Romans* (1988) 1.lix. Dunn speaks of "the distinctiveness of the form Paul created" in Rom, and then goes on to state that "the distinctiveness of the letter far outweighs the significance of its conformity with current literary or rhetorical custom. Parallels show chiefly how others wrote at that period; they provide no prescription for Paul's practice and no clear criterion by which to assess Paul . . . [T]he chief force of the letter lies in its *distinctive* Pauline art and content" (emphasis his).

[53] *Letters* (1973) 27.

[54] Unfortunately, Doty offers no definition of the term "paraenesis," but describes "paraenetic" materials as "by and large traditional materials" which "arise out of community life and thought, and tend to be consistently conservative" (*Letters* [1973] 37). Later on he seems to speak of "paraenesis" as "Paul's ethical teaching materials" (p. 38).

"missing" in First Corinthians and Philippians, and apparently in Second Corinthians as well.[55] As for the letter to Philemon, Doty recommends his readers to compare v. 21, but fails to explain why this should be done. Due to the fact that Doty is only able to point out three letters in which specific "paraenetic" units may be included, sufficient support for the five-part Pauline letter is lacking. In fact, the number of three letters may even be reduced: First, since it is not easily discerned why Doty has restricted the "paraenetic" section of First Thessalonians to 4:1–12 and 5:1–22 (leaving 4:13–18 aside), claiming that these two passages constitute a formally distinct unit,[56] and, second, since it seems indeed plausible that the letter as a whole functions as a "paraenetic" letter,[57] and to speak of a distinct "paraenetic" section within it would therefore be superfluous at best, it may be argued that there are only two letters out of seven in which distinct units could possibly be recognized as "paraenetic,"[58] viz. Romans and Galatians. This strongly suggests that the material labelled "paraenetic" by Doty is

---

[55] See the table on p. 43 in Doty's *Letters* (1973). Doty leaves out the question of "paraenesis" in 2 Cor.

[56] Doty gives no explanation why 4:13–18 should not be included in the "paraenesis"—in fact, this passage is totally left out of consideration. The text in 4:13–18, however, has significant formal commonalities with the surrounding text: In 4:9–10 Paul takes up the topic of "brotherly love" by introducing it with the words περὶ δὲ τῆς φιλαδελφίας, and in 5:1–11 the discussion is περὶ ... τῶν χρόνων καὶ τῶν καιρῶν. In 4:13–18 the subject concerns "those who have fallen asleep," similarly introduced with περὶ τῶν κοιμωμένων. Interestingly, this is the manner in which Paul introduces various subjects in 1 Cor (beginning with περὶ δὲ ὧν ἐγράψατε in 7:1; cf. 7:25; 8:1; 12:1; 16:1, 12) which, according to Doty, lacks a "paraenetic" section.

[57] Convincingly argued by Malherbe, "Moralists" (1992) 278–93.

[58] Of course, that depends on what is meant by the term "paraenesis." Malherbe, for example, defines it as a "moral exhortation in which someone is advised to pursue or abstain from something. . . . [I]t contains useful rules for conduct in common situations and adopts styles that range from censure to consolation" (*Moral* [1986] 124–25). For general discussion of "paraenesis" in the NT, see Popkes, *Paränese* (1996).

more dependent upon contextual factors than a distinctive "Pauline way of writing."⁵⁹

Because of Paul's fairly regular use of epistolary "thanksgivings" (εὐχαριστῶ τῷ θεῷ etc.) at the beginning of his letters, many scholars are of the opinion that they constitute units that are formally distinct from the opening, body, and closing.⁶⁰ Thanksgivings located at the beginning occur in all the letters except Galatians and Second Corinthians, the latter of which includes instead a benediction (εὐλογητὸς ὁ θεός etc.). The "lack" in Galatians is usually explained by reference to the situation addressed in the letter, viz. that because of the departure of the Galatians from his εὐαγγέλιον Paul had little to give thanks for.⁶¹ While I consent to the generally accepted view that thanksgivings should be understood as epistolary formulas,⁶² I consider it doubtful that they constituted formally distinct

---

⁵⁹ It should be noted that Doty does indeed insist that he is not arguing for "one clearly identified Pauline form." Rather, he claims, he is arguing that there is "a basic understanding of structure by which Paul wrote, but that this basic understanding could be modified on occasion, and that the basic understanding itself was something that came into being only gradually" (*Letters* [1973] 21). Yet, his table of "Formal parts of the Pauline letters" (p. 43) shows that he considered the five-part letter to represent the "basic understanding of structure," and that although this structure could be "modified on occasion" such modifications occur in five out of seven instances! It seems more reasonable to conclude that the three- or four-part letter is the basic structure for Paul and that he could modify it (e.g. by formal addition) according to the situation addressed. As Doty himself observes, "every letter represents what Paul thought ought to be addressed to the specific situation" (p. 27).

⁶⁰ So, e.g., O'Brien, "Letters" (1993) 551–52; Weima, *Endings* (1994) 11, who advocate the four-part Pauline letter.

⁶¹ See Schubert, *Form* (1939) 162–63, 184; O'Brien, *Thanksgivings* (1977) 141, 265.

⁶² Against Arzt, "Thanksgiving" (1994), who has argued that Paul could not have been dependent upon epistolary conventions in his use of thanksgivings, simply because "an 'introductory thanksgiving' never existed as a set phrase" (p. 37). By "introductory thanksgiving" he seems to mean either "set phrases of thanksgiving connected with the *formula valetudinis*" (p. 31) or a "combination of a report of a prayer and/or the μνεία–motif with a thanksgiving to God for the addressees" (p.

units in Paul's letters, or a specific Pauline way of introducing the main part of his letters. As frequently found in letters from antiquity,[63] thanks given to God are scattered throughout Paul's letters without any indication of a formally separate section being initiated.[64] This points rather to his flexibility in use of this epistolary formula.[65] The fact that a thanksgiving (or a benediction) is absent in Galatians suggests that Paul's use of it has more to do with the situation at hand than with any epistolary habit of his; at least Paul did not give thanks to God when he wanted to express his "astonishment" (θαυμάζω, 1:6) over his audience's conducts. To be sure, thanksgivings may have been used by Paul in connection with stating the

---

45), or both. But Arzt is not clear on this issue, which makes his study somewhat puzzling. Still, given that I have understood him correctly, he rightly points out the inaccuracy of the phrase *introductory* thanksgiving (as previously observed by Mullins, "Formulas" [1972] 386–87). However, as Reed ("Thanksgivings" [1996]) and Mitternacht (*Forum* [1999] 179–85) have shown, Arzt's (apparent) claim that thanksgivings were not epistolary formulas, has no solid grounds. On the μνεία–motif, see Koskenniemi, *Studien* (1956) 145–48, and the discussion in sec. 3.2.1 below.

[63] See esp. Mullins, "Formulas" (1972) 381–82, 386–87; Arzt, "Thanksgiving" (1994) 33–35; Reed, "Thanksgivings" (1996) 96.

[64] 1 Cor 1:14; 14:18 1 Thess 2:13 (with the verb εὐχαριστῶ); 1 Thess 3:9 (εὐχαριστίαν τῷ θεῷ ἀνταποδοῦναι); Rom 6:17; 1 Cor 15:57; 2 Cor 2:14; 8:16; 9:15 (with χάρις τῷ θεῷ or vice versa); Rom 7:25 (with χάρις or εὐχαριστῶ). Cf. 1 Cor 10:30; 2 Cor 1:11; 4:15; 9:11, 12.

[65] In his influential study of thanksgivings, Schubert noted that 1 Thess contained "at first glance" three separate "thanksgivings" (1:2–5; 2:13–16; 3:9–13), which he then considered to be an "indivisible entity structurally, formally and functionally," i.e. one large "thanksgiving" extending from 1:2 to 3:13. Thus, he concluded that "the thanksgiving is the letter, i.e., the 'main body' of the letter" (*Form* [1939] 16–27; citations on pp. 18, 20, 26; cf. O'Brien, *Thanksgivings* [1977] 143–46; Schnider and Stenger, *Studien* [1987] 42–45). At a closer look, it becomes apparent that a thanksgiving in 2:13–16 is restricted to v. 13 (surely the description of the opposing Jews in vv. 14–16 cannot be a part of a "thanksgiving"!), and that 3:9–13 has a thanksgiving only in v. 9, followed by a "visiting theme" (see sec. 3.2.3 below) in v. 10, and a prayer in vv. 11–13. So, instead of being an "indivisible entity," these passages provide clear examples of Paul's flexibility in his use of thanksgivings.

reason(s) for writing and/or with specifying certain key topics to be discussed later on in the letter, as Paul Schubert once suggested.[66] But it is important to note that thanksgivings constitute single formulas which may or may not be used in combination with other conventional expressions, and should not be extended so as to form whole units incorporating such expressions. Moreover, as for Paul's letter to the Romans, scholars who insist on a distinct Pauline "thanksgiving part" have largely failed to determine and account for its extent, differing widely in opinions on the question where such a unit may end and the body begin.[67] Attempts to solve this problem by speaking of "mixed types"[68] of thanksgivings in Romans (and in 1 Thess) have not proved to be very successful.

Thus, instead of being "a matter of firm and meaningful habit"[69] for Paul, the thanksgiving was an optional epistolary formula, the use of which was shaped by Paul's intention on each occasion as well as his relation to the audience. Whereas thanks given to gods in ancient letters most frequently[70] concern the correspondents' well-being[71] or rescue from danger,[72] Paul's focus is always aimed at his audience with thanks offered be-

---

[66] *Form* (1939) 77, 179–85.
[67] Cf. the various suggestions provided, e.g., by Schubert, *Form* (1939) 5–6, 31–33 ("thanksgiving": Rom 1:8–17); Sanders, "Transition" (1962) 359–60 (1:8–12); O'Brien, *Thanksgivings* (1977) 200–202, 261 (1:8–15 "at least," with 1:16–17 serving as a "bridge passage" into the body); Roberts, "Transitions" (1986) 95 (1:8, followed by a separate prayer section in vv. 9–10). Cf. White's critique of Schubert's and Sanders' attempts to determine the extent of the thanksgivings in his "Introductory" (1971) 91–92.
[68] O'Brien, *Thanksgivings* (1977) 3, 143–46, 197, following Schubert, *Form* (1939) 10–39. Cf. Schnider and Stenger, *Studien* (1987) 46–47.
[69] Schubert, *Form* (1939) 183.
[70] But not exclusively. As Reed, "Thanksgivings" (1996) 96, points out, in P.Mich. 8.473.29 (early 2nd cent. C.E.) the sender gives thanks to the gods because of a certain attribute of a person.
[71] E.g. P.Lond. 1.42.9–10 (168 B.C.E.).
[72] E.g. *UPZ* 1.60 (168 B.C.E.); 2 Macc 1.11–17. See also the discussion in White, "Saint Paul" (1983) 438; idem, "New Testament" (1984) 1741. For further examples from the papyri, see Schubert, *Form* (1939) 158–79; Arzt, "Thanksgiving" (1994) 31–37.

cause of their known, assumed, or expected fidelity.[73] Paul's use of thanksgivings at the beginning of his letters—combined with other epistolary formulas or transitional techniques[74]—may therefore reveal a conscious effort to capture the audience's goodwill (*captatio benevolentiae*)[75] before turning to the main subject. This may even be the primary function of these thanksgivings in the letters of Paul.

It is true that Paul frequently modified standard epistolary expressions in his own peculiar ways, and that he may thus be seen as a bit of an innovator in the field of letter writing. However, there is little reason to infer that he deviated from the general convention in Greco-Roman antiquity to write letters according to the tripartite structure of opening, body, and closing. Paul's thanksgivings and "paraenesis" are therefore constituent parts of the body and should be read as such, i.e. as components of the letter's main message. Unless well informed of a distinctive Pauline way of writing four- or five-part letters, no first century audience of his would have expected anything else from him but a regular three-part letter. Hence, when we read a letter like Romans with a different epistolary structure in view, we are less capable of making out its message within its first century Roman context.

---

[73] Rom 1:8; 1 Cor 1:4–7; Phil 1:3–6; 1 Thess 1:2–10; Phlm 4–7. Cf., however, 2 Cor 1:10–11.

[74] See esp. Roberts, "Transitions" (1986).

[75] So also, e.g., Berger, "Apostelbrief" (1974) 219–24; idem, "Gattungen" (1984) 1047; Aune, *New Testament* (1987) 186; Lampe, *Christen* (1987) 55, 127 n. 11; du Toit, "Persuasion" (1989) 206; Murphy-O'Connor, *Paul* (1995) 62. Cf. Porter, "Paul" (1997) 573. On *captatio benevolentiae* in general, see Wessel, "Captatio" (1994). Cf. the discussion in sec. 3.2.1 below on Paul's *captatio benevolentiae* in Rom.

3. Epistolary Structure of Romans

3.1. Epistolary Opening (1:1–7)

As we recall, the opening of an ancient letter could be decisive for the establishment or manifestation of the social relationship between correspondents. This is because the interpersonal context for the entire discourse was normally established in this part. Studies of the Greek papyri, for instance, show that "the keeping-in-touch aspect of letter writing . . ., which reveals the general character of the correspondents' relationship toward each other, comes to expression primarily through conventions that open or conclude the letter. . . . The writer's presence and disposition in writing is conveyed to the recipient(s) in these two parts of the letter's structure."[76] The opening of Paul's letter to the Romans provides us with an unusual amount of information about the relationship between Paul and the letter's recipients.[77] In fact, "[n]o other known ancient letter from the Graeco-Roman or traditionally Jewish environment contains such an extensive letter opening."[78] This unique extent of the opening would have been identified by the audience, and it probably would have amazed them as well. There is therefore good reason to believe that Paul's audience would have paid special attention to the information provided in this initial section of the letter.

Three elements come into focus in the opening: 1) the identification and status of the sender—Paul, 2) the content of the εὐαγγέλιον θεοῦ, and 3) the identification and status of the recipients. Basically, these elements are expressed through the superscription (1:1), opening extension (vv. 2–6), and adscription (v. 7a).[79]

---

[76] White, *Light* (1986) 219.
[77] Or, at least, Paul's notion of this relationship.
[78] Byrskog, "Epistolography" (1997) 38. Byrskog notes that letter openings could be rather extensive in "the sphere of Pauline influence," as in the letters of Ignatius (n. 42). Titus 1:1–4 would also be an excellent example of this.
[79] On the peculiar Pauline salutation in 1:7b, see above in sec. 2. On the terminology "superscription" and "adscription," see sec. 1.1.

3.1.1. The Superscription (1:1) and the Identification of the Sender

Paul begins the letter by the conventional superscription, viz. stating his name in the nominative case. This is followed by no less than three modifiers: two nouns (δοῦλος, [κλητὸς] ἀπόστολος) and one participle (ἀφωρισμένος). In ancient Greco-Roman letters both superscriptions and adscriptions were frequently expanded by certain titles or roles, epithets, geographical locations, qualifications, or terms of relationship.[80] As for superscriptions specifically, such expansions were prominent in official correspondence,[81] but rarely found in private/personal letters.[82] This is, of course, anything but surprising, since the sender of a letter to friends or relatives was hardly in much need of a detailed presentation, whereas official correspondence typically required at least some sort of presentation. Furthermore, Paul's employment of the perfect passive participle ἀφωρισμένος to designate the particular purpose of his commission closely resembles the way in which Roman officials sometimes presented themselves and their offices in epistolary superscriptions, viz. by standardized forms of

---

[80] See, e.g., 2 Macc 11:34b Κόιντος Μέμμιος, Τίτος Μάνιος, πρεσβῦται Ῥωμαίων τῷ δήμῳ τῶν Ἰουδαίων χαίρειν, P.Tebt. 2.289 (23 C.E.) Ἀπολλώνιος στρατηγὸς Ἀκοῦτι τοπάρχῃ Τεβτύνεως χαίρειν, P.Meyer 6 (125 C.E.) Ἀνδρόνεικος ὁ ἱερεὺς καὶ ἀρχιδικαστὴς τῷ τῆς Ἡρακλείδου μερίδος τοῦ Ἀρσινοΐτου στρατηγῷ χαίρειν. See also the discussion in Reed, *Discourse* (1997) 181–83, and further examples in Exler, *Form* (1923) 24–60.

[81] Roller, *Formular* (1933) 431–33 n. 244; White, *Light* (1986) 200; Reed, *Discourse* (1997) 183. For example, P.Mich. 3.183 (182 B.C.E.) contains a legal agreement with the opening "Eirene, daughter of Orphis, a Macedonian woman, with her guardian, her husband, Agamemnon, son of Chrysermos, a native of Lalassis, to Leontiskos, Thymos and Tesenouphis, greeting" (trans. White, *Light* [1986] 59).

[82] For instance, out of Exler's 220 examples of openings in such letters (which he calls "familiar letters," i.e. "communications between relatives and friends; also other letters which in their expressions betray a certain degree of familiarity"; *Form* [1923] 23) I have only found five clear examples—none prior to the 2nd cent. C.E.—in which the sender's name is modified or expanded in some way (viz. in P.Lond. [P.B.M. in Exler] 3.899; P.Oxy. 6.933; BGU 2.435; P.Stras. 1.37; PSI 3.236; note that the texts of P.Ryl. 2.234 and P.Oxy. 12.1573 are corrupt, the latter of which, however, may probably be regarded as a "business letter").

perfect passive participles.[83] In this respect, Paul's opening words in Romans would no doubt have set the letter in a certain official context. That, in turn, would have been recognized by the audience, who almost certainly were acquainted with characteristic official superscriptions,[84] affecting their reception of the letter's message accordingly. At the same time, the audience would not have considered Paul's choice and number of epithets in the superscription as something extraordinary, but as a natural way of presentation for a person of authority. On the other hand, a comparison with Paul's other extant letters betrays that the amount of modifying epithets in the superscription of Romans is exceptionally large.[85] While the Roman recipients would hardly have been aware of that, it reveals that Paul himself was deeply concerned with pointing out his authoritative status for this particular audience.

Paul presents himself as one who has not been presented before, presumably because this is his initial act of "evangelizing" in Rome (cf. 1:10–14a; 15:22–23).[86] He begins with specifying on behalf of whom he acts. As a "slave (δοῦλος) of Christ Jesus" Paul is devoted to the Jewish Messiah Jesus, who is his master (cf. 1:4). Here, Paul does not use the word δοῦλος to indicate his "humility," as some would have it.[87] On the contrary, defined by the genitive Χριστοῦ Ἰησοῦ, it points to the messianic source of Paul's work and thus his authority.[88] Furthermore, the word δοῦλος echoes scriptural language used of Jewish leaders and prophets chosen by God to carry

---

[83] See Sherk, *RDGE* nos. 28 A 1–2; 58.3; 67.3 (ἀποδεδειγμένος); 26 col. b 7–8; 60 A 2–3 (καθεσταμένος); Josephus, *A.J.* 20.11 (ἀποδεδειγμένος). Cf. also P.Fay. 14.1–2 (124 B.C.E.); P.Oxy. 1.47.2 (83–88 C.E.) (προκεχειρισμένος).

[84] Cf. sec. 1.1 above.

[85] In 1–2 Cor and Gal Paul uses ἀπόστολος only; in Phil he uses δοῦλοι (also referring to Timothy); Paul refers to himself as δέσμιος in Phlm; in 1 Thess such epithets are absent.

[86] Most scholars acknowledge that the extent of Paul's presentation of himself in the opening of Rom may be explained by the fact that he had never been to Rome.

[87] E.g. Schnider and Stenger, *Studien* (1987) 10.

[88] Cf. Jewett, "Ambassadorial" (1982) 13; Brown, "Δοῦλος" (2001); Blumenfeld, *Political* (2001) 308–10. Sass, "Bedeutung" (1941) concludes that δοῦλος in Rom 1:1 is an "Amstbegriff" (p. 32).

out specific tasks in God's plan of salvation.[89] Paul thus places himself within the context of Jewish prophetic tradition, of which audience acquainted with Jewish scriptures would have been well aware.

Paul then proceeds to specify his "official" role in his undertaking as well as its purpose. He has been "called" (κλητός) to be a "messenger"—an "apostle" (ἀπόστολος)—"set apart" (ἀφωρισμένος) for the specific purpose of delivering the message of the εὐαγγέλιον θεοῦ.[90] Paul's terminology implies that he has been specifically chosen and appointed by God to deliver God's "good news." His authoritative status as an apostle of God is thus established.[91] After reading and hearing the letter's superscription, the Roman audience would hardly have failed to grasp Paul's claim of divine authority over those for whom the εὐαγγέλιον was intended.

3.1.2. The Opening Extension (1:2–6) and the Εὐαγγέλιον Θεοῦ

Viewed in its epistolary setting, the placement of the extensive presentation of the εὐαγγέλιον θεοῦ between the superscription and the adscription is certainly striking. Written without this extension, the prescript would have accorded well with a regular letter opening: Παῦλος δοῦλος Χριστοῦ Ἰησοῦ, κλητὸς ἀπόστολος ἀφωρισμένος εἰς εὐαγγέλιον θεοῦ, πᾶσιν τοῖς οὖσιν ἐν Ῥώμῃ ἀγαπητοῖς θεοῦ, κλητοῖς ἁγίοις. The present arrangement, however, is so unique that it is not even found in Paul's other letters. In fact, none of them includes a formal presentation of the εὐαγγέλιον in

---

[89] E.g. Josh 14:7 (Moses); 24:29 (Joshua); Ps 77:70 (David); 2 Esd (Ezra) 9:11 ("the prophets"). See further Sandnes, *Paul* (1991) 146–53. It also reflects intertestamental language used of divinely inspired prophets, e.g. 1QpHab 2:9; 7:5 ("the prophets"). See also Weima, "Preaching" (1994) 340–41, to whom "it appears that Paul is claiming before his Roman readers an authority enjoyed by the prophets" (p. 341).

[90] On Paul's calling and "setting apart" by God for this purpose, see Gal 1:15–16. Paul's terminology in this passage recalls Jer 1:5 and esp. Isa 49:1, 5; see Sandnes, *Paul* (1991) 59–62, 66–70. See also Ch. 4 sec. 2.3.2 below.

[91] Cf. the similar conclusions reached by Weima, "Preaching" (1994) 338–44. See also Holmberg, *Paul* (1978) 76–77; Elliott, *Rhetoric* (1990) 70–77.

the opening.⁹² This suggests two things: first, that Paul had a specific reason to explain to his audience what was meant by the phrase "God's good news," and, second, that the audience would immediately have recognized that this part of the opening was intended to carry special weight for the following discourse.

Paul presents the εὐαγγέλιον θεοῦ as already proclaimed in "holy writings" (γραφαῖς ἁγίαις) of the Jewish prophets (τῶν προφητῶν [θεοῦ]) (1:2). It is therefore no innovation of Paul himself, but in complete continuity with Jewish scriptural proclamation. The "good news" concern God's son,⁹³ Jesus the Messiah (vv. 3–4).⁹⁴ He, a descendant of the royal Messiah David,⁹⁵ was appointed son of God by his resurrection from the dead. Indeed, it is through God's son himself that Paul has received (ἐλάβομεν)⁹⁶ the "grace of apostleship" (χάριν καὶ ἀποστολήν)⁹⁷ to bring about "the obedience of faith (ὑπακοὴν πίστεως) among all the gentiles (ἐν πᾶσιν

---

⁹² The salutatory extension in the opening of Gal (1:4) is placed after the adscription, and is not a formal presentation of the εὐαγγέλιον.

⁹³ Note, however, Hays' suggestion that the phrase περὶ τοῦ υἱοῦ αὐτοῦ should not be read in connection with the noun εὐαγγέλιον, as is usually done, but in connection with the immediately preceding γραφαῖς ἁγίαις, thus yielding the translation "the Gospel of God, which he promised beforehand through his prophets in holy writings about his Son" (*Echoes* [1989] 85).

⁹⁴ It has been customary to hold that Rom 1:3–4 contains a "pre-Pauline formula" taken up by Paul; see most commentaries. For arguments against this view, however, see Davies, *Faith* (1990) 22–23; Scott, *Adoption* (1992) 227–36; and esp. Whitsett, "Son" (2000).

⁹⁵ See discussion in Dunn, *Romans* (1988) 1.12–13.

⁹⁶ It seems best to read ἐλάβομεν here as a "letter writer's plural" (so Turner, *Syntax* [1963] 28). If taken literally, it probably refers to Paul and his co-workers proclaiming God's "good news." But since the superscription does not mention others beside Paul, the latter is less likely.

⁹⁷ Χάριν καὶ ἀποστολήν read as *hendiadys*, i.e. a co-ordination of two items in which the one is dependent upon the other. So also Turner, *Syntax* (1963) 335–36; BDF § 442 (16).

τοῖς ἔθνεσιν) on behalf of his name."⁹⁸ Paul's reference to Jewish "holy writings" shows that he considers his audience to be familiar with these writings⁹⁹—a common basis for both parties—and thus with God's promises proclaimed by the prophets of old. However, if taken at face value, irrespective of the information provided in the subsequent discourse, the very presence of this careful introduction of the εὐαγγέλιον gives the impression that Paul presumes that his readers are largely ignorant of the implications of the recent fulfillment of God's promises, or, at least, that they need to be reminded of the essence and origin of the εὐαγγέλιον.

Although formally distinct from the superscription and the adscription, the opening extension in vv. 2–6 is clearly no digression or "a lengthy parenthesis."¹⁰⁰ As Reed rightly points out, it should be characterized "as a linguistically 'marked' development of [Paul's] subject matter, setting the stage for the rest of the discourse. This would not only be evident to Paul but, more importantly, to Graeco-Roman readers who were exposed to epistolary conventions."¹⁰¹ Apart from being a formal presentation of

---

[98] On the proclamation of God's name among τοῖς ἔθνεσιν, see esp. Isa 66:18–20; Ezek 36:22–23. Cf. also Pss 85:9; 101:13–23; Isa 12:4; 64:1; Ezek 39:7; Amos 9:12.

[99] Cf., e.g., the following: a) 7:1 in which Paul refers to the knowledge of the law (νόμος) by his audience (ἀδελφοί; cf. 1:13); b) a number of passages where Paul seems to presuppose the audience's awareness of, first, which specific writings are attributed to David (4:6; 11:9), Moses (9:15; 10:5, 19), Hosea (9:25), Isaiah (9:27, 29; 10:16, 20–21; 15:12), and "Elijah" (11:2 [ἐν Ἠλίᾳ]), and, second, that ἐν Ἰσαὰκ κληθήσεταί σοι σπέρμα in 9:7 refers to a scriptural passage; c) Paul's presupposition that the historical background of the address of "the scripture" to "the Pharaoh" in 9:17 is known by the audience (the same goes for the references to Sarah and Rebecca [9:9–10], and Jacob and Esau [9:12–13]). For discussion of potential Greek editions of the scriptural texts available to the Roman audience (probably some form of the LXX), see Hays, *Echoes* (1989) x–xi; Stanley, *Paul* (1992) 37–61, 67–79, 340–341; Walser, "Greek" (2001) 148. Cf. the discussion in Ch. 2 sec. 2.2 below.

[100] Dunn, *Romans* (1988) 1.5.

[101] *Discourse* (1997) 182. Cf. Achtemeier, "Judgments" (1997) 13, who objects to the common view that the theme of Rom is found in 1:16–17: "A more appropriate locus for such a theme would be at the beginning of the letter, and in that case

God's "good news," the extension functions as an additional specification not only of the sender but of the recipients as well, and as a thorough explanation of the relationship between these two parties. I will return to this in the following section.

3.1.3. The Adscription (1:7a) and the Identification of the Recipients

As was customary in ancient letters, the adscription stands in the dative case. The letter is explicitly addressed to "all those who are in Rome" (πᾶσιν τοῖς οὖσιν ἐν Ῥώμῃ) modified by three qualifying adjectives descriptive of the recipients, viz. "[God's] beloved" (ἀγαπητοῖς [θεοῦ]), "called to be devout" (κλητοῖς ἁγίοις). As mentioned above, expansions of adscriptions were frequent in ancient letters. The use of qualifying designations specifically was, however, rather stereotyped.[102] From the first century C.E. onward it typically included "(my/our) own" (τῷ ἰδίῳ), "our" (τῷ ἡμετέρῳ), "dearest" (τῷ φιλτάτῳ), or "most honored" (τῷ τιμιωτάτῳ),[103] none of which occur in Paul's letters. Somewhat unexpectedly, designations like these were not restricted to private/personal letters,[104] but were also used in official correspondence, notably of a friendly[105] and/or diplo-

---

1:2–4 would be an admirable candidate, summarizing as it does the economy of salvation and leading into Paul's declaration of his own call to evangelize the gentiles (v. 5)."

[102] See Exler, *Form* (1923) 29–31, 54–56, 62–63; Koskenniemi, *Studien* (1956) 95–104; White, "New Testament" (1984) 1734 n. 9.

[103] E.g. *BGU* 1.37 (50 C.E.) Μυσταρίων Στοτόητι τῶι ἰδίωι πλεῖστα χαίρειν, 4.1079 (41 C.E.) Σαραπίων Ἡρακλείδῃ τῷ ἡμετέρῳ χαίρειν, P.Ryl. 2.231 (40 C.E.) Ἀμμώνιος Ἀφροδισίωι τῷ φιλτάτῳ χαίρειν, P.Oxy. 2.292 (ca. 25 C.E.) Θέων Τυράννωι τῶι τιμιωτάτωι πλεῖστα χαίρειν (a letter of introduction).

[104] In fact, many private/personal papyri in which these designations are used ultimately concern business affairs, e.g. P.Ryl. 2.229 (38 C.E.); 2.230; 2.231; P.Lond. 3.893 (all from 40 C.E.); *BGU* 4.1079 (41 C.E.); 1.37 (50 C.E.); P.Mert. 1.12 (58 C.E.); P.Fay. 110 (94 C.E.); 112 (99 C.E.).

[105] See, e.g., the business instructions and orders of a strategos to a dioiketes (an inferior) in P.Oxy. 2.291 (25–26 C.E.) using τῷ φιλτάτῳ. See also P.Tebt. 2.410 (16 C.E.); P.Oxy. 12.1480 (32 C.E.); 1422 (128 C.E.). Cf. *UPZ* 1.64 (156 B.C.E.) with

matic[106] character. Whereas qualifying designations may be found in Paul's adscriptions elsewhere,[107] the use in Romans exceeds his regular custom. Although it is probably unwise to make too much out of this, both the number and choice of designations point to the apostle's friendly or diplomatic disposition towards the audience.

At first sight, the adscription seems to include a rather general identification of the letter's recipients. However, although the geographical location is a general one, the recipients are not identified solely as residents of Rome. Rather, they are explicitly addressed as those Roman residents who stand in a loving relationship with God to whom they are "called to be devout." In other words, the recipients belong to a specific group of people in Rome recognized by and consecrated to the Jewish God. Moreover, one of the unique features of Paul's opening in Romans is that the identity of the recipients is partly established prior to the formal address in the adscription.[108] Immediately preceding the adscription Paul's audience is directly addressed as being among those gentiles whose obedience of faith Paul was assigned to bring about. As the rest of the gentiles, they are "called to belong to Jesus Christ" (κλητοὶ Ἰησοῦ Χριστοῦ, v. 6). That is, the "good news" about Jesus are intended for them as well. That this is what Paul is saying is clear enough by the coordination of ἐν πᾶσιν τοῖς ἔθνεσιν (v. 5) and ἐν οἷς (v. 6). Paul might as well have written (vv. 5–6): ἐλάβομεν χάριν καὶ ἀποστολὴν εἰς ὑπακοὴν πίστεως ἐν ὑμῖν. But since he is concerned with giving his audience an accurate description of his mission in general and his reasons for writing to Rome in particular, he includes the words πᾶσιν τοῖς ἔθνεσιν. For the audience, these words would have functioned as the initial link between God's "good news" and themselves. It is

---

the designation τὰ ἀδελφῶι. Further examples from the papyri may be found in Exler, *Form* (1923) 54–56. Cf. also Josephus, *Vita* 365–366.

[106] See, e.g., 1 Macc 10:18; 11:30; 12:6; 13:36; 14:20; Josephus, *A.J.* 13.45.

[107] See esp. 1 Cor 1:2, where the adj. ἅγιος is actually a repetition of the verb ἁγιάζω (ἡγιασμένοις [ἐν Χριστῷ Ἰησοῦ], κλητοῖς ἁγίοις). Cf. Phlm 1, in which Philemon is addressed as τῷ ἀγαπητῷ. In Phil 1:1 and 2 Cor 1:1 Paul uses the noun ὁ ἅγιος.

[108] This is also stressed by Dahl, "Missionary" (1977) 75.

precisely at this point in the text that Paul as God's messenger, the "good news," and the audience converge.

While the adscription describes the recipients' current relationship with God, the opening extension in vv. 2–6 explains their relation to the Messiah and to his apostle, Paul. Hence, a hierarchical relationship between the participants is established in the opening, extending from God (vv. 1–2) to God's son, Jesus (vv. 3–4), through Paul (v. 5 [together with v. 1]) to the letter's recipients (vv. 6–7). Paul has thus informed the audience of his status towards them, and vice versa.

3.2. Epistolary Body (1:8–15:33)

The main part of Romans (1:8–15:33) is not exceptionally long among Paul's letters.[109] The body of First Corinthians (1:4–16:18) is similar in length. However, the macrostructural character of the main parts of these two letters differs considerably. The body of First Corinthians may roughly be divided into several sections according to the topics under discussion. These topics are typically introduced by περὶ (δέ) with the genitive (7:1, 25; 8:1, 4; 12:1; 16:1, 12)—a common form of topical introduction in ancient literature, including letters.[110] The usage of περὶ (δέ) in First Corinthians implies that the subject under discussion was previously known to the audience.[111] Paul's letter to the Romans, on the other hand, does not include περὶ (δέ) as an introductory phrase, the use of which would have implied the audience's familiarity with the subject. Generally speaking, the

---

[109] On the length of Rom, Deissmann comments: "Die Länge des Textes darf man nicht gegen die Brieflichkeit geltend machen: es gibt lange Briefe, und es gibt kurze Episteln" (*Licht* [1923] 202–3). Interestingly, in Demosthenes' *Ep.* 3 (widely considered authentic), which is an exceedingly long letter, he writes: "This complaint . . ., though now in outline only (ἐν κεφαλαίῳ) I would gladly enlarge upon a little later in a long letter (δι' ἐπιστολῆς μακρᾶς)" (37).

[110] See esp. Mitchell, "περὶ δέ" (1989) 236–54; Stirewalt, *Paul* (2003) 66–77.

[111] Cf. 1 Thess 4:9, 13; 5:1 (perhaps also 2 Cor 9:1). So Mitchell comments: "By the formula περὶ δέ an author introduces a new topic *the only requirement of which is that it is readily known to both author and reader*" ("περὶ δέ" [1989] 234; emphasis her).

main subject(s) of this letter is gradually worked out with the aid of a dialogical style (chs. 2–11),[112] to be followed up by a lengthy hortatory discourse (chs. 12–15).

A substantial number of scholars share the assumption that the body of Romans is practically devoid of specific epistolary expressions. Analyses of the text's structure have therefore commonly been based either on subject matter, i.e. on Paul's recurrent use of certain "key terms,"[113] or on rhetorical rules of *dispositio*.[114] Typical of the latter approach, decidedly favored in recent scholarship, is the treatment of the text as if Paul had written a rhetorical speech and put it in an epistolary framework. One misguided result of such an approach is that the letter's main part is read as largely unattached to and independent of the opening and closing.

To be sure, the amount of standard epistolary terminology in the body may be somewhat restricted, but not as is usually assumed by scholars. Several such expressions occur at the beginning and end of the body which, I claim, have wrongly been perceived as integral parts either of the opening and closing or of specific units distinct from the body (such as "the thanksgiving"). Moreover, a very common epistolary formula occurs at the middle of the body (approximately) which has received much too little attention in terms of its epistolary context and macrostructural significance for Romans.

---

[112] See Ch. 3 below. To be sure, dialogical elements are also widely employed in 1 Cor, but, unlike Rom, these are mostly confined to rhetorical questions (without explicit answers); see 1:13, 20; 2:11, 16; 3:3–5, 16; 4:7, 21; 5:6, 12; 6:1–9, 19; 7:16; 8:10; 9:1, 4–12, 18, 24; 10:16, 22, 29–30; 11:13–14, 22; 12:15–17, 19, 29–30; 14:6–9; 15:12, 29–30, 32. Cf. the slightly different style in 6:15 (answered by μὴ γένοιτο); 10:18–20; 14:15–17, 26 (with τί οὖν); 15:35 (ἀλλὰ ἐρεῖ τις followed by question posed by Paul's interlocutor), analogous to the dialogical style characteristic of Rom.

[113] See, e.g., Dunn's "Paul's Epistle" (1987).

[114] So, e.g., Wuellner, "Rhetoric" (1976); Jewett, "Argument" (1991); Hellholm, "Amplificatio" (1993); Dormeyer, *New Testament* (1998) 212–13.

3.2.1. The Transition To and Beginning of the Body

Several proposals have been made by scholars as to where Paul initiates the body of his letter. While some suggest that it begins with the so-called disclosure formula in 1:13 (οὐ θέλω δὲ ὑμᾶς ἀγνοεῖν, ἀδελφοί, ὅτι. . .),[115] others claim that it begins with Paul's statement in v. 16[116] (commonly labelled the letter's "theme," together with v. 17). Still others, viewing vv. 16–17 as a part of the opening, hold that the body does not begin until v. 18.[117]

The second and third propositions may be dismissed with reasonable certainty, since they fail to do justice to Paul's grammar by ignoring clear structural markers in the text, viz. the conjunctive γάρ both in v. 16 and v. 18.[118] It is highly unlikely that Paul would have initiated the body of the letter with the particle γάρ. The first suggestion, on the other hand, merits more attention because it is based on the fact that ancient letter writers of-

---

[115] E.g. Sanders, "Transition" (1962) 359–60; White, "Introductory" (1971); Doty, *Letters* (1973) 43; du Toit, "Persuasion" (1989) 208; Elliott, *Rhetoric* (1990) 71, 80–85.

[116] E.g. Schnider and Stenger, *Studien* (1987) 54; Jervis, *Purpose* (1991) 104–7; Fitzmyer, *Romans* (1993) 253–55; Weima, "Preaching" (1994) 346–53.

[117] E.g. Käsemann, *Römer* (1974) v, 1; Wilckens, *Römer* (1978) 1.ix, 15–16; Roberts, "Transitions" (1986); Dunn, *Romans* (1988) 1.27, 37–38, 50.

[118] It is possible that this understanding of the text may at times have been influenced by the arrangement in standard text editions, such as [27]Nestle-Aland, in which vv. 16–17 constitute a separate paragraph with an additional space between v. 17 and v. 18. Holmstrand, *Markers* (1997) 14, rightly asks: "Is it not in fact rather odd to treat three sentences [i.e. 1:16a, 16b, 17] beginning with γάρ as a separate paragraph with a distinct function of its own, namely that of setting out the theme of the entire epistle?" On this arrangement, Elliott comments somewhat ironically: "Numerous commentators follow text editions (e.g., Nestle-Aland[26]) in isolating 1.16–17 as the letter's 'theme', almost as if the superscription περὶ τοῦ εὐαγγελίου or περὶ τῆς δικαιοσύνης θεοῦ stood in the text at this point" (*Rhetoric* [1990] 84 n. 2; cf. idem, *Liberating* [1995] 74–75). Similarly also Achtemeier, "Judgments" (1997) 13.

ten introduced the main part of their letters with a disclosure formula.[119] Sometimes, especially in brief letters, the formula revealed the sender's main or sole purpose with the letter.[120] This, however, does not appear to have been its primary function, since the formula was also used when several different reasons were given for writing.[121] Moreover, although the formula often appeared at the beginning of the letter's main part it was not a transitional formula per se from the opening to the body, but was used at various places within the latter as well.[122]

Indeed, a look at the occurrence of the formula in Paul's letters reveals that his usage was rather fluid in this respect. Besides Romans 1:13, a disclosure formula occurs twice at or near the epistolary opening (2 Cor 1:8; Phil 1:12). More frequently, however, the formula is found within the main part of his letters (Rom 11:25; 1 Cor 10:1; 11:3; 12:1; 1 Thess 4:13).[123] Every instance, inclusive of the former group, conveys an important information to Paul's audience. But none of these occurrences conveys *the* information about the letter's content or Paul's purpose for writing. Rather, the disclosure formula was available to Paul as one of the means by which he could underscore certain parts or aspects of his message.

---

[119] So, e.g., in P.Mich. 1.6.1–2 (257 B.C.E.); P.Köln 1.56.3; P.Oslo.Inv. 1475.3 (1st cent. C.E.); P.Mich. 8.464.3–4 (99 C.E.); P.Oslo 2.50.3 (1st–2nd cent. C.E.); P.Oxy. 8.1155.2–3 (104 C.E.); P.Fay. 123.5–7 (ca. 110 C.E.); P.Giss. 1.11.4 (118 C.E.); 1.13.4–5 (116–120 C.E.). Cf. Demosthenes, *Ep.* 3.1. On the characteristic features of the formula, see esp. Mullins, "Disclosure" (1964). See also Meecham, *Light* (1923) 124; Sanders, "Transition" (1962); White, "Introductory" (1971); idem, *Light* (1986) 207; Reed, *Discourse* (1997) 210–12.

[120] E.g. P.Mich. 8.491.4–5 (2nd cent. C.E.) γεινώσκειν σε θέλω, μήτηρ, ὅτι ἐρρωμένος ἐγενόμην εἰς Ῥώμην ("I want you to know, mother, that I arrived in Rome safely"; trans. White, *Light* [1986] 164).

[121] See esp. P.Mich. 3.203.2–3, 5–6, 8–9, 13–14 (114–116 C.E.).

[122] In addition to P.Mich. 3.203 above, see Sherk, *RDGE* nos. 21, col. 2.6; 49, A 13; 49, B 3; 52.21; Artaxerxes, *Ep.* 2; Josephus, *A.J.* 16.173; P.Oxy. 4.743.27–28 (2 B.C.E.); P.Oslo 3.151.9–10 (1st–2nd cent. C.E.); *BGU* 4.1040.4–5, 15, 28, 29–30 (2nd cent. C.E.); P.Hamb. 2.192.17–18 (3rd cent. C.E.).

[123] Cf. 1 Cor 12:3; 15:1; 2 Cor 8:1; Gal 1:11, with the verb γνωρίζω. Cf. also Col 2:1.

Paul's general employment of disclosure formulas gives therefore little reason to infer that he used such a formula specifically to introduce the body of Romans. It is more likely that by using a disclosure formula in 1:13 Paul's aim was to ensure the audience's attention to and acceptance of his statement that, despite the failure to do so, he had "frequently intended to come" to them.

Elsewhere I have argued that current readings of Romans 1:13–15 are based on inaccurate punctuation and syntax, and suggested a more plausible reading of the passage.[124] A summary account of my arguments and suggestions there are in order, the significance of which will subsequently become apparent for the present discussion.

Most of the syntactical problems scholars have faced in this passage may be overcome by challenging the established punctuation. Thus, instead of a period mark at the end of v. 13, a comma should be read, and instead of following the verse division of the text, a period mark should be placed after the word ἀνοήτοις. Syntactically, this means, first, that the dative phrase Ἕλλησίν τε καὶ βαρβάροις, σοφοῖς τε καὶ ἀνοήτοις is read as an apposition to the preceding dative τοῖς λοιποῖς ἔθνεσιν (i.e. "the rest of the gentiles, Greeks as well as barbarians, wise as well as ignorant"), and, second, that ὀφειλέτης εἰμί in v. 14b forms a construction with the infinitive εὐαγγελίσασθαι in v. 15 (i.e. "I am bound ... to announce the gospel"). Further, the problematic phrase τὸ κατ' ἐμὲ πρόθυμον may be read adverbially as an accusative of respect, with κατ' ἐμέ understood as a circumlocution for the possessive genitive (i.e. "with respect to my goodwill," or, more succinctly, "with [my] goodwill"). All this conforms well with Paul's language elsewhere in his letters; indeed, better in whole than prevailing readings suggest. In order to explain more fully the effects of this reading, I give the following translation of 1:13–15:

> But I do not want you to be ignorant of, brothers, that I have frequently intended to come to you—but was hindered until now—in order that I may reap some harvest among you as I have among the rest of the gentiles, Greeks as well as barbarians, wise as well as ignorant.

---

[124] Thorsteinsson, "Missionary" (2002).

I am bound, then,[125] to announce the gospel with goodwill to you also who are in Rome.

In light of this alternative reading, I have also suggested that the asyndeton in 1:14b (ὀφειλέτης εἰμί etc.) may introduce a new phase in the discourse. The suggestion is strengthened by the fact that Paul sometimes uses asyndeton to signal macrostructural developments in his letters (as evident in Rom 9:1).[126]

The significance of the above reading for the present discussion may now be brought to the fore. First, instead of initiating a new thought in the discourse, the disclosure formula in 1:13 reveals an important information (viz. in vv. 13b–14a) which is closely connected with the preceding text, but less so with the following. In other words, contrary to common opinion, 1:13–15 is not a structural unity. Second, rather than introducing the body of the letter, the disclosure formula and the following in vv. 13–14a constitute the latter part of Paul's initial statements in the body, the former being found in vv. 8–12. This can be seen by the use of πρῶτον μέν in v. 8, which is followed by two explanatory sentences with γάρ (vv. 9 and 11),[127] and then answered by δέ in v. 13.[128] Hence, I can see no compelling reason not to regard 1:8 as the beginning of the body of Romans, immediately following the opening elements of superscription, adscription, and salutation.

As we recall, thanksgiving formulas at or near the beginning of Paul's letters may have had the primary function of initiating his *captatio benevolentiae* (his effort to capture the audience's goodwill).[129] In Romans this for-

---

[125] The adverb οὕτως is here read in an absolute inferential sense. For alternative readings, see Thorsteinsson, "Missionary" (2002) 543–44.
[126] Cf., e.g., 1 Cor 5:1; 6:12; 2 Cor 6:11; Gal 4:12, 21; 6:11; Phil 3:17.
[127] Verse 12 includes a subordinate purpose clause with additional explanation (indicated by τοῦτο δέ ἐστιν) of the preceding purpose clause (εἰς τὸ στηριχθῆναι ὑμᾶς).
[128] Πρῶτον μέν is frequently answered by δέ only; see LSJ, s.v. πρότερος B.III.3.a.
[129] See above in sec. 2. On Rom 1:8 and following as Paul's *captatio benevolentiae*, see also Käsemann, *Römer* (1974) 15; Wilckens, *Römer* (1978) 1.77; Kennedy, *New Testament* (1984) 153; Lampe, *Christen* (1987) 55; Anderson, *Rhetorical* (1996) 184–85; Caragounis, "Obscurity" (1998) 260. Similarly also Elliott, *Rhetoric* (1990) 77–80; Weima, "Preaching" (1994) 346–53.

mula occurs at the beginning of the body (1:8), where Paul gives thanks to God for the audience because of their widely celebrated "loyalty" (πίστις).[130] Somewhat boldly, Paul states that it is being "proclaimed in all the world" (καταγγέλλεται ἐν ὅλῳ τῷ κόσμῳ). Additional acknowledgment of the audience's πίστις was hardly needed. Following the thanksgiving, Paul makes use of another common epistolary formula, viz. the μνεία–motif (v. 9),[131] here combined with a prayer formula (ἐπὶ τῶν προσευχῶν μου, v. 10).[132] In the common letter tradition, the focus of these formulas was particularly aimed at the relationship between the correspondents, the use of which expressed the friendly disposition of the sender(s) towards the recipient(s).[133] Paul's usage of both formulas is therefore well suited for his *captatio benevolentiae* in Romans. By calling no less authority than God as a "witness" (μάρτυς) he further adds force to his statement that he "constantly" (ἀδιαλείπτως) "makes mention" (μνείαν ποιοῦμαι)[134] of the audience in his prayers (τῶν προσευχῶν).[135] The main subject of Paul's prayers,

---

[130] Paul's words in Rom 1:8 are usually taken to mean that he is praising the audience for their acclaimed "Christian faith." Although this is not unlikely, it does not have to be the case. Paul's reference to Jesus Christ concerns his own thanksgiving to God and not the audience's πίστις. Paul may as well be praising the audience for their loyalty to the Jewish way of life (including "Christian") as opposed to the pagan way of life. On the frequent use of the term πίστις and equivalents in relation to *captatio benevolentiae* in official correspondence, see sec. 3.2.2 below.

[131] See, e.g., P.Cair.Zen. 1.59076.2–3 (257 B.C.E.) . . . σοῦ διὰ παντὸς μνείαν ποιούμενος, ὥσπερ δίκαιον ἦν. Koskenniemi informs us that "[d]as μνεία–Motiv gehört zu den allerfestesten Bestandteilen der Brief-Phraseologie und erscheint von den frühesten Anfängen an bis hin zu den christlichen Briefen des 4. Jahrhunderts" (*Studien* [1956] 147). For further examples, see esp. ibid., 145–48; Arzt, "Thanksgiving" (1994) 42–44.

[132] Ancient letter writers sometimes combined the μνεία–motif with a prayer, thus giving it a religious aspect; see, e.g., BGU 10.2006.2–3 (2nd cent. B.C.E.); 2.632.3–6 (2nd cent. C.E.).

[133] See Koskenniemi, *Studien* (1956) 145–48.

[134] On this meaning of the phrase, see LSJ, s.v. μνεία II.

[135] Cf. the diplomatic letter from the Jewish high priest Jonathan (et al.) to the Spartans in 1 Macc 12:6–18. In their effort to renew the nations' "alliance and friendship" (v. 8), the senders note (v. 11): "We therefore remember you

however, is his wish to "somehow sometime at last" (πως ἤδη ποτέ) manage to come to the city of Rome (v. 10). Paul then carefully expresses his desire to see his audience with the strong verb ἐπιποθῶ (v. 11).[136]

At this point, the audience might naturally ask: "If so, why haven't you come already?" Paul answers this hypothetical question by a disclosure formula (v. 13), thus indicating the significance of the statement: "I want you to know . . . that I have frequently (πολλάκις) intended to come to you—but have been hindered until now (ἄχρι τοῦ δεῦρο)." The reason Paul gives for his serious delay (cf. 15:23) is that he has been occupied with "reaping the harvest" among other gentiles, "Greeks as well as barbarians, wise as well as ignorant." This clearly refers to his previous work among gentiles in the eastern part of his missionary province (cf. 15:19–22).[137]

After his carefully worked out *captatio benevolentiae* in 1:8–14a, Paul is prepared to present the main purpose of his writing. Referring to his "goodwill" (τὸ πρόθυμον) towards the audience, he declares that it is his duty (ὀφειλέτης εἰμί) to "proclaim the good news" (εὐαγγελίσασθαι) also to them, as well as to other gentiles (vv. 14b–15). For the audience, this statement comes, of course, as no surprise, since it was already hinted at in the epistolary opening (vv. 5–6). Here, however, it is explicitly stated that Paul's main concern with the letter is to proclaim God's gospel to gentiles in Rome.[138] It may be assumed, then, that this is what he subsequently carries out.

(μιμνησκόμεθα ὑμῶν) constantly (ἀδιαλείπτως) on every occasion, both at our festivals and on other appropriate days, at the sacrifices that we offer and in our prayers (ἐν ταῖς προσευχαῖς), as it is right and proper to remember brothers (μνημονεύειν ἀδελφῶν)." These words clearly function as the senders' *captatio benevolentiae* before turning to the issue of the "many trials and many wars" (v. 13) from which the Jewish nation had suffered, and because of which the nation now sought support from distant "brothers."

[136] Cf. the use of the verb in the similar contexts of Phil 1:8; 2:25–26; 1 Thess 3:6.
[137] On Paul's missionary province, see esp. Gal 2:7–9. Cf. 1:16; 2:2; Rom 1:5–6; 15:15–16, 18.
[138] Cf. Anderson's remarks: "*Formally* the proposition for the letter as a whole might be considered to be v.15. It is this statement (that it is Paul's desire to preach the Gospel to the Roman Christians) that forms the basis for Paul's following remarks

3.2.2. The Παρακαλῶ Sentence in 12:1-2

Apart from the disclosure formula in 11:25 (οὐ γὰρ θέλω ὑμᾶς ἀγνοεῖν, ἀδελφοί), there are few explicit signs of standard epistolary expressions until 12:1. As Carl J. Bjerkelund has shown, the words παρακαλῶ οὖν ὑμᾶς, ἀδελφοί etc. reflect a well known literary form in antiquity, the use of which was particularly prominent in letters and may therefore rightly be described as an established epistolary formula.[139] The formula was employed to express requests of various sorts. The basic characteristics were: 1) a background information of the request, sometimes implied by an inferential conjunction such as διό or οὖν, 2) a verb of request—typically ἀξιῶ, δέομαι, ἱκετεύω, ἐρωτῶ, παρακαλῶ, or the phrase καλῶς ἂν ποιήσαις—the choice of which often reveals the social relationship between the correspondents, and 3) the content of the request.[140] To these a direct address in the vocative was sometimes added.[141] This epistolary formula was widespread in antiquity,[142] used by people of diverse social status and in various situations. Thus it is commonly found, for instance, in a) private petitions to public officials,[143] the sender of which was normally an inferior (i.e. the let-

---

(indicated by the ensuing series of causal conjunctions [γάρ]), and also seems to be reflected upon again at the end of the 'sermon' (15.5ff)" (*Rhetorical* [1996] 185 [his emphasis]). Cf. also Bjerkelund, *Parakalô* (1967) 157; Wedderburn, *Reasons* (1988) 124, 138.

[139] *Parakalô* (1967) esp. 34–111. On the use of παρακαλῶ in speeches, Bjerkelund notes: "παρακαλῶ-Aufforderungen mit direkter Rede sind wir nur selten begegnet, abgesehen von den diplomatischen Ansprachen, deren Funktion und Charakter wir als brieflich bestimmt haben" (pp. 110–11). See also White, "New Testament" (1984) 1744; Reed, *Discourse* (1997) 265–72.

[140] E.g. UPZ 1.42.38–41 (162 B.C.E.) δεόμεθα οὖν ὑμῶν . . . ἀποστεῖλαι ἡμῶν τὴν ἔντευξιν ἐπὶ Διονύσιον, P.Oxy. 4.745.7–8 (ca. 1 C.E.) ἐρωτῶ οὖν σε μὴ ἄλλως ποιῆσαι.

[141] E.g. P.Mich. 8.485.9 (ca. 105 C.E.) διὸ παρακαλῶ σε, ἄδελφε . . .

[142] For Latin equivalents, cf., e.g., Cicero, *Quint. fratr.* 2.14; *Ep. Brut.* 12.2, 4; Seneca, *Epp.* 19.1; 20.1; Pliny, *Ep. Tra.* 4.6; 6.2 (cf. Trajan's response in 7); 11 and passim.

[143] E.g. P.Mich. 1.29 (256 B.C.E.), a letter addressed to the official Zenon from a native Egyptian widow. As in most petitions, the letter opens with the "To B from

ter of petition proper);[144] in b) various familiar requests,[145] sometimes implying efforts of persuasion;[146] in c) letters of recommendation;[147] or in d) official requests or exhortations, whether the correspondents were of equal[148] or non-equal[149] status. As a rule, the epistolary situation called for the appropriate form, the decisive element of which was the verb of request chosen by the sender.[150]

A" formula, indicating the sender's inferiority. It concludes with the words (lines 11–13): δέομαι ὂν σοι καὶ εἰκετεύω, μέ με παραελκύσῃς. γυνή ἰμὶ χέρα. εὐτύχι ("Therefore, I beg and entreat you, that you not put me off. I am a widowed woman. Farewell"; trans. White, *Light* [1986] 46).

[144] See esp. White, "Introductory" (1971) 93–94; idem, *Light* (1986) 194–96.

[145] E.g. P.Oxy. 2.294.28–30 (22 C.E.) ἐρωτῶ δέ σε καὶ παρακαλῶ γράψαι μοι ἀντιφώνησιν περὶ τῶν γενομένων ("I ask and beseech you to write me a response concerning the present matters"; trans. Reed, *Discourse* [1997] 267–68), a letter from Sarapion to his brother.

[146] E.g. P.Oxy. 4.744.6–7, 13–14 (1 B.C.E.) ἐρωτῶ σε καὶ παρακαλῶ σε, ἐπιμελήθητι τῷ παιδίῳ. . . . ἐρωτῶ σε οὖν ἵνα μὴ ἀγωνιάσῃς ("I urge and entreat you, be concerned about the child. . . . Therefore I urge you not to worry"; trans. White, *Light* [1986] 111–12), a letter from Hilarion to his wife (or sister).

[147] E.g. P.Oxy. 2.292.3–7 (ca. 25 C.E.) Ἡρακλείδης ὁ ἀποδιδούς σοι τὴν ἐπιστολὴν ἐστίν μου ἀδελφός· διὸ παρακαλῶ σε μετὰ πάσης δυνάμεως ἔχειν αὐτὸν συνεσταμένον ("Herakleides, who carries this letter to you, is my brother. Wherefore, I entreat you with all my power to regard him recommended"; trans. White, *Light* [1986] 118).

[148] E.g. Josephus, *A.J.* 8.52 διὸ παρακαλῶ σε συμπέμψαι τινὰς τοῖς ἐμοῖς εἰς Λίβανον τὸ ὄρος κόψοντας ξύλα ("I therefore request you to send some men along with mine to Mount Lebanon to cut timber"), a letter from king Solomon to Eiromos, the Tyrian king.

[149] E.g. Welles, *RCHP* no. 14.12–13 παρακαλοῦμεν δὲ καὶ εἰς τὸν λοιπὸγ χρόνον τὴν αὐτὴν ἔχειν αἵρεσιν πρὸς ἡμᾶς ("[W]e summon you for the future to maintain the same policy of friendship toward us"; trans. Welles), a letter from king Ptolemy II to the council and people of Miletus.

[150] In light of all this, it should be clear that the term "petition" preferred by some scholars, esp. Mullins, "Petition" (1962), as a general designation of the formula under discussion is insufficient and somewhat misleading. The term implies a much more limited use of it than the ancient documents actually attest. While Mullins' brief study of petitions among the Oxyrhynchus papyri is valuable for re-

In his survey of the verb παρακαλῶ and its equivalent ἐρωτῶ, Bjerkelund found that these were used in most types of letters. The closest parallels to Paul's usage, however, are found in official correspondence, particularly in Hellenistic royal letters of a diplomatic character:

> Die Schreiben offiziellen Charakters haben sich als das ergi[e]bigste Material erwiesen. Doch soll der Abstand zwischen privaten Briefen mit παρακαλῶ und den entsprechenden offiziellen Schreiben nicht übertrieben werden. Denn nicht in allen Dokumenten der letzten Kategorie sind wir auf Aufforderungen mit παρακαλῶ gestossen. Diesen sind wir nur in solchen begegnet, die ausgesprochen persönlichen Charakter haben, d. h. in Schriftstücken, die sich den Privatbriefen nähern. Das Interessante an diesen Briefen ist, dass παρακαλῶ hier in einem gepflegten diplomatischen Stil erscheint, der sich durch Jahrhunderte hindurch unverändert erhalten hat. Dieser Stil war Griechen und griechisch sprechenden Juden bekannt. Sowohl Könige wie auch Städte machten von ihm Gebrauch. . . . Die besten Beispiele für die Wohlabgewogenheit dieses Stiles finden wir in einigen hellenistischen Königsbriefen.[151]

Often being answers to particular requests, but sometimes written at the sender's own initiative, these letters served the basic function of establishing or assuring the goodwill of certain groups of people, cities, or nations towards the royal authority involved. This purpose was typically accomplished by showing mutual goodwill. Hence the frequent occurrences of words like εὔνοια, σπουδή, and προθυμία in this type of letters, as well as expressions of gratitude (εὐχαριστία etc.) and praise (ἔπαινος etc.) of the recipients, notably because of their loyalty (πίστις etc.).[152]

---

search into ancient petitionary letters, he has wrongly made this material sufficient basis for generalizations about the request formula in Paul's letters.

[151] *Parakalô* (1967) 110; cf. pp. 73–4, 86, 108.

[152] Examples of this terminology in official letters are abundant. See, e.g., Welles, *RCHP* nos. 6; 11; 13; 14; 15; 25; 26; 31; 32; 34; 35; 38; 49; 50; 52; 63; 66; 67; Sherk, *RDGE* nos. 14.50–55; 18.1–14, 42–48; 26 col. a 10–13; 34; 35; 38; 47.37–47; 58.73–84, 85–93; Philip, *Ep.* 5; 2 Macc 1:10–18; 9:19–27; *Let. Aris.* 35–40; Philo, *Legat.* 276–329; *CPJ* 2.153; Apollonius of Tyana, *Ep.* 53; Josephus, *A.J.* 8.51–52 (cf. 57); 13.45, 48; 20.11–14. Cf. Demosthenes, *Ep.* 1.3, 10. Cf. also the description of the "diplomatic letter" (πρεσβευτική) in Pseudo-Libanius, *Ep. Char.* 76, and in Menander Rhetor 2.423.6–424.2. See also discussions in

Out of several alternative verbs of request, the choice of παρακαλῶ was no mere chance. Since it expressed at once the sender's politeness and goodwill towards the recipients, the verb was well apt for the letter's diplomatic purpose. Whereas the use of verbs like ἀξιῶ or δέομαι normally indicated inferiority,[153] παρακαλῶ was appropriate for a superior concerned with sustaining his or her authoritative status without being unnecessarily and unwisely commanding.[154] In other words, the verb could have the diplomatic function of neither being commanding nor begging,[155] but somewhere in between depending on the larger context. This is the reason why the sense of παρακαλῶ could vary from "asking" or "appealing" to "urging" or "exhorting" and the like.

An illustrative example of how the epistolary situation could determine the language of the request is found in a letter sent to Erythrea from king Antiochus II (ca. 260 B.C.E.).[156] Following the epistolary opening, Antiochus describes how Erythrea's envoys had approached him bringing him a present and expressing the city's goodwill and gratitude towards the royal house (lines 6–12):

Bickermann, "Bellum" (1932) 63–64; Mosley, *Envoys* (1973) 93–95; Spicq, "εὐνοέω"; idem, "προθυμία" (1978–82); Mitchell, "Envoys" (1992) esp. 658–61.

[153] Apparently, this does not apply to Paul's use of δέομαι as a verb of request in 2 Cor 5:20; 10:2; Gal 4:12 (Paul never uses ἀξιῶ). For discussion of these interesting occurrences, see Mitternacht, *Forum* (1999) 200–232.

[154] Cf. the comments of Pseudo-Demetrius, *Ep. Typ.* 1, on the "friendly" (φιλικός) type of letter: "The friendly type . . . is one that seems to be written by a friend to a friend. But it is by no means (only) friends who write (in this manner). For frequently those in prominent positions (ἐν ὑπάρχοις κείμενοι) are expected by some to write in a friendly manner to their inferiors (ὑποδεεστέρους) and to others who are their equals (ἴσους). . . . There are times, indeed, when they write to them without knowing them (personally). They do so, not because they are close friends and have (only) one choice (of how to write), but because they think that nobody will refuse (ἀντερεῖν) them when they write in a friendly manner, but will rather submit and heed what they are writing (ὑπομενεῖν καὶ ποιήσειν περὶ ὧν γράφουσιν)."

[155] Bjerkelund, *Parakalô* (1967) 188.

[156] Welles, *RCHP* no. 15 (trans. his). See also Bjerkelund's analysis in *Parakalô* (1967) 62–63.

Having discoursed on the good-will (τῆς εὐνοίας) which you have always felt toward our house and on the gratitude (τῆς εὐχαριστίας) which your people entertain toward all its benefactors generally, and likewise on the esteem which your city enjoyed under the former kings, they asked (ἠξίουν) with all earnestness (σπουδῆς) and zeal (προθυμίας) that we should be friendly to you and should aid in advancing the city's interests in all that refers to glory and honor.

Antiochus then informs the recipients of his response to their request (lines 12–16):

> We have then accepted in a friendly spirit the honors and the wreath and the present also, and we praise (ἐπαινοῦμεν) you for being grateful (εὐχαρίστους) in all things—for you seem generally to pursue this as your policy. We have therefore from the beginning entertained good-will (εὔνοιαν) toward you . . .

Later in the letter, the king puts forth his own request (lines 30–34; the text is slightly corrupt):

> We summon (παρακαλοῦμεν) you also, remembering (μνημονεύοντας) that (we have always) tried earnestly . . . good-will (εὔνοιαν) as is just and . . . consistent with your previous actions . . . that you will remember (μνημονεύσειν) suitably those (by whom) you have been benefitted.

Whereas the verb ἀξιῶ is quite properly used of the envoys' petition before the king, the king himself uses παρακαλῶ as a polite, diplomatic verb of exhortation.[157]

As an expression of request, Paul frequently employs the verb παρακαλῶ,[158] the sense of which varies somewhat according to the larger context. In Romans 12:1 Paul uses παρακαλῶ in all likelihood as a refined verb of exhortation, resembling the diplomatic usage above. The subsequent se-

---

[157] Note that in some royal letters, which contain answers to requests from city councils, παρακαλῶ is used for the cities' actual or potential requests, with the sense of the verb ranging from "asking" to "exhorting"; see Welles, *RCHP* nos. 31.13, 24; 32.12–13, 23; 34.5–6, 17–18 (ἀξιῶ in line 13); 52.32. These letters, however, differ from the one above in that they do not contain any request from the king himself.

[158] Rom 12:1; 15:30; 16:17; 1 Cor 1:10; 4:16; 16:12, 15; 2 Cor 2:8; 6:1; 8:6; 9:5; 10:1; 12:8, 18; Phil 4:2; 1 Thess 2:12; 4:1, 10; 5:14; Phlm 9, 10. Cf. the use of ἐρωτῶ in Phil 4:3; 1 Thess 4:1 (with παρακαλῶ); 5:12.

ries of imperative expressions strongly suggest this, as does Paul's reference to his authority in v. 3 (λέγω[159] γὰρ διὰ τῆς χάριτος τῆς δοθείσης μοι παντὶ τῷ ὄντι ἐν ὑμῖν etc.), which clearly echoes Paul's claim of authority over non-Jews in the epistolary opening (1:5). This sense of παρακαλῶ would have been easily recognized by an audience familiar with official correspondence. Once again, then, Paul's language in relation to his employment of a widespread epistolary formula sets his letter in a certain official context.

It should be urged in this light that it is unlikely that Paul's audience would have taken the verb παρακαλῶ as a fixed technical term for introducing a distinct hortatory ("paraenetic") section within the letter, with no necessary dependence upon the preceding discourse. Paul does not use the verb here—or anywhere else in his letters—in this way, as has sometimes been asserted.[160] In fact, ancient documents hardly attest such usage at all,[161] which indicates that it would not only have been foreign to Paul but to his audience as well. It is much more probable that παρακαλῶ would simply have been one among several verbs from which Paul could choose in order to set forth his request. Because of its semantic flexibility this verb would have been the most appropriate for Paul's purpose, viz. to allow for hortatory weight in his request. Put differently, it is the larger context that gives παρακαλῶ an exhortative sense and not vice versa.

All basic characteristics of the request formula are present in Romans 12:1–2: 1) background information is implied by the conjunction οὖν, 2) the verb of request is, of course, παρακαλῶ, and 3) the content of the request is stated by its grammatical object παραστῆσαι τὰ σώματα ὑμῶν etc.

---

[159] Cf. the authoritative tone of λέγω in 1 Cor 7:8; 2 Cor 6:13; 7:3; 8:8; Gal 5:2; 1 Thess 4:15; Phlm 21.

[160] So, e.g., Grabner-Haider, *Paraklese* (1968) 7 (on Rom 12–15 as "Paraklese"); Ortkemper, *Leben* (1980) 19–21 (on Rom 12–13 as "Paränese"). Bryan, *Romans* (2000) 194, states: "I appeal to you (*parakalô . . . humas*) is the normal expression with which to introduce *parainesis*, and signals what is to come." This is simply incorrect.

[161] See Bjerkelund, *Parakalô* (1967) 58, 87, 189.

and, if the infinitive form is original,[162] μὴ συσχηματίζεσθαι . . . ἀλλὰ μεταμορφοῦσθαι etc. as well. As sometimes found in request formulas elsewhere, Paul addresses his audience directly with the vocative ἀδελφοί. This address both enhances Paul's politeness and creates a sense of presence, thus contributing to the audience's mutual goodwill.

With Romans 12:1 the discourse enters a new stage. This becomes evident when several converging features are considered: First, Paul's concluding hymn in 11:33–36 (ending with the adverb ἀμήν), second, the use and content of the request formula in 12:1–2, and, third, the general, almost sweeping, change of form from this point onward. Not only does the text subsequent to Paul's request differ from the preceding by the now dominant use of imperative language but also, as we shall see in Chapter Three below, by the total ceasing of the dialogical exchanges of questions and answers so prominent in chapters 3–11. The inferential conjunction οὖν within the request formula in 12:1–2 would have told the audience that by now the basis of Paul's request had been set out. They would have recognized that the occasion of the request consisted indeed of the preceding discourse as a whole.[163] As their reading and hearing proceeded, the audience would probably have understood also that 12:1–2 functioned simultaneously as a summary of the following hortatory discourse.

In terms of the epistolary structure of Romans, the following inference may be drawn. Due, first, to the central position and function of request formulas in ancient letters in general, many of which have requests as their sole or main occasion and purpose, second, to the central role played by the request formula in Romans 12:1–2, which not only has the preceding discourse in its entirety as its basis, but also functions properly as a summary of the subsequent one, and, third, to the unmistakable change of form oc-

---

[162] The earliest MSS show evidence of some uncertainty whether the impv. or the inf. was the original form. Whereas P^{46} B* *pm* include the two impvs. (cf. [27]Nestle-Aland), A B^2 D* *pm* have infs. in both places. The latter form is also partly supported by ℵ D^2 *pc* in which μεταμορφῶ (only) is read in the inf. The reading of A (two infs.) was preferred by von Soden in his 1913 edition of the text, and noted as a reading of equal value in the margin of Westcott and Hort's edition of 1881.

[163] See esp. Furnish, *Theology* (1968) 98–106. Cf. Berger, "Apostelbrief" (1974) 229; Smiga, "Romans 12:1–2" (1991).

curing at this point in the text, the hortatory request in 12:1–2 constitutes the structural center of Paul's letter.[164]

3.2.3. The Confidence Expression and Visiting Theme in 15:14–29

In 15:14 Paul expresses his confidence (πέπεισμαι) in the audience that they are indeed "full of goodness (μεστοὶ ἀγαθωσύνης), filled with all knowledge (πεπληρωμένοι πάσης γνώσεως), capable also of admonishing one another (δυνάμενοι καὶ ἀλλήλους νουθετεῖν)." Stanley N. Olson's study of confidence expressions in ancient letters reveals that several, somewhat stereotypical forms of expressions were in use, the parallels of which are mostly related to function. In general, the confidence expression is closely tied to the purpose of the letter and "the tone of confidence is more pragmatic than sincere—though it may be both."[165] As a rule, the expression occurs in letters that include requests of some kind.[166] Even if the letter had other purposes as well, the confidence expression was linked to particular requests made in it, and was meant to avoid the appearance of harshness and/or to urge the recipients to act as requested.[167]

By expressing his confidence in the audience in Romans 15:14 Paul exhorts them to act according to his earlier hortatory request, namely, the one in 12.1–2 and elaborated upon in 12:3–15:13.[168] The function of Paul's

---

[164] On the request formula in Gal 4:12 as the decisive turning point of that letter, cf. Hansen, "Paradigm" (1994) 195–201; Mitternacht, *Forum* (1999) 200–232; idem, "Foolish" (2002) 419–23; Dahl, "Paul's letter" (2002) 134–39, 141–42. Mitternacht describes Gal as a "halb-offizieller, frei gestalteter Petitionsbrief" (*Forum* [1999] 231).

[165] "Confidence" (1985) 283–84.

[166] E.g. P.Mich. 8.485.17–19 (ca. 105 C.E.) μέντοι πείθομαί σε μηδὲ εν διστάζειν ἐν τοῖς προκειμένοις ("I trust you, however, to show no hesitation whatever in the aforesaid matter"; trans. Olson, "Confidence" [1985] 285), after making the specific request by the formulaic διὸ παρακαλῶ σε, ἄδελφε . . . (line 9).

[167] Cf. also White, *Apostle* (1999) 69.

[168] Generally speaking, Paul's discourse in 12:3–15:13 concernes the issue of mutual love and respect, several aspects of which are worked out in further details: acceptance and maintenance of current status (esp. 12:3–8); brotherly love (ἀγάπη)

expression is to "undergird the letter's requests or admonitions by creating a sense of obligation through praise," thus "increasing the likelihood of a favorable hearing."[169] Paul's subsequent words about his manner of writing "rather boldly" (τολμηρότερον, v. 15) may also soften the authoritative force of "some points" (ἀπὸ μέρους)[170] of his letter. Simultaneously, however, these words function so as to point out to the audience that Paul has in fact the authority to write in this way—he might even have written more boldly!—"because of the grace given to me by God to be a minister of Christ Jesus to the gentiles in the sacred service of God's good news" (διὰ τὴν χάριν τὴν δοθεῖσάν μοι ὑπὸ τοῦ θεοῦ εἰς τὸ εἶναί με λειτουργὸν[171] Χριστοῦ Ἰησοῦ εἰς τὰ ἔθνη, ἱερουργοῦντα τὸ εὐαγγέλιον τοῦ θεοῦ, vv. 15–16). While this utterance clearly recalls Paul's presentation of his commission and message in the letter's opening,[172] it also alludes to 12:3 where

---

(esp. 12:9–18; 13:8–10); τὸ ἀγαθόν vs. τὸ κακόν (esp. 12:21–13:4; cf. 13:11–14); judging one another (esp. 14:4–23); welcoming one another (esp. 14:1; 15:1–7).

[169] Olson, "Confidence" (1985) 289, 295. Olson has treated the confidence expressions under four headings "which are determined by the relationship of the expression to the purpose of the letter" (p. 283): 1) confidence of the addressee's compliance to the writer's request; 2) confidence as the reason for making a request; 3) confidence with an apology for the request; and 4) confidence expressions as the request or command. Between these groups is a "considerable similarity of function" (ibid.). Olson's words on p. 289, cited above, do not refer to Rom specifically but to letters in group 1) (he includes Gal, Phlm, and 2 Thess in this group). Olson considers the expression in Rom 15:14 rather to belong to group 3). However, this latter group is concerned with expressions "which appear with an apology for writing, advising, or requesting at all" (p. 291). This does not seem to be the case in Rom 15:14 where Paul apologizes—if he indeed does so—for his *manner* of writing, but not for writing at all. My analysis above suggests that the expression in Rom 15:14 has more similarities with Olson's first group of expressions.

[170] On other potential meanings of this phrase, see Kaye, "Romans" (1976) 42–43; Dunn, *Romans* (1988) 2.858–59. These "points" are not necessarily restricted to chs. 12–15.

[171] On Paul's use of the term λειτουργός, cf. Rom 13:6. See also Jewett, "Ambassadorial" (1982) 16.

[172] See Olsson, "Rom 1:3f" (1972–73) esp. 262–64.

he claims to be addressing the audience "through the grace given to me" (διὰ τῆς χάριτος τῆς δοθείσης μοι). This latter reference is of particular importance since the figurative sacrificial terminology in 15:16, "so that the offering of the gentiles may be acceptable, sanctified by the holy spirit" (ἵνα γένηται ἡ προσφορὰ τῶν ἐθνῶν εὐπρόσδεκτος, ἡγιασμένη ἐν πνεύματι ἁγίῳ), is actually a restatement of the one found at the structural center of the letter, viz. in 12:1: "present your bodies as a living sacrifice, holy and acceptable to God" (παραστῆσαι τὰ σώματα ὑμῶν θυσίαν ζῶσαν ἁγίαν εὐάρεστον τῷ θεῷ).

All this suggests that Paul's focus in 15:14–16 is aimed at exhorting the audience to act according to his hortatory request in 12:1–2. Paul does this in a diplomatic way. By linking together an expression of confidence and "factual" accounts of his apostolic ministry, the impression is given that the sender of the letter is a benevolent figure in an authoritative position. At the same time, Paul frames the main part of his letter by addressing the audience in much the same manner as he had done at its beginning, viz. by expressing his goodwill towards them. This is not only shown by Paul's praising statement in 15:14 (cf. 1:8) but also by the number of allusions in 15:17–29 to his visiting remarks in 1:10–14a.[173]

Robert W. Funk's essay of 1967, "The Apostolic *Parousia*: Form and Significance," has long served as a model for scholars[174] stressing the formal aspects and correlations between Romans 15:14–29 (or 33) and 1:8ff. In his study, Funk identified several "more or less discrete section[s]" in Paul's letters "on the basis of both form and content, as specifically concerned with the apostolic *parousia*," i.e. "the presence of apostolic authority and power." Of these passages Funk considered Romans 15:14–33 to be "the most elaborate and formally structured," thus basing his analysis primarily on this text.[175] As Mullins rightly observed, however, Funk's "apostolic

---

[173] These correlations have been the subject of many studies, the following of which are particularly helpful: du Toit, "Persuasion" (1989) 198–208; Weima, "Preaching" (1994) 354–58.

[174] E.g. White, "New Testament" (1984) 1744–50; idem, *Light* (1986) 219–20; Schnider and Stenger, *Studien* (1987) 92–107; Jervis, *Purpose* (1991) 110–31.

[175] "*Parousia*" (1967) 249–51, 253.

parousia" is hardly consistent enough formally to be identified as a distinct epistolary form. Its variations suggest instead that we are dealing with a common epistolary theme, viz. the theme of visiting or "visit talk."[176] Paul's announcement of his planned visit to Rome is therefore constituent of a much more extensive and fluid literary practice than Funk assumed,[177] often being mixed with other common themes, such as the theme of letter writing (cf. Rom 15:15).[178] Funk was nevertheless right in his judgment that Paul's visiting comments often were combined with the issue of his apostolic authority;[179] an issue evidently present in Romans 15:14–29. Furthermore, while Paul's visiting remarks sometimes function as a threat or a warning,[180] they also serve the purpose of stressing Paul's affection for

---

[176] "Visit Talk" (1973). So also Aune, *New Testament* (1987) 190; Weima, "Preaching" (1994) 353–54.

[177] Funk's narrow approach brought him, for instance, to the conclusion that since "the apostolic *parousia* is normally attached to the theological body of the letter, preceding *paraenesis*," the structure of Rom as a whole seemed rather "odd." Consequently, he made the curious suggestion that "Rom. 1:1–15:13 may well have been conceived by Paul as a general letter, to be particularized and dispatched, as the occasion demanded, to other well-known churches which he had not founded or visited. . . . Paul needed only to fill in the address and, if the occasion required it, add a personalized form of the apostolic *parousia* at the end, in order to be able to dispatch this generalized summary of his gospel to yet another church" ("*Parousia*" [1967] 268). Needless to say, Funk considered it "possible" that the references to Rome in 1:7, 15 were secondary. Cf. Knox, "Note" (1955–56) on whose reading Funk is partly depended.

[178] Cf. esp. P.Mich. 3.203 (114–116 C.E.). Further examples are found in Mullins, "Visit Talk" (1973) 352–57; Reed, *Discourse* (1997) 216. See also Koskenniemi, *Studien* (1956) 111–12. References to past, planned, or desired visits are frequent in Paul's letters. Besides Rom, see esp. 1 Cor 4:18–20; 16:2–7; 2 Cor 1:15–16, 23; 2:1–3; 9:4; 12:14, 20–21; 13:1–2, 10; Gal 4:20; Phil 2:24; 1 Thess 2:17–18; 3:6, 10; Phlm 22.

[179] "*Parousia*" (1967) esp. 249, 258–62.

[180] E.g. 1 Cor 4:18–20; 2 Cor 9:4; 12:21; 13:2, 10; Gal 4:20; Phil 1:27–28.

his audience as well as indicating his goodwill towards them.[181] As we have seen, the latter function is central in Romans 15:14–29.

At the beginning of the letter's body (in 1:8–14a) Paul had spoken of his great longing to visit the audience and the reasons for not having been able to do so. In 15:14–29 he returns to this, both by providing further details for his delay—he had been occupied with proclaiming the "good news" in the east (vv. 19b–22)[182]—and by intensifying his desire for a visit with a long series of "visit talk" (vv. 22, 23, 24, 28, 29). In addition, Paul lists out his travelling plans: He no longer has any room for work in the eastern regions and intends to pass through Rome on his way to Spain (vv. 23–24). However, Paul now informs his audience that before this may take place he has to make a trip to Jerusalem (vv. 25–27). Although this may have sounded surprising in light of Paul's recurrent mention of his yearning to make a visit, it would not necessarily have amazed the audience. They would probably have realized this already by the extent and content of the letter itself. After all, why would Paul have written a letter with such an extensive exposition of God's "good news" if a visit to Rome was at hand?

3.2.4. The Παρακαλῶ Sentence in 15:30–32 and the Closing of the Body (15:33)

In 15:30–32 Paul makes an additional request with the same epistolary terminology as we saw in 12:1: 1) the background information is provided in the request itself (vv. 31–32),[183] 2) again, the verb of request is παρακαλῶ, and 3) the content is that the readers are to "strive together" (συναγωνίσασθαι) with Paul in prayer to God concerning Paul's impending journey. Paul also adds the personal address ἀδελφοί.[184] Unlike the earlier instance in 12:1, the context here gives no definite reason to read παρακαλῶ otherwise than in the plain sense of "asking" or "appealing."

---

[181] E.g. Phil 1:8, 26; 2:24; 1 Thess 2:17–18; 3:6, 10; cf. 1 Cor 16:5–7, 17; 2 Cor 7:6–7. See also Mitchell, "Envoys" (1992) esp. 658–61.
[182] Cf. Byrne, "Rather Boldly" (1993) 94–95 with n. 37.
[183] I.e. by ἐν τῇ Ἰουδαίᾳ (v. 31; cf. v. 25); ἡ διακονία μου ἡ εἰς Ἰερουσαλήμ . . . (v. 31; cf. vv. 25–27); ἐλθὼν πρὸς ὑμᾶς . . . (v. 32; cf. vv. 23–24, 28–29).
[184] Omitted by P[46] and B, but supported by ℵ A C D and the majority of MSS.

In his visiting remarks elsewhere Paul sometimes alludes to God's intervening power by referring to the importance of divine approval of his travelling activity.[185] Occasionally, Paul appeals to his recipients to affect God's will through prayer,[186] implying that their partaking could have some effect on the completion of his intended visit. In Romans 15:30–32 Paul has extended this kind of appeal by asking his audience to offer prayers to God not only for his planned visit to Rome (v. 32) but also for his rescuing from "the unbelievers (τῶν ἀπειθούντων) in Judea" (v. 31a), as well as for the proper performance of his official duties (ἡ διακονία, v. 31b). By doing so, Paul asks and thus invites his audience to take active part in his mission "by becoming his co-agonists [συναγωνίσασθαι] in prayer to God on his behalf."[187] Paul's request may therefore reveal a further attempt to increase the probability of the audience's acceptance of his message in the letter, this time by creating a sense of obligation through participation. Instead of simply being passive readers/listeners, the recipients thus become actively engaged in Paul's ministerial work and partly responsible for his visit to Rome. If everything goes according to the common prayer of Paul and the audience, he will eventually, "through God's will," come "with joy" (ἐν χαρᾷ) and "take a rest together with" them (συναναπαύσωμαι ὑμῖν).

Paul closes the body of his letter in 15:33 by the peace wish ὁ δὲ θεὸς τῆς εἰρήνης μετὰ πάντων ὑμῶν. This is a somewhat regular way for Paul to end the main part of his letters.[188] Jeffrey A. D. Weima, among others, has argued that the peace wish was instead the initial part of the closing in Paul's letters.[189] I am not convinced. In any case, the Roman audience

---

[185] E.g. Rom 1:10; 1 Cor 4:19; 16:7; 1 Thess 3:11. Cf. P.Mich. 8.492.18–19 (2nd cent. C.E.); P.Oxy. 14.1666.15–17 (3rd cent. C.E.).
[186] Phlm 22; cf. 2 Cor 1:10–11; Phil 1:19. Cf. also P.Col. 4.66.22–23 (ca. 255 B.C.E.); Cicero, *Fam.* 52.4.
[187] Pfitzner, *Agon Motif* (1967) 122.
[188] See esp. 2 Cor 13:11b; 1 Thess 5:23; cf. Gal 6:16. A peace wish does neither occur in 1 Cor nor Phlm. The occurrence in Phil 4:9b has sometimes been used as an argument against the literary integrity of the letter, but see Reed, *Discourse* (1997) 270–72, for counter-arguments.
[189] *Endings* (1994) 87–104 (on Rom specifically, see pp. 215–30). Similarly also Gamble, *Textual* (1977) 67–73; Jervis, *Purpose* (1991) 139, 155.

would most likely have taken the peace wish as properly signifying the closing of the body, both due to its concluding character and because of Paul's introduction of Phoebe immediately following (see below). If original,[190] the adverb ἀμήν at the end of 15:33 would also have served as a clear marker of this.

3.3. Epistolary Closing (16:1–24)

Paul denotes the closing of his letter by introducing one of his co-workers, Phoebe, who is on her way to Rome (16:1–2). This is followed by a lengthy list of greetings, mostly from Paul himself (vv. 3–15), but also—subsequent to the interrupting admonition in vv. 17–20—from several of his co-workers and compatriots. Instead of the more common farewell wish, Paul includes his regular "grace benediction" (v. 24)[191] which marks the end of his letter.[192]

---

[190] Omitted by P[46] A and few others, but supported by ℵ B C D and the majority of MSS. It is possible that the omission in P[46] may be explained by its addition of (the secondary) 16:25–27 (which ends with ἀμήν) immediately after the peace wish. Somewhat surprisingly, the potential presence of ἀμήν in 15:33 is totally ignored by Weima in his thorough study of the peace wish (see the previous n.).

[191] Due to the omission of 16:24 in the earliest MSS, modern text editions (e.g. [27]Nestle-Aland) include the verse in the apparatus only. For a summary support of this decision, see Metzger, *Textual* (1975) 540. Gamble, on the other hand, has argued convincingly that this verse may originally have been omitted because of an intrusion of the (inauthentic) doxology in vv. 25–27: "Once the doxology began to find a firm place at the end of ch. 16 the benediction of 16:24 became problematic: there were too many concluding elements. There was a growing tendency to omit 16:24, but [the benediction in] 16:20b was satisfactory enough to be retained. . . . Thus the primary form of the text at the conclusion of the letter was 16:20b+21–23+24" (*Textual* [1977] 132). Whereas Gamble's suggestion (pp. 93–94) that the double benediction (in v. 20b and v. 24) may be explained by 16:1–20 being Paul's autograph and vv. 21–24 being written by his scribe Tertius (v. 22) seems rather speculative, one has to consider the fact that the real "intruder" here is the benediction in v. 20b and not the one in v. 24 (see below in sec. 3.3.3).

[192] While the doxology in 16:25–27 may be a fine summary of Paul's letter, it probably is secondary. See esp. Gamble, *Textual* (1977) 16–29, 107–24, who has suc-

3.3.1. The Introduction of Phoebe (16:1–2)

Paul's introduction of Phoebe, who may have been the letter's carrier,[193] is in many ways reminiscent of the ancient letter of recommendation (ἡ ἐπιστολὴ συστατική or *litterae commendaticae*),[194] sometimes labelled the letter of introduction (ἡ ἐπιστολὴ παραθετική).[195] Paul's selection of words[196] shows without doubt that he wrote Romans 16:1–2 with this par-

---

ceeded in making the highly complex textual history of Rom apprehensible. Gamble concludes that "the doxology must be judged an editorial product added to the [secondary] short form of Romans [1:1–14:23] in order to provide that form of the letter with a suitable conclusion" (p. 124). So also—each from a different perspective—Schmithals, *Römerbrief* (1975) 108–24; Elliott, "Language" (1981); Trobisch, *Entstehung* (1989) 70–79; Müller, *Schluß* (1997) 208–12; and most commentaries on Rom (e.g. Lietzmann, Käsemann, Cranfield, Dunn, Fitzmyer). See also Gamble, "Redaction" (1975) 410–11; Metzger, *Textual* (1975) 533–36, 540. Weima, *Endings* (1994) 217–19, 229–30, chooses to side with the authenticity of this "wandering doxology," the choice of which seems to call for his omission of v. 24.

[193] Although not explicitly stated in the text, this seems likely. For a general discussion of postal systems in Greco-Roman antiquity, see Purcell, "Postal" (1996). See also Stirewalt, "Evaluation" (1969) 179–90; idem, *Paul* (2003) 1–19; Epp, "New Testament" (1991) esp. 43–55; Bruce, "Travel" (1992) esp. 649–50; Llewelyn, "Sending" (1995) 339–49.

[194] According to Pseudo-Demetrius, in this type of letter "we write on behalf of one person to another (ὑπὲρ ἄλλου πρὸς ἄλλον γράφομεν), mixing in praise, at the same time also speaking of those who had previously been unacquainted as though they were (now) acquainted" (*Ep. Typ.* 2). Cf. Cicero's remarks in this light: "I have shown Paccius both in word and deed how heavily a recommendation (*commendatio*) from you counts. Accordingly he is in my inner circle, though I had never met him previously" (*Att.* 89.1). In P.Oxy. 12.1587.20 (late 3rd cent. C.E.) the letter type is labelled συστατικῶν γραμμάτων.

[195] Cf. Pseudo-Libanius' remarks: "The commending style (συστατική) is that in which we commend (συνιστῶμεν) someone to someone. It is also called the introductory style (παραθετική)" (*Ep. Char.* 8). For general discussion of this epistolary type, see Stowers, *Letter* (1986) 153–65; Klauck, *Briefliteratur* (1998) 75–79, with further references.

[196] See esp. Keyes' "Greek" (1935), some parts of which must be supplemented and corrected by Cotton, "Greek" (1984).

ticular type of letter in mind.[197] Frequently, personal recommendations or introductions in antiquity were written in forms of independent letters,[198] of which the main or sole purpose was the recommendation or introduction itself.[199] As Harry Y. Gamble has pointed out,[200] however, these were not restricted to independent letters, but could also be included at the end of more extensive ones.[201] The personal introduction in Romans 16:1–2 may thus be conceived as a natural part of the letter,[202] properly signifying the closing of the letter.

---

[197] Richards suggests that Paul's use of a "well-written *litterae commendaticae*" in Rom 16:1–2 may be explained by his employment of a professional secretary: "Paul dictated the letter and then told Tertius [see 16:22] to write a commendation for Phoebe" (*Secretary* [1991] 171). But, as Richards himself observes (p. 182), "[o]ne must first show that the *litterae commendaticae* was a form with which Paul was unlikely to be familiar" before arguing that Rom 16:1–2 necessarily called for a secretary. That Paul at least was aware of this particular epistolary type is shown in 2 Cor 3:1 where he explicitly refers to ἐπιστολαὶ συστατικαί. In light of this reference, it is not unreasonable to assume that Paul was acquainted with some regular forms of the type as well.

[198] E.g. P.Cair.Zen. 1.59032 (ca. 257 B.C.E.); *BGU* 8.1871 (61 B.C.E.); P.Mert. 2.62 (7 C.E.); P.Oxy. 2.292 (ca. 25 C.E.); P.Herm. 1 (1st cent. C.E.); Plato, *Epp.* 14; 15; Isocrates, *Ep.* 4; Aeschines, *Ep.* 6; Chio, *Epp.* 2; 8; Horace, *Ep.* 1.9; Apollonius of Tyana, *Ep.* 107; Pliny, *Ep. Tra.* 87; and passim in Cicero's letter collection.

[199] Cf. Cicero, *Fam.* 5.1: "I had not intended to write you any letters except of recommendation (*litteras commendaticias*). . ."

[200] *Textual* (1977) 84–87.

[201] See esp. Cicero, *Fam.* 64.3; 337.8; *Att.* 19.11 (cf. *Fam.* 72.4; 328.4; 371.7; *Att.* 220.3). In a letter to one of his friends, Cicero remarks: "Every letter I write to Caesar or to Balbus carries a kind of statutory bonus (*accessio* [=addition]) a recommendation of yourself (*commendationis tuae*), and not the standard sort but phrased with some special indication of my regard (*benevolentiae*) for you" (*Fam.* 27.1). See also Plato, *Ep.* 13; Pol. *Phil.* 14.1. Interestingly, Socr., *Ep.* 30 begins with an introduction of the letter's carrier, only to be shortly reminded of at the end of the letter.

[202] Against the so-called Ephesian hypothesis; see below in sec. 3.3.3.

3.3.2. Closing Greetings (16:3–16, 21–23)

Greetings in ancient letters may be classified into first-person, second-person, and third-person types of greetings, corresponding to the person of the verb in use.[203] The first-person type is used when the letter's sender (or writer) wants to greet someone directly. The second-person type of greeting, on the other hand, is an indirect salutation in which the sender asks the recipient(s) to deliver greetings to someone for him or her. "In this way, the writer of the letter becomes the principal and the addressee becomes his agent in establishing a communication with a third party who is not intended to be among the immediate readership of the letter."[204] In the third-person type of greeting the sender becomes the agent through whom a third party greets the recipient(s) or a fourth party.

The only example of the first type in the letters of Paul is the one in Romans 16:22, viz. the greeting to the letter's recipients from Paul's scribe, Tertius.[205] The use of second-person types of greetings in vv. 3–16a is the most extensive of its kind in Paul's letters. These verses include no less than sixteen instances of the verb ἀσπάζομαι, the object being one (vv. 5b, 6, 8, 10a, 11a, 12b), two (vv. 7, 9, 12a, 13), or an indefinite amount of persons (vv. 5a, 10b, 11b, 14, 15, 16a). Similarly, vv. 16b, 21–23 constitute the longest list of third-person type of greetings in the letters of Paul. The verb ἀσπάζομαι is used four times, expressing greetings to the recipients not only from αἱ ἐκκλησίαι πᾶσαι τοῦ Χριστοῦ[206] but from several specifically named individuals as well.

Viewed in its contemporary epistolary context, the lengthy list of greetings in Romans is in itself nothing unique. A number of letter writers de-

---

[203] See esp. Mullins, "Greeting" (1968) 418–22. Cf. also Koskenniemi, *Studien* (1956) 148–51; Weima, *Endings* (1994) 39–45.

[204] Mullins, "Greeting" (1968) 420.

[205] On Tertius as Paul's scribe, see esp. Richards, *Secretary* (1991) 170–72. Cf. also Bahr, "Paul" (1966) 465–66. For general discussion of professional letter writing in Greco-Roman antiquity, see Poster, "Economy" (2002).

[206] Cf. the general, yet somewhat more restricted, third-person greetings in 1 Cor 16:19a (αἱ ἐκκλησίαι τῆς Ἀσίας), 20a (οἱ ἀδελφοὶ πάντες); 2 Cor 13:12b (οἱ ἅγιοι πάντες); Phil 4:21b (οἱ σὺν ἐμοὶ ἀδελφοί), 22a (πάντες οἱ ἅγιοι).

voted large parts of their letters to personal greetings.[207] However, such greetings were mainly[208] characteristic of correspondence between close relatives or well acquainted friends.[209] Since that can hardly apply to Paul's letter, in which he addresses previously unacquainted people, the extent of the greetings in Romans may come as a surprise. In fact, a comparison with Paul's other letters, which he indeed wrote to previous acquaintances, reveals several notable differences in this respect. First, Romans includes by far the most extensive list of greetings. Second, more importantly, Romans is also the only letter in which Paul asks his recipients to deliver greetings to particular individuals. Second-person types of greetings are otherwise restricted to Paul's general request that his recipients are to "greet one another with a holy kiss" (1 Cor 16:20b; 2 Cor 13:12; 1 Thess 5:26 ["all the brothers"]) or that they "greet every saint in Christ Jesus" (Phil 4:21).[210] To be sure, the greeting with a "holy kiss" (φιλήματι ἁγίῳ) is also included in Romans (16:16a), but not until the verb ἀσπάζομαι has been used fifteen times. Significantly, the majority of the persons greeted in vv. 3–15 are carefully described and/or introduced, with a large part of the descriptions closely connected to Paul himself (e.g. v. 3: τοὺς συνεργούς μου, v. 5b: τὸν ἀγαπητόν μου, v. 7: τοὺς συγγενεῖς μου καὶ συναιχμαλώτους μου, v. 8: τὸν ἀγαπητόν μου, v. 9b: τὸν ἀγαπητόν μου, v. 11a: τὸν συγγενῆ μου).

---

[207] See, e.g., P.Oxy. 2.300 (late 1st cent. C.E.), with almost half the letter devoted to greetings. See also *BGU* 16.2659 (ca. 21 B.C.E.–5 C.E.; greetings: at least 1/3 of the letter); P.Oslo.Inv. 1475 (1st cent. C.E.; 1/3); P.Mich. 8.466 (107 C.E.; 1/5); 8.481 (ca. 1/4); 8.491 (nearly 1/3); 8.490 (ca. 1/5); *BGU* 2.632 (1/2–1/3); Sel.Pap. 1.121 (nearly 1/3) (all from the 2nd cent. C.E.). In comparison, greetings in Rom comprise ca. 1/26 of the letter, which, however, is much more extensive than the examples provided here.

[208] For example of greetings in a letter that shows signs of "less intimate relationship" (White, *Light* [1986] 172) between the correspondents, see P.Mich. 8.475 (early 2nd cent. C.E.; greetings: nearly 1/4 of the letter).

[209] Exler, *Form* (1923) 116; White, *Light* (1986) 196–97; Weima, *Endings* (1994) 39, with further references.

[210] There are no second-person types of greetings in Gal and Phlm, the former of which has no greetings at all.

Third, with the sole exception of Paul's letter to Philemon,[211] the third-person greetings in Romans are the only ones in which certain specifications and descriptions are supplied to the individuals mentioned, again typically related to Paul himself (συνεργός [μου], συγγενεῖς [μου], ξένος [μου], οἰκονόμος, ἀδελφός).

What all this suggests is that it would have been of secondary importance for Paul to actually have greetings delivered to the persons mentioned in 16:3–15. After all, "Paul may know some of these individuals or groups only by reputation."[212] It is also improbable that Paul delivered greetings from some of his friends and co-workers (vv. 21, 23) simply and solely by request. It is more likely that Paul's primary concern was to ensure the acceptance of the εὐαγγέλιον among his Roman audience by making evident the extent and nature of his relationship with a large group of people (including Phoebe),[213] by whom the letter's message and Paul's status could be supported.[214] In other words, the primary function of the greetings in Romans 16 was to further establish Paul's authority as an apostle with a mission "to bring about the obedience of faith among all the gentiles" (1:5).

---

[211] In Phlm 23 Epaphras is specified as ὁ συναιχμάλωτός μου ἐν Χριστῷ Ἰησοῦ, and in v. 24 four individuals are described as οἱ συνεργοί μου. This letter is, of course, unique among Paul's letters in that it is written to (although certainly not addressed to!) one person only.

[212] Meeks, *Urban* (1983) 56. See also Gamble, *Textual* (1977) 47–48; Lampe, "Roman" (1991) 219–20.

[213] For prosopographic analysis of these persons, see Sanday and Headlam, *Romans* (1902) 418–29; Lietzmann, *Römer* (1971) 125–28; Meeks, *Urban* (1983) 55–63; Lampe, *Christen* (1987) 128–53; idem, "Roman" (1991). See also Stowers, *Rereading* (1994) 74–82.

[214] So also Gamble, *Textual* (1977) 91–92; Lampe, *Christen* (1987) 127; Jervis, *Purpose* (1991) 150–57; Weima, "Preaching" (1994) 358–65; idem, *Endings* (1994) 222–23, 225–30.

3.3.3. The Admonition in 16:17–20: A Foreign Text?

Ever since the early nineteenth century the actual context and destination of Romans 16 has been disputed. In light of the chapter's content and, especially, its complicated textual history, a number of scholars have argued that originally this chapter did not belong to Romans but more likely constituted a separate letter or a fragment of a letter addressed to a community in Ephesus (the so-called Ephesian hypothesis).[215] As laid out above, there seem to be no good reasons to doubt the Roman address of the introduction of Phoebe (vv. 1–2) together with the concluding greetings (vv. 3–16, 21–23). When it comes to the admonition in vv. 17–20, however, the question becomes more urgent.

The arguments for a non-Roman context of 16:17–20 have primarily been based upon two observations. First, the sudden "change of tone" in v. 17, i.e. from a friendly to a harsh and authoritarian one, may suggest that Paul is here addressing a community towards which he already has an established authority. Second, the content of vv. 17–20 does not appear to fit well with the preceding text of the letter.[216] Against the former argument it should be pointed out that the "tone" in the passage may not be that harsh after all. As discussed earlier, the phrase παρακαλῶ δὲ ὑμᾶς, ἀδελφοί (v. 17) is suggestive of literary conventions of introducing refined requests or exhortations (cf. 12:1; 15:30).[217] If, on the other hand, it may be judged fair to infer that the tone is somewhat authoritarian at this point, that should in no way come as a surprise. On the contrary, in light of my analysis above,

---

[215] For overview of and arguments against this hypothesis (existing in several versions), see esp. Gamble, *Textual* (1977). See also Ollrog, "Röm 16" (1980); Lampe, *Christen* (1987) 124–53; idem, "Roman" (1991) 216–21; Fitzmyer, *Romans* (1993) 57–64.

[216] So, e.g., Knox, "Romans" (1954) 661: "This paragraph, in view of the newness of the *subject matter* and the abrupt *change of tone*, raises as serious a question as to the original connection of this chapter with the letter to the Romans as does the preceding paragraph of greetings" (emphasis mine; cf. pp. 365–68). For general discussion of arguments along these lines, see Donfried, "Romans 16" (1970) 49–52; Gamble, *Textual* (1977) 52–55.

[217] See Bjerkelund, *Parakalô* (1967) 160, and the discussion in sec. 3.2.2 above.

this is rather what we should expect in Paul's letter. Hence, the claim for a non-Roman address of 16:17–20 cannot be based on a "change of tone" in the passage—a rather subjective criterion indeed. The latter argument is more to the point. The content of the passage seems in fact to be somewhat loosely connected to the letter as a whole. But it is practically impossible to determine whether this is the case or not.[218] For that purpose, too little scholarly agreement exists on the actual message of Paul's letter. A judgment based entirely on content contributes therefore little to the search for a reasonable solution.

One important argument for the non-Roman address of 16:17–20 is to be added to the ones above, the force of which, in my view, has not been sufficiently emphasized.[219] Having evaluated the standard arguments for and against the Ephesian hypothesis (i.e. with respect to ch. 16 as a whole), Gamble set out to analyze Paul's epistolary conclusions within the context of ancient Greco-Roman letter writing. In Hellenistic letters (i.e. Greek papyri as well as Greek and Latin "literary" letters) he found "a generally consistent order in which the selected elements are ranged: greeting, health wish, final wish and date." He further observed that "[a]dmonitions and requests for letters usually precede all of these formulaic items. This progression of elements tends to be maintained no matter what particular formulae are omitted . . ."[220] Similar findings were made in the letters of Paul: "[T]he primary formulaic elements are consistently ranged in a structural sequence," viz. hortatory remarks, wish of peace, greetings, and gracebenediction, and "[c]oncluding hortatory remarks tend to precede all of these [i.e. the other] formulaic items, but the sequence of formal elements is occasionally interrupted by the insertion of a brief warning or request" (referring to 1 Thess 5:25–27; Gal 6:17; 1 Cor 16:22). Nevertheless, Gamble insisted that "[n]o matter what else occurs in the conclusions or which

---

[218] Cf., e.g., the unsuccessful attempt of Schmithals, "Irrlehrer" (1965), to show that the passage belongs to a corpus of Pauline "antignostische Polemik" (p. 172). Cf. also Jewett's "Ecumenical" (1995) 105–8, and the response of Sampley, "Romans" (1995) 127–28.

[219] See, however, Erbes, "Zeit" (1909) 131, 146; Ollrog, "Röm 16" (1980) esp. 226–34.

[220] *Textual* (1977) 65.

of these formulaic elements is omitted, the sequence as such is never violated.... The epistolary conclusions, then, show a high degree of regularity in components and structure."[221] As for Paul's letter to the Romans, Gamble concluded that "in terms of letter-form and style everything speaks in favor of the integrity of the letter"[222] (i.e. Rom 1–16 as a whole, except for 16:25–27).

While I basically agree with Gamble on this, it seems to me that he failed to follow up his task at one point. He did not account for the anomalous placement of 16:17–20 within the closing of the letter. Without further notice, he simply observed that "[t]he sequence is then 'interrupted' by the hortatory remarks of 16:17–20."[223] This "interruption" may, however, be an important clue to the inappropriateness of the passage to Romans, as the following points exhibit.

First, (hortatory) remarks introduced by the phrase παρακαλῶ δὲ ὑμᾶς, ἀδελφοί are normally found preceding the closing greetings in Paul's letters (1 Cor 16:15–18; 1 Thess 5:12–25;[224] cf. 2 Cor 13:11). This is also the case with Romans 15:30–32. At times, Paul inserts some brief comments at the end, such as a curse (1 Cor 16:22) or a charge (1 Thess 5:27), but these are always placed after the closing greetings. Besides Romans 16:17–20, Paul never interrupts the greetings with comments of any sort, not even brief ones.

Second, not only does the passage in 16:17–20 break the greeting list, but, more importantly, it is strangely placed *within* the list of third person greetings. Thus, instead of being placed between the second person and third person greetings, which would have minimized its "interruptive" effect, it immediately follows the greeting ἀσπάζονται ὑμᾶς αἱ ἐκκλησίαι πᾶσαι τοῦ Χριστοῦ (v. 16b)[225] and precedes the greeting ἀσπάζεται ὑμᾶς

---

[221] *Textual* (1977) 82–83.
[222] *Textual* (1977) 94–95.
[223] *Textual* (1977) 88. This shortcoming of Gamble's study is also recognized by Fitzmyer, *Romans* (1993) 63.
[224] The verb ἐρωτῶμεν in v. 12 is functionally equivalent to παρακαλοῦμεν in v. 14; see Bjerkelund, *Parakalô* (1967) 17.
[225] Some ancient scribes (see esp. D* F G) apparently found this placement inappropriate and placed αἱ ἐκκλησίαι πᾶσαι τοῦ Χριστοῦ at the end of v. 21.

Τιμόθεος etc. (v. 21).[226] Considering the authoritative force of the former greeting, this would naturally be the most proper and effective place for an interpolation containing polemic against those who do not follow "the teaching" (τὴν διδαχήν, v. 17).[227]

Third, the benediction in 16:20b which closes the passage in vv. 17–20 is clearly superfluous. As a rule, Paul ends his letters with a benediction (1 Cor 16:23; 2 Cor 13:13; Gal 6:18; Phil 4:23; 1 Thess 5:28; Phlm 25), which means that it would be a serious deviation from such a regular custom not to do so in this letter. Therefore, the benediction in v. 24 should be considered original, while the one in v. 20b most likely is the closing of a foreign text.[228]

There is nothing in 16:17–20 that definitely speaks against Paul's authorship of it. Neither grammar, vocabulary,[229] nor style is substantially differ-

---

[226] Efforts of some scholars to provide a "psychological" explanation of this peculiar placement are highly conjectural. See esp. the dramatized attempt of Lietzmann, *Römer* (1971) 127: "[M]an hat den Eindruck, als ob nun am Ende des Schreibens der Apostel mit ganz plötzlich auflodernden Impuls die bis dahin geübte Zurückhaltung durchbricht, deutlich die Gegner kennzeichnet, die Römer lobend ermahnt und zuversichtlich seine Hoffnung auf den Sieg des Guten ausspricht. Er mag dem Schreiber Tertius plötzlich . . . die Feder aus der Hand genommen haben, um selbst ein paar eindringliche Worte hinzuzufügen—dann gibt er sie ihm zurück, und fährt (mit v. 21) ruhig wie vorher fort, Nachträge zu diktieren, langsam und mit Pausen: in einer solchen ist v. 22 geschrieben"! To Knox, "Romans" (1954) 664, there is "no better way of explaining" the present form of the text. Cf. also Sanday and Headlam, *Romans* (1902) 429; Dunn, *Romans* (1988) 2.906–7; Weima, *Endings* (1994) 96, 123.

[227] So also Ollrog, "Röm 16" (1980) 232.

[228] The same goes for the so-called peace benediction in v. 20a. Weima, *Endings* (1994), has attempted to account for the "unique occurrence, placement and form" of this "striking" benediction (p. 96), but, unfortunately, he has not allowed for the possibility that it may be secondary.

[229] In spite of the several *hapax legomena* identified by Ollrog in the passage ("Röm 16" [1980] 230). In most cases, vocabulary does not offer a very reliable criterion by which to judge whether or not any given passage in Paul's letters is authentic or an original component of the letter concerned. After all, we do not have access to all the letters he actually wrote (a large portion perhaps, but nonetheless an un-

ent from Paul's. But that does not mean that the passage originally belonged to the text of Romans. Nor does it mean that it necessarily was written by Paul. It may have been a fragment of another letter by him, or it may as well have been written by one of Paul's followers well acquainted with his manner of writing. Hence, although there is virtually no textual evidence for the passage ever being separate from the rest of the chapter, the arguments above strongly suggest that 16:17–20 should not be assigned any weight for the interpretation of Romans.

4. Epistolary Setting of Romans

There has been no lack of scholarly proposals concerning the difficult question what specific kind of a letter Romans may constitute.[230] Yet, no proposal has gained enough support to allow one to speak of a majority view, let alone consensus. The basic problem with Romans in this respect is that there are as few "either-or" categories pertinent to the letter as there are many "both-and." The letter simply resists any clear-cut classification.

Although I will make some relevant suggestions in this regard, my intention here is not to engage directly in this urgent but tangled discussion. Such an undertaking is beyond the immediate scope and purpose of the present study. My aim is somewhat broader, namely, to apply recent research into epistolary types and settings in Greco-Roman antiquity to assess

---

known one), and can therefore hardly determine with any certainty which vocabulary would or would not have been distinctively "Pauline."

[230] E.g. on Rom as 1) a "protreptic" letter, cf. Stowers, *Letter* (1986) 114; Aune, "Romans" (1991); Guerra, *Romans* (1995) esp. 1–22 (see also Berger, "Gattungen" [1984] 1140); 2) a "paraenetic" letter: Elliott, *Rhetoric* (1990) 85–86, 94–104; 3) an "epideictic" discourse: Wuellner, "Rhetoric" (1976); Aune, *New Testament* (1987) 219; Nanos, *Mystery* (1996) 207–18; 4) a "diatribal epistle": Porter, *Idioms* (1994) 300 (cf. his "Scribe" [2002] in which he perceives "the entire book as a diatribe" [p. 406]); 5) an "ambassadorial" letter: Jewett, "Ambassadorial" (1982); 6) a "[Selbst]Empfehlungsschreiben": Köster, *Einführung* (1980) 575; 7) a "Friedensmemorandum": Haacker, "Römerbrief" (1990); 8) an "εὐαγγέλιον": Roosen, "Genre" (1964).

the specific letter setting in which Romans was written, which, in turn, may shed some further light on the relationship between Paul and the Roman audience.

Before turning to the question of the epistolary setting of Romans, I will reflect upon the complications encountered in classifications of ancient epistolary literature, as well as upon the potential advantages of such attempts.

4.1. Classifications of Ancient Letters: Some Problems and Benefits

The task of providing an inclusive classification of letters in Greco-Roman antiquity is highly intricate, to say the least. Whereas research in this area has resulted in large amount of information proved to be helpful for the undertaking, at the same time it has made more and more clear how extremely complicated it is.[231] Of course, both the process and outcome of such an effort depends much on the point of departure and criteria chosen at the outset. By this I mean whether it is preferred to focus specifically on the aspects of form, function,[232] or content[233] of the documents. Concen-

---

[231] Cf. the classifications in the following works: Dziatzko, "Brief" (1897); Sykutris, "Epistolographie" (1931); Schneider, "Brief" (1954); Schmidt, "Epistolographie" (1967); Doty, "Classification" (1969); idem, *Letters* (1973) 4–8, 15–17; Dahl, "Letter" (1976); Berger, "Gattungen" (1984) 1326–39; White, "New Testament" (1984) 1732–33; idem, "Greek Letters" (1988) 88–95; Stowers, *Letter* (1986); idem, "Letters" (1992); Aune, *New Testament* (1987) 160–69; Bauckham, "Pseudo-Apostolic" (1988) 469–78; Classen, "Paulus" (1991) 5–8; Müller, "Brief" (1994) 63–69; Levens et al., "Letters" (1996); Trapp, "Letters" (1996); Salles, "L'épistolographie" (1996) 86–92; Görgemanns, "Epistolographie" (1997); Görgemanns and Zelzer, "Epistel" (1997); Neumann and Schmidt, "Brief" (1997); Klauck, *Briefliteratur* (1998) 71–73. On Jewish letters specifically, see Alexander, "Epistolary" (1984) 583–88.

[232] This is the point of departure in Pseudo-Demetrius' *Ep. Typ.* and Pseudo-Libanius' *Ep. Char.* In his functional approach, Stowers, *Letter* (1986), distinguishes between letters of friendship, family letters, letters of praise and blame, and letters of exhortation and advice (divided into several subtypes). His classification is useful, but not an inclusive one since several important groups of letters (e.g. of-

tration on one or two of these closely connected but distinct features may perhaps result in a classification that covers most surviving products of letter writing in antiquity. But one in which all these aspects are equally considered is practically impossible to arrive at. The reason is obvious: Extant letters from antiquity betray a considerable variation of form, function, and content. Thus, on the functional aspect alone, M. Luther Stirewalt comments: "Letters are . . . as varied in function as are the possibilities of social intercourse."[234] Similarly, one might insist that varieties of content correspond to varieties of social communication.

The problem at hand may be illustrated by the following general examples. The Greek "documentary" papyri from Egypt show a high degree of formal constancy and their contents are relatively uniform. Functional aspects, however, are not always as easily detected. Thus, there is good reason to classify these letters according to form and/or content, but less so according to function.[235] Many of the Greek and Latin "literary" letters, on the other hand, written by or attributed to prominent philosophers or rhetoricians, include only a minimal amount of specific epistolary expressions—some of them to such an extent that they have even been denied the label "letter"—and the issues discussed are diverse. Therefore, grouping them according to form is virtually out of the question and the criterion of content is not very effective either. The aspect of function, however, is usually far more prominent in the "literary" letters and thus more helpful as a classificatory criterion.

---

ficial letters) are mostly ignored (cf. the criticism of Aune, *New Testament* [1987] 162).

[233] As often noted by scholars (e.g. Aune, *New Testament* [1987] 161), Cicero appears to have distinguished between several types of letters according to content (cf., e.g., *Fam.* 5.1; 48.1; 225.1). His remarks, however, hardly reflect any systematic classification and sometimes show more concern for style than content.

[234] *Studies* (1993) 1. Cf. Stowers, *Letter* (1986) 15–16.

[235] Cf. Exler, *Form* (1923) 23; Meecham, *Light* (1923) 40–45 (P.Oxy.); Koskenniemi, *Studien* (1956) 47–53; White, *Light* (1986) 193–98.

These broad examples, representing two opposite poles, so to speak, in the field of ancient epistolography,[236] suffice to point out the complications involved in any work of classification. Numerous letters may, of course, be located somewhere along the line between the two groups (e.g. many official letters). Today, most scholars recognize—at least in theory—that this is the case with Paul's letters. On the one hand, his letters are written according to a fairly regular and consistent macrostructural pattern and are thoroughly furnished with conventional epistolary terminology, though not as stereotyped as in the Greek papyri. On the other, Paul's literary style shows many close resemblances to stylistic features rarely found among the papyri but characteristic of some "literary" letters,[237] the use of which often accentuates functional aspects of the discourse. As Gamble observes, "[o]n the whole, early Christian letters combine the familiarity of the private letter, the authority and community address of the official letter, and the expository and didactic functions of the philosophical letter."[238]

In light of all this, it seems reasonable to ask if there is any advantage at all in attempting to locate individual letters in this diverse and perplexed field of ancient literature. In the words of Dieter Mitternacht: "Warum systema-

---

[236] Roughly the same "opposite poles" were referred to by Deissmann when he presented his influential distinction between a "real, non-literary" letter ("Brief") and an "artistic, literary" one ("Epistel"); see *Licht* (1923) 116–19, 193–98, esp. 194–95 ("Der Brief ist ein Stück Leben, die Epistel ist ein Erzeugnis literarischer Kunst"). Cf. Dziatzko, "Brief" (1897). Criticism of Deissmann's distinction is found in most subsequent literature on ancient epistolography; see esp. Doty, "Classification" (1969) 183–92; Thraede, *Grundzüge* (1970) 1–4; Stowers, *Letter* (1986) 17–20. See also Richards, *Secretary* (1991) 211–16; Anderson, *Rhetorical* (1996) 93–97. In his study of Greek terms for letter and letter writing in antiquity, Stirewalt concludes that "[t]he dual, English terminology, letter or epistle, is non-Greek and misleading. The Greek terminology avoided such a distinction" (*Studies* [1993] 87). Pearson and Porter, "Genres" (1997) 151, suggest that "it is probably better to see features such as audience, situation, and the character of the content as differentiating one set of letters from another set of letters, rather than as differentiating letters from epistles."

[237] Cf., e.g., the dialogical style in Seneca's letters; see further Ch. 3 below.

[238] *Books* (1995) 37; cf. p. 95 on Paul's letters specifically. See also White, *Light* (1986) 220. Differently Koester, "Writings" (1991) 357.

tisieren, warum nicht jeden Brief in seiner eigenen Gestalt und für sich allein lesen?" To this question Mitternacht provides the ample answer "Weil auch Briefe sich trotz aller Vielfalt in Kategorien unterscheiden lassen und weil sie Träger von Indikatoren sind, die erst dann erkannt werden, wenn sie in verschiedenen Briefen identifiziert und systematisch erfasst werden. Die Systematisierung dient dem modernen Ausleger als heuristisches Werkzeug."[239] Put differently, since most letter writers made use of specific literary markers which were thought to be appropriate, favorable, or even necessary in particular epistolary situations, it is important to explore if applications of such markers may be traced in the letter concerned, and if it may be beneficial to compare these with uses in other works of the genre, and thus perhaps gain a better understanding of the letter as a whole. It must continually be kept in mind, however, that although there evidently existed several distinct types of letters in antiquity, relationships and boundaries between them were often quite fluid.[240] According to the shared opinion of ancient epistolary theorists, "the letter type must be appropriate to the nature of the relationship that exists between the sender and the recipient as well as to the particular occasion for writing."[241] As for categorizations of Paul's letters, it seems best to allow of a high degree of flexibility.[242]

4.2. Ancient Epistolary Settings and Paul's Letter to the Romans

M. Luther Stirewalt has approached the problem of classification from a broad perspective, grouping the letters according to the inclusive settings in which they functioned. According to him, ancient epistolary settings are either 1) normative, 2) extended, or 3) fictitious. Basically, they differ "according to the degree to which the correspondents and the contexts move

---

[239] *Forum* (1999) 172.
[240] Cf. Stirewalt, *Studies* (1993) 1 n. 1: "In the conduct of daily life [ancient] letters cover many activities, and they defy neat or complete classifications" (cf. p. 26). Similarly also Dahl, "Letter" (1976) 539; Buss, "Principles" (1980).
[241] Weima, "Epistolary" (2000) 328.
[242] Cf. White, "Mission" (1993) 145.

from reality to imaginary construct."[243] Because of its wide scope, Stirewalt's categorizing provides a useful ground for my approach to Romans and the specific aspects with which I am concerned. In the following, I will discuss the epistolary settings in reverse order.

4.2.1. Fictitious Settings and Paul's Letter

Fictitious settings are those in which "the writer impersonates another and composes a message in that person's name. . . . The dispatch of the letter is of no real concern, and co-respondents have no necessary contemporary reality."[244] Applications of the letter form in school exercises[245] and as an entertainment[246] are typical of these settings.

Obviously, Paul's letter to the Romans does not belong to this category of letter settings. Neither is there any reason to believe that the letter is pseudonymous, nor does the irrelevance of the contemporary reality of the correspondents apply to the letter. In short, it seems safe to assume that Paul's letter does not fall in group with literature of entertainment and fictitious school exercises.

---

[243] *Studies* (1993) 1–2. In light of this explanation, the term "normative" may be inapt (see, however, sec. 4.2.3 below), but since I have not been able to find a better term for this category I will use Stirewalt's. To speak, e.g., of "genuine" settings would be rather misleading because extended settings (and, in a sense, even fictitious ones) hold a grain of "genuineness."

[244] Stirewalt, *Studies* (1993) 3; see also p. 20.

[245] Among these Stirewalt includes elementary copy-writing (e.g. P.Fay. 19.16–20 [2nd cent. C.E.]) and exercises in literary composition (e.g. P.Bon. 5 [3rd–4th cent. C.E.]) or in writing on philosophical and ethical topics (e.g. the collections of Diogenes, Heraclitus, Phalaris, and Pythagoras). Also included are pseudonymous letters written to preserve or defend certain philosophical doctrines (e.g. many of the letters attributed to Crates and Diogenes). According to Stirewalt, Chion's letter-romances may both be regarded as school exercises and as literature of propaganda or entertainment, and the same goes for some of the letters of Aeschines, Euripides, and the Socratics (*Studies* [1993] 20–24).

[246] Among letters of entertainment Stirewalt includes the mimic-erotic letters (e.g. Aeschines, *Ep.* 10) and the entertaining letters of Alciphron (*Studies* [1993] 24–25).

4.2.2. Extended Settings and Paul's Letter

According to Stirewalt, extended settings supply the contexts "in which writers publicize non-epistolary topics for a group of people, identified or unidentified, and known or assumed to be interested."[247] What is involved is therefore both an extension of the letter's audience beyond the explicitly identified recipients and an extension of the letter's "conventional subject matter."

> [T]he intentionally wider audience and non-epistolary character of the subject-matter are characteristics of the letters under this heading. The audience consists of known and unknown people, the latter included only for their assumed interest in the subject of the document. That subject is not to maintain intimate relationships nor to conduct business of state between or among rulers and subjects. It makes available to whomever it may concern some knowledge or position which the writer feels need to publicize.[248]

Stirewalt counts letters on technical and professional subjects, and for propaganda, as representatives of extended settings. The context in which these letters flourished was mainly provided by the Greek rhetorical and philosophical schools, particularly the latter. The large number of ancient references to "letters" and "books of letters" written by prominent philosophers—Plato, members of the Academy, Aristotle's successors in the Lyceum, Epicureans, Stoics, and Cynics—indicate the wide employment of the letter form in this context. Except for the Cynic letters,[249] the references may be to authentic letters used for instruction, propaganda, and controversy. While some of the extant philosophical letters probably are authentic (e.g. those of Epicurus), many are pseudonymous.[250]

Considering the vast field of literature under discussion, it is not surprising to come across some potential flaws in Stirewalt's elaboration of extended settings. It is, for instance, not always easily seen where he intends to distinguish between extended and fictitious settings; some of the letters

---

[247] *Studies* (1993) 3.
[248] Stirewalt, *Studies* (1993) 15.
[249] On the Cynic letters, see esp. Malherbe, *Cynic* (1977) 1–34.
[250] *Studies* (1993) 15–17, with references.

and letter collections to which he refers appear to belong to both settings. But this is wholly in line with what was pointed out above (in sec. 4.1) and of minor concern for the present discussion. What is more important is Stirewalt's overlooking of the need to clarify what he regards as a "non-epistolary topic" and, conversely, a "conventional subject matter" in an ancient letter. The vagueness of this phraseology is not very helpful when attempting to locate individual writings within extended settings. Fortunately, however, Stirewalt seems to have advanced his definition when he speaks instead of the "non-epistolary character of the subject-matter" as one of the two main characteristics of these letter settings, the other being the "intentionally wider audience" (see above). Given that by the former Stirewalt means the absence of conventional epistolary terminology in the body of the letters—the part in which the subject matter is submitted and worked out—it may be ascertained whether Paul's letter to the Romans is to be placed within these letter settings or not.

First, as amply demonstrated above, characteristic epistolary terminology is found in the main part of Paul's letter as well as in the opening and closing. Not only is this seen at the beginning and end of the body but in its middle as well, the latter constituting, I have argued, the letter's center in terms of its epistolary structure. Thus, the criterion of "non-epistolary character of the subject-matter" does not apply well to Romans. Second, as for the "intentionally wider audience," nothing suggests that this would have been the case with Romans. Nowhere is it substantiated in the letter that Paul intended to address a wider audience than the letter's identified recipients,[251] viz. a specific, contemporary group of people in Rome.[252] Apparently, then, Romans does not correspond to this second characteristic of letters written in extended settings.

---

[251] Against Jervell, "Jerusalem" (1971), who has not only maintained that Paul had a wider audience in mind when he wrote the letter, but, more amazingly, that Paul's letter to the Romans was "primarily directed to Jerusalem" (p. 56). Jervell bases his argument chiefly on (his interpretation of) Paul's words in 15:30–32, but, as Fitzmyer puts it, "that is to allow the tail to wag the dog" (*Romans* [1993] 725).
[252] See further Ch. 2 below.

This conclusion does not mean, however, that the discussion of extended settings can now be put aside. One discernible group of letters written within these settings remains to be considered, namely, a cluster of ancient letters identified and termed by Stirewalt as "letter-essays."[253] This subgroup of professional and technical letter types[254] requires special attention since it has in fact been suggested that Romans may be classified as a "letter-essay."

Scholars' attention to Stirewalt's work on the "letter-essay" was primarily called by Karl P. Donfried.[255] In 1974 he published an article on Paul's letter to the Romans at the close of which he noted that Stirewalt's work "is indeed very suggestive and deserves to be well tested by subsequent scholarship." Donfried then presented two significant aspects of the "letter-essay" which, in his view, had the potential of shedding some light on the "summary character of Romans" and its "'public' character." Rather than insisting that Romans was a "letter-essay," Donfried cautiously remarked that this part of his article "must remain quite tentative until such time when far more research is carried on in the total field of ancient epistolography and particularly into that segment which Stirewalt has identified as the letter-essay."[256] In 1977 Stirewalt's essay was included in Donfried's edited volume *The Romans Debate*, though as an appendix, "because it does not deal directly with Romans" but "presents us with untold parallel and background material."[257] In the second edition of this volume (1991), however, the essay appeared without further notice among other contributions—all on Romans—as if it were a study of Paul's letter. As a matter of fact, scholars have repeatedly treated Stirewalt's work as a study of Romans, either strongly implying[258] or even asserting[259] that Stirewalt did classify Paul's

---

[253] See his "Letter-Essay" (1977) (summarized in *Studies* [1993] 18–20). Stirewalt's essay was initially presented to the 1971 SBL Epistolography Seminar.
[254] *Studies* (1993) 18; cf. "Letter-Essay" (1977) 170.
[255] "Presuppositions" (1974); reprinted in idem (ed.), *Romans Debate* (1991) 102–25, to which references are made here. See also Doty, *Letters* (1973) 7–8, 15.
[256] "Presuppositions" (1974) 121–25.
[257] Donfried, "Introduction 1977" xlvi.
[258] E.g. Dunn, *Romans* (1988) 1.lix; Fitzmyer, *Romans* (1993) 68–69.

letter as a "letter-essay" in it. But Romans is nowhere mentioned in this study of his, simply because he "did not have in mind any one of Paul's letters"[260] when he wrote it. Bearing this in mind, we may now turn to Stirewalt's influential essay and thereafter to Paul's letter.

Fifteen documents were selected by Stirewalt to represent the "letter-essay": three letters by Epicurus; equally many by Dionysius of Halicarnassus; seven of Plutarch's writings; The Martyrdom of Polycarp; and Second Maccabees.[261] According to Stirewalt, these writings constitute a category of their own, agreeing in form, style, function, and content. Although written in genuine letter settings, "they are losing some of the form, phraseology, and structure of the letter and are incorporating the more impersonal,

---

[259] E.g. Wedderburn, *Reasons* (1988) 8–9; Aune, "Romans" (1991) 109; Klauck, *Briefliteratur* (1998) 230; Miller, "Romans Debate" (2001) 334.

[260] Stirewalt, *Paul* (2003) 107 n. 77. In his *Studies* (1993) 18 n. 56, Stirewalt merely observes: "Donfried identifies some influence of the letter-essay on Romans," referring to Donfried's "Presuppositions" (1974). In fact, it is only in his very recent work, *Paul* (2003), that Stirewalt attempts to place Rom among the "letter-essays," explicitly stating that, by doing so, he is following the lead of Donfried and others (see ibid.). It is noteworthy, however, how reluctant Stirewalt appears to be in this classification, inferring little more than that Rom "reflects the setting of the letter-essay" (p. 107) and taking into close consideration some notable differences between Paul's letter and the "letter-essay" (see esp. p. 108). It is also worth observing that, according to Stirewalt, "Paul's letters [including Rom] are 'real' letters, written communication between two identifiable parties, in an historical context, on subjects that arise out of their relationships." This description, however, accords not with extended settings (in which the "letter-essays" were written) but with normative settings (cf. below). Moreover, it seems to me that Stirewalt's arguments for Rom having been written for a wider audience (as were the "letter-essays") betray an inapt measure of psychologizing of Paul himself at the point of composing his letter (see esp. pp. 110–12).

[261] Among other writings "approximating letter-essays," Stirewalt includes *Let. Aris.*; Josephus, *C. Ap.* (see 1.320; 2.296). See "Letter-Essay" (1977) 154–55 n. 23. Cf. also p. 151 n. 6, for other writings by Plutarch which "contribute to the letter-essay or reflect its influence," e.g. the consolating letter to his wife in *Mor.* 608B–612B.

objective style of the monograph."[262] The intimacies of private correspondence are dropped, and the intended audience extends beyond the identified recipients. Moreover, the distinguishing feature of the writings—indeed, the one that initially led to Stirewalt's gathering of them[263]—is that they are "all supplementary in some way to another writing usually by the same author or substitute for a work projected by him."[264] Publication of the "letter-essay" could also be of significance:

> Publishing a letter-essay is especially important when it supplements a previously published work and when the writer must defend a position he has taken. . . . The publicizing of the letter-essay was much more academic [than that of the official letter as a publicly recorded statement]; it was an article for professional journal, a monograph written on request and dedicated *in honorem*. The letter-essay was developed and used in highly literate communities. It was instruction and argument *in writing*; it was often supplementary to a previously *published* work. It was a supplement or substitute to other writing; the official letter and the personal letter were, on the other hand, extensions of oral communications.[265]

Epicurus' letter to Pythocles is illustrative:

> To aid your memory you ask me [in your letter] for a clear and concise statement respecting celestial phenomena; for what we have written on this subject elsewhere (τὰ γὰρ ἐν ἄλλοις ἡμῖν γεγραμμένα) is, you tell me, hard to remember, although you have my books constantly with you (συνεχῶς αὐτὰ βαστάζεις). I was glad to receive your request and am full of pleasant expectations. We will then complete our writing and grant all you ask. Many others besides you will find these reasonings useful . . . So you will do well to take and learn them and get them up quickly along with the short epitome (τῇ μικρᾷ ἐπιτομῇ) in my letter to Herodotus.[266]

---

[262] "Letter-Essay" (1977) 148.
[263] "Letter-Essay" (1977) 163.
[264] "Letter-Essay" (1977) 148.
[265] "Letter-Essay" (1977) 170 (emphasis original).
[266] D.L. 10.84–85. Epicurus' letter to Herodotus (D.L. 10.34–83) is also included among Stirewalt's "letter-essays."

Irrespective of the several weaknesses apparent in Stirewalt's study,[267] this summary account of it suffices to elucidate the considerable exertion needed if Paul's letter to the Romans is to be fitted into the category "letter-essay." None of the given criteria that may characterize and distinguish this group of writings from others seem to apply to Paul's letter. First, unlike the "letter-essays," most of which include only limited amount of epistolary expressions at the very beginning, Romans is patently structured according to the standard opening, body, and closing, with common epistolary terminology found in every part. Second, as pointed out above, nothing in the letter itself suggests that it was intended for a wider audience.[268] Third, and most importantly, nowhere does Paul state that his letter is a supplement or

---

[267] First, the (vague) formal agreement between the selected writings does not say much about them being "letter-essays"; it only suggests that they were written in a letter setting. Second, it is far from clear how many of the writings were actually intended for a wider audience. This is neither stated, e.g., in Epicurus' letter to Menoeceus (D.L. 10.122–135), nor the first three of Plutarch's selected letters (*Mor.* 138B–146A; 172B–208A; 464E–477F). Third, in this light, the only solid agreement between these writings seems to be found in their explicitly stated function, viz. to supplement or substitute for previous (published) works. That, however, excludes Epicurus' letter to Menoeceus from being a "letter-essay." In fact, this letter differs from the others in almost every respect: It is, e.g., "more consistently epistolary and contains no statement concerning its derivation or relation to other works of Epicurus" ("Letter-Essay" [1977] 149); different from the other documents, "[t]he method or manner of presentation is not explicitly described" (p. 158); the body of the letter is "more epistolary-personal than in any other of the examples" (p. 160), this letter being the "one full exception" to the body "almost rigidly cast in the objective third person or editorial first person" (p.163). Interestingly, Stowers classifies Epicurus' letter as a "protreptic letter" along with Rom (*Letter* [1986] 114, 116–18).

[268] Arguably, the general character of the letter may point in this direction. However, as I have already discussed above and will return to in the following, this character may be explained by the fact that Paul is basically using the letter to proclaim his gospel to its recipients. Against Stirewalt's recent claim that Rom includes only a "generalized address" in its opening (*Paul* [2003] 46; cf. p. 111 with n. 87), see my discussions in sec. 3.1.3 and Ch. 2 sec. 2.1.1.

substitute for a previous writing or writings. Hence, Paul's letter to the Romans is not a "letter-essay" as defined by Stirewalt.[269]

4.2.3. Normative Settings and Paul's Letter

The remaining category of ancient epistolary settings Stirewalt describes as "normative." They are considered normative, first, because they enclose actual correspondence, and, second, because they provide basic formal models for derivative uses. These are the settings of official and private/personal[270] letters, the former of which were the generating source of other applications of the medium.[271]

> In these settings the sender writes in his own name, to addressees known directly or indirectly to him, in an actual, contemporary context. In these settings letter-writing is social / political activity, conducted in the private and in the public sectors. In general a normative setting consists of relationships defined by the measure of acquaintance, the relative status, and reciprocal roles between two parties. This general social setting becomes particularized in the identity of the parties and in the subject addressed in the letter. The subject arises out of the relation-

---

[269] It is interesting to note that, although Bauckham would define the "letter-essay" less restrictively than Stirewalt does, viz. that it is not essential that it should be supplementary to another writing, he rejects the proposition that Rom should be classified as a "letter-essay" ("Pseudo-Apostolic" [1988] 472 with nn. 12, 13).

[270] Stirewalt speaks interchangeably of "personal," "familiar," and "personal familiar" letters.

[271] Stirewalt, *Studies* (1993) 4–10, 25–26, 85. The various uses of the epistolary form originally evolved out of letters written for administrative, military, and diplomatic purposes, soon to be employed in the service of bureaucrats and lesser officials (examples may be found in White, *Light* [1986]). At an early stage, the letter form was adapted by common people for private purposes. Although basic features of private/personal letters (see esp. Koskenniemi, *Studien* [1956] 35–47; cf. Thraede, *Grundzüge* [1970] 125–79) seem to have their antecedents in official ones, a reciprocal relationship between the two types eventually developed, so that the former came to affect the latter no less than the other way round; see Welles, *Royal* (1934) xlii–xliii; White, *Light* (1986) 191–92; Stirewalt, *Studies* (1993) 9–10.

ship. It is a communicative exchange, a true co-respondence, linking the parties and affecting an aspect of their lives.[272]

Compared to the findings above (in sec. 3), there is good reason to believe that Paul's letter to the Romans was written within a normative setting. As we have seen, Romans shows ample signs of being an actual communication developed in a contemporary context. The recipients remain in focus throughout the letter and its subject is by and large worked out in relation to them. The way in which Paul addresses his audience strongly suggests that, instead of being directed to anyone interested in the subject (characteristic of extended settings), Paul's message was mainly or solely intended for the audience identified in the letter. Gamble is therefore right in his judgment that "it is clear that no interpretation of Romans will be adequate if it fails to make sense of the fact that in Romans we have a letter addressed to a specific community and, as it appears, only to that community."[273] Paul's manner of addressing the audience suggests further that he knew well with whom he was conversing. That does not mean that he had a first-hand knowledge of every one or any of these people in Rome; on the contrary, the letter provides little evidence that he did.[274] Rather, it means that the Roman audience was known to Paul precisely as he addressed them, namely, as a group of people basically united by common convictions of a particular way of life.

We have also seen how distinctly Paul's employment of epistolary terminology is based on characteristic official correspondence. While there are elements also which are sought from the more intimate private/personal letter, the number and nature of similarities with official letter writing in particular locates his letter firmly within such a context.[275] Moreover, Stire-

---

[272] Stirewalt, *Studies* (1993) 2.
[273] *Textual* (1977) 137.
[274] On the greetings in Rom 16, see Ch. 2 sec. 1.2 below.
[275] It is worth noting that, in his *Paul* (2003), Stirewalt argues convincingly that Paul adopted and modified the official letter in most of his correspondences. "Paul saw himself as a representative of Christ ministering between the Lord and the people of the ecclesiae. It was an authoritative position in the religious community similar to that of numerous officials in the secular world" (pp. 25–26). However, Stirewalt does not apply these insights of his to Rom, which, according to him, comes

walt's description of letter writing in normative settings as a "social activity" applies well to Paul's language in Romans. This is well discernible in the epistolary expressions, in which the relative status of and social relationship between Paul and his audience is regularly manifested. Paul's use of this terminology is clearly meant to establish a hierarchical relationship—albeit a "brotherly" one—the force of which is prominent not only in the opening (1:1–7) but also at the letter's structural center (12:1–2; cf. v. 3) and in the immediate context of the confidence expression (15:14–16; cf. vv. 17–21). According to Paul's presentation, he is a divinely appointed apostle, assigned by God to carry on a mission towards a certain group of people, and the letter's recipients are explicitly addressed as belonging to this particular group.

Provided that the subject of the letter "arises out of the relationship," which continually is seen through the lens of Paul's apostolic office and mission and the recipient's subordinate status, it may be inferred that Paul was using the letter primarily to perform his missionary duty of proclaiming God's "good news" to this audience.

Concluding Summary

Paul's letter to the Romans is written according to the regular tripartite structure of Greco-Roman letters, viz. opening (1:1–7), body (1:8–15:33), and closing (16:1–24). Conventional epistolary terminology is found not only in the opening and closing but at the beginning, middle, and end of the body as well. Paul's choice and use of such terminology betrays well his status towards the letter's recipients. Romans is not a rhetorical speech in an epistolary framework.

The opening sets the letter immediately in a certain official context, but here appear several features characteristic of official letter writing. The opening presents a hierarchical relationship between the correspondents,

---

closer to being a "letter-essay." My analysis above suggests that he might well have done so. On the official character of Paul's letters, cf. also Schubert, *Form* (1939) 145; Dahl, "Paul" (1977) 7–8; Koester, "Writings" (1991) 356–59; Gamble, *Books* (1995) 95.

defined by the sender's divinely ordained authority vis-à-vis the recipients. In spite of its length, the body of the letter is relatively well stocked with standard epistolary expressions, the macrostructural significance of which has received undue scholarly attention. In particular, this is the case with Paul's hortatory request in 12:1–2 which, in terms of epistolary structure, properly serves as the letter's structural center. Again, the way in which Paul employs formulaic language in the body shows affinities mainly with official letters, especially those of a diplomatic character. The closing greetings, on the other hand, are more in line with typical procedures in private/personal correspondence. These are meant to substantiate Paul's claim to authority as an apostle, and thus to increase the likelihood of the recipients' acceptance of the letter's message. It is likely that the admonition in 16:17–20 was not an original part of Paul's letter to the Romans.

While Paul's letter is far from easily classified in terms of identifiable epistolary types, the setting in which it was written aligns itself mostly with the settings of official and private/personal correspondence, viz. normative settings. That suggests that Romans is to be read as a letter which was written and dispatched to a particular group of people in a specific, contemporaneous situation. The subject of the letter arose out of the relationship between the sender and the recipients, out of Paul's God-given assignment to be the recipients' apostle and to proclaim to them God's "good news." The letter *is* Paul's proclamation and exposition of these "good news." Every component of Romans is dependent upon this relationship between Paul and his audience.

Chapter Two

The Intended Audience of Romans

Introduction

Given that Paul's letter to the Romans is written within a normative setting,[1] it may be assumed at the outset that its intended audience[2] is identical to the letter's explicitly identified recipients. In the epistolary adscription, Paul addresses his letter to "all those in Rome who are God's beloved, called to be devout" (1:7a). As discussed above,[3] one of the exceptional features of Paul's opening in Romans is that the letter's recipients are partly identified prior to the formal adscription: They are included among the people to whom Paul was appointed apostle, namely, non-Jews. In other words, the rather general identification of the letter's recipients in the adscription has already been demarcated by Paul's introductory account of his mission to "all the gentiles" (vv. 5–6). Hence, the letter is addressed to all those gentiles in Rome who stand in a loving relationship with God.

As will be discussed in more details below, this identification of the recipients of Romans is reinforced by several explicit addresses later in the letter. In 1:13, for example, Paul compares the Roman audience to "the rest of the gentiles" among whom he has been "reaping the harvest," and goes

---

[1] See Ch. 1 sec. 4.2.3 above.
[2] By "intended audience" I simply mean the people to whom Paul intended to write. Information about who they were is both explicitly and implicitly provided by the text; cf. Reichert, *Römerbrief* (2001) 102. Observe that the intended readers are not necessarily those who *actually* received and read the letter when it eventually arrived in Rome. We can only speculate as to who these "empirical readers" were; cf. Stowers, *Rereading* (1994) 22.
[3] See Ch. 1 sec. 3.1.3.

on to state that it is his duty to "proclaim the gospel" to the former also (vv. 14b–15). In 11:13 he explicitly addresses his readership as "gentiles," and toward the end of the epistolary body Paul speaks of his authority to write "boldly" to the audience because of his divinely ordained status as a "minister of Christ Jesus to the gentiles" (15:15–16).

It is worth noting that in no other extant letter by Paul is the audience so distinctly identified as in Romans. Yet, for various reasons, interpreters of Romans have been very reluctant to take Paul's explicit addresses at face value and thus considering the letter to be addressed to gentiles. Although most reject the early view of Ferdinand Christian Baur that Paul was primarily writing to people of Jewish origin,[4] the overwhelming majority of scholars still insist or simply take for granted that Paul's letter was intended for Jews as well as gentiles, albeit primarily the latter.[5] This assumption was

---

[4] "Zweck" (1836); reprinted in his *Paulus* (1845) 334–416. Baur has been followed, e.g., by Zahn, *Römer* (1910) 18–20; Krieger, "Römerbrief" (1959); Fahy, "Romans" (1959); Watson, *Paul* (1986) 88–105; Mason, "Not Ashamed" (1994). Cf. also Vielhauer, *Geschichte* (1975) 179–81; Kettunen, *Abfassungszweck* (1979) 73–81; Guerra, *Romans* (1995) 22–42, who strongly emphasize a Jewish presence in the audience.

[5] Regardless of major interpretative differences in other respects, so most standard commentaries (e.g. Weiss, Sanday and Headlam, Dodd, Althaus, Lagrange, Barrett, Schmidt, Käsemann, Cranfield, Schlier, Michel, Wilckens, Dunn, Stuhlmacher, Fitzmyer, Wright). So also, e.g., Bartsch, "Situation" (1965); Wiefel, "Community" (1970) 92–96; Williams, "Purpose" (1971); Minear, *Obedience* (1971) 43–44; Drane, "Why" (1980); Beker, *Paul* (1980) 69–93; Bruce, "Romans Debate" (1981–82) 178–86; Brown and Meier, *Antioch and Rome* (1983) 109–11; Sanders, *Paul* (1983) 183–84; Theobald, "Warum" (1983); Lampe, *Christen* (1987) 54–58; Wedderburn, *Reasons* (1988) 44–65; Kaylor, *Community* (1988) 17–18; Brown, "Reflections" (1990) 105–7; Jervis, *Purpose* (1991) 82; Jeffers, *Conflict* (1991) 13–15; Becker, *Paulus* (1992) 351–58; Campbell, *Gospel* (1992) 21–22; Niebuhr, *Heidenapostel* (1992) 137–41; Myers, "Romans" (1992) 820; Sanders, *Schismatics* (1993) 215–19; Walters, *Ethnic* (1993) 63–64, 90; Boers, *Justification* (1994) 77–142; Chae, *Paul* (1997) 43; Brändle and Stegemann, "Formation" (1998) 123–25; Lane, "Social" (1998) 206–7; Caragounis, "Obscurity" (1998) 248–52; Alvarez Cineira, *Religionspolitik* (1999) 380–83; Dabourne, *Purpose* (1999) 63–75; Carter, *Paul* (2002) 135.

rightly challenged some time ago by Johannes Munck who argued for a purely gentile audience of the letter.[6] Munck's assessment is now being refined by an increasing number of scholars.[7]

As will become clear, the question of Paul's intended audience is far too important for the understanding of the letter as a whole to be left open.[8] It is my contention that prevailing answers to this question are not justified by Romans itself and that herein lies a primary cause for much of the perplexity that has enclosed the interpretation of this letter, including chapter 2.

Arguments for Jews being among Paul's intended audience have both been based on Romans itself as well as external sources for the historical circumstances behind the letter. The arguments are basically centered on the following: 1) the identity of the "weak" and the "strong" in Romans 14–15; 2) Paul's greetings at the end of the letter; and 3) various aspects of chapters 1–11 which, together with certain implicit addresses, allegedly indicate a Jewish readership. The first two focus mainly on external factors, viz. the potential composition of "Roman Christianity" at the time when Paul wrote his letter, whereas the last claims to be mostly concerned with internal elements.

---

[6] See his *Paul* (1959) 196–209. For a recent appraisal of Munck's work, see Donaldson, *Paul* (1997) 19–22.

[7] See esp. Suhl, "Anlaß" (1971) 126–30; Elliott, *Rhetoric* (1990) 9–104, 290–92; Stowers, *Rereading* (1994) 21–33, 36, 287–89; Achtemeier, "Judgments" (1997) 4–9; Nanos, "Jewish" (1999); Gager, *Paul* (2000) 101–2, 106–8; Engberg-Pedersen, *Paul* (2000) 185–86. Cf. also Klein, "Purpose" (1969) esp. 36–37; idem, "Romans" (1976); Fraikin, "Function" (1986); Tomson, *Paul* (1990) 59–62; Stendahl, *Final* (1995) 12–13; Nanos, *Mystery* (1996) 75–84; Donaldson, *Paul* (1997) 251–57; Cosgrove, *Israel* (1997) 86 with n. 40; Brawley, "Multivocality" (2000) 76–77; Whitsett, "Son" (2000) 669 n. 27; Reichert, *Römerbrief* (2001) 101–46; Keck, "*Pathos*" (2001) 81–82, 89–90; Gaston, "Romans" (2002) 129–35; Wagner, *Heralds* (2002) 33–36.

[8] Against Cranfield's opinion that "we ought . . . to leave this question open" (*Romans* [1975] 1.21), a question which for him is actually tantamount to the question of the ethnic make-up of the "Roman church."

But before proceeding any further, a note on terminology is in order. In his letter, Paul speaks of Jews and gentiles primarily in ethnic terms. That is, the primary distinction he makes and takes for granted is between those who are of Jewish origin and those who are not.[9] To refer to "Jewish Christians" and "gentile Christians" in relation to the letter's recipients is almost certainly anachronistic and thus potentially misleading. None of these terms are used by Paul himself and, although he sometimes makes some distinction, for example, between those Jews who recognize Jesus as Messiah and those who do not (e.g. Rom 9–11), the terms "Jewish Christians" and "gentile Christians" reflect chiefly a later historical development which Paul could know nothing of. If preferred, they should at least be used with great caution. To refer, for instance, to Paul himself as a "gentile Christian"[10] is not very helpful for an already tangled terminology.[11] Thus, in the present study I will endeavor to avoid the use of phrases like "Jewish/gentile Christians." Instead, in line with Paul's own terminology in Romans, I will refer to Jews and gentiles in terms of ethnic origin.

In this second chapter, I will argue that neither external nor internal evidence gives ample support to the (still) prevailing opinion that those whom Paul addressed in his letter were partly of Jewish origin. I will first deal with

---

[9] On the significance of ethnic origin for (most) Jews in antiquity, see Cohen, *Beginnings* (1999) 132–39, 156–62, 169 and passim. See also the discussion below in Ch. 4 sec. 2.3.

[10] So Watson, *Paul* (1986) 95; Marcus, "Circumcision" (1989) 74. Cf. also Guerra, *Romans* (1995) 22. This kind of terminology is not only misleading but also highly obscure. Though the phrase "gentile Christian" may be designed as a designation of those followers of Jesus who advocated a "less Jewish" way of life (so Paul, according to many), Paul was obviously not a "gentile." Even the word "Christian" should be used with caution; wrongly applied, it can overshadow Paul's Jewish identity.

[11] It should be noted that this terminology is not applied univocally by scholars. On the one hand, "Jewish Christians" and "gentile Christians" are used for those Jesus believers who are of Jewish origin and those who are not of Jewish origin (resp.); i.e. in terms of ethnic distinction. On the other hand, the terms are used of those Jesus believers who advocate a "more Jewish" way of life/religion and a "less Jewish" way of life/religion (resp.); i.e. in terms of ideological and/or religious orientation. Cf. also Brown, "Not Jewish" (1983).

the external sources which have been utilized for identifying the audience of Romans (sec. 1). My basic claims will be, first, that studies of the letter's audience would profit much by making a methodological distinction between the questions of what can be known of the composition of "Roman Christianity," on the one hand, and Paul's intended audience, on the other, and, second, that primary weight should be given to identifying the audience based on information in the letter itself. Accordingly, I will devote the second section of the chapter to an assessment of the internal evidence at hand, viz. the information provided by Paul about his readership. But let us first address external factors relating to the possible composition of "Roman Christianity."

1. Presuppositions in the Study of Paul's Audience: The Composition of "Roman Christianity"

The scholarly discussion of Paul's audience in Romans is firmly tied to the ongoing quest of the occasion and purpose of the letter—the so-called "Romans Debate."[12] The debate has resulted in many valuable studies on the historical background of Romans, both with respect to Paul's own situation at the time he wrote the letter as well as the potential situation of the letter's recipients. As for the latter, however, it seems to me that scholars are not cautious enough when attempting to identify Paul's intended audience through historical reconstruction of the origin and development of "Roman Christianity" prior to Paul's letter. Not only is this a precarious undertaking, since the earliest extant document from the city of Rome that speaks of God's "good news" about Jesus is Romans itself, but it is also methodologically suspect. It is true that Paul's letter may say something about the Jesus movement(s) in Rome, but does the make-up of such a movement necessarily say anything definite about the audience Paul intended to address? I will argue that it does not.

---

[12] See esp. Donfried (ed.), *Romans Debate* (1991); Jervis, *Purpose* (1991) 11–28; Reichert, *Römerbrief* (2001) 13–75; Mil'er, "Romans Debate" (2001).

1.1. Romans 14–15 and the Claudian Edict

Paul's references to the "weak" and the "strong" in Romans 14–15 play an important role in the scholarly discussion of the letter's recipients. Some even take these references as a point of departure in identifying Paul's audience.[13] The "weak" and the "strong," it is commonly argued, represent two groups of people actually present in Rome, about whom Paul was informed. The former group is to be identified with "Jewish Christians" and/or "Judaizing gentiles," while the latter group is composed of "gentile Christians" and possibly some Jews who had given up their Torah observance.[14] It is assumed that there were tensions or divisions between the two groups and that (one of) Paul's main purpose(s) with his letter was to bring about unity and harmony between them.

These tensions, in turn, are thought to have been greatly affected some years earlier by the so-called Claudian edict, i.e. the decision of the emperor Claudius to expel Jews from Rome because of certain disturbances. The view that the edict of Claudius is decisive for the reading of Romans has been widespread during the last four decades.[15] It is conjectured that a large

---

[13] Esp. Minear, *Obedience* (1971); Watson, *Paul* (1986) 88–105. Cf. also Reasoner, *Strong* (1999) esp. 221–39; Carter, *Paul* (2002) 128–37.

[14] The scholarly discussion is sketched in Reasoner, *Strong* (1999) 1–22.

[15] Apparently beginning with Marxsen, *Einleitung* (1963) 88–97; further developed in Wiefel, "Community" (1970) 92–96; and endorsed, e.g., by Donfried, "Presuppositions" (1974) 104–6; Gamble, *Textual* (1977) 136–37; Drane, "Why" (1980) 216–19; Bruce, "Romans Debate" (1981–82) 177–86; Kümmel, *Einleitung* (1983) 268–71; Brown and Meier, *Antioch and Rome* (1983) 108–9; Theobald, "Warum" (1983) 8–11; Stuhlmacher, "Purpose" (1986) 235; Watson, *Paul* (1986) 91–98; Wedderburn, *Reasons* (1988) 54–65; Marcus, "Circumcision" (1989) 72; Tomson, *Paul* (1990) 61–62; Crafton, "Vision" (1990) 320–25; Elliott, *Rhetoric* (1990) 47–59, 95–96; Haacker, "Römerbrief" (1990) 39–40; Moiser, "Rethinking" (1990); Jeffers, *Conflict* (1991) 12–13; Becker, *Paulus* (1992) 352–57; Walters, *Ethnic* (1993) 56–66, 84–92; idem, "Romans" (1998) 176–79; Wright, "Romans" (1995) 34–35, 62–63; Brändle and Stegemann, "Formation" (1998); Lane, "Social" (1998) 198–214; Caragounis, "Obscurity" (1998) 250–51; Alvarez Cineira, *Religionspolitik* (1999) 1–8, 371–404; Dabourne, *Purpose* (1999)

number of Jews, including "Jewish Christians," were driven out of Rome and when the latter returned—subsequent to Claudius' death—"Roman Christianity" had become predominantly gentile so that the "Jewish Christians" found themselves in a minority and vulnerable position. This then is the alleged situation of the community Paul addresses in Romans.[16]

There is no need here to go into the Claudian edict in detail. This thoroughly discussed edict is well known and so are also the diverse uncertainties surrounding it.[17] In short, according to Suetonius (early 2nd cent.), Claudius "expelled from Rome Jews who, at the instigation of Chrestus, were constantly making disturbances" (*Iudaeos impulsore Chresto assidue tumultuantis Roma expulit*).[18] It is widely held that by "Chrestus" Suetonius means "Christus," i.e. Jesus, and that the turmoils were being caused by disagreements about him and his message.[19] Suetonius does not provide any specific date of the expulsion. According to Acts 18:2, however, when Paul met Aquila and Priscilla in Corinth around 50 C.E., they had "recently" (προσφάτως) arrived from Italy "because Claudius had ordered all Jews (πάντας τοὺς Ἰουδαίους) to leave Rome." This seems to agree with

---

70–71; Carter, *Paul* (2002) 125–43; and in several commentaries (e.g. Cranfield, Schlier, Michel, Wilckens, Dunn, Ziesler, Fitzmyer, Wright).

[16] In his recent commentary on Rom, Wright seems to speak for many when he states: "This historical sequence produces a situation into which Romans fits like a glove" ("Letter" [2002] 406).

[17] See esp. the detailed discussion in Riesner, *Frühzeit* (1994) 139–80; Botermann, *Judenedikt* (1996); Alvarez Cineira, *Religionspolitik* (1999) 194–214.

[18] *Claud.* 25.4. Or: "Since the Jews constantly made disturbances at the instigation of Chrestus, he [i.e. Claudius] expelled them from Rome," as the LCL trans. would have it, in agreement with Acts 18:2 that "all Jews" were expelled.

[19] So, e.g., Wiefel, "Community" (1970) 92–96; Lüdemann, *Paulus* (1980) 183–95; Smallwood, *Jews* (1981) 210–16; Lampe, *Christen* (1987) 4–9; Riesner, *Frühzeit* (1994) 144–48, 172–77; Botermann, *Judenedikt* (1996) 87–102, 132–40; Alvarez Cineira, *Religionspolitik* (1999) 201–16. For contrary opinions, see Frend, *Martyrdom* (1965) 160–61; Benko, "Edict" (1969); idem, "Criticism" (1980) 1056–62; Slingerland, "Chrestus" (1989); idem, "Suetonius" (1992); Judge, "Judaism" (1994) 361–62; Gruen, *Diaspora* (2002) 36–41; Mitternacht, "Current" (2003) 524–25. Rutgers, *Heritage* (1998) 181–82, 191–97, prefers to leave the question open.

the date offered by the fifth century Christian writer Paulus Orosius, namely 49 C.E.[20] Dio Cassius (early 3rd cent.) does also recount some unrest among the Roman Jews to which Claudius responded, but this is said to have taken place in 41 C.E., and Dio explicitly states that the emperor "did not drive [the Jews] out" (οὐκ ἐξήλασε [τοὺς Ἰουδαίους]).[21] Thus, Dio's account may perhaps refer to an earlier incident.

Now, the problems involved in using this material as a point of departure for reconstructing a situation into which Paul directs his letter are substantial. First, the date of the expulsion is not altogether clear. Orosius, whose suggestion of 49 C.E. is usually accepted, claims that he got his information from a report by the Jewish historian Josephus, but this cannot be verified since the report is no longer extant, if it ever was. Such a verification is desirable, indeed, since it is difficult to rely on Orosius in matters of historical details.[22] The account in Acts is probably more reliable. Unfortunately, however, it is somewhat ambiguous in this respect because Luke does not actually state that Aquila and Priscilla had recently come from the city of Rome, only that they had recently come from Italy (ἀπὸ τῆς Ἰταλίας)—whatever the range of the word "recently" may have been for Luke. At any rate, the lack and nature of the sources on the date of the event cannot but give rise to some chronological uncertainty.

Second, and more importantly, the only potential link between the Claudian edict and the Jesus movement in Rome is Suetonius' text. Although it is possible that "Chrestus" in his record really is a misspelling of "Christus,"[23] it must be judged unlikely. Considering the fact that Sueto-

---

[20] *Hist. adv. pag. lib.* 7.6.
[21] *Hist. Rom.* 60.6.6.
[22] See Chesnut, "Eusebius" (1992) 697–99: "Orosius' *History against the Pagans* . . . was a very bad history. It was neither well organized nor coherent, and constantly confused myth and legend with real historical events" (p. 697). See also Slingerland, "Suetonius" (1992).
[23] The terms "Christus" (χριστός) and "Christianus" (χριστιανός) were often misspelled as "Chrestus" (χρηστός) and "Chrestianus" (χρηστιανός) in antiquity. See further Botermann, *Judenedikt* (1996) 72–95.

nius was well familiar with the Christians,[24] and that he specifically mentions an individual by a known name[25] as directly responsible for the riot, there is little basis for concluding that "Christianity" was involved. The suggestion that Suetonius had merely copied an earlier report, yet realizing the actual reference to Jesus Christ, seems strained.[26] It is also telling that Luke does not imply that the expulsion of Jews from Rome had anything to do with followers of Jesus (cf. esp. Acts 28:21–22). Nor does he identify Aquila and Priscilla as such in his account.

Third, it is unclear how many and who were expelled from Rome on this occasion. There is good reason to doubt Luke's accuracy of "all Jews" being involved, due both to his hyperbolic use of the word "all" (πᾶς) elsewhere in Acts[27] and the improbability of thousands of people being driven out from the city at this particular point.[28] The latter also applies to the alterna-

---

[24] See *Nero* 16.2: "Punishment was inflicted [by Nero] on the Christians, a class of men given to a new and mischievous superstition" (*afflicti suppliciis Christiani, genus hominum superstitionis novae ac maleficae*). Suetonius' description implies that it is first here that he mentions the Christians in his work on the Roman emperors (Claudius, of course, being discussed prior to Nero). Note also that two of Suetonius' close acquaintances, Tacitus (*Ann.* 15.44) and Pliny the Younger (*Ep. Tra.* 96), were no strangers to the Christians.

[25] The name Chrestus is well attested in ancient documents; see Benko, "Edict" (1969) 410–13; Botermann, *Judenedikt* (1996) 57–58.

[26] Suggested by Botermann, *Judenedikt* (1996) 95–102. She concludes: "Da sich kein Kandidat für den unbekannten jüdischen Messiasprätendenten Chrestus gefunden hat, sollten wir den Chrestus nehmen, den wir kennen, den, über den in den Jahren nach der Kreuzigung allenthalben in den Synagogen gestritten worden ist" (p. 102). This is an argument from silence.

[27] See 1:18, 19; 2:5, 45; 3:9, 11; 4:16, 21; 8:10; 9:35; 17:21; 19:17. Cf. 2:47; 19:27; 21:30 (with ὅλος).

[28] Suggestions of the number of 1st cent. Roman Jews range from ca. 20 to 60 thousand; see Penna, "Juifs" (1982) 328; Barclay, *Jews* (1996) 295. A recent survey of the scholarly discussion may be found in Hedner-Zetterholm, "Communities" (2001) 132–33. If 20–60,000 Jews were expelled from Rome, that would hardly have gone unnoticed by Josephus only several years later. In fact, "the expulsion order is not noted in any Jewish source as a disaster for the Jews of Rome" (Murphy-O'Connor, *Paul* [1996] 333).

tive, but common, reading of Suetonius' text, viz. that "the Jews" were expelled without further qualifications. It seems most likely that only or mainly those directly involved in the unrest were forced out, but how many these were cannot be determined by Suetonius' account. Given the dispersion of Roman synagogues[29] and the autonomy each one of them appears to have had,[30] and that Roman authorities normally took measures against Jews for ad hoc reasons,[31] these actions were probably carried out on a local level. Furthermore, if the disturbances were caused by disputes over the message of and about Jesus, the assumption that "gentile Christians" stayed at home while "Jewish Christians" were banished is not as obvious as many assume. It cannot be taken for granted that the distinction between Jews and sympathizing gentiles, let alone "Jewish Christians" and "gentile Christians," would have been evident to the Roman authorities at this point.[32] Thus, if Jesus was the issue at stake, a number of "gentile Christians" would probably have been expelled as well.

All this demonstrates the uncertainties relating to the edict of Claudius in general, as well as the speculations inevitably inherent in utilizing this material for reconstructing "Roman Christianity" in particular. The Claudian edict is therefore not of much value for the interpretation of Paul's letter.[33] It follows that there is virtually no external evidence for any "suddenly Gentile-only churches"[34] in Rome at the time Paul wrote his letter, nor for any disunity between "Jewish Christians" and "gentile Christians." As Jerome Murphy-O'Connor puts it, "[t]he Jewish vacuum, which is essen-

---

[29] See Barclay, *Jews* (1996) 316; Richardson, "Synagogues" (1998).
[30] See esp. Williams, "Structure" (1994).
[31] Rutgers, "Policy" (1998). Cf. also Gruen, *Diaspora* (2002) 15–53.
[32] Cf. the discussion in Cohen, *Beginnings* (1999) 25–68, 140–74 and passim.
[33] Similar conclusions are reached, e.g., by Murphy-O'Connor, *Paul* (1996) 9–15, 333; Nanos, *Mystery* (1996) 372–87; Achtemeier, "Judgments" (1997) 5–7; Keck, "Judgments" (1997) 22–24; Gaston, "Reading" (2000) 37–38; Tellbe, *Paul* (2001) 152–56; Reichert, *Römerbrief* (2001) 95–96; Wagner, *Heralds* (2002) 33–34.
[34] Wagner, *Heralds* (2002) 33.

tial to the theory that the content of Romans was determined by a unique feature of Christianity in the Eternal City, is a myth."[35]

As for the identification of the "weak" and the "strong" in Romans 14–15, careful attention must be paid to what is explicitly stated in the passage and what is not. There is not much in the text itself that suggests that Paul is here dealing with groups of "Jewish Christians" and "gentile Christians." He certainly does not identify them as such. The different attitudes towards eating, drinking, and judging days described in the text are no sure indicators of Jewish versus gentile dispositions.[36] These issues are all known to have been dealt with by non-Jews in the Greco-Roman world. Indeed, the "weak" vegetarian in 14:2 and the abstention from wine (14:17, 21) fits rather badly with Jewish practices in antiquity.[37] Moreover, the fact that Paul identifies himself explicitly with the "strong" (15:1) strongly speaks against equating them with "gentile Christians." Hence, while it is possible that the people depicted in the passage exemplify actual groups of people in Rome,[38] Paul's references to the "weak" and the "strong" in Romans 14–15 do not imply a mixed audience of Jews and gentiles.[39]

---

[35] *Paul* (1996) 333.

[36] See Meeks, "Judgment" (1987) 291–93; Reichert, *Römerbrief* (2001) 271–333, esp. 323–25. Cf. also Karris, "Romans" (1974); Schmithals, *Römerbrief* (1975) 95–107; Stowers, "Reason" (1990) 281–86; Sampley, "Weak" (1995); Glad, *Paul* (1995) 213–35.

[37] Despite occasional examples to the contrary; see Minear, *Obedience* (1971) 9–10; Watson, *Paul* (1986) 94–98; Dunn, *Romans* (1988) 2.799–802.

[38] I am not convinced that they do. Paul seems to be mostly concerned with portraying different "types" of persons or dispositions, rather than with actual groups of people in Rome; cf. esp. Glad, *Paul* (1995) 217–35.

[39] The similarities between Rom 14–15 and 1 Cor 8–10 are well known and need not be discussed here (the classic study is Karris, "Romans" [1974]). As often pointed out, however, there are also some significant differences between the two texts (see Donfried's response to Karris in "Presuppositions" [1974]). That, on the other hand, does not exclude the possibility that both discourses could have grown out of the same ideological and/or theological soil, and that 1 Cor 8–10 may therefore to some extent be illuminative for the understanding of Rom 14–15, and vice versa. For an up to date discussion of the relationship between these pas-

1.2. Paul's Greetings in Romans 16

It is commonly thought that the identity of the persons greeted in Romans 16:3–15 may be illustrative both of the composition of "Roman Christianity" and of Paul's intended audience. Whereas the former may perhaps be true, the latter is not.

As discussed above,[40] the type of epistolary greeting employed in this passage is a second-person type (ἀσπάσασθε).[41] This is the form of an indirect salutation in which the sender of a letter bids the reader(s) to greet certain people on his or her behalf. What is to be noted here is that this type was used when the sender wanted greetings to be delivered to someone who was not among the immediate audience.[42] This aspect of Paul's greetings in Romans 16:3–15 has been entirely overlooked by interpreters of the letter.[43] If Paul's choice of salutatory form is to be taken seriously it must be concluded that, instead of being descriptive of the letter's audience, these

---

sages, see Reasoner, *Strong* (1999) 25–37. Reasoner himself sides with those who would underscore the differences between the two texts.

[40] In Ch. 1 sec. 3.3.2. There I argued that Paul's primary concern with this extensive list of greetings was to (further) establish his credibility and authority as an apostle.

[41] Also used in v. 16a in which the formulaic "greet one another with a holy kiss" is used. Cf. 1 Cor 16:20b; 2 Cor 13:12a. Note also the general character of the second-person type of greetings in Phil 4:21a; 1 Thess 5:26.

[42] Mullins' explanation is worth repeating: "In this way, the writer of the letter becomes the principal and the addressee becomes his agent in establishing a communication with a third party who is not intended to be among the immediate readership of the letter" ("Greeting" [1968] 420).

[43] According to Weima, *Endings* (1994) 108, "a second-person greeting functions almost as a surrogate for a first-person greeting." He fails, however, to provide any support for this claim. His decision to disregard both the distinction between first-person and second-person greetings as well as the regular function of the latter with respect to Rom 16:3–15, is chiefly based on his presupposition that there were "several house churches at Rome" and that "Paul expected his letter to be read in all the churches of Rome." Weima asks the right question in this light: "Why then did Paul not use the more personal first-person greeting?" but gives no adequate answer to his question. Müller simply ignores the different types of greetings in his treatment of the closing of Rom (*Schluß* [1997] 216–17), and makes no mention of Mullins' important study cited above.

greetings suggest that the persons meant to be greeted should *not* be counted among those to whom Paul wrote the letter. In other words, the greetings in Romans 16 say nothing conclusive about the identity of Paul's intended audience.

1.3. The Distinction between the Composition of "Roman Christianity" and Paul's Intended Audience

Research into the historical circumstances in Rome is of great significance for the understanding of Romans, because Paul's letter is not a timeless writing but a document framed by a specific history and written with specific audience in mind. It must be accepted, however, that we do not have the evidence required for reconstructing a Christian community in Rome prior to Paul's letter. Hence, the starting point for an historical inquiry about the recipients of Romans should be the following: Paul's intended audience is the audience testified by the letter itself. As simple as this may sound, the fact is that this has not been considered carefully enough by commentators on Romans. Instead, the letter has repeatedly been read in light of some vague historical reconstruction and with particular preconceived audience in mind which then is forced into the letter.[44] This, I believe, is a critical mistake which currently presents one of the most important challenges facing interpreters of Romans. Historical inquiry would do well to ask first for whom Paul's letter was intended, and then what can be known of such an audience in the city of Rome around the middle of the first century.

---

[44] To take but one enlightening example: In his *Einleitung* (1983), Kümmel initially remarks that Rom portrays its audience "unzweideutig als Heidenchristen." Having provided several examples of this fact, Kümmel then asserts: "Indessen ist die römische Gemeinde sicher nicht rein heidenchristlich gewesen. Schon die Entstehungsgeschichte macht einen judenchristlichen Einschlag in der römischen Christengemeinde wahrscheinlich, auch wenn nach dem Judenedikt des Claudius die judenchristliche Minderheit stark dezimiert worden sein wird; doch können seit 54 auch wieder Judenchristen zugewandert sein. . . . Wenn Kap. 16 zum Röm gehören sollte . . ., beweisen 16,7.11 das Vorhandensein von ehemaligen Juden in der römischen Gemeinde" (pp. 270–71).

The present study, however, can focus upon the former question only. What is of primary importance to note here is what really has stood at the center of the discussion above: Whatever the composition of "Roman Christianity" may have been when Paul wrote Romans, he was not necessarily speaking both to people of Jewish and gentile origin.[45] In other words, even if there existed an ethnically mixed group(s) of Christ believers in Rome—wholly separated from the Jewish community or not—that does not mean that Paul wanted to speak to everyone involved. A distinction must be made between potential knowledge of "Roman Christianity" and of the people addressed in Paul's letter, the fusion of whom cannot simply be assumed. This methodological principle is vital for any study of Paul's intended audience in Romans.

2. Paul's Intended Audience according to Romans

Steve Mason has recently criticized the approach taken by the greater part of scholars who have dealt with the question of Paul's readership in Romans: "Most critics recognize a conflict between the heart of the argument (1.16–11.36), which seems directed toward Judaeans, and notices in the letter's opening and closing sections that seem to address Gentiles (1.5–6, 13–15; 11.13; 15.15–17). But this tension has usually been resolved by privileging the references to Gentiles."[46] Claiming that Paul wrote Romans exclusively to "Christian Judaeans," Mason insists instead that "the bulk of the letter . . . should be given interpretative priority"[47] over the "opening

---

[45] This is also stressed by Fraikin, "Function" (1986) 95; Stowers, *Rereading* (1994) 21–33; Nanos, *Mystery* (1996) 76; idem "Jewish" (1999) 284; Tellbe, *Paul* (2001) 159. Engberg-Pedersen's "minimalist point" is worth citing: "In the congregations to whom Paul is writing there will have been some Christ-believing Jews. But he did not necessarily write *to* them too. It is sufficient to see him as writing to the gentile Christ-believers in those congregations" (*Paul* [2000] 185–86; emphasis his).

[46] "Not Ashamed" (1994) 255. See also Mason's "Paul" (1993) 152–54, 166–80.

[47] "Not Ashamed" (1994) 276. By "the bulk of the letter" Mason seems to mean 1:16–11:36 (= "the heart of the letter"). He is, however, not consistent in his de-

and closing sections" in this respect. On the basis of "the external evidence"[48] and the assumption that "the heart of the letter" posits audience of Jewish origin,[49] he infers that not even the explicit addresses in the letter indicate gentile readership. According to Mason, then, Romans includes no references at all to an audience of gentile origin.[50]

The methodology opted for by Mason is not very helpful for the study of Paul's audience in Romans; indeed, I find it detrimental for research into Paul's letter—or any letter, for that matter. I have already pointed out the significance of making a primary distinction between what can be known of "Roman Christianity" around the middle of the first century, on the one hand, and Paul's intended audience, on the other. More to the point for the present discussion, whatever the conclusions about the identity of the audience either in the letter's explicit or implicit references may be, the former must take precedence over the latter. It will not work to treat the implied as explicit and vice versa. Implicit references are, by definition, less evident than explicit ones and thus more depended upon interpretation. This must be taken seriously in any attempt to determine the recipients of an ancient letter like Romans. Though an approach such as Mason's is rarely advocated openly in Pauline scholarship, a tendency to read the ex-

---

termination of the letter's macrostructure, which makes his discussion rather puzzling. He sometimes considers 11:13 to be found at "the end of the letter body" ("Paul" [1993] 174) and sometimes within "the closing section" (see above). Either way, Mason's "closing section" is amazingly extensive.

[48] Mason finds that the Claudian edict offers "no support for the putative shift from Judaean to Gentile Christianity," and that "we cannot simply infer from Nero's action [against Christians] that Roman Christianity was predominantly non-Judaean by 64 CE" ("Not Ashamed" [1994] 266, 268; on Nero's persecution of Christians, see Tacitus, *Ann.* 15.44). Though I agree with Mason about the former, I do not think that such external evidence should be used as a ground upon which the reading of Rom is to be built (see the discussion above).

[49] This will be discussed in sec. 2.2 below.

[50] At the very closing of his essay Mason remarks: "Of course, there may have been some Gentiles among the Roman Christians, perhaps Judaean sympathizers or even proselytes, but the letter does not deal with their particular concerns" ("Not Ashamed" [1994] 287). I must admit that it remains a mystery to me how Mason can come to this conclusion dealing with this letter!

plicit through the lens of the implicit may often be detected in studies on the readership of Paul's letter.[51]

In the following, I will begin with discussing Paul's most explicit references to his audience, which, again, should be given primary weight for the study. I will then consider what kind of information may be found in some of the letter's more implicit references and assess the nature and value of such information.

2.1. Explicit References to the Letter's Audience

It is generally acknowledged that the passages in Romans 1:5–7, 13–15; 11:13; 15:15–16 (approximately) include the letter's most explicit references to its readership. It is also widely recognized that in these Paul addresses an audience of gentile origin.[52] Objections to this agreement occasionally arise, however. In the following analyses, these will be dealt with in due course.

2.1.1. Romans 1:5–7

Romans 1:5–7 is a pivotal passage for determining the identity of the letter's recipients. This is the place in the letter where Paul has the formal option of stating to whom he is writing. Correspondingly, this is the place where the audience gets to know for whom Paul's message is meant.

I have already dealt with this passage above in terms of ancient epistolary openings.[53] It will be useful to iterate the main points of that discussion here. First, whereas the qualifying terms descriptive of the recipients in the adscription (1:7a) imply the sender's friendly disposition towards them, Paul's presentation of himself in the opening clearly has an official tone of

---

[51] Of course, a strict line between the explicit and implicit cannot always be drawn. What I treat in sec. 2.1 as "explicit references to the letter's audience" are those generally taken in Pauline scholarship to be the most explicit ones. These are passages which include direct addresses in the 2nd per. pl. and in which distinct information is provided about the audience's identity.

[52] See esp. the detailed discussion in Reichert, *Römerbrief* (2001) 101–46.

[53] See Ch. 1 sec. 3.1. Cf. also the introduction to the present chapter.

superiority. Second, the content of the adscription is largely reliant on the information previously provided in Paul's unique opening extension (vv. 2–6). The adscription itself designates the Roman recipients as a group of people that enjoys a loving and sacred relation to the Jewish God. This says something about the religious and social context of the audience, but little about their ethnic identity. At this point, however, the readers have already been informed that they are included among "all the gentiles" to whom Paul was appointed apostle (vv. 5–6). In other words, at the beginning of his letter Paul tells the audience that he has a specific task to perform among all non-Jews, and that since they belong to this particular group of people, he is now writing a message to them by his divine authority as apostle to the gentiles.

In his attempt to show that Romans was addressed "primarily to Jewish Christians," Francis Watson argues that the phrase ἐν οἷς in 1:6 does not imply that the recipients are themselves gentiles but that they "live in the midst of Gentiles."[54] The words καὶ ὑμεῖς κλητοὶ Ἰησοῦ Χριστοῦ, then, refer to and imply a comparison with Paul's own calling described in v. 1. Thus, according to Watson, "'You too' [καὶ ὑμεῖς] probably means 'you as well as me', for Paul has spoken of himself in 1:1 as having been 'called', and in 1:5 he states that his call has taken him among the Gentiles. Paul is saying: 'You too are called by Jesus Christ in the midst of Gentiles, just as I am.'" But how are we to construe such a comparison? In 1:1 Paul does not state that he is κλητὸς Ἰησοῦ Χριστοῦ but that he is κλητὸς ἀπόστολος. Is Watson perhaps suggesting that the letter's recipients were called to be *apostles* "in the midst of Gentiles," "just as" Paul?[55] That seems unlikely since

---

[54] *Paul* (1986) 103.
[55] This is the implication in Mason, "Not Ashamed" (1994) 269: "Both he [i.e. Paul] and his readers are called to be *among* the Gentiles. . . . That Paul means to evoke Israel's mandate among the nations/Gentiles . . . seems likely from his remarks in 15.16" (emphasis original). Cf. also Mason's "Paul" (1993) 171–72, where he asserts: "Paul has just described himself as 'called' (κλητός) of Jesus Christ (1:1) to be 'among (ἐν) the Gentiles' (1:5); now he says that the Romans are called (κλητοί) of Jesus Christ and among (ἐν) the Gentiles (1:6)." This is a misleading representation of Paul's text.

Watson observes later on that "1:6 does not exclude Gentile Christians,"⁵⁶ and thus does not insist that the addressees here are solely "Jewish Christians." But Watson is not clear on this issue; neither has he explained sufficiently why we should read the comparative καὶ ὑμεῖς in light of Paul's remarks in the superscription instead of the immediately preceding ἐν πᾶσιν τοῖς ἔθνεσιν, upon which the relative ἐν οἷς ἐστε καὶ ὑμεῖς is grammatically dependent.

In his rather cursory treatment of the text's grammar, Watson refers to and finds support in comments on the passage made by C. E. B. Cranfield. So does Mason also,⁵⁷ who follows Watson's reading. But neither of them notes how cautiously Cranfield's observations are phrased. He writes: "If κλητοὶ Ἰησοῦ Χριστοῦ is taken closely with the preceding words, the point intended must presumably be that the Roman Christians too (who are in some sense ἐν τοῖς ἔθνεσιν) are κλητοὶ Ἰησοῦ Χριστοῦ as well as Paul (described as κλητὸς ἀπόστολος in v. 1)." Indeed, both Watson and Mason fail to mention that Cranfield himself does not appear to find this reading feasible:

> But there seems to be no reason for inserting this just here: the natural place for it would surely be after πᾶσιν τοῖς οὖσιν ἐν Ῥώμῃ. We should probably therefore put a comma after ὑμεῖς, and understand the words to mean: 'among whom are you also, you who are called . . .' In this case, what is emphasized is that the Roman Christians also are ἐν τοῖς ἔθνεσιν, and a plausible motive for inserting the words just here is not far to seek, namely, Paul's desire to indicate that the Roman church, though not founded by him, is nevertheless within the sphere of his apostolic commission, and that he therefore has a right to address it in the way he is doing.⁵⁸

It is true that Cranfield, mainly concerned with the composition of "the Roman church," seeks to downplay the value of the text in Romans 1:5–6 for determining the identity of Paul's audience. He holds, for example, that the relative clause in v. 6 "is really parenthetic; for a statement about the

---

⁵⁶ *Paul* (1986) 104.
⁵⁷ "Not Ashamed" (1994) 269. Unlike Watson, Mason excludes gentiles from being addressed here.
⁵⁸ *Romans* (1975) 1.67–68.

people addressed is unexpected before the datives of v. 7 [i.e. the adscription] and, placed where it is, disturbs the flow of the salutation."[59] However, such an "unexpected" placement of the clause would almost certainly have had the opposite effect on Paul's audience. It would have appeared emphatic rather than parenthetic. Cranfield notes also that the words ἐν οἷς ἐστε καὶ ὑμεῖς "could quite as well simply refer to its [i.e. the church's] geographical situation in the midst of the Gentile world."[60] In a footnote he suggests further that "[h]ad the thought been of the church's being made up mostly of Gentiles, ἐξ ὧν . . . would probably have been more natural than ἐν οἷς."[61] But this suggestion is quite unnecessary. The text's grammar does not demand that Paul uses ἐξ ὧν here. On the contrary, ἐν οἷς seems to be well or even more appropriate. Paul's point is surely not restricted to telling the addressees in 1:6 "of whom" they are.[62] Rather, he

---

[59] *Romans* (1975) 1.67.

[60] *Romans* (1975) 1.68. This is also argued, e.g., by Heckel, "Heiden" (1994) 292. But, though one ought perhaps to grant that there may have been some overlapping between Paul's apostleship being, on the one hand, exclusively focused upon gentiles, and, on the other, directed at all those living "among the nations" (cf. Scott, *Paul* [1995] 121–80), Paul's later statement in this very letter about him being an "apostle to gentiles" (εἰμι ἐγὼ ἐθνῶν ἀπόστολος, 11:13), and not just an "apostle among the nations," at least speaks against the geographical sense. Rom is in fact the only letter in which Paul uses the phrase ἐθνῶν ἀπόστολος. It is also worth noting that when in 16:3–4 Paul speaks of his "co-workers," Prisca and Aquila, he states that "all the congregations of the gentiles" (πᾶσαι αἱ ἐκκλησίαι τῶν ἐθνῶν) give their thanks to them. He does not mention any congregations "among the nations/gentiles." Cf. also Gal 1:16; 2:2, 7–9; 1 Thess 2:16a, on Paul as apostle to the gentiles.

[61] *Romans* (1975) 1.68 n. 2; referring also to Schlatter, *Gerechtigkeit* (1952) 23. Cf. Beker, *Paul* (1980) 76, who notes that Schlatter was preceded by W. J. Mangold (1884) in making this suggestion. More recently, the proposal has been taken up by Guerra, *Romans* (1995) 26.

[62] Neither is his point restricted to stating "no more than the obvious fact—that the Roman church is in the midst of the gentile world" (Bryan, *Romans* [2000] 218). Regardless of the question whether or not the term "Roman church" is appropriate here, how likely is it that Paul's recipients were in need of knowing such an "obvious fact"?

wants to stress that they, as other gentiles, are under the sphere of his apostolic mission, which, in turn, explains his concern for writing in the first place. Hence his use of the inclusive ἐν οἷς. This may also explain why Paul does not simply profess that gentiles are subject to his apostolic mission but that "all" (πᾶσιν) gentiles are, an emphatic word echoed in the adscription (πᾶσιν τοῖς οὖσιν ἐν Ῥώμῃ, 1:7a).

Watson, to be sure, certainly recognizes the possibility that the phrase ἐν οἷς may mean that the addressees are themselves gentiles, but he dissmisses it because in that case "the Roman Gentile Christians are being seen as the objects of Paul's missionary activity, just like any other Gentiles." This he finds unlikely "for the addressees are *already* 'called by Jesus Christ' (1:6)."[63] But the phrase κλητοὶ Ἰησοῦ Χριστοῦ cannot serve as a basis for such a weighty conclusion.[64] Even if the audience's "calling" has in some way and to some extent already occurred, that does not seem to prevent Paul for considering them as being "the objects" of his mission. In fact, that is precisely what he explicitly states a few lines later in his letter (1:14b–15), and it is to these lines we now turn.

2.1.2. Romans 1:13–14a, 14b–15

In 1:13–14a Paul addresses the audience directly and ranks them among "the rest of the gentiles, Greeks as well as barbarians, wise as well as ignorant." He then states in vv. 14b–15 that it is his duty to "proclaim the gospel to you also who are in Rome."[65] Thus, it can scarcely be questioned that Paul addresses his audience here as gentiles.

---

[63] *Paul* (1986) 103 (emphasis his).
[64] Actually, it seems better to take Ἰησοῦ Χριστοῦ here as poss. gen., thus "called to belong to Jesus Christ." So also, e.g., Dunn, *Romans* (1988) 1.19. Watson's reading is also found, e.g., in Cranfield, *Romans* (1975) 1.68.
[65] On this division and reading of the text, see Thorsteinsson, "Missionary" (2002), and the discussion above in Ch. 1 sec. 3.2.1.

Yet, Watson argues differently.[66] He admits that in these passages Paul surely expresses his wish to undertake a mission to gentiles in Rome, but insists that this does not concern Paul's audience: "Paul does not mean that his readers are themselves to be the objects of his missionary activity . . ., but is simply addressing them as inhabitants of Rome—hence, 'to you who are in Rome' (1:15)."[67] However, it is not entirely accurate that Paul is "simply addressing" his readers as inhabitants of Rome, as if this were the letter's second adscription. Watson's summary reading of 1:15 misses two crucial points: the presence of the verb εὐαγγελίσασθαι and the object of this verb. There can be little doubt that the verb εὐαγγελίσασθαι means here "proclaiming (the) good news"[68] and that its grammatical object is the personal pronoun ὑμῖν. Thus, contrary to Watson's claim, Paul explicitly declares that his addressees are themselves to be the objects of his missionary activity, just as "the rest of the gentiles" have been. Watson's attempt to minimize the relation between these groups of people by asserting that καὶ ἐν ὑμῖν (v. 13) and καὶ ὑμῖν (v. 15) are used "somewhat loosely" totally lacks support.

---

[66] So does Mason also ("Not Ashamed" [1994] 270–73). His arguments, however, include a number of misreadings of Paul's text. Mason's main point is that καθὼς καὶ ἐν τοῖς λοιποῖς ἔθνεσιν in 1:13 neither relates to the previous address to the letter's audience (καὶ ἐν ὑμῖν) nor concerns Paul's missionary work in the East. Instead, 1:13 implies that Paul "will harvest some fruit both among the Judaean-Christians of Rome, in passing, and then continue the mission for which he was called among the western *Gentiles*" (p. 270; emphasis his). Thus, according to Mason, "the remainder of the Gentiles" are actually gentiles in the West, to whom the "barbarians" and the "ignorant" in 1:14 apply. His point of departure in this interpretation is Paul's statement in 15:24, 28 about his planned mission to Spain. But, against Mason, it must be pointed out that Paul's mission to Spain is not the issue here; it is nowhere hinted at in Rom 1. Neither is the text's grammar flexible enough to justify Mason's reading (see esp. his translation of 1:13–16 on p. 273). Cf. also Reichert's critique in *Römerbrief* (2001) 105 n. 20.

[67] *Paul* (1986) 103.

[68] The verb does not imply that Paul merely introduced or "set forth the gospel" to "Jewish Christians," as Watson claims (*Paul* [1986] 104), referring to Gal 2:2 where the wording, however, is quite different: ἀνεθέμην αὐτοῖς τὸ εὐαγγέλιον ὃ κηρύσσω ἐν τοῖς ἔθνεσιν.

Furthermore, Watson's "real problem" with the text, viz. the apparent contradiction between Paul's desire to proclaim his gospel in Rome and his "principle" expressed in 15:20 of not proclaiming it "where Christ has been named" (εὐαγγελίζεσθαι οὐχ ὅπου ὠνομάσθη Χριστός), should not be allowed to govern the interpretation of what Paul says at the beginning of his letter where no such principle is alluded to. Paul's words in 15:20 are spoken in another context and what he means by these words is not entirely clear.[69] Even if it may be considered likely that in Romans 15:20 we have Paul's missionary principle operative everywhere at all times,[70] and that Christ had already "been named" in Rome, to what extent Paul's addressees were "Christians" should be left more open to discussion. The length, content, and character of Romans, all these factors suggest that Paul himself at least regarded the Roman audience as (still) being in need for his proclamation and exposition of the "good news." As Nils A. Dahl once put it: "What Paul does in his letter is what he had for a long time hoped to do in person: he preached the gospel to those in Rome."[71] Whether that accords with the rest of the letter or not, in Romans 1:13–15 we have the *stated* occasion and purpose of Paul's letter. Verses 13–14a, together with vv. 8–12,

---

[69] Cf. the divergent conclusions reached, e.g., by Klein, "Purpose" (1969); Pedersen, "Überlegungen" (1985); Wedderburn, *Reasons* (1988) 26–29; Scott, *Paul* (1995) 136–49, 162; Nanos, *Mystery* (1996) 39, 245 n. 17. Nanos points out that, contrary to common opinion, Paul may as well have been referring to the city of Jerusalem, "where the Christ was 'named' [ὠνομάσθη]."

[70] Cf. Cranfield, *Romans* (1979) 2.763 n. 1: The neuter participle φιλοτιμούμενον indicates "a general principle which has in the past governed, in the present governs, and in the future still will govern, Paul's missionary practice."

[71] "Missionary" (1977) 77. Cf. Jervis, *Purpose* (1991) 163–64: "Paul was chiefly exercising his apostolic mandate in the letter." It was "intended specifically for the believers at Rome so that they too would become part of his 'offering' of 'sanctified' and 'obedient' Gentiles [cf. Rom 12:1–2; 15:15–16]. . . . The function of Romans is to preach the gospel by letter to the Christian converts at Rome." The comments of Dabourne, *Purpose* (1999) 67, are also worth citing: "If the gospel was not at the centre of Paul's attention when he began the letter, he certainly went out of his way to give the Romans the impression that it was. If he wanted to move away from the gospel after that, he would have needed to do something to alert his Roman listeners."

concern the occasion, and vv. 14b–15 announce the purpose. Both have already been hinted at in the epistolary opening.

In short, there seems to be no good reason to doubt that in these passages Paul addresses his audience directly as gentiles.

2.1.3. Romans 11:13

In 11:13 Paul turns directly to the audience with the words ὑμῖν δὲ λέγω τοῖς ἔθνεσιν ("But to you gentiles I say . . ."), referring to his authority as "apostle to gentiles" (ἐθνῶν ἀπόστολος), a phrase only found in Romans. Here we have perhaps the clearest example of the letter's intended audience being of gentile origin.

That Paul's address in Romans 11:13 is directed at gentiles is, of course, beyond question.[72] It is not a matter of much debate whether the addressees here belong to the Roman audience or not.[73] What is sometimes dis-

---

[72] Watson, for example, sees no reason to doubt that "in 11:13ff Paul directly and explicitly addresses the Gentile Christians in Rome." He comes to the conclusion, however, that Paul's argument is "surely intended to be read and noted by Jewish Christians," and then proceeds to discuss the text as if it were explicitly addressed to the latter group (*Paul* [1986] 170–73).

[73] Mason appears to be alone in arguing otherwise; see his "Paul" (1993) 174–75; "Not Ashamed" (1994) 273–74. He even finds it "remarkable" that "scholars cite 11:13 as proof of a Gentile readership in Rome." According to Mason, the whole of Paul's argument in chs. 9–11 is "in the abstract" and the gentile addressees in 11:13 are not among the Roman audience (11:13–32 being a "rhetorical aside"). Rather, they are Paul's earlier converts in the East, spoken to "in imaginary convocation, for obvious rhetorical effect" for his "Judaean-Christian" readership. Mason's arguments for this interpretation are both farfetched and forced. Not only has he transformed the explicit into implicit (cf. the introduction above to this section) but also turned a direct address in the 2nd per. pl. into an imaginary address equal to the ones found in the 2nd per. sg. Indeed, Mason believes the latter to provide more reliable information about Paul's audience than the address in 11:13 (cf. "Paul" [1993] 168; "Not Ashamed" [1994] 256–61). But this kind of approach cannot be accepted. If we are to take direct addresses such as the one in 11:13 as fictitious addresses "in the abstract," how can we say anything about the identity of the people to whom Paul wrote his letter? Furthermore, as Reichert

puted, however, is whether Paul's address applies to the letter's readership as a whole or just a portion of it. Some scholars hold that at this point Paul turns specifically to the non-Jewish part of his mixed audience of Jews and gentiles. According to this reading, the shift of readership is indicated by the particle δέ, thus: "Now I am speaking to you Gentiles" (RSV; NRSV), or "I turn now to you Gentiles."[74]

But this is to overestimate the function of δέ here.[75] It is not the particle δέ that is emphatic in 11:13; neither is indeed the apposition τοῖς ἔθνεσιν. Rather, the force lies in the personal pronoun ὑμῖν. The shift indicated in v. 13, then, is a turn from the previously prominent third person language to a more specific second person language, i.e. a change of focus from those being spoken of to those being spoken to.[76] From 9:1 onward Paul has fo-

---

rightly points out, the formula οὐ γὰρ θέλω ὑμᾶς ἀγνοεῖν together with the address ἀδελφοί in 11:25 strongly suggest that 11:13–32 as a whole is directly addressed to the letter's immediate audience (*Römerbrief* [2001] 107).

[74] Fitzmyer, *Romans* (1993) 612. Cf., e.g., Zahn, *Römer* (1910) 506–8; Michel, *Römer* (1978) 346; Siegert, *Argumentation* (1985) 166, 227; Stuhlmacher, *Römer* (1989) 151.

[75] See esp. Stowers, *Rereading* (1994) 287–89, who rightly points out that the Greek here "does not justify the idea, 'now at this point in the discourse'" (p. 288). Stowers paraphrases 11:13–15 as follows: "Yes, I am addressing you gentiles in this letter *but* you should understand that my very ministry to the gentiles has direct relevance to the salvation of my fellow Jews and their salvation to your own" (ibid.; italics his). Observe also the uncertainty in the MS tradition as to which particle is the proper one here. Due to this uncertainty, Güting and Mealand suggest that Paul's text originally had asyndeton: "We conjecture ὑμῖν λέγω τοῖς ἔθνεσιν. Tradition supplies us with three alternatives: δέ ℵ A B P 0151; γάρ D F G L Ψ 049 056; οὖν C, which are best explained by the assumption of an original blank" (*Asyndeton* [1998] 28).

[76] So also Hort (quoted in Sanday and Headlam, *Romans* [1902] 324): "[T]he context appears to me decisive for taking ὑμῖν as the Church itself, and not as a part of it. In all the long previous discussion bearing on the Jews, occupying nearly two and a half chapters, the Jews are invariably spoken of in the third person. In the half chapter that follows the Gentiles are constantly spoken of in the second person. Exposition has here passed into exhortation and warning, and the warning is

cused upon his non-Christ believing kinsmen, who are definitely not among the audience, whereas Paul's readers have mainly stood in the background. In 11:13, however, he turns directly to his audience and explains to them their status with respect to these kinsmen. Paul is saying: "But as for *you*, my readers. . ." The reason for Paul explicitly identifying his audience (ὑμῖν) at this point, viz. with the designation τοῖς ἔθνεσιν, appears to be both to connect them with the foregoing statements about the relationship between gentiles and Paul's kinsmen (vv. 11–12),[77] as well as to underline their subordination to him as ἐθνῶν ἀπόστολος (v. 13b) before severely reminding them about their vulnerable position as God's people (vv. 16–24).[78] It is worth observing that in 15:15–16 Paul will again appeal to his right as an apostle to the gentiles to speak boldly to his audience.

Hence, it seems most likely that in Romans 11:13 Paul addresses his audience as a whole, whom he also explicitly identifies as gentiles.

2.1.4. Romans 15:15–16

Immediately following the epistolary expression of confidence (15:14),[79] Paul declares that he has written to his audience (ἔγραψα ὑμῖν) "rather boldly" (τολμηρότερον) on some points so as to "remind" them (ἐπαναμιμνῄσκων ὑμᾶς). This, he says, is fully warranted by the grace given to him

---

    exclusively addressed to Gentiles; to Christians who had once been Jews not a word is addressed."

[77] I.e., to paraphrase Paul's words here: "My readers, you yourselves being gentiles, as the ones I have just spoken of, should know that. . ." Cf. Niebuhr, *Heidenapostel* (1992) 172: "So bindet Paulus die Adressaten, indem er sie als τὰ ἔθνη anredet, direkt ein in das Heilsgeschehen, das er unmittelbar zuvor grundsätzlich zur Sprache gebracht hat: Die Adressaten selbst gehören zu denen, die aufgrund des Unglaubens in Israel Anteil am Heil gewonnen haben und erst recht künftig von der Annahme Israels profitieren werden."

[78] Note also that there is no indication of a shift of audience in 11:25 (with ἀδελφοί, cf. 12:1), subsequent to which the address is clearly directed at gentiles. There is no good reason either to doubt that Paul addresses his audience as a whole in 11:25.

[79] See above in Ch. 1 sec. 3.2.3.

by God to be a "minister of Christ Jesus to the gentiles." Paul then proceeds to explain the purpose of this task of his. It is a sacred service, a service for the gospel of God intended to make "the offering of the gentiles acceptable, sanctified by the holy spirit."

The words ἔγραψα ὑμῖν make it clear that Paul is addressing his audience as a whole in these verses (cf. ἀδελφοί μου in v. 14).[80] Paul does not identify this readership as distinctly as he had done in the passages discussed above. However, the reason and purpose given for Paul's way of writing his reminder strongly suggest that the "you" (ὑμῖν) consist of the very people placed under his apostleship, viz. gentiles. First, Paul explains to his audience that he has written to them somewhat boldly "because of" (διά with the acc.) his ministry to the gentiles given to him by God.[81] That is, this states the reason why it would be proper for Paul to address his audience in such a daring manner. Verse 18 is also telling: "For I shall not dare (τολμήσω) to say anything except of what Christ has accomplished through me for the obedience of the gentiles (εἰς ὑπακοὴν ἐθνῶν)." Second, in this same context, Paul elucidates the purpose and goal of his ministry. He is a priestly servant of God's εὐαγγέλιον, with the aim of bringing about an acceptable and holy offering of the gentiles.[82] By implication, it is Paul's very proclamation of the εὐαγγέλιον that will eventually result in such an offering.[83] That, in turn, is a just motive for at times being somewhat bold in the exposition of the gospel for the Roman audience.

---

[80] Note also the presence of ἀδελφοί in v. 15 in many MSS, including P[46].

[81] I.e. διὰ τὴν χάριν τὴν δοθεῖσάν μοι ὑπὸ τοῦ θεοῦ εἰς τὸ εἶναί με λειτουργὸν Χριστοῦ Ἰησοῦ εἰς τὰ ἔθνη. It makes little difference if this statement is taken with the participle ἐπαναμιμνήσκων instead of the main verb ἔγραψα (so Käsemann, *Römer* [1974] 378). Either way, it is Paul's authority as an apostle and the readers' inferiority in that respect that is under discussion.

[82] I.e. ἱερουργοῦντα τὸ εὐαγγέλιον τοῦ θεοῦ, ἵνα γένηται ἡ προσφορὰ τῶν ἐθνῶν εὐπρόσδεκτος, ἡγιασμένη ἐν πνεύματι ἁγίῳ.

[83] Cf. Jervis, *Purpose* (1991) 164: "The function of Romans is to encourage the Roman believers to enter Paul's apostolic orbit so that they may be included within his 'offering' through having heard his preaching." Cf. also Phil 2:17.

Thus, the context of Paul's direct address in 15:15 is strikingly similar to the ones in 1:5–7, 13–15; 11:13,[84] in which he spoke of his apostleship to gentiles and in which he explicitly identified his audience as such. It may therefore be concluded that the people addressed here are gentiles as well.

2.2. Implicit References to the Letter's Audience

If the letter's most explicit addresses attest an audience of non-Jewish origin, why is Paul so concerned with Jewish issues in Romans, particularly in chapters 1–11? And why does he write as if he assumes that his readers are fully initiated into the quintessence of Judaism? Does he not address Jews directly at some points in his letter?

These pressing questions have long haunted interpreters of Romans. Werner Georg Kümmel explains: "Röm trägt einen Doppelcharakter: er ist im wesentlichen Auseinandersetzung des paulinischen Ev[angeliums] mit dem Judentum, so daß der Schluß, die Leser seien Judenchristen, nahezuliegen scheint; und doch enthält der Brief Aussagen, die die Gemeinde bestimmt als heidenchristlich kennzeichnen."[85] Whereas this "double character" of Romans has occasionally led to doubts about the integrity of the letter,[86] or to suggestions of non-Roman addressees,[87] most scholars opt for the solution that Paul is partly addressing people of Jewish origin in his letter. Yet, this solution does not answer the question why Paul depicts his readers so distinctly as gentiles—and gentiles only—in the letter's explicit addresses, most of which are in fact found at or within those epistolary portions where the interpersonal context for the letter as a whole comes to clearest expression.

---

[84] Cf. also Paul's appeal to his authority towards his readers in 12:3 (λέγω γὰρ διὰ τῆς χάριτος τῆς δοθείσης μοι παντὶ τῷ ὄντι ἐν ὑμῖν), immediately following the hortatory request in 12:1–2 (see the discussion above in Ch. 1 sec. 3.2.2).

[85] *Einleitung* (1983) 270. The "double character" of Rom is discussed thoroughly in Elliott, *Rhetoric* (1990) 9–67 and passim. See also Nanos, "Jewish" (1999) 293–95.

[86] E.g. Schmithals, *Römerbrief* (1975); Scroggs, "Paul" (1976).

[87] Jervell, "Jerusalem" (1971).

But what indications are there in Paul's letter that may imply a Jewish readership? These are said to be three: 1) The subject under discussion in chapters 1–11 is thoroughly Jewish; 2) Paul's scriptural citations and allusions seem to presuppose an audience of Jewish origin; and 3) Paul appears to address (Jesus believing) Jews directly at various points in the letter or at least include them in some of his direct addresses. All these aspects are, of course, interrelated. In the following, I will deal with the first two under the same heading and the third separately. Two questions will guide my discussion. First, do the letter's more implicit references to its readership allow us either to exclude the explicitly identified audience or to infer that others must be included among the ones addressed? Second, what additional information do the implicit references provide concerning the letter's intended audience?

2.2.1. Jewish Issues and Scriptural References in Romans

In Romans 1–11 in particular Paul deals with some fundamental aspects of Judaism as they relate to the "good news" about Jesus. These include reflections on what it means and takes to be a Jew, the (dis)advantages of circumcision, the value of the Jewish Law, and the current as well as future status of those Jews who do not share the belief in Jesus as Messiah. Paul's discourse is thoroughly furnished with both overt and covert references to Jewish scriptures, the use of which clearly shows that Paul envisaged his audience to be well versed in these particular writings.[88]

Does this contradict Paul's explicitly identified audience? That is, does this necessarily presuppose Jewish readers and exclude gentile ones? Not at all. Paul's speaking about Jews and Judaism does not make the audience Jewish. Neither do Paul's scriptural references. Instead, the basic implications of these factors are that the people addressed in the letter are or have been operative within a Jewish community. And that pertains not only to Jews but to (former) gentile adherents to Judaism as well. Even scholars who see Jews among Paul's intended audience acknowledge this, more or

---

[88] On scriptural quotations and allusions in Rom, see esp. Hays, *Echoes* (1989) 34–83; Stanley, *Paul* (1992) 83–184. Cf. also Ch. 1 sec. 3.1.2 above.

less readily. For instance, claiming that "the focus and scope of Paul's argument contradict the exclusively Gentile character of the Roman church," and that "on the basis of internal evidence, Romans seems mainly a dialogue with Jews," J. Christiaan Beker nevertheless has to admit that "the frequent allusions to the Old Testament and Jewish terminology in Romans, and a statement like Rom. 7:1 ('I am speaking to those who know the law'), are intelligible even when Paul addresses the 'Gentile' majority of the Roman church."[89] When Anthony J. Guerra asks "to whom would the extraordinary cluster of concerns evident in Romans 1.2–4, namely, the continuity between gospel and Scripture, the Davidic Messiahship of Jesus Christ, and the adoptionist formula of 1.4, be directed?" his initial answer is "undoubtedly Jewish Christians in Rome." Later on, however, Guerra adds that Paul's scriptural allusions in the passage "would be relevant only to 'Jewish Christians' . . . doubtless including a good number of ethnic Gentiles, especially God-fearers and proselytes."[90] For some reasons, Guerra does not take into full account this latter insight of his. Similarly, yet somewhat more reluctantly, Douglas A. Campbell states: "Paul discusses Jewish themes extensively in Romans, but this is a strategy which would make little sense if his audience were entirely Gentile (and had not been subject to Jewish teaching)." He concludes that Romans posits "at least a partially Jewish-Christian audience" because "it seems that several stylistic and substantive features of Romans assume a significant degree of Jewish knowledge on the part of at least some of its recipients."[91] While Campbell's premise is certainly valid, his inference seems to be drawn too rapidly. As Campbell himself implies (albeit within parenthesis), the Jewish themes in Romans would make sense to a gentile audience who had been "subject to Jewish teaching." Why, then, pass over such a readership which

---

[89] *Paul* (1980) 76–77. Actually, Beker's "internal evidence" seems to be somewhat dependent upon his conception of the composition of the "Roman church."
[90] *Romans* (1995) 25–26. Guerra uses the term "Jewish Christians" "as a category designating Christians who abide by some or all of the ritual commandments of Judaism" (p. 22).
[91] *Rhetoric* (1992) 15–16, 19.

would correspond well with Paul's explicitly identified audience, and add instead a "Jewish-Christian" one which is not as easily identified?

A case to compare here is Paul's letter to the Galatians. Despite his attention to more or less "Jewish issues" and his quotations from Jewish writings in this letter, few scholars would insist that Paul's addressees are others than non-Jews. Why is it assumed, then, that Romans is any different in this respect? Presumably because of certain preconceived ideas of the ethnic composition of the audience to which Paul is writing (see above), and/or because of some implicit references to the letter's audience which may appear to presuppose Jewish addressees. As for the latter, E. P. Sanders even claims that "Romans is unique in the Pauline correspondence in containing so many clues to the presence of Jewish Christians among the readership. The other letters contain no such clues."[92] But where are these "clues" and what do they consist of? To these questions I now turn.

2.2.2. Various Potential References to the Letter's Audience

Among the most common arguments for Jewish or "Jewish Christian" addressees in Romans is the presence of a supposedly Jewish interlocutor in chapters 2–4, particularly chapter 2. The Jewish identity of this person, it is argued, shows that Paul must have had at least a partly Jewish audience in mind when he wrote the letter. However, arguments of this kind do not take into sufficient consideration the nature of Paul's invention of a conversational partner in his letter.[93] When Paul addresses such a person he is not directly addressing the letter's audience but a fictitious individual whose participation in the discourse is meant to say something to the audience. It is extremely difficult to identify the audience with any certainty on the basis of such a dialogue. Even if the interlocutor in chapters 2–4 is thought by Paul to be Jewish, that does not necessarily mean that the audience must (partly) be Jewish. As Stanley K. Stowers has shown, for instance, it is quite possible that Paul is creating a fictitious debate with a "Jewish teacher"

---

[92] *Paul* (1983) 184.
[93] This will be discussed more thoroughly in Ch. 3 below.

(from 2:17 onward) which his gentile audience is meant to overhear.[94] Although I disagree with Stowers and others concerning the interlocutor's identity (see Ch. 4 below), Stowers' conclusions elucidate well the problem involved in attempting to determine the letter's audience on the basis of an imaginary dialogue. Whatever the specific identity of Paul's interlocutor(s), it cannot be used a priori to determine to whom Paul is writing. Methodologically, it would be more appropriate to reverse the question: Does the letter's intended audience tell us anything about the identity of the interlocutor?

It is sometimes held that Paul's words in 1:16 about the εὐαγγέλιον being "God's power for salvation" both to "Jews and Greeks" imply that he is addressing both groups concerned. But Paul does not address the audience directly in this verse as "Jews and Greeks." He merely explains that God's εὐαγγέλιον has relevance not only to Jews but to non-Jews as well, the latter of whom are subject to Paul's apostolic sphere (1:5, 13–15). Similarly, in 9:24 where he observes that God "has called us not only from Jews but also from gentiles" he does not say that his readers are both Jews and gentiles. Rather, he is stating in general terms that those who believe in Jesus as Messiah ("we") derive from both groups. Paul's use of the first person plural is furthermore highly intricate, resulting in many instances in which it is far from easily detected who are meant to be included.[95]

In 4:1 Abraham appears to be referred to as "our forefather according to (the) flesh" (τὸν προπάτορα ἡμῶν κατὰ σάρκα, cf. 9:10). It is commonly argued that the "we" in the verse could only have included those of Jewish birth, and thus that Paul's audience must have been at least partly Jewish. But several factors advise us not to draw hasty conclusions about the letter's

---

[94] *Rereading* (1994) esp. 143–75, 231–50.
[95] See Cranfield, "Changes" (1982) 283–7, who notes that "it is often difficult, or maybe impossible, to be sure whether in a particular occurrence of the first person plural the 'we' is thus limited [i.e. to Paul and the addressees in question] or includes Christians quite generally" (p. 283). Cranfield remarks that "there is scope for a good deal of further, and more careful, investigation of the occurrences of the first person plural in Paul's epistles" (p. 287). The present writer knows of no such study. With respect to Paul's references to co-sender(s) in his letters, see, however, Byrskog, "Co-Senders" (1996).

audience on the basis of this verse. First, the weight of 4:1 in this respect is heavily diminished by textual uncertainties—the verse is "textkritisch eine crux."[96] Second, the words "our forefather" do not call for Jewish readers, as shown in vv. 11–12, 16–18. This fact is also substantiated, for instance, by First Corinthians 10:1 where Paul refers to the Israelites in the wilderness as "our fathers" (οἱ πατέρες ἡμῶν). Few interpreters would claim that Paul was not addressing people of gentile origin in this letter or that "we" in 10:1 necessarily included Jews. Third, in addition to its ambiguous syntactical position,[97] the sense of the phrase κατὰ σάρκα in Romans 4:1 is by no means clear. If taken with τὸν προπάτορα ἡμῶν, which seems to be the least problematic reading, it may refer to physical descent, but it may also allude to the manner in which Abraham received the fatherhood in question.[98] The latter alternative neither requires a Jewish "we" nor excludes a gentile one. Fourth, as several scholars have argued, 4:1 may well include the question "Have we found Abraham to be our forefather according to the flesh?"[99] Such a question would seem peculiar if coming from a Jew addressing a fellow Jew.

These factors suffice to show that we cannot attach much importance to 4:1 in the task of identifying Paul's audience, and that it cannot be taken for granted that Jews must have been included in the "we" referred to in the verse.

---

[96] Wilckens, *Römer* (1978) 1.260. The inf. εὑρηκέναι is variously placed in the MS tradition and absent from several MSS, including B. See further Metzger, *Textual* (1975) 509–10.

[97] The phrase κατὰ σάρκα may be taken either with the inf. εὑρηκέναι or the immediately preceding τὸν προπάτορα ἡμῶν.

[98] Cf. Stowers, *Rereading* (1994) 234, who submits the following translation of 4:1–2a (the "Jewish teacher" asks): "What then will we say? Have we found Abraham to be our forefather by his own human efforts [that is, according to the flesh]? For if Abraham was justified by works, he has a reason for boasting." Paul then answers (vv. 2b–3): "But not before God [ἀλλ᾿ οὐ πρὸς θεόν]. For what does the scripture say? . . ." While I disagree with Stowers on the Jewish identity of Paul's interlocutor (see Ch. 4 below), I agree with him on this division of the dialogue.

[99] See Hays, "Abraham" (1985); Palmer, "τί οὖν;" (1995); Campbell, "Towards" (2002) 374–91. Cf. also Ch. 4 sec. 4.2 below.

In 7:1 Paul states that he is speaking to "those who know the Law." This has often been thought to call for Jewish addressees,[100] but such an explanation is really unnecessary. Indeed, the fact that Paul makes this mention at all strongly suggests the opposite, viz. that the addressees here are of non-Jewish origin. There would have been no reason for him to add this observation to an address to Jews, since no Jew would not have "known the Law." What Paul's remark reveals instead is that he presupposes at least some familiarity with the Law by his readership.

In 15:7 Paul addresses the audience directly and urges them to "welcome one another" (προσλαμβάνεσθε ἀλλήλους) just as Christ had "welcomed" (προσελάβετο) them "for the glory of God" (εἰς δόξαν τοῦ θεοῦ). His following comment about Christ having become a "servant of circumcision" (διάκονον περιτομῆς, v. 8) is sometimes taken to imply that Jews must be included in this address. But that is probably not the case. While the syntax in vv. 8–9 is difficult,[101] it is fairly clear that the addressees in v. 7 are precisely those whom Christ had welcomed "for the glory of God." Immediately preceding this verse, Paul had prayed that the audience might "together with one voice glorify (δοξάζητε)" God (v. 6). In vv. 8–9 he explains that Christ had become a "servant of circumcision" in order to confirm God's promises to the patriarchs, but that the gentiles are to "glorify" (δοξάσαι) God for God's mercy. Thereafter follows a series of scriptural quotations in which this same thought is expressed, namely, the glorification of God by the gentiles (vv. 9b–12).[102] Thus, the addressees in v. 7, the

---

[100] E.g. recently by Boers, *Justification* (1994) 87. Boers rightly asks: "Would he speak like that to Jews?" but then proceeds to argue that "what follows in 7:1c–6 could not have been addressed to gentiles; it concerns specifically those who are under the Law." Provided that Boers is right in this latter respect, it must be noted that Paul's words may as well concern those *gentiles* who are or have been "under the Law."

[101] See Wagner, "Christ" (1997); Lambrecht, "Syntactical" (2000).

[102] It is worth noting that Paul's vision here of gentiles glorifying God is the reverse of his description of the sinful gentile world in 1:18–32, esp. vv. 21–25. For discussion of this passage, see Ch. 4 sec. 2.1 below.

ὑμᾶς whom Christ had welcomed for the glory of God, in all likelihood belong to this particular group of people.[103]

In sum, there is little which may be suggestive of another audience than the one explicitly identified in the letter. While we should perhaps expect at least some common traits between Paul's interlocutor(s) and the audience, the fact that the interlocutor is a fictitious person prevents us from determining the audience on the basis of his or her identity. Paul's general remarks about the relevance of the εὐαγγέλιον (1:16; cf. 9:24) and his use of the intricate first person plural (4:1; 9:24) do not necessitate a Jewish readership. As for 7:1 and 15:7–9, it is not only unnecessary to postulate Jewish addressees but it may even be a mistake to do so. These passages actually appear to confirm the identity of Paul's intended audience as gentiles.

There are in fact further features in the letter which verify this conclusion. First, in 8:15 Paul declares to his readers that they have now received a "spirit of adoption" (πνεῦμα υἱοθεσίας), but in 9:4 it is stated of the Israelites that "the adoption" already belongs to them (ὧν ἡ υἱοθεσία). That suggests that Paul's readership does not belong to the latter group. Second, in chapters 9–11 Paul speaks to his audience about the Jewish nation, "my own people, my kinsmen according to flesh" (τῶν ἀδελφῶν μου τῶν συγγενῶν μου κατὰ σάρκα, 9:3; cf. 11:1), and it is quite clear that the latter are referred to in terms of ethnicity and religious heritage. They are often contrasted with gentiles (e.g. 9:30–31; 11:11–14, 25, 28, 30–31) and always spoken of in the third person plural. Third, Paul's epistolary request in 12:1–2, which, of course, is aimed at the readership as a whole, is followed by an appeal to his authority towards the audience (λέγω γὰρ διὰ τῆς χάριτος τῆς δοθείσης μοι παντὶ τῷ ὄντι ἐν ὑμῖν, v. 3). It seems reasonable to assume that this applies to his authority as an apostle to the gentiles (cf. 1:5–6, 13–14a; 11:13; 15:15–16), and that he thus addresses his readers here as such. Further examples can and might be provided,[104] but these suffice to demonstrate that the letter's more implicit references to its audience correspond well to its explicitly identified readership.

---

[103] So also Whitsett, "Son" (2000) 664–72.
[104] Cf. the discussion in Ch. 4 sec. 2.1.2 below.

It would probably be unwise to maintain that there were actually no Jews present when Paul's letter was eventually read in the city of Rome, or that Paul himself thought so. But, whatever the actual circumstances were at the moment of reading, the conclusion must be that the people whom Paul addressed in Romans were of gentile origin only. The fact that Paul presupposes considerable knowledge of Jewish principles on the part of the audience may partly explain the letter's "double character." Romans is directed to non-Jews, but precisely those non-Jews who had been or still were operative within a Jewish community in Rome.[105]

Concluding Summary

Whereas Pauline scholarship appears to be gradually moving away from the view that the intended audience of Romans was partly of Jewish origin, the majority still seems to maintain that it was. This understanding has mostly been based, first, on certain presuppositions about the composition of "Roman Christianity" at the time when Paul wrote his letter, and, second, on certain aspects of the letter itself which are thought to presuppose Jewish readers. As for the former, it is of primary importance to distinguish between potential knowledge of "Roman Christianity" around the middle of the first century, on the one hand, and the people to whom Paul intended to write, on the other. This methodological principle is essential for studies of Romans, not least because of the almost total lack of sources informative of "Roman Christianity" prior to Paul's letter. Information about the audience of Romans is instead to be sought in the letter itself.

The letter's most explicit references to its readership, including the one in the epistolary opening, attest an audience of gentile origin. Such references should, by definition, take precedence over more implicit ones. A survey of the latter type, on the other hand, brings to light an audience the identity of whom accords well with the explicitly identified recipients. Implicit references neither exclude the gentile audience from being addressed nor do they necessarily call for a Jewish readership of which no mention is made in

---

[105] There is no way of knowing the extent of such a group, but it should be pointed out that the number of people included does not have to be large.

the most explicit ones. At the same time, it is evident that Paul was writing not to gentiles at large but to a certain group of gentiles whose knowledge of Jewish writings and experience of Jewish ways of life was substantial. Every aspect of Paul's message in Romans must be read in light of this particular audience.

Chapter Three

The Dialogical Style and Epistolary Interlocutor in Romans 2–11

Introduction

Peculiar to Paul's letter to the Romans is the extensive use of a dialogical style. While some of his other extant letters also include examples of such a style,[1] these are comparatively casual and do not seem to be used consistently so as to characterize major portions of the letters. In Romans the style of a dialogue is initiated in chapter 2 by a direct address to a certain individual in the second person singular, followed in chapter 3 by a series of questions and answers which from that point onward occur regularly through chapter 11. With Paul's epistolary request in 12:1–2, however, the discourse takes a different shape: Whereas second person singular addresses appear now and then, exchanges of questions and answers are entirely absent. Instead, imperative language prevails.

For any discussion of Paul's interlocutor(s) in Romans 2 it is requisite to pay careful attention to the way in which a dialogical style such as that applied by Paul was used in ancient Greco-Roman literature, epistolary in particular. While this is certainly not an easy task, I will attempt to cope with this requirement in the present chapter, with the focus specifically aimed at the questions of function and identity. To begin with, I will attend to previous research in this area, first by describing some basic traits of this literary style, and then by focusing on the divergent kinds of literature and settings in which it was employed (sec. 1). Subsequently, the ancient

---

[1] See esp. 1 Cor 4:7; 6:15; 7:16, 21; 8:10–11; 10:18–20; 14:15–17, 26; 15:35–37; Gal 2:17; 3:19, 21.

understanding of the epistolary medium as a dialogical form will be discussed (sec. 2). In section 3 the use of interlocutors in Greco-Roman letters will be analysed, both in formal terms as well as in terms of function and identity. Finally, before moving on to the more detailed discussion of Romans 2 in Chapter Four, a general assessment of Paul's use of an interlocutor(s) in Romans 2–11 will be presented, with respect specifically to the macrostructural function of the dialogical style (sec. 4).

1. Paul's Letter and the Greco-Roman "Diatribe"

It has long been recognized that Paul's dialogical language in Romans closely parallels the ancient literary style come to be known in modern scholarship as the Greco-Roman "diatribe." While it is doubtful that the term "diatribe" can properly be used in a generic sense,[2] it may nonetheless be useful as a descriptive term for the distinctive dialogical style employed in a certain set of ancient writings,[3] both Greek and Latin. These include works of Bion of Borysthenes (fragments),[4] Teles, Musonius Rufus (fragments), Seneca, Epictetus (as recorded by Arrian), Plutarch, Dio of Prusa, and Maximus of Tyre. Others have also been mentioned.[5] Many of the works were written or spoken in a didactic context,[6] intended to persuade

---

[2] See esp. Donfried, "Presuppositions" (1974) 112–19; Stowers, *Diatribe* (1981) 7–78; Schmeller, *Paulus* (1987) 1–54. Cf. also Trapp, "Sermons" (1997) 1974 n. 100. For the view that the "diatribe" was a genre in Greco-Roman antiquity, see Porter, "Argument" (1996); cf. idem, "Diatribe" (2000).

[3] Against Anderson, *Rhetorical* (1996) 218. Yet, the potentially misleading term must be used with caution, of which a quotation mark may serve as a reminder.

[4] On the difficulties involved in locating the fragmentary quotations of Bion by Teles, see Stowers, *Diatribe* (1981) 50–53. Stowers himself concludes that "Bion is certainly not a major source for the style of the diatribe" (p. 51).

[5] See the overview of scholarly suggestions in Schmeller, *Paulus* (1987) 33–36, several of which seem to posit a rather vague boundaries of definition.

[6] Stowers, *Diatribe* (1981) esp. 48–78, has argued convincingly that the "diatribal" works of the authors listed above (except Bion) grew out of a school setting: "Teles, Epictetus, Musonius Rufus and Plutarch headed formal philosophical

or exhort the audience concerned to adopt or adhere to particular views or ways of life.

1.1. Basic Characteristics of the "Diatribe" Style

Though formal traits may vary markedly from author to author and from text to text, several shared and distinctive elements may be discerned for this type of literary style.[7] The most basic and prominent one—and with which I am mainly concerned in the present study—is the presence or invention of an interlocutor in the text, i.e. a conversational partner who responds to or raises questions, objections, or new points in the flow of the discourse. Another, interrelated characteristic would be the writer's or speaker's direct and sometimes abrupt address to a certain individual using the second person singular. The address typically involves censure of some sort and may include such biting vocatives as ταλαίπωρε, *infelix*, or *miser*, or the more neutral ἄνθρωπε. More often than not the person addressed in this way is or will be engaged in the discussion as the speaker's or writer's conversational partner.

The dialogue between the writer/speaker and the interlocutor typically consists of concise exchanges of questions and answers, the former often serving as an objection to what has already been stated. The interlocutor may either have the role of answering questions posed by the writer/speaker (in line with the Socratic dialogue), or raising questions—often based on

---

schools while Dio Chrysostom and Maximus of Tyre created their discourses for situations which have some of the basic characteristics of a school, most important of which is the student-teacher relationship. Seneca has fictitiously created this student-teacher relationship with its dialogical style in his letters to Lucilius" (p. 76). See also idem, "Diatribe" (1988) 73–75. This conclusion has been sharply criticized by Schmeller, *Paulus* (1987) esp. 46–52. But see Stowers' Review of Schmeller (1989), and Malherbe, "Moralists" (1992) 318–19; White, *Apostle* (1999) 76–77.

[7] See esp. Bultmann, *Stil* (1910) 10–64; Stowers, *Diatribe* (1981) 20–21, 50–78, 85–93, 125–33; idem, "Diatribe" (1988) 75–76. See also Capelle and Marrou, "Diatribe" (1957) 998; Berger, "Gattungen" (1984) 1130–32; Reiser, *Sprache* (2001) 184–87.

false conclusions—the response to which is then provided by the writer/speaker. Sometimes these roles are mixed. Questions and objections are frequently introduced by words and phrases such as τί οὖν, τί δέ, ἀλλά, *quid ergo*, *at*, etc. When rejected, strong negatives such as μὴ γένοιτο, οὐ-δαμῶς, and *minime*, may be used.

There are two basic ways in which the interlocutor enters the discussion. On the one hand, this is clearly marked by a verb of saying, such as "you say," "you might say," or "someone says."[8] On the other, the interlocutor simply joins in with a comment or question without such explicit indication. In the latter case, the identity of the one speaking may at times be somewhat ambiguous.

1.2. Identifying the "Diatribal" Interlocutor: The Problem of Distinct Settings

Three influential monographs have been issued entirely devoted to the Greco-Roman "diatribe" in relation to the letters of Paul. Only one of them, however, pays due attention to the function and identity of the "diatribal" interlocutor, viz. Stanley K. Stowers' *The Diatribe and Paul's Letter to the Romans* (1981).[9] In his survey of the ancient sources for this particular style,[10] Stowers observes that "a chief characteristic of the dialogical element of the diatribe" is the "marked ambiguity and lack of clarity" about

---

[8] Usually some forms of φημί, λέγω, *inquio*, or *dico*. Various examples may be found in Stowers, *Diatribe* (1981) 126 with nn.

[9] The other two are Bultmann's *Stil* (1910) and Schmeller's *Paulus* (1987). Bultmann's discussion of the interlocutor's identity is rather dispersed and surely reflects too much dependence on Epictetus' *Diatr.* (see, e.g., pp. 11–12), as already pointed out by Bonhöffer, *Epiktet* (1911) 179 n. 1. Although Schmeller does to some extent touch upon the question of the interlocutor's identity (see esp. pp. 22–24), his focus is not specifically aimed in that direction.

[10] Stowers recognizes Teles, Epictetus, Musonius Rufus, Dio of Prusa, Plutarch, Maximus of Tyre, Seneca, and, to a limited extent, Philo of Alexandria, as the primary sources for the "diatribe" style (see *Diatribe* [1981] 48–78).

the interlocutor's identity.[11] The identity may at times be determined with reasonable certainty, particularly when the writer/speaker addresses some figure from history or mythology, or a personified thing or concept.[12] But as a rule the question is more open. Sometimes the interlocutor may exemplify common opinion or a certain type of person, and sometimes he or she may represent the specific audience to whom the author is writing or speaking.[13] The boundaries between these are, however, often quite fluid. Indeed, "there is often little distance between the real audience and the fictitious interlocutor."[14] According to Stowers, the very ambiguity about the interlocutor's identity reflects a decisive part of the "diatribal" function. While the individual addressed may be imaginary (e.g. a specific type of person) it is actually the intended audience that is the prime target: "In diatribal address to the interlocutor there is a calculated duality or ambiguity by which the teacher [or writer/speaker] could speak indirectly to his students [or audience] and at the same time vigorously censure students [or those among the audience] whose vices corresponded to the imaginary interlocutor's."[15] This also applies to the "diatribal" exchanges of questions and answers:

> The author or speaker in the diatribe addresses and responds to both his real audience and a fictitious one. As the author slips back and forth between the two levels this ambiguity allows the audience to be caught up in the simulated dia-

---

[11] *Diatribe* (1981) 73. Ultimately concerned with Rom, Stowers deals with the "diatribal" interlocutor from two angles, viz. "Address to the Imaginary Interlocutor" (ch. 2 in his work) and "Objections and False Conclusions" (ch. 3). Note that in my summary account of Stowers' study I sometimes combine these two aspects more than he does.

[12] See Stowers, *Diatribe* (1981) 90–92.

[13] See discussion with examples in Stowers, *Diatribe* (1981) 50–75, 101–10.

[14] Stowers, *Diatribe* (1981) 99.

[15] *Diatribe* (1981) 110. Cf. on p. 180: "The dialogical element of the diatribe does grow out of the argument or represents what is typical, but it is directed toward a specific group with which the teacher has a certain relationship. The typical is addressed to the particular pedagogical needs of the audience" (a response to G. Bornkamm's thesis about Rom being Paul's "last will and testament," the content of which has little, if anything, to do with the situation of the audience).

logue, the question-and-answer . . . process. . . . Through objections the teacher [or author/speaker] rhetorically simulates the student's [or audience's] input into the 'discussion.'[16]

But, in order that this may function properly, is it not necessary, or at least preferable, that there exist some commonalities or connections between the interlocutor and the audience addressed? According to Stowers, the fictitious objector is "often anonymous, colorless and almost without any identity."[17] The exception to this rule usually occurs either if the objector may be identified with a person addressed previously in the second person singular or if the interlocutor can clearly be identified with the audience. However, the "striking characteristic . . . of the phenomenon of objections and false conclusions is the looseness and variability of their usage. There is a lack of concern for maintaining the fiction of the interlocutor on a consistent level." Moreover, "the objector throughout a discourse only sometimes represents a consistent position, type of person or school of thought."[18] Stowers comes to the conclusion that this pertains to Paul's letter to the Romans as well.[19]

At this point, an important question must be raised. Is it at all helpful to consult all the various sources attesting the use of a "diatribe" style in the attempt to identify Paul's interlocutor in Romans? Surely the nature and setting of the communicative medium used at each occasion must also be seriously considered. After all, there is an obvious difference between actual dialogues taking place, say, within the walls of a classroom, and fictitious dialogues in literary works. There is also a fundamental difference between a lecture or a speech—even if written—and a letter—even if read aloud,

---

[16] *Diatribe* (1981) 140. Cf. pp. 177–78.
[17] *Diatribe* (1981) 129, with references to R. Hirzel and A. Oltramare.
[18] *Diatribe* (1981) 129.
[19] *Diatribe* (1981) 134–35. Cf. p. 117 on Paul's addresses to imaginary interlocutors in the letter: "Paul censures the pretentious and arrogant *Gentile* (or all men?) in 2:1–5, the pretentious *Jew* in 2:19[*sic*]–24, the pretentious and arrogant *Gentile Christian* in 11:17–24 and the pretentious *Christian* in 14:14[*sic*] & 10" (emphasis mine). Cf., however, Stowers' different approach in his more recent *Rereading* (1994) 22–33 and passim.

viz. the difference between the presence and absence of the author.[20] Of the ancient sources for the "diatribe" listed above, letters are only found among the works of Seneca and Plutarch. Most of the others constitute either classroom discussions or lectures and/or speeches delivered by the authors themselves, some of which were noted down by students more[21] or less[22] verbatim. The basic problem with this type of literature is that we do not always know whether an actual dialogue has been recorded or not.[23] The discourses of Epictetus, for example, include without doubt a major source material, both formally and functionally, for the Greco-Roman "diatribe" in general and for the use of the style by Paul in particular.[24] But when it comes to the more specific question of identifying the "diatribal" interlocutor, Epictetus' discourses prove to be somewhat problematic. The reason is that, while most of the discourses show potential signs of the "diatribal" interlocutor being a literary invention built in the lectures, many of them are evidently recorded as actual dialogues taking place in Epictetus' classroom.[25] Thus, it is often very difficult to know whether the interlocutor is a real person or a fictitious one.[26] As for other "diatribal" lectures and speeches, similar inferences may be drawn. It is not always possible either to know if, how, and to what extent the orator or lecturer might have given

---

[20] As discussed above in the introduction to Ch. 1.

[21] The scholarly majority follows Hartmann, "Arrian" (1905) in taking Epictetus' *Diatr.* as Arrian's stenographic records of his teacher's lectures or discussions with his students. In his introductory letter to Lucius Gellius, Arrian calls them ὑπομνήματα (see the LCL ed.).

[22] As in the case of Epictetus' teacher, Musonius Rufus, whose lectures are extant only in fragments; see van Geytenbeek, *Musonius* (1963) 7–12. It is unlikely that Musonius wrote anything himself.

[23] Thus even Stowers, *Diatribe* (1981) 128, notes: "In the sources which record oral speech much has been lost which was communicated through intonation and gesture. There are a few instances where real objections from the audience seem to occur in Epictetus and Dio, but again, it is very difficult to determine this with certainty." Cf. also Schmeller, *Paulus* (1987) 24.

[24] See esp. Malherbe, "Μὴ γένοιτο" (1980).

[25] E.g. 1.2; 1.5; 1.11; 1.13; 1.14; 1.15; 1.26; 2.4; 2.14; 2.24; 2.25; 3.1; 3.4; 3.6; 3.7; 3.9; 3.22.

[26] This is also partly acknowledged by Stowers, *Diatribe* (1981) 55–56.

the audience an implication of the interlocutor's identity at the moment of speaking, or to know whether the orator/lecturer was addressing a real person or not. Conversely, in most cases it is practically impossible to know if, how, and to what extent the audience might have effected the speaker's use of a "diatribal" interlocutor.

Hence, whereas research into the "diatribe" style is extremely important for adding to our understanding of Romans, it is questionable whether utilization of every type of "diatribal" work when attempting to identify Paul's interlocutor in the letter may be useful or even legitimate. I suggest that a more helpful way may be to examine analogous elements in Greco-Roman documents of the same genre as that of Romans, viz. letters. The reason for this is twofold. First, approaching the problem from this angle minimizes the extent of it because of the relatively similar settings and basic confines of the epistolary genre. Put differently, as soon as the dialogical style is used in a letter it becomes subject to and limited by, not only the genre's prevailing norms and boundaries, but also the relationship existing between author and audience. Second, full advantage has not been taken of the sources available for this sort of style in ancient letters. Instead, scholars have almost exclusively focused on the letters of Seneca. That is in itself anything but amazing, since they constitute no doubt the most important source extant in this respect.[27] However, a survey of Greco-Roman letters reveals that there are many others in which a conversational partner is invented and used for the sake of the author's argument and/or message. While "diatribal" elements in other types of writings may have had their impact on epistolographers,[28] it is likely that the ancient understanding of the epistolary medium also effected the use of a dialogical style in ancient letters.

---

[27] Curiously, however, Schmeller, *Paulus* (1987), almost totally ignores Seneca's letters in his study of the "diatribe" and Paul's letters (cf. index on p. 483).

[28] In this regard, Malherbe's remark is well to the point: "More important than questions of derivation or dependency [of the "diatribe"] is that of function" ("Moralists" [1992] 320).

2. The Ancient Letter as a "Kind of Written Conversation"

The most basic function of the ancient letter was to be a surrogate for oral communication.[29] This is amply reflected both in the unanimity among ancient epistolary theorists of likening the letter to an actual conversation, and by comments of epistolographers either on their own letter writing or on letters in general.

In the oldest extant work on epistolary theory (ca. 1st cent. B.C.E.–1st cent. C.E.) we are told that Artemon claimed that "a letter ought to be written in the same manner as a dialogue (διάλογον), a letter being regarded by him [i.e. Artemon] as one of the two sides of a dialogue (τὸ ἕτερον μέρος τοῦ διαλόγου)."[30] For the author of a letter attributed to the Cynic philosopher Diogenes (probably dating from the 1st cent. B.C.E.), the forcefulness of letters consisted in their functional equivalence to actual dialogues: "For letters are worth a great deal (δύνανται) and are not inferior to conversation with people actually present (οὐχ ἥττονα τῆς πρὸς παρόντας διαλέξεως)."[31] Cicero frequently referred to his letters as a kind of conversation.[32] He even stated that, in times of distress, he sometimes wrote letters just to have a "talk" with his friends and thus ease his mind: "I have nothing to write about. . . . But since my distress of mind is such that it is not only impossible to sleep but torment to be awake, I have started this scrawl without any subject in view, just in order as it were to talk to you (*tecum ut quasi loquerer*), which is my only relief."[33] Although Seneca was far from impressed by the trivialities with which Cicero "filled" his correspon-

---

[29] See, e.g., Cicero, *Fam.* 417.1: "Now that I cannot talk to you face to face (*cum coram tecum loqui non possim*), what could I like better than writing to you or reading your letters?" Cf. *Phil.* 2.7, in which Cicero describes the letter as *amicorum colloquia absentium*.

[30] Demetrius, *Eloc.* 223. For discussion of Demetrius' subsequent critique of this notion, cf. Koskenniemi, *Studien* (1956) 43–44; Thraede, *Grundzüge* (1970) 22–23. On the date of the work, see the introduction to Ch. 1 above.

[31] *Ep.* 3.8–9. On the date of the letter, see Malherbe, *Cynic* (1977) 14–15.

[32] E.g. *Att.* 139.1; 164.2; 280.2; 295; 325; *Quint. fratr.* 1.45; 14.1. Cf. *Fam.* 216.1 (a letter to Cicero from Cassius Longinus).

[33] *Att.* 177.1. Cf. 151.4; 164.1.

dence,³⁴ he shared the latter's views on the dialogical nature of the letter: "I prefer that my letters should be just what my conversation (*sermo*) would be if you and I were sitting in one another's company or taking walks together."³⁵

This conception of the medium constituted a common ground also in later epistolary theory. In an appendix to his *Ars rhetorica* devoted to letter writing, Julius Victor (4th cent. C.E.) taught that "[s]ometimes it is agreeable to write as though you were conversing with the person actually present (*quasi praesentem alloqui*)," as "amply found in Cicero's letters."³⁶ Even more insistent was his contemporary, Gregory of Nazianzus, when he urged that "everyone knows that one should avoid prose-like style [in letters] so far as possible, and rather incline towards the conversational (τὸ λαλικόν)."³⁷ Thus, it comes as no surprise that sometime during the fourth to sixth century C.E. the letter would be described in general terms as a "kind of written conversation (ὁμιλία τις ἐγγράμματος) with someone from whom one is separated. . . . One will speak in it as though one were in the company of the absent person (ἐρεῖ δέ τις ἐν αὐτῇ ὥσπερ παρών τις πρὸς παρόντα)."³⁸

This basic understanding of the letter is also frequently manifested in the letters' specific language and literary style. Numerous letters from antiquity are furnished with dialogical elements giving the impression that an actual conversation is taking place in or by the letter. Besides the widespread use of rhetorical questions,³⁹ this is most distinctly effected by exchanges of

---

[34] *Ep.* 118.1–2.
[35] *Ep.* 75.1. Cf. 27.1; 55.9–11; 67.2.
[36] *Rhet.* 27. He noted, however, that this pertained only to "personal/private" (*familiares*) letters (as distinct from "official/commercial" [*negotiales*] letters).
[37] *Ep.* 51.4. The latter style Gregory considered to be a mark of epistolary clarity (σαφήνεια), providing an example of it himself earlier in the letter by an invention of an interlocutor (3).
[38] Pseudo-Libanius, *Ep. Char.* 2.
[39] Rhetorical questions are, of course, employed in various kinds of literature. In ancient letters specifically they are so prevalent that they may even be found in the rather stereotyped "documentary" papyri, e.g. P.Oxy. 4.744.11–13 (1 B.C.E.);

questions and answers. The most straightforward examples of this sort of language occur when the author of the letter is directly responding to or answering particular questions or statements put forth in previous letters addressed to him or her. For instance, when Cicero begins one of his letters to his brother with the question "What, *you* afraid of interrupting me?"[40] he is responding to a letter in which Quintus apparently expressed some hesitance to come for a visit. Similarly, when Cicero quite unexpectedly cries out in a letter to Atticus "Good gracious! (*Sed heus tu!*) Do you approve of corn doles to Athens?"[41] he is questioning some of Atticus' conducts previously recounted by the latter. In cases like these, the statements concerned are paraphrased as questions before a response is given, thus intensifying the impact of it. Sometimes the statements are simply restated and then replied to in an interrogative form, as in the opening words of Pliny the Younger in a letter to Cornelius Tacitus: "So you recommend Julius Naso as a candidate for office. Naso to me? It might be me to myself! (*quid si me ipsum?*)."[42] Information previously provided by the addressee may also be slightly hinted at before reacted to in this manner. Thus Cicero opens a letter: "Apenas had hardly gone when your letter came. Really? (*Quid ais?*) Do you think he won't propose his law? Pray speak a little more clearly (*Dic, oro te, clarius*), I hardly think I caught your meaning."[43]

All this adds a dialogical aspect to the writing. The dialogue, however, is not framed as actually taking place within the letter but primarily by the very exchange of letters, the letter thus properly functioning as "one of the two sides of a dialogue." In other words, this type of dialogical style does not include any invention of an interlocutor within the letter itself. Nevertheless, it illuminates well the dialogical nature of the epistolary medium and thus why the letter could properly be described as a "kind of written

---

BGU 3.846.15–16 (2nd cent. C.E.). See texts and discussion in Deissmann, *Licht* (1923) 134–36, 153–58; White, *Light* (1986) 111–12, 181–82.

[40] *Quint. fratr.* 12.1 (italics original in trans.).
[41] *Att.* 121.2 (trans. Winstedt [no. 6.6.2]).
[42] *Ep.* 6.9.1.
[43] *Att.* 82.1 (trans. Winstedt [no. 4.8a.1]).

conversation." The step towards creating an epistolary interlocutor was not a giant one.

3. Epistolary Interlocutors in Greco-Roman Antiquity

A considerable number of ancient letters are extant in which the author has created an imaginary dialogue with the aid of a conversational partner—an epistolary interlocutor.[44] Most significant are the voluminous letter collections of Cicero and Seneca which are richly furnished with such a dialogical style. Although widely neglected in this respect, Cicero's collection provides us with valuable information on how an interlocutor could be used in letters, not only by Cicero himself but also by some of his correspondents. The fact that his letters were known and studied already in the first century C.E. also adds to their value.[45] Seneca's letters are even more important because of his more extensive, calculated, and consistent employment of an interlocutor.[46] As we shall see, uses of imaginary partners in dialogue are made by other Greco-Roman epistolographers as well.

---

[44] I.e. "epistolary interlocutor" is here used for any given conversational partner in a letter, the dialogue with whom is more or less fictitious (cf. the description of the "diatribal" interlocutor in sec. 1.1 above).

[45] See Seneca, *Epp.* 21.4; 97.3; 118.1–2. Cf. Pliny, *Epp.* 1.2.4; 9.2.2; Plutarch, *Cic.* 24.4, 6–7; 36.5; 37.2–3; 40.3; *Comp. Dem. Cic.* 1.2; Quintilian, *Inst.* 6.3.109, 112; 8.3.32, 34–35; 11.1.21; Suetonius, *Aug.* 3.2; *Gramm.* 14; *Jul.* 9.2; 49.3; 55.1; *Rhet.* 2. Indeed, only shortly after Cicero's death in 43 B.C.E. did Cornelius Nepos (ca. 99–ca. 24 B.C.E.) have access to Cicero's "sixteen [or eleven] volumes of letters sent to Atticus" (*Att.* 16). On publication and copies kept of Cicero's letters, cf. *Fam.* 261.1; *Att.* 410.5. On Cicero's preservation of Atticus' letters, see *Att.* 177.10.

[46] It has been a matter of some dispute whether Seneca's letters may be considered "real" letters or not. The reason for this is mostly grounded in their literary character. Thus, in her influential study of the letters, Cancik argued that the letters "bewußt komponiert und zu Gruppen geordnet sind" and constitute therefore "ein literarisches Werk" (*Untersuchungen* [1967] 53; cf. pp. 4–7). It must be kept in mind, however, that Cancik's work was written in times when the distinction between a "letter" and an "epistle" was still commonly favored among scholars

In the following, I will first describe some basic formal features relating to the use of interlocutors in ancient letters, and then focus on aspects of function and identity.

3.1. Formal Features of Epistolary Interlocutors

The mere fact that interlocutors are present not only in long letters but in short ones as well points to versatile applications of the style by epistolographers. For instance, in a very brief letter attributed to Diogenes, the author sets out to argue that "one should not wed nor raise children." He is, however, immediately confronted with an objection: "'But (ἀλλά) life will become devoid of people. For from where,' you will ask (ἐρεῖς), 'will the succession of children come?'" The author then swiftly concludes the letter by expressing his unconcern for the extinction of humanity.[47] The frequency of interlocutors in one and the same letter does not have to be affected by the length of it either. In one of Plato's longer letters, for example, the author makes use of an interlocutor, but despite the letter's extent the usage is confined to one instance only (indicated by τις ἂν εἴποι).[48]

As in the "diatribe," it varies if the words of an epistolary interlocutor are explicitly marked as such or not. If they are, a verb of saying is used. If not, this may be indicated by other means (see below). Whether an author

---

(see, e.g., pp. 61, 71–73; cf. Sevenster, *Paul* [1961] 23–25). It must also be observed that the collection includes letters which are highly divergent in character (cf., e.g., *Epp.* 46, 55, 86 with 94, 95). I can see no cogent reason why the letters should not be regarded as "real" letters—even if "literary"—sent from Seneca to Lucilius. Whereas many of the letters may have been written in extended settings, i.e. with wider audience in mind (see 21.3–5; cf., however, 7.11–12), a number of Seneca's references to previous letters from Lucilius suggest that the latter may have had more to do with the correspondence than Cancik and others have claimed (e.g. 2.1–4; 3.1; 9.1; 21.1; 29.1; 31.1; 39.1; 40.1–2; 42.1–2; 46; 67.3; 69.1; 71.1; 72.1; 74.1; 75.1; 79.1–2, 4, 7; 83.1–7; 85.1; 88.1; 89.1–2; 96.1, 3; 100.1; 102.1–5; 108.1; 112; 113.1; 114.1; 117.1; 120.1). According to Seneca himself (118.1), the correspondents had made the agreement that Lucilius would write first and Seneca would then answer.

[47] *Ep.* 47. Cf., e.g., Cicero's very short *Att.* 287.
[48] *Ep.* 8.355A.

chooses a verb of saying or not to indicate the involvement of an interlocutor appears to be casual and the two modes are often mixed within the same letter. Thus, in one of his letters to Atticus, Cicero's imaginary partner in conversation ("Atticus") poses two questions, the former marked by a verb of saying, the latter not:

> Our Gnaeus [i.e. Pompey] is marvellously covetous of despotism on Sullan lines. *Experto crede* (εἰδώς σοι λέγω); he has been as open about it as he ever was about anything. 'And is that the man you want to be with?' you will say (*inquies*). Believe me, it is the obligation that moves me not the cause, as in Milo's case or—but enough. 'Is the cause not a good one then?' An excellent one, but remember that it will be abominably conducted.[49]

Conversely, in Cicero's description of his meeting with Julius Caesar, no verb of saying is used when the interlocutor ("Atticus") first enters the discussion, only later on:

> Caesar's closing remark, which I had almost forgotten, was hateful. He said that if he could not use my advice, he would use those he could get and go to any length. 'So (*igitur*) you have seen him to be as you have described him. Did you heave a sigh?' Indeed I did. 'Tell me the rest (*cedo reliqua*).' What more is there to tell? . . . 'Come,' you will say (*inquies*), 'do not dwell on past mistakes. Even Pompey, our leader, has made many.'[50]

When an interlocutor is meant to represent or speak for the letter's recipient(s)—which typically is the case (see below)—it is sometimes difficult to determine if the author of the letter is inventing the words, i.e. creating an interlocutor, or simply restating some words previously uttered by the re-

---

[49] *Att.* 174.3–4. Cf. the same procedure in 164.2; Seneca, *Epp.* 4.4, 9; 13.7–8; 14.12, 15–16; 76.1–2; Apollonius of Tyana, *Ep.* 58.

[50] *Att.* 187.3 (Winstedt's trans. with some modifications [no. 9.18.3]). Note that Shackleton Bailey reads the text differently, assuming that Atticus' words are quotations from his letter to Cicero (see n. 2 ad loc. in the LCL). But this is unlikely since it seems to be first in this letter that Cicero describes his meeting with Caesar (thus, e.g., *cedo reliqua* hardly refers to Atticus' previous words, as Shackleton Bailey claims). Cf. the same procedure in 130.6–7; Seneca, *Epp.* 5.6–7; 20.2, 7, 10–11; 84.8, 11; Pliny, *Ep.* 9.26.8, 10.

cipient(s).[51] If a verb of saying is used the actual source of the words may often be determined, but that depends on the specific form of the verb. For example, as a rule, Cicero either uses the present tense *inquis* or the future tenses *inquies*[52] and *dices*[53] to mark the involvement of an interlocutor. While the future form cannot but signify imaginary words—even if likely or expected—the present form gives no such straightforward information in itself. It is both used when Cicero is clearly referring to actual words previously stated by the recipient,[54] and when he is inventing the words himself,[55] thus resulting in many unclear uses of *inquis* in this respect.[56] The most ambiguous instances, however, are those in which no verbs of saying are used.[57] In that case, the immediate context may provide information about the actual source of the words, particularly if references to letters previously received from the recipient(s) are made.

Epistolary interlocutors are often presented not by a verb of saying but by other means. One form of introducing questions and/or objections from a

---

[51] In a sense, the words may of course be fictitious even if previously uttered, viz. when the author of the letter is making use of them for the sake of the argument and not in a way they were originally used or meant to be used.

[52] *Att.* 21.5, 8; 40.1; 91.5; 92.1, 2; 95.2; 113.1; 115.15, 26; 121.3; 132.3; 142.1; 152.2; 166.2; 171.3; 174.3; 187.3; 198.1; 287.1; 387.1; 400; *Fam.* 74.2; 189.3; 213 (x2); 215.3; 231.3; 234.9; *Quint. fratr.* 4.4. Cf. *Ep. Brut.* 11.3 (from Brutus to Cicero); 26.4 (from Brutus to Atticus). Seneca never uses the fut. form *inquies* in his letters to Lucilius.

[53] *Att.* 36.2; 39.1; 74.5; 80.2, 3; 82.3; 90.7; 91.3; 92.2; 94.4; 103.3; 114.3; 123.2; 129.2; 132.3; 164.2; 200.2; 218.3; 294.3; 384; *Fam.* 197.1; 202.2; 393.1. Cf. Seneca, *Epp.* 5.7; 41.4; 64.3; 82.21; Pliny, *Epp.* 2.10.5; 3.9.27; 4.29.3; 5.8.7; 8.14.2; 9.26.10.

[54] E.g. *Att.* 116.8; 169.1; 217.2; 342.2; 381.3. Cf. Seneca, *Epp.* 67.3; 100.10; Pliny, *Ep.* 5.21.1.

[55] E.g. *Att.* 13.6; 128.5; *Fam.* 189.2. Cf. Seneca, *Ep.* 12.6, 10, 11 and passim; Pliny, *Epp.* 1.6.1; 4.9.17; 9.6.1.

[56] E.g. *Att.* 112.3; 116.5; 121.1; 126.11; 130.6–7; 132.1; 134.2; 153.6; 161.4; 174.5; *Fam.* 71.3; 96.4; 197.1–2. Cf. Seneca, *Epp.* 2.4; 8.1; 17.1, 5; 27.1; 45.2; 56.3; 82.1; Pliny, *Epp.* 6.23.1; 7.3.1; 7.4.2.

[57] Cf., e.g., Cicero, *Att.* 27.2; 153.4; 155.1; 188.2; Seneca, *Epp.* 42.2–3; 96.4; 107.5; 112.3.

partner in dialogue is to use interrogative phrases such as τί οὖν, *quid ergo*, etc. For instance, after mentioning his resolution of avoiding the popular watering-place Baiae, Seneca introduces an interlocutor ("Lucilius") whose comments are meant to steer the argument towards a more general course:

> Baiae is a place to be avoided, because, though it has certain natural advantages, luxury has claimed it for her own exclusive resort. 'What then (*quid ergo*)? Should any place be singled out as an object of aversion?' Not at all (*minime*). But just as, to the wise and upright man, one style of clothing is more suitable than another . . . so there are places also, which the wise man or he who is on the way toward wisdom will avoid as foreign to good morals.[58]

Similarly, in an answer to Atticus, Cicero writes:

> Just as I was folding up this letter, a night-bird courier arrived with a letter from you. . . . I had assigned 1 December to Axius, the 2nd to you, and the day of my arrival, i.e. 30 November, to Quintus. This then is all I have for you, nothing new. 'Why bother then to write (*quid ergo opus erat epistula*)?' And when we are together, and chatter away with whatever comes into our heads? Surely there is *some* value in *causerie*, in which the mere interchange of talk is agreeable, even if there is nothing behind it.[59]

Another, less explicit, way of introducing an interlocutor without a verb of saying is the employment of adversative or inferential conjunctions. For example, when Pliny, in a letter to his friend Lupercus, compares the style of Homer to that of Greco-Roman oratory, he is met with the objection "But surely (*at enim*) orators are different from poets!"[60] Or, when Seneca attempts to argue that lost friends may be replaced by new ones, the interlocutor ("Lucilius") raises the objection "But (*sed*) new friends will not be the same!" to which Seneca responds "No, nor will you yourself remain the

---

[58] *Ep.* 51.1–2. Cf. 35.1; 36.4; 40.8; 47.15; 56.15; 66.14, 38; 74.26, 31; 75.8; 84.8; 88.20; 95.36; 98.1, 16; 108.5.

[59] *Att.* 248.2 (italics original in trans.). Or, as Winstedt suggests (no. 12.1.2): "I had arranged for [dates etc.] . . . So please count on that: there is no new arrangement. 'What's the use of writing then?'"

[60] *Ep.* 9.26.8 (the LCL trans. slightly modified).

same; you change with every day and every hour."[61] Of course, conjunctions alone do not guarantee the presence of an interlocutor in the text. Whether they may be indicative of this, ultimately depends on the context.

At times, an author's immediate response to a statement may serve as the only or safest indication of the involvement of a dialogical partner. In the following example, Seneca's repeated reply to an assertion which probably reflects common opinion suggests that he is conversing with such a partner:

> I am glad to learn . . . that you [i.e. Lucilius] live on friendly terms with your slaves. This befits a sensible and well-educated man like yourself. 'They are slaves (*Servi sunt*).' No, rather (*immo*) they are men. 'Slaves!' No, rather (*immo*) they are comrades. 'Slaves!' No, rather (*immo*) they are unpretentious friends. 'Slaves!' No, rather (*immo*) they are our fellow-slaves, if one reflects that Fortune has equal rights over slaves and free men alike.[62]

A somewhat more problematic example is found in a letter by Plutarch addressed to a certain Paccius. Plutarch has been discussing some virtuous philosophers when someone poses a question. Besides the introductory τί οὖν, there is little in the phrasing of the question that prevents it from being raised by Plutarch himself. However, Plutarch's following words suggest that he is responding to an imaginary interlocutor:

> 'What, then, prevents (our) imitating such men as these (τί οὖν κωλύει μιμεῖσθαι τούτους)?' Have you [sg.] failed in your canvass for an office? You will be able to live in the country and look after your own affairs. Were you repulsed in wooing the friendship of some great man? Your life will be free from danger and trouble. Have you, again, . . .[63]

In sum, corresponding to formal features of the "diatribe" style, epistolary interlocutors are introduced in various ways, sometimes explicitly with a verb of saying and sometimes less explicitly with an interrogative phrase or

---

[61] *Ep.* 104.12 (the LCL trans. slightly modified). Cf. 7.5 (*sed*), 9 (*ergo*); 9.16 (*tamen*); 36.2 (*at*); 42.2–3 (*at*); 67.7 (*tamen*); 78.17 (*sed*); 85.25 (*at*); 88.36 (*at*); 90.17 (*tamen*); 94.38 (*at*); 96.4 (*sed*); 99.9 (*sed*); 112.3 (*at*); 115.17 (*at*); 119.7 (*at*). Cf. also, e.g., Cicero, *Att.* 153.4 (*at*); 155.1 (*at, igitur*); 188.2 (*igitur*); 164.2 (*igitur*); Plutarch, *Tranq. an.* 467E (ἀλλά).
[62] *Ep.* 47.1 (the LCL trans. slightly modified).
[63] *Tranq. an.* 467D.

with a conjunction only. The immediate context is often decisive for determining whether or not an interlocutor is involved.

This survey reveals that imaginary partners in dialogue were both more amply and more widely employed by Greco-Roman epistolographers than Pauline scholarship has taken notice of. In view, however, of the common notion of the letter as a "kind of a written conversation," this outcome should in no way come as a surprise. We may now turn to the more critical questions of function and identity.

3.2. Function and Identity of Epistolary Interlocutors

The intended function of the epistolary interlocutor appears to be analogous to that of the "diatribal" interlocutor. The conversational partner is used as a device to develop the argument as desired, for instance, by enabling the epistolographer to respond in advance to potential objections to what is being uttered in the letter. Moreover, the interlocutor is essentially intended as an object of identification for the audience, thus activating their engagement in the discourse at the moment of reading and/or listening. In this way, the readership is invited to turn, as it were, from object to subject in the process of perusal.[64]

Interlocutors are used in all kinds of epistolary settings, whether fictitious, extended, or normative. A good example of an imaginary partner in dialogue in a fictitious setting occurs in the letter of Diogenes cited above (in sec. 3.1). Epistolary interlocutors in extended settings are, for instance, found in Plutarch's letter to Paccius (also cited above) and many of Seneca's letters. As for normative settings, some of Pliny's letters exemplify this use, but the most illuminating examples from these settings are without doubt found in the letters of Cicero.

---

[64] Cf. Stowers' observations on how Lucilius enters Seneca's text, so to speak, by the latter's use of an interlocutor: "In ancient thought the letter mediates the presence of the writer to the recipient, but in the dialogical element of Seneca's letters there is the fiction of the recipient, Lucilius, coming into the presence of the writer, Seneca" (*Diatribe* [1981] 73–74).

It is important to observe that the main difference between the epistolary settings in this regard lies not in the identity of the interlocutor him/herself. Rather, the difference lies in the question of whom the dialogue with the interlocutor is meant to have an affect on. Thus, in normative settings the primary target is the letter's recipient(s), while in extended settings it is both the recipient(s) as well as a wider audience.[65]

Similar to the "diatribe" style, the epistolary interlocutor may represent different groups and views of people, such as the immediate audience, specific types of persons, or common opinion. Unlike many of the "diatribe" texts, however, a general, verifiable,[66] norm may be discerned in this respect. As a rule, the epistolary interlocutor represents and/or speaks for the letter's recipient(s). That is, utterances made by the former are presented as concurrently coming from the latter. When this is not the case, that tends to be specifically indicated. In light of the widespread understanding of the letter as a kind of a dialogue with an absent audience as if present—an understanding thus presumably shared by audiences at large—this seems indeed to be a logical presumption. Nevertheless, the following examples will show this to be the operative principle.

In the letters of Cicero the imaginary dialogical partners consistently speak for the letters' recipients. This is clear enough by Cicero's rather plain use of the style in this regard, especially because of his preference for identifying the interlocutor explicitly by a verb of saying. Even the minority cases in which he does not make use of such a verb show this to be true.[67] To be sure, Cicero occasionally turns away from the letter's recipient in an imaginary address to someone else (i.e. in an apostrophe),[68] but, when he does,

---

[65] Fictitious settings are of little concern for the present study (cf. Ch. 1 sec. 4.2 above).

[66] Cf. the discussion above in sec. 1.2.

[67] Cf., e.g., *Att.* 130.6; 153.4; 155.1; 164.2; 188.2; 248.2; some of which, however, possibly include references to previous letters received.

[68] Note that the term "apostrophe" does not have a univocal reference in scholarly works. For Stowers, e.g., "apostrophe" simply denotes a direct address to someone (*Diatribe* [1981] 79–81 and passim); so also Anderson, *Rhetorical* (1996) 165 (cf. index, p. 297). I use the term more literally, and thus more narrowly, for the turning away from the audience to address someone else; cf. Lausberg, *Handbuch*

he is very explicit both about the mode of address and the identity of the person addressed.[69]

What goes for Cicero, also applies to those of his correspondents who make use of an interlocutor.[70] The same holds true for Pliny, whose dialogical style, however, is relatively scanty.[71]

Plutarch's conventions in this respect are not as easily verified since his use of an interlocutor is virtually confined to one letter, viz. his lengthy letter to Paccius referred to above.[72] However, even this piece of writing gives support to the general principle of identity. Throughout the first half of the letter the conversational partner evidently represents the letter's recipient, Paccius.[73] When a different interlocutor enters the stage, this is explicitly designated with a verb of saying together with the indefinite pronoun τις.[74]

The best examples available are found in the letters of Seneca. Yet, his application of the dialogical style is by far the most complex one. Some basic statistics may therefore be helpful. A survey of the epistolary collection shows that, out of a maximum of 100 letters in which a conversational partner is surely invented,[75] at least 65 include the recipient, Lucilius, exclusively as the interlocutor. Moreover, in approximately 15 letters one interlocutor represents Lucilius while another (or others) represents someone else, and in about 12 letters the conversational partner exclusively speaks for

---

(1960) 377–79; Rowe, "Style" (1997) 139. On various uses of "apostrophe" (ἀποστροφή) in ancient rhetorical theory, see Anderson, *Glossary* (2000) 25.

[69] E.g. *Att.* 134.3; 141.2.

[70] E.g. *Fam.* 79.3; 149; 325.3; *Ep. Brut.* 11.3; 26.4.

[71] For examples, see sec. 3.1 above (with nn.).

[72] *Tranq. an.* This letter is included among Stirewalt's "letter-essays"; see above in Ch. 1 sec. 4.2.2. On the potential character of the text as a "letter-essay," see esp. 464E–F.

[73] Cf. esp. 464E–465A; 467D–468E.

[74] Viz. φῆσαι τις ἄν ("someone may say") in 469D.

[75] At least 24 out of Seneca's 124 letters contain no immediately apparent interlocutor. These include *Epp.* 1, 3, 10, 11, 21, 30, 32, 38, 39, 46, 50, 55, 57, 61, 62, 69, 72, 79, 80, 97, 103, 105, 114, 120. Perhaps, the following might also be added to the list: *Epp.* 41, 48, 49, 53, 60, 83, 91, 101, 106, 122.

someone else than Lucilius. In several letters an interlocutor's presence and identity is too obscure to be determinable.[76] A closer examination reveals further that, in those letters in which Lucilius himself does not occur as an interlocutor, Seneca routinely identifies his conversational partners by the words *dicet aliquis* ("someone will say")[77] or by the verbs *inquit* and *inquiunt*,[78] sometimes with the general meaning "it is said" or "some say" etc. In these letters, apostrophic addresses tend to be clearly marked also.[79] The procedure is roughly similar in letters which include shifts of interlocutors from Lucilius to someone else or vice versa. This may be indicated by changing the form of the verb *inquis* to *inquit* (or the other way round),[80] by a shift from *inquis* to *dicet aliquis*,[81] or simply by stating "I now turn to X" (*transeo/venio ad aliquem* etc.).[82] In some letters within this group, however, the exact boundaries between interlocutors is very vague.[83]

In view of Seneca's elaborate use of the dialogical style it is difficult to avoid some generalizations in a wideranging analysis like this.[84] Still, on the whole, the analysis gives good reason to conclude that even Seneca substantiates the basic rule of identity.

Before summing up and moving on to Paul's letter, one detail must be addressed. Unlike Romans, the letters discussed above have individual recipients (i.e. those identified as such). It seems reasonable to assume that an identification with a single interlocutor would have been more straightforward for one person than for two or more. The problem, however, is that the vast majority of extant letters from Greco-Roman antiquity in which a conversational partner is created have individual recipients and not multi-

---

[76] E.g. *Epp.* 28, 48, 49, 53, 60, 91, 94.
[77] *Epp.* 16, 86. Cf. 81.11.
[78] *Epp.* 85, 92, 95, 102, 117.
[79] *Epp.* 33, 70, 77, 89, 110. Cf. 99 (embedded letter to Marullus).
[80] *Epp.* 87, 109, 113, 121. Cf. 74.
[81] *Epp.* 47, 81.
[82] *Ep.* 88.9, 14.
[83] *Epp.* 7, 65, 66, 78, 82, 118, 124.
[84] Cf., e.g., the somewhat different inferences drawn by Stowers, *Diatribe* (1981) 71–73.

ple like Romans.[85] A solution to the problem might, of course, be sought in some of the non-epistolary "diatribe" texts. Indeed, there is no lack of examples in these texts which clearly exhibit how an individual interlocutor, either speaking or spoken to, could represent plural addressees,[86] which, in turn, reflects the dialogue's often loose boundaries between the singular and the plural in this respect. But, as urged above, one has to be very cautious when making use of this potentially misleading material in the specific attempt to identify epistolary interlocutors. Fortunately, however, ancient letters are not totally devoid of individual interlocutors used as representatives for more than one recipient. In a letter to his associates M. Brutus and Cassius, D. Brutus evidently uses the singular *inquis* to mark an imaginary question posed by the recipients. Having briefly described the correspondents' political position subsequent to their assassination of Julius Caesar, D. Brutus forms a question calling for his own advisory opinion: "'What then is your advice?' you ask ('*Quid ergo est' inquis 'tui consili?*'). We must give way to Fortune, leave Italy, go to live in Rhodes or anywhere under the sun...."[87]

In sum, then, in accord with the dialogical nature of the epistolary medium, conversational partners are widely employed in ancient letters. Moreover, the sources available give ample support to the general principle of identity, viz. that, unless otherwise stated or implied, the epistolary interlocutor represents or speaks for the letter's recipient(s), thus functioning as an object of identification for the latter. It may be assumed on this basis also that in any given letter an interlocutor remains the same unless otherwise indicated. With this information I turn now to Paul's letter to the Romans.

---

[85] One reason for this may be that inventions of interlocutors appear to have been considered specifically apt in private/personal correspondence (cf. Julius Victor, *Rhet.* 27, cited above in sec. 2), which more often than not included letters sent between individuals.

[86] See, e.g., Epictetus, *Diatr.* 1.3.1–4; 1.9.18–21; 2.6.1–5; 2.16.11–13; 2.17.35–38; 3.22.36–44; Maximus of Tyre, *Or.* 1.7; 7.4.

[87] Cicero, *Fam.* 325.3 (the LCL trans. slightly modified).

4. The Epistolary Interlocutor in Romans 2–11: Macrostructural Aspects

The ways in which Paul indicates the involvement of an interlocutor in Romans varies considerably. If Seneca's use of the dialogical style is complex, Paul's is no less. While he frequently employs verbs of saying, it is first in 9:19 that such a verb occurs in the second person singular (ἐρεῖς, cf. 11:19) and first in 10:18 that it occurs in the first person singular (λέγω, cf. 10:19; 11:1, 11). Otherwise, and more typically, Paul uses the first person plural (ἐροῦμεν, 3:5; 4:1; 6:1; 7:7; 8:31; 9:14, 30). This use makes it sometimes difficult to identify the one speaking because of its inclusive potentials. The most involved cases, however, arise when Paul shifts back and forth between the singular and the plural (e.g. 3:5–9).

Paul utilizes also miscellaneous interrogative phrases to mark a question posed by an interlocutor, τί οὖν in particular (3:1, 9; 6:15; 9:19; 11:7) but others as well (e.g. 3:7, 27; 9:32). Adversative conjunctions may also serve this function (ἀλλά, followed by a verb of saying; 10:18, 19). On some occasions, however, it is not clear whether the one speaking is Paul himself or his interlocutor (e.g. 3:3; 4:10; 8:31b–35).

Nevertheless, whilst several details of the dialogue are uncertain the reading of which must be determined by the immediate context, one thing seems certain: It is Paul's very employment of the dialogical style which characterizes and steers the macrostructure of Romans 2–11. This is specifically effected, first, by a direct address in the second person singular (ch. 2), and then (chs. 3–11) by the use of inferential questions the regular occurrence of which more or less guides the argument until the closing of chapter 11. From chapter 12 onward exchanges of questions and answers cease to occur. Typically, the questions draw a false inference from what has previously been stated, to which Paul often responds by the strong negation μὴ γένοιτο or the like.[88] Potential cases of such macrostructural

---

[88] White, *Apostle* (1999) 82 n. 60, remarks somewhat humorously that a "modern equivalent of Paul's strong reaction is the popular expression 'Hell, no!'"

markers in chapters 3–11 include the following (questions on left; immediate responses on right):[89]

τί οὖν . . . ἢ τίς . . .; (3:1)	πολὺ κατὰ πάντα τρόπον (3:2)
εἰ . . . μή . . .; (3:3)	μὴ γένοιτο (3:4)
εἰ δέ . . . τί ἐροῦμεν; μή . . .; (3:5)	μὴ γένοιτο (3:6)
εἰ δέ . . . τί ἔτι . . .; καὶ μή . . .; (3:7-8)	ὧν τὸ κρίμα ἔνδικόν ἐστιν (3:8)
τί οὖν; προεχόμεθα; (3:9)	οὐ πάντως (3:9)
ποῦ οὖν ἡ καύχησις; (3:27)	ἐξεκλείσθη (3:27)
διὰ ποίου νόμου; τῶν ἔργων; (3:27)	οὐχί, ἀλλά . . . (3:27)
νόμον οὖν καταργοῦμεν . . .; (3:31)	μὴ γένοιτο (3:31)
τί οὖν (ἐροῦμεν); (4:1)	
τί οὖν ἐροῦμεν; ἐπιμένωμεν . . . ; (6:1)	μὴ γένοιτο (6:2)
τί οὖν; ἁμαρτήσωμεν . . . ; (6:15)	μὴ γένοιτο (6:15)
τί οὖν ἐροῦμεν; ὁ νόμος ἁμαρτία; (7:7)	μὴ γένοιτο (7:7)
τὸ οὖν ἀγαθόν . . .; (7:13)	μὴ γένοιτο (7:13)
τί οὖν ἐροῦμεν πρὸς ταῦτα; (8:31)	
τί οὖν ἐροῦμεν; μή . . .; (9:14)	μὴ γένοιτο (9:14)
ἐρεῖς μοι οὖν· τί (οὖν) ἔτι μέμφεται; (9:19)	ὦ ἄνθρωπε . . . (9:20)
τί οὖν ἐροῦμεν; ὅτι . . .; (9:30)	δικαιοσύνην δέ . . . (9:30)
διὰ τί; (9:32)	ὅτι οὐκ . . . ἀλλ᾽ . . . (9:32)
ἀλλὰ λέγω, μή . . .; (10:18)	μενοῦνγε (10:18)
ἀλλὰ λέγω, μή . . .; (10:19)	
λέγω οὖν, μή . . .; (11:1)	μὴ γένοιτο (11:1)
τί οὖν; (11:7)	
λέγω οὖν, μή . . .; (11:11)	μὴ γένοιτο (11:11)

Stowers has greatly enriched our understanding of the dialogical style applied in Romans. Followed by a number of scholars,[90] Stowers has argued

---

[89] On the macrostructural function of the questions and answers in Rom, cf. also Stowers, *Diatribe* (1981) 79–81, 119–22, 148–52, 155–56, 164–65, 172; Campbell, "Romans III" (1981) 30–34; Boers, "Problem" (1982) 185–87; Palmer, "τί οὖν;" (1995) 213–18.

that Paul's conversational partner in 3:1–9 is the very person previously addressed in 2:17–29.[91] He has further suggested that the dialogue in 3:1–9 is resumed in 3:27 with the same interlocutor engaged in the discussion.[92] According to Stowers, the dialogue continues until the closing of chapter 4 when this particular interlocutor "vanishes"[93] and Paul's address is (again) explicitly directed to the letter's audience.

While I basically agree with Stowers that the identity of the interlocutor in chapters 3–4 is the same as that of the one in 2:17–29, I find little support in the text for his claim that this person "vanishes" at the end of chapter 4. Stowers does not provide any clear reason for this either. Rather, the reason seems primarily to be grounded in his identification, on the one hand, of Paul's interlocutor from 2:17 onward as Jewish, and, on the other, of the letter's intended audience as gentiles. Accordingly, "something new happens in the discourse at 4:23, when Paul . . . returns explicitly to his readers for the first time since 1:15."[94] Remarkably, however, Stowers also insists that the passage in which this "something new happens" is firmly tied to the foregoing text: "The argument and discourse of 2:17–5:11 fit together so tightly that any division poses difficulties. Paul's discussion with the fictitious Jewish teacher about the fate of the gentiles unifies the section."[95] The passage in 4:23–5:11, then, "reads well as a section that draws conclusions from the preceding argument and provides hortatory application for the letter's audience."[96] Indeed, it is even "likely that 4:23–5:11

---

[90] Explicitly so, e.g., by Elliott, *Rhetoric* (1990) 135–41; Aune, "Romans" (1991) 115; Fitzmyer, *Romans* (1993) 325; Palmer, "τί οὖν;" (1995); Gager, *Paul* (2000) 107, 114–18; Engberg-Pedersen, *Paul* (2000) 217. Cf. also Campbell, "Towards" (2002) 358–59. Interestingly, Anderson draws a similar conclusion in spite of his disapproval of Stowers' approach (*Rhetorical* [1996] 186, 193).

[91] "Dialogue" (1984) esp. 714–22; idem, *Rereading* (1994) 159–75, 231.

[92] *Diatribe* (1981) 155–74. See also Stowers, "Dialogue" (1984) 721–22; idem, "Ἐκ πίστεως" (1989); idem, *Rereading* (1994) 231–37.

[93] *Diatribe* (1981) 167. Cf. his *Rereading* (1994) 247.

[94] *Rereading* (1994) 249.

[95] *Rereading* (1994) 231.

[96] *Rereading* (1994) 249.

forms the hortatory conclusion to the first four chapters."[97] The tension in Stowers' reading here comes further to expression in his treatment of the motif of "boasting." This motif is important in Paul's dialogue with his interlocutor, first appearing in 2:17 and then invoked in 3:27 and 4:2.[98] However, although the Jewish interlocutor has "faded from view," according to Stowers, "the final answer to his boasting will be provided—to the letter's audience—only in 5:1–11."[99] Hence, "[t]he final answer to the teacher's boast comes as an exhortation to the gentile audience: Boast not in works of the law but in the reconciliation and hope that God has wrought for you through Jesus Christ! (5:1–11)."[100] This sounds as if Paul's interlocutor was meant to represent the gentile audience all along.

In light of the foregoing analysis of epistolary interlocutors, it seems legitimate to ask if Paul's interlocutor in Romans may be identical throughout chapters 2–11. While I cannot go into every detail of Paul's dialogical style in the present study the primary focus of which is aimed at the opening segments of the dialogue, a positive answer to this question would presumably result in a more straightforward reading of the letter and thus more economic than currently is the case.[101]

According to Stowers, the interlocutor who poses such questions as τί οὖν ... (3:1), τί ἐροῦμεν (3:5), τί οὖν (3:9), and τί οὖν (ἐροῦμεν) (4:1) is different from the person(s) who subsequently asks, for instance, τί οὖν ἐροῦμεν (6:1), τί οὖν (6:15), τί οὖν ἐροῦμεν (7:7), τί οὖν ἐροῦμεν ... (8:31), τί οὖν ἐροῦμεν (9:14), τί οὖν ἐροῦμεν (9:30), and τί οὖν (11:7). In formal terms, that does not seem to be likely. On the contrary, as the overview presented further above indicates, formal features of the dialogue give

---

[97] *Rereading* (1994) 247.
[98] In his *Diatribe* (1981) Stowers suggests that the "questions about boasting in 3:27 and 4:1 [*sic*] form an *inclusio* for the dialogue" (p. 168). This is, however, difficult to explain in view of the fact that the dialogue continues in 4:9–10 (see p. 172) and that the discussion of "boasting" is not completed until 5:2, 3, 11 (subsequently only in 15:17).
[99] *Rereading* (1994) 247.
[100] *Rereading* (1994) 250.
[101] Cf. the "minimalist" methodological approach advocated by Engberg-Pedersen, *Paul* (2000) 180–81.

no evident indications of a shift of an interlocutor, not even when there is a considerable space between dialogical exchanges of this kind. These features suggest instead that the interlocutor remains the same throughout the discourse, and thus that he/she is used much more consistently in the letter than scholars have usually thought. That, in turn, gives Paul's argumentative structure a coherent and progressive character. Because the interlocutor typically draws false conclusions from what has been stated, the correction of which is then provided by Paul with further elucidation, it may be said that the interlocutor—and those whom he/she speaks for—is gradually being led by Paul towards some desired point in the discourse. That point seems to be reached at 12:1, where the exchanges of questions and answers disappear, and where Paul presents his hortatory request based on the foregoing text as a whole.

Whatever conclusions are reached in terms of the macrostructural function of Paul's dialogical style in Romans, it is clear that the role played by the interlocutor in the letter largely depends on the identity of the person(s) addressed in the second person singular in chapter 2. It is Paul's direct address to this imaginary person(s) which sets the stage for the following dialogue, something which the audience may very well have recognized, both due to the nature of the epistolary medium as a "kind of written conversation" and because of analogous applications of interlocutors by other epistolographers. It is Paul's address to a certain "man" (ἄνθρωπε) in 2:1 which opens the fictitious conversation taking place in the letter. The questions of this person's identity, his or her relation to the person addressed in v. 17, and the identity of the latter, are thus decisive for the subsequent dialogue which occupies the bulk of Romans. The above questions constitute the primary focus of the final chapter of this study.

Concluding Summary

Paul's invention of an imaginary interlocutor in Romans has much in common with the Greco-Roman "diatribe," formally as well as functionally. However, when it comes to the more specific task of identifying the interlocutor, the value of non-epistolary "diatribal" texts as comparative material turns out to be somewhat problematic. More reliable in this respect are ancient documents of the epistolary genre in which uses are made of fictitious partners in conversation. Such a dialogical style would have been considered proper for most letters because of the widespread notion of the epistolary medium as a "kind of written conversation."

A survey of Greco-Roman letters reveals a more widely established application of imaginary partners in dialogue than most Pauline scholars have taken heed of. While uses of such interlocutors show basic formal and functional similarities with the "diatribe" style, the specific identity of an epistolary interlocutor may normally be determined according to the following procedure. As a rule, the interlocutor is meant to speak for or represent the letter's recipient(s) and thus to function as an object of identification for the latter. Otherwise, that tends to be specifically indicated. It follows that the interlocutor remains the same throughout the letter in question, unless otherwise stated or implied. This latter principle appears to apply to the dialogical exchanges in Romans 2–11, strongly suggesting that the interlocutor remains identical throughout these chapters. It is the very employment of a dialogical style with a fictitious interlocutor which dominates and guides the macrostructure of Romans 2–11, the stage for which is set by Paul's direct address to a certain individual in chapter 2.

Chapter Four

Paul's Interlocutor in Romans 2

Introduction

In Chapter One above we saw that Romans shows ample signs of being a letter written to a particular group of people in a setting in which the subject of the letter arises out of the relationship between the correspondents. Paul utilizes the letter as a means by which to fulfill his missionary task, namely, to proclaim God's "good news" to gentiles in Rome.

Correspondingly, in Chapter Two we found out that Paul did not write to people who were not subject to his authority and missionary intentions. The audience to whom Paul wrote his letter consisted of people of gentile origin.

In his epistolary preaching and exposition of the "good news," Paul makes use of a literary technique well suited for such a purpose. Chapter Three offered a survey of the close formal and functional resemblances between Paul's dialogical style in Romans and the Greco-Roman "diatribe" which was typically applied within a didactic context. As a rule, the readers or listeners in question were supposed to identify themselves with the imaginary partner in conversation. My own investigation of the employment of interlocutors in letters specifically suggested a general principle by which the identity of these may be ascertained. Unless otherwise stated or implied, the interlocutor represents or speaks for the letter's recipient(s). From this principle another followed, viz. that, unless otherwise stated or implied, the interlocutor is identical throughout the discourse. As for the latter, I argued that formal features do not suggest otherwise for the dialogical exchanges in Romans 3–11. As for the former principle, the following hypothesis presents itself. In principle, Paul's interlocutor(s) in Romans is representative of the letter's gentile audience and the one(s) with whom the audience should identify. This hypothesis must be tested against Paul's use of a conversational partner or partners in Romans 2, since this chapter sets the stage for the entire dialogical discourse in the letter, and it is in this chapter where the identity of Paul's interlocutor(s) is established.

With this larger context and framework in view, I now turn to the analysis and reading of Romans 2 with the primary focus of attention aimed at the identity of Paul's imaginary addressee in 2:1–5 and in 2:17–29. I will begin with analyzing the text's coherence and argumentative flow, i.e. the way in which its components connect internally, not least on the grammatical level (sec. 1). The second section offers a linear reading of the text with respect specifically to the question of identity. This section occupies the core of the analysis. A brief assessment of the functional aspect follows (sec. 3), and, finally, some implications for the subsequent dialogue in Romans will be discussed (sec. 4). A concluding summary of this chapter will be provided in the general Conclusions.

1. Continuity in Romans 2

Paul's discourse in Romans 2 is characterized by a dialogical style replete with uses of the second person singular. No other passage by Paul is so richly furnished with this type of language.[1] Paul begins the chapter with a direct and rather abrupt address to a certain individual, severely indicting him[2] for practicing the very vices he judges others for. The second person singular address continues through v. 5, with the sole exception of v. 2

---

[1] Only Rom 11:17–24 comes close to Paul's use of the 2nd per. sg. here. Apart from (clear) scriptural quotations, it occurs also in 8:2; 9:19–20; 10:9; 12:21; 13:3–4; 14:4, 10, 15, 20–22. Except for 1 Cor, in which it is used rather randomly (4:7; 7:16, 21, 27–28; 8:10–11; [12:21]; 14:16–17; 15:36–37), the 2nd per. sg. occurs rarely or not at all in Paul's other letters (excl. Phlm): 2 Cor 12:9 (the "Lord" addresses Paul); Phil 4:3 (Paul addresses one of the recipients directly); Gal 2:14; 4:7; 6:1. The 2nd per. sg. is never used in 1 Thess.

[2] In the following, I will take the liberty to speak of this person in masculine terms. Not only is this done for convenience, but also due to the context of male circumcision in the chapter.

where the inclusive first person plural occurs. While vv. 1–2 consist of clear-cut statements, vv. 3–4 include two rhetorical questions, the unexpressed answers to which are then responded to in v. 5. In vv. 6–16, however, Paul's discourse differs in that the text is marked by a more general third person language. Subsequently, the second person singular address is resumed and remains in force throughout vv. 17–29, though the scope of address seems to be broadened a bit in vv. 28–29. Again, rhetorical questions are prominent. The series of questions and answers initiated in 3:1 is the point at which the second person singular address ceases.[3] Hence, the feature which both distinguishes and unites Romans 2 is Paul's use of the second person singular.

In this section, I will first consider the coherence of the text in 2:6–16 and its connection with the foregoing, and then turn to the question of the relationship between Paul's second person singular addresses in 2:1–5 and 2:17–29, without attempting to determine specifically the (ethnic) identity of the interlocutor(s). That will be done in the subsequent section (sec. 2).

1.1. The Unity and Immediate Context of Romans 2:6–16

It is important to note that although there is a marked stylistic change in 2:6, the boundary between v. 5 and v. 6 is very vague. Grammatically, there is no division at all between these verses since v. 6 is made up of a relative clause modifying the genitive τοῦ θεοῦ in v. 5. Moreover, the appeal to scripture in v. 6 that God "will render to everyone according to his deeds" (ἀποδώσει ἑκάστῳ κατὰ τὰ ἔργα αὐτοῦ)[4] is primarily put forth as a substantiation of Paul's claim that his interlocutor in vv. 1–5 will not es-

---

[3] It does not occur again until 8:2 (if σε is the reading to be preferred) and thereafter first in 9:19 where an epistolary interlocutor is clearly involved (indicated by a verb of saying): ἐρεῖς μοι οὖν· τί οὖν ἔτι μέμφεται; etc., followed by the voc. ὦ ἄνθρωπε.

[4] From Prov 24:12 (ὃς ἀποδίδωσιν ἑκάστῳ κατὰ τὰ ἔργα αὐτοῦ) or Ps 61:13 (σὺ ἀποδώσεις ἑκάστῳ κατὰ τὰ ἔργα αὐτοῦ). Cf. also Job 34:11; Jer 17:10; Sir 16:12–14; *1 En.* 95.5; 100.7; *Jos. Asen.* 28.3; *L.A.B.* 3.10. Helpful discussions of Paul's scriptural quotation in Rom 2:6 are found in Snodgrass, "Justification" (1986) esp. 77–79; Hays, *Echoes* (1989) 41–43.

cape God's wrath on the day of judgment. Verses 5–6, culminating in the scriptural quotation of the latter, serve therefore as a response to the interlocutor's implied point of view by revealing to him the actual state of affairs. What follows (vv. 7–16) constitutes a further development of Paul's reference to judgment according to deeds (v. 6) on the "day of wrath and revealing of God's righteous judgment" (v. 5). In other words, vv. 7–16 offer a commentary on vv. 5–6.[5]

The chain of reasoning in this eschatologically colored discourse, extending from the day of judgment in vv. 5–6 to the day of judgment in v. 16, strongly speaks for its unity. So do also structural markers in the passage, viz. connecting particles and conjunctions,[6] the basic function of which is to assist the reader in perceiving the relations between the text's constituent parts.[7] That there is an integral connection between vv. 7–8 and v. 6 is clear enough by the former's grammatical dependence on the latter in that the predicate of both v. 7 and v. 8 is the verb ἀποδώσει in v. 6. This verb seems also to function as the predicate in vv. 9–10, which makes a break at this point unlikely despite the asyndeton in v. 9.[8] Any marked division between v. 9 and the foregoing is furthermore ruled out by the fact that vv. 9–10 constitute a chiastic iteration of the basic statements in vv. 7–8,[9] adding only that what is stated pertains both to Jews and Greeks. Verse 11,

---

[5] Cf. Snodgrass, "Justification" (1986) 80.

[6] On the use of particles and conjunctions in the NT, see Thrall, *Particles* (1962); Turner, *Syntax* (1963) 329–41; Porter, *Idioms* (1994) 204–17. Cf. also the helpful studies of Reed, *Discourse* (1997) 89–93, 118–19; Holmstrand, *Markers* (1997); Güting and Mealand, *Asyndeton* (1998); Levinsohn, "Constraints" (1999).

[7] Cf. Burkitt, "Punctuation" (1927–28) 397: "In a certain sense the punctuation of an ancient Greek work is no part of the original tradition; a properly written Greek paragraph goes in theory from the beginning to the end without punctuation, the beginnings and the due subordination of the several sentences being sufficiently indicated by the appropriate particles."

[8] Asyndeton is sometimes indicative of a break in Paul's discourse; e.g. Rom 9:1; 1 Cor 5:1; 6:12; 2 Cor 6:11; Gal 4:12, 21; 6:11; Phil 3:17. For discussion of asyndeta in the letters of Paul, see Güting and Mealand, *Asyndeton* (1998) esp. 10–23.

[9] Cf. Jeremias, "Chiasmus" (1958) 149; Grobel, "Retribution-Formula" (1964); Jüngel, "Chiasmus" (1972). See also Louw, *Semantic* (1979) 2.45–51; Harvey, *Listening* (1998) 123–24.

then, gives a further explanation of this latter aspect, as indicated by the particle γάρ: Reward and punishment will be allotted to Jews and Greeks on equal terms, for God shows no partiality. Thus, the ἑκάστῳ in v. 6 has been confirmed.[10] Verses 12–14, all introduced with γάρ, elaborate directly upon the information provided in vv. 6–11 about God's impartial judgment, with gradual adjustment of focus. In the words of Max Pohlenz: "Die vier Sätze in V. 11–14 werden alle durch γάρ eingeleitet; sie sind also die Glieder einer Kette, von denen eins immer durch das folgende begründet oder erläutert wird. Der ganze Gedankengang bringt aber die Ausführung der These von 2,6 ἀποδώσει ἑκάστῳ κατὰ τὰ ἔργα αὐτοῦ mit spezieller Aufteilung auf die Juden und Heiden, die durch den Begriff des Gesetzes nötig wird."[11] With the indefinite relative pronoun οἵτινες directly following upon v. 14, vv. 15–16 supply the final link in this "chain," concluding with reference to the day of judgment previously spoken of in vv. 5–6.[12]

This suggests that it would impair the logic and flow of Paul's discourse in vv. 6–16—or vv. 1–16 for that matter—to part the text at v. 12, as proposed by many interpreters of the letter, editors of the Greek text included. The editors of the 27th Nestle-Aland edition, for instance, denote such a division being designed by the author by beginning a new paragraph with v. 12, thus curiously ignoring the conjunctive γάρ in the verse. That such decisions in modern text editions can have an effect on translations and interpretations of the text is hardly to be doubted.[13] On the division commonly made between v. 11 and v. 12, N. T. Wright rightly remarks that "[i]t goes against the grain to cut off a Pauline sentence beginning with γάρ from that which precedes it," but nevertheless determines to "turn now to

---

[10] Similarly Bornkamm, "Gesetz" (1963) 97: "Dem ἑκάστῳ (v. 6) entspricht ἐπὶ πᾶσαν ψυχὴν ἀνθρώπου τοῦ κατεργαζομένου τὸ κακόν (v. 9) und παντὶ τῷ ἐργαζομένῳ τὸ ἀγαθόν (v. 10)."

[11] "Paulus" (1949) 74 n. 15. Cf. also Bornkamm, "Gesetz" (1963) 98–100.

[12] Cf. Saake, "Überlegungen" (1972–73) on the reference to vv. 5–6 in v. 16. Saake has also convincingly shown the weaknesses of Bultmann's suggestion that v. 16 is a secondary gloss ("Glossen" [1947] 200–201).

[13] Cf., e.g., the following trans.: RSV, NRSV, TEV, NAB, JB, MOFFATT.

the paragraph which precedes 2.17 in the Nestle-Aland text, i.e. 2.12–16."[14]

Less reluctant in this respect is Jouette M. Bassler.[15] In an attempt to isolate Paul's announcement of God's impartiality in v. 11 as a theological axiom, Bassler holds that 1:16–2:11 and 2:12–29 constitute two "firmly bracketed" and "discrete" units, and that v. 11 "to a strong degree structures the argument," functioning as "the pivotal point in the argument, summarizing 1:16–2:10 and introducing 2:12–29."[16] The analytical criteria upon which Bassler's claims are based are what she calls "formal evidence,"[17] viz. those of inclusion (ring-structure) and word chain. "These," she says, "have the advantage over more subjective criteria in that they are based on purely formal characteristics of the text. Thus they provide an objective indication of the contours of Paul's thought-units, which can then be tested by appealing to logic and content."[18] That the text in 1:16–2:11 constitutes a unity is chiefly established by the criterion of inclusion, viz. the observation that 2:9–10 restates the ideas introduced in 1:16–18, most clearly by echoing the phrase Ἰουδαίῳ τε πρῶτον καὶ "Ελληνι from 1:16. The unity of 2:12–29, on the other hand, is mostly grounded on the criterion of word chain. Here Paul's "introduction" of the word νόμος (v. 12), and later on περιτομή (v. 25), is decisive: "Thus the word-chain ἀνόμως-

---

[14] "Law" (1996) 143. Cf., however, Wright's comments in his more recent "Letter" (2002) 440 with n. 60.

[15] *Impartiality* (1982) esp. 121–54. Bassler's arguments are summarized in her "Impartiality" (1984), and iterated more recently in her "Centering" (1995) 164–66. Bassler is followed explicitly, e.g., by Davies, *Faith* (1990) 49–67; Carras, "Romans 2,1–29" (1992) 188 n. 12; Tobin, "Controversy" (1993); Yinger, *Paul* (1999) 146–56; Engberg-Pedersen, *Paul* (2000) 212–15. Cf. also the similar approaches in Schmithals, *Römerbrief* (1975) 13–14; Schmeller, *Paulus* (1987) 232–86.

[16] "Impartiality" (1984) 44–45.

[17] I.e. "evidence that is independent of the logic or content of the argument and thus do not permit us to prejudge the conclusion on the basis of what we think Paul is trying to say" (*Impartiality* [1982] 123).

[18] "Impartiality" (1984) 45. Bassler's choice of criteria is based on Fischer's "Forms" (1977).

νόμος-περιτομή-ἀκροβυστία unites the argument of 2:12–29 and marks it off from the surrounding verses."[19]

Bassler's arguments are unconvincing. Though the criteria of inclusion and word-chain may sometimes be useful, both can be slippery. Surely there is a conceptual connection between Ἰουδαίῳ τε πρῶτον καὶ "Ελληνι in 1:16 and 2:9–10, but the inference that this connection exhibits a calculated formal inclusion seems unwarranted. The mere repetition of words or phrases does not always provide a safe indicator of such an inclusion. The theme of "divine impartiality" is certainly significant for Paul's argument,[20] but this theme is subordinated to the statement about divine judgment according to deeds in 2:6, which is expounded not only in vv. 7–11 but in vv. 12–16 as well. Paul's discussion of Jews, non-Jews, and God's impartiality does not cease to be the center of attention in what follows after v. 11. Moreover, the stylistic shift occurring at 2:1 makes Bassler's "deliberate ring-structure" in 1:16–2:11 highly problematic. She states: "Thus even though 2:1 marks a change in style, it does not mark a change in thought. The basic content of the argument remains the same."[21] Here, Bassler's analysis appears after all to be based on some "more subjective criteria" rather than "purely formal characteristics of the text" (see above). The same goes for the second person singular address resumed in 2:17, the stylistic change at which is altogether ignored by her.

At first glance, Bassler's claim that a new element of thought is initiated in 2:12 by the "introduction" of the word νόμος seems to be well-founded. In fact, some of her critics also favor a (minor) division between v. 11 and v. 12 on similar grounds.[22] However, the newness in v. 12 may prove to be

---

[19] "Impartiality" (1984) 50. Bassler also adds some "stylistic" features in the passage which, according to her, present a "ring-like appearance" supporting the claim about the unity of 2:12–29. Remarkably, however, she pays no attention to the obvious stylistic change occurring at v. 17 with the resuming of the 2nd per. sg. Cf. her *Impartiality* (1982) 137–54.

[20] But, as Elliott, *Rhetoric* (1990) 122, rightly points out, Paul's aim is not to argue *for* God's impartiality; rather, he argues *from* it (cf. 2:6).

[21] "Impartiality" (1984) 48. Cf. *Impartiality* (1982) 131.

[22] E.g. Dunn, *Romans* (1988) 1.viii, 77–79, 94–95; Fitzmyer, *Romans* (1993) 98, 296–98.

more apparent than real. It is true that the word νόμος occurs for the first time in this verse, but it seems reasonable to presume that the concept itself has to some extent been inherent in Paul's discussion prior to v. 12, probably ever since he first made a verbal distinction between "Jews and Greeks" (1:16).[23] To Paul's readers, who were of course no strangers to Judaism,[24] it would have been evident that what distinguished Jews from non-Jews was first and foremost the former's possession of God's νόμος. The readers would thus have been aware of the fact that when Paul in 2:6–11 spoke of God's impartial judgment of Jews and Greeks according to their deeds, the function and value of the Jewish Law was or would be at stake. The mention of the word νόμος comes therefore hardly as a surprise at this point in Paul's discourse; on the contrary, it would have been expected. Hence, although it may otherwise be significant that Paul uses the word νόμος first in v. 12, the mere occurrence of it does not give rise to any division of the text at variance with its flow and structural markers. Furthermore, seen in this light, it appears that Bassler's word-chain ἀνόμως-νόμος-περιτομή-ἀκροβυστία is somewhat partial. Why exclude the words which launched this dichotomy in the first place, viz. "Jews and Greeks"? Why not the word-chain Ἰουδαῖος-Ἕλλην-ἀνόμως-νόμος-περιτομή-ἀκροβυστία (in order of appearance)? That would entail a considerably different structure from that proposed by Bassler.

All in all, Bassler seems to be quite right in stressing the topical continuity in Paul's text, but less so in her choice and assessment of criteria for its formal structure. A recognition of the dialogical style functioning as a prominent feature in the macrostructure of Romans would be more helpful. So would also an acknowledgment of the unity and the expository and subordinate character of the discourse in 2:6–16.

In sum, each of vv. 7–10 in Romans 2 is grammatically dependent on v. 6, which, in turn, modifies the genitive τοῦ θεοῦ in v. 5. The ensuing series of clauses introduced with γάρ (vv. 11–14), followed by a sentence linked by the relative pronoun οἵτινες (vv. 15–16), imply also that vv. 11–16 de-

---

[23] Cf. Bornkamm, "Gesetz" (1963) 98: The concept of νόμος "ist freilich, auch ohne daß er expressis verbis gebraucht wird, von 1,18 ab zur Genüge vorbereitet."
[24] See esp. in Ch. 2 sec. 2.2 above.

fine further the foregoing statements. Contrary to common opinion, Paul's text does not allow of any division between v. 11 and v. 12. Hence, Paul's discourse in vv. 6–16 as a whole continually points back to v. 5, in which Paul exposed the interlocutor's wretched position on the day of judgment. That implies that the focus of vv. 6–16 is still very much within the scope of Paul's indictment of his interlocutor in vv. 1–5.

1.2. Romans 2:17–29 as a Resumption of Paul's Address in 2:1–5

Most scholars recognize the stylistic correspondence between Paul's addresses in 2:1–5 and 2:17–29. As James D. G. Dunn observes, in 2:17 "[t]he diatribe style of the opening verses (2:1ff.), which had been allowed to lapse from 2:6, is now resumed."[25] This particular point is scarcely controversial. A matter of debate, however, is whether the resuming of the second person singular address implies a change of interlocutor or not. Neil Elliott, for instance, insists that in 2:17 "[t]here is an obvious shift to a new conversation partner: 'But you, for your part—' (εἰ δὲ σύ). The person now addressed is specifically a Jew."[26] Joseph A. Fitzmyer, on the other hand, states: "In 2:17 the 'Jew' is explicitly mentioned, and vv 1–16 merely lead up to that identification."[27] Dunn concurs: "With vv 17–24 the identity of the interlocutor becomes explicit: a (typical) Jew whose views Paul knew 'from inside'."[28]

The question of the interlocutor's (ethnic) identity will be dealt with in detail in the next section. Meanwhile, I wish to pave the way for the present discussion by noting that Paul does not actually state that the person addressed in 2:17 *is* a Jew. Rather, this person is depicted as someone who wants to be *called* a Jew. As we shall see, the difference is a crucial one. My purpose in this section, however, is to substantiate the claim that Paul's address in 2:17–29 is a direct continuation of the preceding text, and that the same interlocutor is involved throughout the chapter.

---

[25] *Romans* (1988) 1.108.
[26] *Rhetoric* (1990) 127.
[27] *Romans* (1993) 297.
[28] *Romans* (1988) 1.108.

We have already seen that, as a rule, an epistolary interlocutor tends to remain the same throughout a discourse unless and until otherwise indicated. Now, provided that the interlocutor in 2:1–5 is not a Jew, the word Ἰουδαῖος in 2:17 may appear to be such an indicator, as Elliott maintains. But, again, Paul's address in 2:17 does not imply unambiguously that this individual is a Ἰουδαῖος. The word Ἰουδαῖος is therefore not a reliable sign of a shift to a new interlocutor in 2:17. A number of factors suggest instead that there is no such shift, but that the interlocutor in 2:17–29 is the very person addressed earlier in 2:1–5.

The similarities between 2:1–5 and 2:17–29 are not only stylistic. Even the substance of Paul's indictments in these passages is strikingly uniform. The interlocutor in 2:1–5 is censured for judging the misdeeds of others while doing the same things himself, and for falsely believing that he will nonetheless escape God's judgment. It is not the interlocutor's judging per se that is condemned by Paul; neither is it the judging itself that will be the cause for God's wrath on the day of judgment. Rather, it is the fact that the person acts sinfully, in spite of his opinion or appearance to the contrary. The interlocutor is dissembling and inconsistent. He is not who he claims to be or presumes that he is. Correspondingly, the interlocutor in 2:17–29 both claims to be something that he really is not and does the very things he tells others not to do. He thinks he has what it takes to be a "Jew," but does not behave as one and is unaware of the fact that he will eventually be judged by others. Precisely as the person in 2:1–5, the person in 2:17–29 acts contrary to God's will and is charged with being double-faced.

Thus, there is a close resemblance between Paul's indictments in 2:1–5 and 2:17–29. But there are also certain differences. The focus of the latter is somewhat more detailed than that of the former. Elliott is therefore right in this respect when he observes that "[t]he second apostrophe, in 2.17–29, differs markedly from the first [i.e. in 2:1–5]. . . . [T]his characterization is developed much more fully than in the first apostrophe."[29] Now, this might support the view that Paul is dealing with two different interlocutors, as Elliott infers. However, when the differences between the two passages are considered in light of the progress of the discourse from the be-

---

[29] *Rhetoric* (1990) 127.

ginning of the chapter onward the "much more fully" developed characterization in 2:17–29 merely turns out to be expected.

As we saw above, 2:5–6 constitutes a refutation of the interlocutor's false conviction about being safe on the day of judgment, where the scriptural quotation in v. 6 provides the proof to the contrary. The subordinate position of vv. 7–16, which basically constitute a commentary on v. 6, show that these verses substantiate and amplify further Paul's charges against his interlocutor. Read linearly, the text grants no good reasons to doubt that the letter's audience would have perceived vv. 6–16 as a direct continuation of Paul's address in vv. 1–5. What is to be noted here is that the range of subjects in vv. 6–16 gradually becomes more specific with one particular point at the core of the argument, viz. that it will be decisive on the day of judgment to have done what God's Law requires.

To begin with, Paul's partner in dialogue is confronted with the fact that God will judge everyone according to deeds, both Jews and non-Jews (vv. 6–11). The interlocutor is then informed that those who sin ἀνόμως will have no chance whatsoever before God. They will perish ἀνόμως (v. 12a), whereas those who sin ἐν νόμῳ will be judged διὰ νόμου (v. 12b). Paul's argument is somewhat puzzling here. The immediate context seems to demand that v. 12 concerns those who are "without the Law" (ἀνόμως), i.e. gentiles, as compared to those who are "within the Law" (ἐν νόμῳ), i.e. Jews.[30] And yet, such a reading seems suspect because there is actually no comparison made in v. 12 either between the fate of those ἀνόμως and those ἐν νόμῳ, or the criteria through which those ἀνόμως and those ἐν νόμῳ are to be judged. Instead, v. 12a focuses exclusively upon the *fate* of those who sin ἀνόμως—they will "perish." Paul does not state that they will be judged ἀνόμως, only that they will perish ἀνόμως. In v. 12b, on the other hand, Paul concentrates on the *criterion* used when those who sin ἐν νόμῳ will be "judged." He does not mention their fate specifically. Hence, the issues dealt with in v. 12a and v. 12b are two different things (note also that v. 12b is not linked with v. 12a by δέ but by καί). Dunn attempts to amplify the comparative element by downplaying the difference between

---

[30] See, e.g., the discussions in Räisänen, *Paul* (1983) 25–26, 101–9; Dunn, *Romans* (1988) 1.95–96.

the verbs ἀπολοῦνται and κριθήσονται, translating the latter as "'condemned' as no less serious than 'perish'."[31] But this is almost certainly not the meaning of κριθήσονται here. Would this be the proper meaning in v. 16, for example, where God is said to κρίνειν men through Christ Jesus? I think not, and neither does Dunn. Is it not more likely that if Paul wanted to refer to those "without the Law" he would have used a phrase such as χωρὶς νόμου (cf. 3:21) instead of ἀνόμως? And does it not speak against his claims elsewhere to gather that Paul is stating here that those "without the Law" will simply perish? Hence, I am inclined to agree with Stanley K. Stowers that the adverb ἀνόμως should be read not as "without the Law" but as "lawlessly" or "in a lawless manner."[32] Taken thus, Paul is saying that whoever (whether Jew or gentile) has acted outrageously against God's precepts will eventually be wiped out. Verse 12a seems thus to summarize the statements made in vv. 8–9.

Moreover, Paul continues, it will not suffice to be a mere "hearer" of the Law (οἱ ἀκροαταὶ νόμου). Rather, one has to be a "doer" of the Law (οἱ ποιηταὶ νόμου) in order to be "justified" (δικαιωθήσονται, v. 13). Paul informs his interlocutor (v. 14) that there may indeed be some gentiles who actually do what the Law requires (τὰ τοῦ νόμου ποιῶσιν), although they, unlike Jews, have no claim to the Law by birth (τὰ μὴ νόμον ἔχοντα φύσει).[33] Such gentiles, says Paul, will show that "the work of the Law" (τὸ

---

[31] *Romans* (1988) 1.96.

[32] *Rereading* (1994) 134–42. Cf. LSJ s.v. ἄνομος: "lawless, impious." Stowers translates 2:12 as follows: "For all who have sinned in a lawless manner, shall perish in a manner befitting lawlessness. All who have sinned while living within the law, shall have their case judged by the law" (p. 139). Cf. also Gaston, "Paul" (1979) 71 n. 60, who translates ἀνόμως as "godlessly." Cf. further Rom 6:19; 1 Cor 9:21; 2 Cor 6:14.

[33] That φύσει is to be taken with the participle ἔχοντα, instead of the verb ποιῶσιν ("do by nature"), has been argued convincingly by Cranfield, *Romans* (1975) 1.156–57; Achtemeier, "Some Things" (1984) 255–59; Stowers, *Rereading* (1994) 138–42; Wright, "Law" (1996) 144–45; Gathercole, "Law" (2002) 35–37. So also Snodgrass, "Justification" (1986) 80; Finsterbusch, *Thora* (1996) 17–19; Bergmeier, "Gesetz" (2000) 52–53. For arguments to the contrary, see Dunn, *Romans* (1988) 1.98–99.

ἔργον τοῦ νόμου) is "written on their hearts" (γραπτὸν ἐν ταῖς καρδίαις αὐτῶν)[34] on the day when God judges "men's concealment" (τὰ κρυπτὰ τῶν ἀνθρώπων), according to Paul's "good news," through Christ Jesus (vv. 15–16).

This, then, is the information in light of which Paul turns again directly to his interlocutor. The charges now brought against him reflect the essence of this information. They revolve around his transgression of the Law and, consequently, his defenseless position before God. Paradoxically, the interlocutor boasts in God and the Law (vv. 17–20, 23), but in reality he violates the Law and thus dishonors God (vv. 21–24). That, in turn, makes him no better off than those who sin ἀνόμως and will perish accordingly (v. 12). In fact, he will not only be judged by gentiles who keep the Law (v. 27; cf. v. 14) but will as well be considered unworthy of God's praise, for whom outward appearance is nothing but men's hearts everything (vv. 28–29; cf. v. 16). Hence, the most straightforward explanation why the characterization in 2:17–29 is more detailed than the one in 2:1–5 is that vv. 17–29 elaborate on information already provided in vv. 1–16.

There is therefore good reason to disagree with Elliott that there is an "obvious" shift to a new interlocutor in 2:17. The words εἰ δὲ σύ do not imply this either, as Elliott assumes. On the contrary, it is far more likely that the emphasis put on σύ, shown by its redundancy,[35] is meant to point back to the σύ in 2:1–5 (see esp. the emphatic σύ in v. 3) in order to signal that the direct address to this same person is now resumed.[36] Moreover,

---

[34] A probable allusion to Jer 38:33 (δώσω νόμους μου εἰς τὴν διάνοιαν αὐτῶν καὶ ἐπὶ καρδίας αὐτῶν γράψω αὐτούς). Cf. Isa 51:7 (λαός μου οὗ ὁ νόμος μου ἐν τῇ καρδίᾳ ὑμῶν). For further discussion, see Gathercole, "Law" (2002) 40–43.

[35] The pronoun is redundant because the 2nd per. sg. is expressed by the form of the verb ἐπονομάζῃ.

[36] Unfortunately, the presence of the particle δέ is not of much help to us here. We might consult Callow's study of its use in 1 Cor ("Δέ" [1992]), in which she concludes that "when Paul is developing an argument by a succession of points, linearly, the use of δέ is appropriate and frequent. . . . δέ characteristically occurs where there is linear development of thought . . . it marks new development in the progression of the message" (pp. 191–92). We might also turn to Levinsohn, "Constraints" (1999), who describes δέ "as a particle that constrains the material

Elliott's rendering "But you, for your part—" might be proper if the text would read σὺ δέ . . . But this is not what Paul says. His address begins, not with an absolute statement which might perhaps be expected if he were turning to a different interlocutor, but with a conditional clause: "But if you . . ." Unfortunately, interpreters often tend to downplay the conditional element here, even to the extent of exchanging the "if" for a "since," as if Paul's utterance were unconditional altogether. But this, I think, is a fault which probably goes hand in hand with the tendency among some scholars to treat the protasis (the "if" part) of first class conditional clauses (sometimes called "real" conditions) as if the thing assumed in it necessarily is true or real. However, as D. A. Carson reminds us, "[i]n a first class condition the protasis is assumed true for the sake of the argument, but the thing actually assumed may or may not be true. To put it another way, there is stress on the reality of the assumption, but not on the reality of the content that is assumed."[37]

What, then, does Paul's mode of expression in Romans 2:17 tell us? First, it denotes that there is a condition involved—an "if." Second, it informs us that something is possibly true for the sake of the argument. Paul is saying: "But if you . . . [in view of the information just provided], then . . ."[38] That, in turn, strongly suggests that the interlocutor in 2:17–29 is the very person previously addressed in 2:1–5. In other words, the σύ in 2:17 is the "man" (ἄνθρωπε) in 2:1.

---

associated with it to be processed as a new discourse unit that builds on and develops from the previous material" (p. 320). But, although this may tell us something about the development of Paul's text, the particle δέ does not by itself determine if Paul turns to a new interlocutor in 2:17 or not.

[37] *Fallacies* (1984) 81. See also Porter, *Idioms* (1994) 256–57.

[38] Note, however, that the conditional clause is defective in that it lacks the apodosis; see further sec. 2.3.2 below.

2. The Identity of Paul's Interlocutor in Romans 2

Having reached the conclusion that the same interlocutor is involved throughout Romans 2, I turn now to the question of identity. As any linear reading requires, I will first pay attention to Paul's statements in the passage immediately preceding chapter 2, viz. 1:18–32. The logical connection between this passage and Paul's address in 2:1 will then be considered, subsequent to which a reading of chapter 2 will be presented in terms of the main focus of this study.

2.1. Paul's Indictment of Gentiles in Romans 1:18–32

After his epistolary opening (1:1–7) and his *captatio benevolentiae* (vv. 8–14a), Paul sets out the main purpose of his letter: His missionary duty urges him to announce God's "good news" (εὐαγγελίσασθαι) to the gentiles in Rome (vv. 14b–15). The postulates of these "news"[39] had already been declared in the opening, viz. that they concern God's son, Jesus the Messiah, through whom Paul had received the specific assignment of bringing about obedience among all the gentiles (vv. 2–5). Now Paul explains that he has no occasion for being ashamed of the εὐαγγέλιον, because it is the power of God for salvation to *everyone* (παντί) who has faith, not only the Jew but the Greek as well (v. 16). For what the εὐαγγέλιον reveals (ἀποκαλύπτεται) is God's righteousness which leads to faithfulness (εἰς πίστιν), confirming that God is faithful (ἐκ πίστεως) to the promise that it is the righteous one (ὁ δίκαιος) who shall live (v. 17).[40]

---

[39] It may be misleading to use the word "news" here, since it is clearly important to Paul's argument that his message is not based on something new: the εὐαγγέλιον had been προεπηγγείλατο διὰ τῶν προφητῶν αὐτοῦ [i.e. τοῦ θεοῦ] ἐν γραφαῖς ἁγίαις (1:2).

[40] I have chosen to paraphrase v. 17 rather freely, presuming that my readers are acquainted with more traditional and literal renderings of this much discussed text. Presentations of the interpretative difficulties encountered in the verse, such as the problematic phrasing ἐκ πίστεως εἰς πίστιν, may be found in most standard commentaries. I find Elliott's reading particularly helpful and his arguments for it convincing: "Paul has no reason to be put to shame, because it is *God's* integrity

However, this is not the only thing that is revealed. Paul's announcement has a dark side as well. For God's wrath (ὀργὴ θεοῦ), he says, is revealed (ἀποκαλύπτεται) against all impiety and unrighteousness (πᾶσαν ἀσέβειαν καὶ ἀδικίαν) of those men (ἀνθρώπων) who by their unrighteousness (ἐν ἀδικίᾳ) suppress the truth (v. 18). Unlike the righteous one who will live (v. 17), these unrighteous men will only encounter the wrath of God.[41] According to Paul, they should have acknowledged God's eternal power and divinity, the reality of which has always been plain to them, but since they have failed to do so they are without excuse (ἀναπολογήτους, vv. 19–20). In spite of their knowledge of God, they did not glorify (ἐδόξασαν) or give thanks to God as God. Instead, they became futile in their reasoning (διαλογισμοῖς) and their foolish hearts (καρδία) were darkened (v. 21). Pretending to be wise, they became fools and exchanged the glory (δόξαν) of God for despicable images (vv. 22–23). Therefore (διό), God handed them over (παρέδωκεν αὐτούς) in the desires of their hearts (ἐν ταῖς ἐπιθυμίαις τῶν καρδιῶν αὐτῶν) to impurity (ἀκαθαρσίαν) for bodily dishonor (v. 24). These men exchanged the truth of God (τὴν ἀλήθειαν τοῦ θεοῦ) for a lie (τῷ ψεύδει) and revered (ἐσεβάσθησαν) and worshiped (ἐλάτρευσαν) the creature instead of the creator (v. 25). For this reason (διὰ τοῦτο), says Paul, God handed them over (παρέδωκεν αὐτούς) to dishonorable passions (πάθη ἀτιμίας), resulting in unnatural sexual relations (vv. 26–27). And since they refused to acknowledge God, God handed them over

---

that is revealed through the preaching of the gospel (1.17), an effectual revelation 'from faith'—that is, proceeding from God's faithfulness—'to faith'—creating faithfulness where there was none, life where there was death, so that 'out of faithfulness the righteous shall live'. The verses tell what happens when Paul does what he says he wants to do among the Romans: in the gospel the power of God is at work, faith is created, God's righteousness is thus revealed" (*Rhetoric* [1990] 111–12; italics his; cf. also pp. 82–85).

[41] In v. 32 Paul states that they are indeed "worthy of death" (οἱ τὰ τοιαῦτα πράσσοντες ἄξιοι θανάτου εἰσίν). Cf. Theobald, "Zorn" (2001) 76–77: "Wie σωτηρία und ὀργή konträre Begriffe sind [cf. 1 Thess 5:9], so gilt das natürlich auch von 'Leben' und 'Tod'. Es überrascht deshalb nicht, wenn dem letzten Wort der *propositio* [1:16–17], ζήσεται, im letzten Vers der sich anschließenden prophetischen Gerichtsrede das ἄξιοι θανάτου von V.32 gegenübertritt."

(παρέδωκεν αὐτούς) to a reprobated mind (ἀδόκιμον νοῦν), to do what is improper (ποιεῖν τὰ μὴ καθήκοντα), so that they became filled with all kinds of unrighteousness (πάσῃ ἀδικίᾳ) and horrible vices (vv. 28–31). Despite their knowledge of the fact that those who do such deeds (οἱ τὰ τοιαῦτα πράσσοντες) are worthy of death, such men (οἵτινες) not only do these deeds (αὐτὰ ποιοῦσιν) but even approve of others who do them (τοῖς πράσσουσιν, v. 32).

In sum, according to Paul, the people described in 1:18–32 have "no excuse" (ἀναπολογήτους, v. 20) for not having acknowledged and worshiped God properly, and because they failed to do so God "handed them over" (παρέδωκεν αὐτούς, vv. 24, 26, 28) to all kinds of vices, to "impurity" (ἀκαθαρσίαν, v. 24), to "dishonorable passions" (πάθη ἀτιμίας, v. 26), and to a "reprobated mind" (ἀδόκιμον νοῦν, v. 28).

In the following, I will first discuss the identity of the people spoken of in 1:18–32, and then point out the often neglected importance of this passage for Paul's subsequent discourse in Romans.

2.1.1. Paul's Indictment as a Characteristic Jewish Polemic

Scholars have long recognized that Paul's description in Romans 1:18–32 closely parallels standard Hellenistic Jewish polemic against the gentile world.[42] Wiard Popkes states: "Man kann fast sagen, daß sich in Röm 1. 18–32 kaum etwas findet, was nicht traditionsgeschichtlich vorgeformt wäre."[43] Particularly noteworthy are the many affinities between Paul's text and Wisdom of Solomon 11–15,[44] a writing which may have been known

---

[42] For discussion and overview of these parallels, see, e.g., Schulz, "Anklage" (1958); Bornkamm, "Offenbarung" (1966) esp. 12–26; Schlier, "Heiden" (1966); Bussmann, *Themen* (1971) 108–22, 143–90; Stowers, *Rereading* (1994) 83–100. See also most standard commentaries, among which Kuss, *Römerbrief* (1957) 1.30–56, is particularly helpful.

[43] "Aufbau" (1982) 493.

[44] Cf. also, e.g., *Sib. Or.* 3.8–45; *Let. Aris.* 134–141, 152; *Jub.* 22.16; *T. Naph.* 3.3–4; Philo, *Abr.* 135–136; *Spec.* 3.37–42; *Contempl.* 59–64.

to Paul.[45] Making a sharp distinction between Jews (the righteous) and non-Jews (the ungodly), the author of Wisdom narrates how "the ungodly were tormented when judged in wrath" (μετ' ὀργῆς κρινόμενοι ἀσεβεῖς ἐβασανίζοντο, 11:9):[46]

> In return for their foolish and wicked thoughts (ἀντὶ δὲ λογισμῶν ἀσυνέτων ἀδικίας αὐτῶν), which led them astray to worship irrational serpents and worthless animals (ἄλογα ἑρπετὰ καὶ κνώδαλα εὐτελῆ), you [i.e. God] sent upon them a multitude of irrational creatures to punish them, so that they might learn that one is punished by the very things by which one sins (δι' ὧν τις ἁμαρτάνει διὰ τούτων κολάζεται, 11:15–16).... But judging (κρίνων) them little by little you gave them an opportunity to repent (τόπον μετανοίας), though you were not unaware that their origin was evil (πονηρὰ ἡ γένεσις αὐτῶν) and their wickedness inborn (ἔμφυτος ἡ κακία αὐτῶν), and that their way of thinking would never change (οὐ μὴ ἀλλαγῇ ὁ λογισμὸς αὐτῶν εἰς τὸν αἰῶνα, 12:10–11).... Therefore those who lived unrighteously (βιώσαντας ἀδίκως), in a life of folly, you tormented through their own abominations (βδελυγμάτων). For they went far astray on the paths of error, accepting as gods those animals that even their enemies despised; they were deceived (ψευσθέντες) like foolish infants (12:23–24).

In spite of their ignorance, these impious and unrighteous people have no excuse for not having worshiped God properly:

> For all people (πάντες ἄνθρωποι) who were ignorant of God were foolish (μάταιοι) by nature (φύσει); and they were unable from the good things that are seen (ἐκ τῶν ὁρωμένων ἀγαθῶν) to know the one who exists, nor did they recognize the artisan while paying heed to his works (13:1).... Yet again, not even they are to be excused (οὐδ' αὐτοὶ συγγνωστοί); for if they had the power to know so much that they could investigate the world, how did they fail to find sooner the Lord of these things? (13:8–9)

Furthermore, as if it were not enough to err about the knowledge of God (τὴν τοῦ θεοῦ γνῶσιν, 14:22),

---

[45] Scholars generally agree that either Paul knew the work or both authors relied on similar traditions.

[46] I am indebted here to the NRSV trans. of Wis.

they no longer keep either their lives or their marriages pure, but they either treacherously kill one another, or grieve one another by adultery, and all is a raging riot of blood and murder (αἷμα καὶ φόνος), theft and deceit (κλοπὴ καὶ δόλος), corruption (φθορά), faithlessness (ἀπιστία), tumult (τάραχος), perjury (ἐπιορκία), confusion over what is good (θόρυβος ἀγαθῶν), forgetfulness of favors (χάριτος ἀμνηστία), defiling of souls (ψυχῶν μιασμός), sexual perversion (γενέσεως ἐναλλαγή), disorder in marriages (γάμων ἀταξία), adultery (μοιχεία) and debauchery (ἀσέλγεια, 14:24–26). . . . But just penalties (τὰ δίκαια) will overtake them on two counts: because they thought wrongly (κακῶς) about God in devoting themselves to idols, and because in deceit they swore unrighteously (ἀδίκως) through contempt for holiness (14:30).

The parallels to Paul's account are clear enough. There is little doubt that for Paul and his audience the people described in Romans 1:18–32 belonged to the non-Jewish world. What would, however, have sounded foreign to Paul and his ancient readers is the surprising claim of some modern readers that the passage was meant to account for the sinfulness of all human beings, Jews included. C. E. B. Cranfield, for example, holds that although "Paul has in mind primarily the Gentiles" he is simultaneously "describing the basic sinfulness of fallen man as such, the inner reality of the life of Israel no less than of that of the Gentiles."[47] The reasons for this interpretation, according to Cranfield, are threefold: 1) Paul does not explicitly refer to those described in 1:18–32 as gentiles or Greeks, but uses the general term "men" (ἄνθρωποι); 2) the description of men's idolatry in v. 23 "echoes the language used of Israel" in Psalm 105:20 (MT 106:20) and Jeremiah 2:11; 3) "the main point of 2.1–3.20 is precisely that the Jew,

---

[47] *Romans* (1975) 1.105. Cf. also the similar conclusions reached by Bassler, *Impartiality* (1982) 122–23, 195–97. Bassler, however, stretches her case. At first she observes that "[c]ertainly Paul has patterned his argument here according to traditional Jewish polemics against Gentiles but . . . one cannot maintain that in Chapter 1 Paul had *only* Gentiles in mind." But then she continues: "Although he employs an argument traditionally directed against the Gentiles, he clearly signals that it was also, *if not primarily*, appropriate to the Jews" (p. 122; the latter emphasis mine). Here Bassler has curiously transformed the "not only gentiles" into a "if not primarily Jews."

who thinks himself entitled to sit in judgment on the Gentiles, himself does the very same things that he condemns in them."

The first argument carries little weight. As we saw above, the author of Wisdom of Solomon can even speak of "all men" (πάντες ἄνθρωποι) without Jews being included (13:1). More to the point, Paul does not say that the ἄνθρωποι against whom God's wrath is revealed are just any men—let alone all humans—but precisely *those* men who (ἀνθρώπων τῶν) suppress the truth and are without excuse because they should have recognized God's eternal power and divine nature, albeit invisible, through God's creation of the world.[48] Such description could hardly have applied to Jews, who certainly enjoyed a more immediate access to the truth about God.

The second argument appears to carry more weight. However, although there are some verbal similarities in v. 23 with Psalm 105:20 and Jeremiah 2:11, it is to be noted that Paul in no way indicates that he is alluding to scripture. Such allusion would not have been evident to his readers either, since v. 23 simply includes a typical description of gentile ungodliness which, needless to say, was commonly associated with idolatry. That, in turn, would be a more than enough cause for stating openly (e.g. by καθὼς γέγραπται) that Israel was included. But Paul does not do that. Hence, if he had these particular texts from scripture in mind, which I doubt, Paul made use of and adapted them to suit his own purpose.[49] Moreover, an in-

---

[48] I find it surprising how frequently interpreters take πᾶσαν in 1:18 to denote that Paul was speaking of God's wrath against "all men." This is not expressed in Paul's text. Rather, πᾶσαν qualifies not ἀνθρώπων but ἀσέβειαν καὶ ἀδικίαν: God's wrath is revealed against "all impiety and unrighteousness. . ."

[49] Note that Jer 2:11, after mentioning gentiles (ἔθνη) who change (ἀλλάξονται) their gods, speaks of God's nation changing (ἠλλάξατο) *their* "glory" (τὴν δόξαν), not God's. Similarly, Ps 105:20 states that the people of Israel changed *their own* "glory" (ἠλλάξαντο τὴν δόξαν αὐτῶν), not God's (so in MT). There is no comprehensive list either covering all sorts of images as in Rom 1:23 ("images resembling a mortal human being or birds or fourfooted animals or reptiles"). Instead, the image in Ps 105:20 is limited to that of an ox (cf. Exod 32). Cranfield suggests a comparison with the list of images in Deut 4:16–18, a suggestion which seems however to speak against his argument, since this text includes not an accusation

clusion of Jewish idolatry in v. 23 only works if the verse is read out of context. It is beyond question that the people spoken of in vv. 22–23 are the same as those described both before and after these verses in 1:18–32, and it is beyond reasonable doubt that neither Paul nor his readers would have understood these latter descriptions as referring to Jews.

The weaknesses of Cranfield's third argument will be elucidated below (in sec. 2.2). Suffice it to point out the methodological danger involved in reading the text in reverse, so to speak. To infer that because (or if) Paul accuses Jews in chapter 2 they *must* be included among those spoken of in 1:18–32 is a *non sequitur*.[50]

Some scholars see in Romans 1:18–32 an allusion to the story in Genesis 2–3 of the "fall of Adam."[51] But the plausibility of such readings seems remote, not only due to the lack of evidence for the Genesis story being anything more than vaguely "echoed" in a portion of Paul's text, but also because they rest on an anachronistic conception of the role played by the figure of Adam in pre-70 C.E. Jewish literature.[52] Notions of the sinfulness of all humanity being caused by Adam's transgression against God ("original sin") appear to have been non-existent in Paul's own time.[53]

---

but a standard warning against idolatry which, by implication, was practiced among other nations.

[50] This kind of approach also characterizes the study of Popkes, "Aufbau" (1982), for whom Paul's letter is "im wesentlichen ein dialogus cum Judaeo" (p. 494).

[51] E.g. Hooker, "Adam" (1959–60); Wedderburn, "Adam" (1980); Longenecker, *Eschatology* (1991) 173–74; Garlington, *Faith* (1994) 34–37; Dunn, *Theology* (1998) 91–93; Bryan, *Romans* (2000) 78, 82–83.

[52] Levison, *Portraits* (1988), has shown that interpretations of the story of Adam varied widely in early Judaism, and that questions of the effects of Adam's transgression were a matter of little interest prior to the fall of Jerusalem in 70 C.E. For further arguments against this understanding of Rom 1:18–32, see Stowers, *Rereading* (1994) 83–100.

[53] "Adam, as the first human, commits the first sin, and God punishes sin. But extant pre-70 Jewish literature does not make the leap to connect human sinfulness with primeval sin" (Stowers, *Rereading* [1994] 87–88). Paul will speak of Adam's transgression later in his letter, viz. in 5:12–21, but, as Dunn points out, there "his theme is original *death* more than original *sin*" (*Romans* [1988] 1.273 [emphasis his]).

Hence, Paul's account in 1:18–32 is best understood as falling in ranks with characteristic Jewish indictments of gentiles. The passage does not present ideas foreign to Paul himself,[54] but expresses fundamental Jewish convictions about non-Jews wholly shared by Paul.[55] This means that at the very outset of his preaching of the εὐαγγέλιον Paul seeks to describe or, better perhaps, remind his readers of their own gentile background.[56] And it is a sharp reminder indeed.

God's "handing over" of the gentiles (παρέδωκεν αὐτούς) to sinful ways of life (vv. 24, 26, 28) is a recurrent theme in the passage.[57] In close line with the Wisdom of Solomon, the theme conveys God's rule over the whole world by stressing that God is not an agent only in Jewish history but in non-Jewish as well. It was God's own will that the impious and unrighteous would suffer from an existence filled with abomination. Their situation is therefore understood as a direct result of a divine punishment. By implication, it is not up to these people themselves to alter the situation; it wholly depends on God's will. It is noteworthy, however, that Paul takes great care to point out that the gentiles are no victims of an inequitable punishment. On the contrary, their miserable condition is fully deserved, a just and necessary consequence of their rejection of God. They are thus

---

[54] Against Schmeller, *Paulus* (1987) 232–86, followed by Porter, "Romans 1.18–32" (1994), who propose that Rom 1:18–32 is actually made up of views held by Paul's Jewish "opponent" addressed in 2:1, against which Paul intends to argue (similarly also Dunn, *Romans* [1988] 1.78–93, as discussed below). I detect no hints of this in Paul's text.

[55] Cf. esp. Gal 2:15: ἡμεῖς φύσει Ἰουδαῖοι καὶ οὐκ ἐξ ἐθνῶν ἁμαρτωλοί.

[56] Cf. the vices listed in Gal 5:19–21, which Paul calls "the works of the flesh" (τὰ ἔργα τῆς σαρκός), and which he claims to have spoken of earlier (προεῖπον) to the gentile addressees in Galatia. It is not unlikely that this refers to his initial preaching of the εὐαγγέλιον to the Galatians. Interestingly, he notes that he then told them that "those who do such deeds (οἱ τὰ τοιαῦτα πράσσοντες) will not inherit the kingdom of God"; cf. Rom 1:32: "those who do such deeds (οἱ τὰ τοιαῦτα πράσσοντες) are worthy of death." Cf. also 1 Cor 6:9–11; 12:2; 1 Thess 1:9–10; 4:2–7.

[57] Cf. esp. Klostermann, "Vergeltung" (1933); Jeremias, "Rm 1,22–32" (1954).

"without excuse" (ἀναπολογήτους)—a point of central import in the passage.[58]

2.1.2. The Gentile Condition

It is not merely past episodes in gentile history which are most biting in Paul's discourse. Rather, it is the disclosure of the fact that the condition described is still very much in force. While Romans 1:18–32 is dominated by past tense narrative, it is framed by references to current state of affairs. It begins with statements uttered mainly in the present tense (vv. 18–20), followed by a lengthy exposition of past events and circumstances (vv. 21–31), the enclosing of which is then marked by turning again to uses of the present tense (v. 32). The text, however, is anything but clearly cut in this way. Its flow is continuous, effecting an interwoven context of past and present. It is to be noted that, although the verb ἀποκαλύπτεται in v. 18 undeniably has some future connotation (cf. 2:5),[59] it is nonetheless used in the present tense, precisely as in v. 17. That implies that the revelation spoken of by Paul is not just something which will happen in the future. It is Paul's very proclamation of the gospel which reveals God's past, present, and future wrath against the gentile world. By returning to the present tense at the closing of the passage (v. 32) Paul indicates that the vicious dispositions and deeds listed in the preceding are features which still characterize the gentile world. Thus, Romans 1:18–32 is not only concerned with the past—the gentile "background"—but also with the present—the gentile condition. References to history are employed to explain and substantiate this condition. According to Paul's bitter reminder, then, the divine punishment once imposed upon gentiles is still in effect and, unless otherwise decided by God, it remains so. To put it differently, Paul is not only saying here to his gentile readership "you once were. . ." but also "beware, you are still. . .!"

---

[58] Rightly so Popkes, "Aufbau" (1982) 500: "Inhaltlich ist 'unentschuldbar' als zentrales Stichwort zu bezeichnen."

[59] For recent discussion, see Eckstein, "Gottes Zorn" (1987); Theobald, "Zorn" (2001) 74–86.

It is, of course, a basic message of Paul's εὐαγγέλιον that God has now determined to give the unrighteous an opportunity to repent and glorify God properly and thus be justified (see esp. 3:21–26). And Paul's addressees have evidently already embraced this offer to some extent.[60] But it is important to take notice of the tension in Paul's letter between the past and the present, between "once" and "now."[61] The stage for this tension is set by the gentile portrayal in 1:18–32, the significance of which for the subsequent discourse should not be overlooked.[62] In chapter 6, for instance, the threats of the gentile condition as a present reality are conspicuously expressed. Paul urges his audience not to let sin rule in their mortal body (σώματι) to obey the body's desires (ταῖς ἐπιθυμίαις, v. 12; cf. 1:24),[63] nor to offer (παριστάνετε) their members to sin as weapons of unrighteousness (ὅπλα ἀδικίας, v. 13; cf. 1:18, 29), but to offer (παραστήσατε) themselves to God, as if having been brought from death to life, and their members to God as weapons of righteousness (ὅπλα δικαιοσύνης). Paul thanks God (v. 17) that the addressees, who once were slaves of sin (ἦτε δοῦλοι τῆς ἁμαρτίας),[64] became obedient from the heart (ἐκ καρδίας, cf. 1:21, 24)[65] to the pattern of teaching (τύπον διδαχῆς) to which they were handed over (εἰς ὃν παρεδόθητε, contrast 1:24, 26, 28).[66] Significantly, however, he is nonetheless compelled to speak to them in human terms (ἀνθρώπινον λέγω) due to the weakness of their flesh (διὰ τὴν ἀσθένειαν τῆς σαρκὸς ὑμῶν). Just as they had offered (παρεστήσατε) their members as slaves of impurity (τῇ ἀκαθαρσίᾳ, cf. 1:24) and of greater and greater lawlessness (τῇ ἀνομίᾳ εἰς τὴν ἀνομίαν), they should now (νῦν) offer (παραστήσατε) their members to righteousness (τῇ δικαιοσύνῃ, contrast

---

[60] See esp. 1:7, 8, 11–12; 6:2–4, 17–18, 20–22; 7:5–6; 8:9, 15; 11:30; 13:11.
[61] Cf., e.g., 3:21, 25–26; 5:6–11; 6; 7:5–6, 24–25; 8:1; 13:11–14.
[62] Beker's assertion that "typical Gentile sins do not fill the pages of Romans (except for 1:18–32)" (*Paul* [1980] 88) is certainly stunning.
[63] Cf. also 13:14; Gal 5:16–17; 1 Thess 4:5.
[64] Cf. Paul's remarks in 1 Cor 6:9–11; 12:2 about the Corinthian addressees.
[65] Note the variant reading in A: ἐκ καθαρᾶς καρδίας, cf. 1:24 (the phrase occurs also in 1 Tim 1:5; 2 Tim 2:22).
[66] For a different reading of the problematic phrase εἰς ὃν παρεδόθητε τύπον διδαχῆς, see Dunn, *Romans* (1988) 1.343–44.

1:18) for consecration (v. 19). Thus, even "now" the menaces of 1:18–32 hover over Paul's audience.

The addressees' weakness spoken of in 6:19 comes to further expression in 7:7–25. Here, a certain individual, who probably is meant to represent the gentile readership,[67] describes and laments over his inability to follow the Jewish Law, because of the very weakness of the flesh. The case in point (cf. 13:9) is the person's failure to comply with the Law's prohibition against desire (ἐπιθυμία, vv. 7–8; cf. 1:24; 6:12). The person, who once lived without the Law (v. 9a), tells how sin made use of the Law in order to produce in him all kinds of desires. According to this individual, the primary cause for this lies not with the Law (vv. 12, 13) but with the individual himself: "For I know[68] that the Law is spiritual (πνευματικός), but I am of the flesh (σάρκινος), sold under sin" (v. 14). This explains further his incapacity to conform to the will to do good (vv. 15–23; cf. Gal 5:17). Hence the bitter exclamation: "What a wretched man (ἄνθρωπος) I am! Who will rescue me from this body (τοῦ σώματος) of death?" (v. 24). Paul's subsequent response (cf. σε in 8:2) is to declare that there is now (νῦν) no condemnation for those who are in Christ Jesus (8:1). What the Law could not do, in that it was weakened by the flesh (ἐν ᾧ ἠσθένει διὰ τῆς σαρκός),[69] God has done by sending God's own son in the likeness of sinful flesh, thus condemning sin in the flesh (v. 3). This apparent tension between "once" and "now" is followed up in v. 13 where Paul, in spite of previous statements in the chapter, has reasons to warn his readers that if they live according to the flesh (κατὰ σάρκα) they will surely die (cf. 1:32). If they, on the other hand, by the spirit put to death the deeds of the body

---

[67] The identity of this person is, of course, hotly debated; for a recent overview, see Dodd, *Paradigmatic 'I'* (1999) 222–30, with further references. I am in basic agreement with Kümmel, *Römer 7* (1974) 74–138, that the ἐγώ of 7:7–25 does not represent Paul himself but stands for a fictitious person. The possibility that the text contains Paul's autobiographical reflections is almost certainly ruled out by v. 9: ἐγὼ δὲ ἔζων χωρὶς νόμου ποτέ (cf. Gal 1:13–14; Phil 3:5–6).

[68] Here I read οἶδα μὲν γάρ instead of οἴδαμεν γάρ (so [27]Nestle-Aland). The μέν is answered by δέ in v. 14b.

[69] Dunn rightly observes that "the inadequacy of the law lies not in itself but in the conditions in which it has to operate" (*Romans* [1988] 1.419).

(τὰς πράξεις τοῦ σώματος, cf. Gal 5:24) they will live. That Paul has in mind here the sorts of bodily dishonor described in 1:24–31 is likely.

Most enlightening in this respect are Paul's words in his hortatory request in 12:1–2, the occasion of which is the preceding discourse as a whole.[70] The antitheses of the existence delineated here to the one in 1:18–32 is striking and seems deliberate. Instead of devoting their bodies to various dishonorable conducts (1:24, 26–27), Paul's addressees are to offer (παραστῆσαι, cf. also 6:13, 16, 19) their bodies (τὰ σώματα ὑμῶν) as a living sacrifice, holy and acceptable to God. Such would be their reasonable worship (τὴν λογικὴν λατρείαν ὑμῶν),[71] in contrast to the erroneous worship denounced in 1:18–32 (esp. vv. 21, 23, 25 [ἐλάτρευσαν]). The readers are not to be conformed to this age (τῷ αἰῶνι τούτῳ). Rather, instead of being ruled by a reprobated mind (ἀδόκιμον νοῦν, 1:28), they are to be transformed (μεταμορφοῦσθε) by the renewing of their minds (τῇ ἀνακαινώσει τοῦ νοός) and thus to determine (δοκιμάζειν ὑμᾶς) what is God's will, what is good and acceptable and perfect (contrast τὰ μὴ καθήκοντα etc. in 1:28–31). In other words, at the letter's very structural center, where Paul sums up the basic goal in his proclamation of the εὐαγγέλιον, he summons his audience to transform their lives in absolute contrast to the gentile condition described in 1:18–32.

Hence, the tension expressed in Romans 1:18–32 between the past and present state of gentiles is repeatedly alluded to by Paul in his subsequent message. Indeed, I suggest that this is one of the passages Paul has in mind when in 15:15–16 he says that, on account of his authority as a minister of

---

[70] Cf. Ch. 1 sec. 3.2.2 above.

[71] Paul's use of the adj. λογικήν is somewhat baffling. It is often taken to denote some kind of "spiritual" worship, but the connection between such a worship and the bodily sacrifice, though figurative, is not readily apparent. Reichert, *Römerbrief* (2001) 238–48, suggests that ἡ λογικὴ λατρεία has to do with "sprechender Gottesdienst," but even this reading seems to neglect the physical aspect of the worship pled for. By translating the word as "reasonable" I want to retain the potential relation to reason (λόγος), but at the same time accentuate the comparative element in Paul's text, i.e. the comparison between "once" (cf. 1:18–32) and "now" (12:1–2). Cf. Betz, "Christianity" (1991) esp. 335–39, who also points out a number of allusions here to 1:18–32 (overlooked by Reichert).

Christ Jesus to the gentiles, he has on "some points" (ἀπὸ μέρους) written to the Roman audience "rather boldly" (τολμηρότερον) so as to "remind" them (ἐπαναμιμνῄσκων ὑμᾶς).[72] I take this to mean that Paul regards it as his duty to remind his gentile addressees of their actual position *qua* gentiles (cf. also 11:11–32).

2.2. Paul's Gentile Interlocutor in Romans 2:1–5

Having concluded that Romans 1:18–32 presents not merely a characteristic Jewish description of the gentile world but also Paul's own convictions in that respect, and that this passage is of central importance for the letter's message, I now turn to Paul's interlocutor in Romans 2. I shall begin by engaging scholarly discussions about how Paul's address in 2:1 may relate to the preceding discourse, and then analyze chapter 2 in view of the identity of Paul's imaginary partner in dialogue.

2.2.1. The Διό Debate: The Connection between Romans 2:1 and 1:18–32

Many aspects of the scholarly discussion of the identity of Paul's interlocutor in Romans 2:1–5 are reflected in what might be termed the "διό debate," viz. disputes over the proper function of the conjunction διό in 2:1 (for δι' ὅ: "wherefore"). The various proposals have been conveniently summarized by Cranfield in his commentary on Romans.[73] Among these, three suggestions stand out as having gained most support: 1) that διό has lost its inferential weight and is here used as a "colorless transition particle," thus not following logically upon what precedes;[74] 2) that it draws a con-

---

[72] For more detailed discussion of this passage, see above in Ch. 1 sec. 3.2.3 and Ch. 2 sec. 2.1.4.
[73] *Romans* (1975) 1.140–41.
[74] So, e.g., Lietzmann, *Römer* (1971) 37–39 ("farblose Uebergangspartikel"); Käsemann, *Römer* (1974) 50; Michel, *Römer* (1978) 112–13.

clusion from the sentence immediately preceding (1:32);⁷⁵ and 3) that διό with its full inferential force looks back to 1:18–32 as a whole.⁷⁶

The first suggestion is actually no more persuasive than attempts to explain away the problem, for instance, by arguing that διό is a scribal error for δίς,⁷⁷ or that 2:1 simply is a secondary gloss.⁷⁸ A survey of Paul's usage of διό shows that there are no instances of it being used as a "colorless transition particle."⁷⁹ Though the referential scope may vary,⁸⁰ διό always marks a conclusion drawn from the preceding. That, however, seems to be of little concern to scholars who choose to follow this suggestion. Presupposing—either by way of a backward reading from 2:17 or by regarding it as self-evident—that the interlocutor in 2:1 is a Jew, these scholars are forced to disregard the inferential function of διό, since it cannot convincingly be maintained that the indictment against gentiles in 1:18–32 tells something about Jewish conduct. Otto Kuss, for example, begins his discussion with rejecting the non-inferential function of διό, but in effect this is exactly what his reading unfolds, due to his decision that the interlocutor in 2:1 must be "the Jew" addressed in 2:17.⁸¹ Similarly, Heinrich Schlier comments on 2:1: "Der richtende Mensch ist hier der Jude. Dieser ist es natürlich nicht ausschließlich, aber er vertritt den Typus des nicht nur gelegentlich, sondern grundsätzlich moralisch urteilenden Menschen. So taucht sein Name auch erst später auf (V. 9f.), und noch später (V. 17ff.) erst steht

---

[75] So, e.g., Zahn, *Römer* (1910) 104; Flückiger, "Unterscheidung" (1954). Cf. also Weiss, *Römer* (1899) 100–101, who thinks that διό draws an inference from 1:28–32.

[76] So, e.g., Sanday and Headlam, *Romans* (1902) 55; Cranfield, *Romans* (1975) 1.141; Wilckens, *Römer* (1978) 1.123–24; Fitzmyer, *Romans* (1993) 299.

[77] Fridrichsen, "Jude" (1922) 187.

[78] Bultmann, "Glossen" (1947) 200: "Alle Schwierigkeiten verschwinden, wenn man den Vers als Glosse aushebt."

[79] See (excl. scriptural references) Rom 1:24; 4:22; 13:5; 15:7, 22; 1 Cor 12:3; 14:13; 2 Cor 1:20; 2:8; 4:16; 5:9; 12:7, 10; Gal 4:31; Phil 2:9; 1 Thess 3:1; 5:11; Phlm 1:8.

[80] Cf., e.g., Rom 15:7 with 2 Cor 1:20.

[81] *Römerbrief* (1957) 1.60–61.

er eindeutig im Licht der Ausführungen."[82] Having recognized that 1:18–32 spoke of the gentile world, Schlier simply ignores the presence of διό in 2:1.

The second proposal, viz. that διό denotes an inference drawn from 1:32, merits some attention because this would seem to correspond to the use of διό in 1:24 (cf. διὰ τοῦτο in v. 26). However, this solution is almost certainly ruled out by the contrasting statements made in 1:32 and 2:1. In the former, the persons spoken of are said to "approve" (συνευδοκοῦσιν) of those who practice the vices discussed. In the latter, the interlocutor is charged with "judging" (κρίνων, κρίνεις) those who do such deeds. Thus, διό cannot mark a conclusion being drawn directly and solely from the preceding sentence, since it clearly does not follow from Paul's charge against those who *approve* of others' vices (1:32) that the one who *judges* others is "therefore" without excuse (2:1). C. K. Barrett's effort to pass over the logical contrast by arguing that διό connects 2:1 with 1:32a, while v. 32b is "parenthetic," is strained.[83]

The proposition that διό points to 1:18–32 as a whole is to be preferred. Thus understood, neither is διό deprived of its basic inferential function (as in the first suggestion) nor is the conclusion it marks at odds with Paul's reasoning (as in the second suggestion). That διό alludes to the whole passage and not just a portion of it is furthermore strengthened by the stylistic change in 2:1, where Paul turns from the general third person language characteristic of 1:18–32 to a direct address in the second person singular. Verbal allusions in 2:1 to the earlier part of 1:18–32 support this as well, such as the word ἀναπολόγητος (cf. ἀναπολογήτους in 1:20). This means, in other words, that 1:18–32 as a whole provides the cause (διό) for the interlocutor in 2:1 being "without excuse" when he judges others. This conclusion corresponds well with Johannes P. Louw's and Eugene A. Nida's assessment of the function of διό (and διόπερ): These are "relatively emphatic markers of result, usually denoting the fact that the inference is self-evident—'therefore, for this reason, for this very reason, so then'. . . . What

---

[82] "Juden" (1966) 38. For Schlier's discussion of Rom 1:18–32, see his "Heiden" (1966).
[83] *Romans* (1957) 43.

precedes constitutes the reason, but the result may be effectively introduced by referring back to the reason."[84]

That this is the basic function of διό in 2:1 is indeed currently advocated by the bulk of interpreters. However, there is a wide disagreement about what implications this may have for the identity of Paul's interlocutor. And here the question of the proper function of διό often fades away. It seems to me that the different conclusions reached in this respect depend largely upon the way in which scholars approach the text as text, i.e. whether they prefer to read it (more) linearly and progressively (in this case, from 1:18 onwards) or (more) reversely or retrogressively (from 2:17 backwards).

Endorsed by many, Cranfield's reading may serve as an example of the latter approach. His starting point is the following: "That in 2:17ff Paul is apostrophizing the typical Jew is clear; but there is no explicit indication before v.17 that it is the Jews whom he has in mind." Having provided some "weighty reasons for thinking that Paul had the Jews in mind right from 2.1,"[85] he then—and only then—turns to the question of the function of διό in 2:1. He finds that the suggestion that it looks back to 1:18–32 as a whole

> is surely the most natural solution; but its acceptance has been hindered, particularly for those who feel sure that Paul has the Jews in mind right from the beginning of chapter 2, by the common assumption that in 1.18–32 he is concerned *exclusively* with the Gentiles. And, on this assumption, it is indeed difficult to see any sense in which 2.1 can be said to follow from 1.18–32. How can it follow from the fact that the Gentiles fall under the condemnation declared in 1.18–32 that the Jew is without excuse if he judges?

Cranfield's answer is that "in 1.18–32 (though no doubt Paul has especially in mind the sins of the Gentile world) it is not exclusively the sin of the Gentiles which is being declared, but the sin of all men. The διό then presents no difficulty." In 2:1, then, "Paul himself, it is scarcely to be doubted, was thinking especially of the typical Jew."[86]

---

[84] L&N § 89.47 with n. 7.
[85] Most, if not all, of these "weighty reasons" fall under categories dealt with below.
[86] *Romans* (1975) 1.137–42; quotations on pp. 137, 138, 141–42 (italics his).

I find this kind of approach and reasoning altogether unacceptable. To begin with, a backward reading of the text can be utterly misleading and is to be avoided as far as possible.[87] After all, would Paul's audience have reasoned as Cranfield does? Would Paul himself have wanted his audience to reason in such a way? As Stowers observes, "[t]exts normally progress from a beginning to an ending. The reader's knowledge and understanding progress as the text provides information and allusions to cultural codes, other texts, and appeals to protocols of persuasion."[88] Would Paul, then, have intended his audience to read the letter repeatedly in order to perceive fully the reverse reference assumed by Cranfield and others? Hardly. Paul was writing, not a theological treatise to be understood only after a careful study,[89] but a letter. Perhaps we may call it theological or didactic or even doctrinal, but a letter it is nonetheless, the message of which, as in other genuine letters, progresses from beginning to end. While I grant that the identity of Paul's interlocutor becomes more and more explicit in the flow of the discourse, when read in proper order the text affords no good reason to infer that Paul turns his address to a Jew in 2:1 nor that his readers would have perceived it so. In the words of R. Dean Anderson: "Keeping in

---

[87] Thus, I strongly dissent from Fitzmyer's proposal that one can discern the structure of Rom "most easily by beginning with the end of the letter and working forward [backward?]" (*Romans* [1993] 96). Cf. also Wright's reverse reading in his "Law" (1996), though it should be noted that he does not focus specifically upon 2:1–11, since he is mostly concerned with the question of the Law in the chapter (first mentioned in v. 12).

[88] *Rereading* (1994) 30.

[89] Dabourne's critique of Pauline scholarship is apropos (*Purpose* [1999] 31–33): "[T]he model of the apostle implicit in most Pauline studies is of Paul as a scholar writing for other scholars. This Paul is a curious amalgam of first- and twentieth-century models, writing theological arguments for the first numbers of *NTS* or *ZNW*, AD 56. . . . The problem is that we treat Paul's texts as though he were doing what scholars do when they write for each other. . . . We make Paul in our own image when we work on the assumption that he was doing the kind of thing we do, and when we unconsciously treat the text as though what we are looking for is what he intended his readers to find, even though we are not his intended readers. [This phenomenon] has turned Paul into a scholar and his letters into abstruse scholarly writings, however situational and polemical."

mind the necessity of reading an ancient text *linearly* . . ., one cannot expect the reader to have interpreted the διό of 2.1 as referring to anything else but the foregoing."[90] Hence, unless simply swept over, the inferential conjunction διό indicates that the judging individual addressed in 2:1 is "without excuse" (ἀναπολόγητος) precisely because he is one of the people described previously in 1:18–32, viz. gentiles, the very people who are "without excuse" (ἀναπολογήτους, 1:20) because they failed to acknowledge and worship God properly.

Moreover, Cranfield's widely accepted explanation of the causal connection between 2:1 and 1:18–32 strikes me as surprisingly illogical. He admits that 1:18–32 as a whole provides the reason for Paul's interlocutor in 2:1 being "without excuse," thus taking into account the inferential function of διό. He also admits that the former text describes "especially" the gentile world. But then he goes on to argue that in 2:1 Paul "was thinking especially of the typical Jew." (In fact, Cranfield's subsequent discussion takes for granted that Paul had the Jew exclusively in mind.) How can it follow from Paul's indictment "especially" of the gentiles that the Jew is "especially" without excuse when he judges others? Surely we must give Paul credit for being more consistent than this! It seems reasonable to assume that if Paul, in his lengthy account of 1:18–32, wanted to expose the reasons for Jews in particular being without excuse, he would have striven to describe especially and explicitly the sins of the Jewish people instead of the gentile world. Expressively, Cranfield has to read Jews into 1:18–32 in order to justify his logic. But even if we were to allow for the possibility that Jews are partially included among the people described in 1:18–32, it still does not follow that the passage gives reasons for Jews "especially" being inexcusable.

In a recent study on Romans 1–5, Simon J. Gathercole has also attempted to solve this problem. Having found that 1:18–32 speaks of gentiles, that 2:1–5 addresses a Jew, and that διό draws an inference from the former passage as a whole, Gathercole contends that "the logic of the ar-

---

[90] *Rhetorical* (1996) 189 n. 476 (his emphasis). Anderson, however, takes 1:18–32, and thus 2:1, as referring to "mankind in general" (discussed below). On the linear reading of ancient texts, see also Kennedy, *New Testament* (1984) 5–6.

gument is: 1:18–32 They are without excuse and subject to judgment because of their wickedness (because God's wrath is on the wicked). 2:1 Therefore you are *also* without excuse and subject to judgment because you *also* do wicked deeds."[91] Though more subtly, Gathercole's solution is as contrived as that of Cranfield. The logic of Paul's argument is not entirely as the former describes it. There is no "also" in Paul's text; he does not say διὸ ἀναπολόγητος εἶ καὶ σύ. This "also" has been inserted by Gathercole in order to make a (slightly) better sense of the logical connection between the two passages as he perceives it.[92] And Gathercole is by no means alone in seeking to overcome the problem, whether explicitly or implicitly, by means of such an insertion.[93] I will return to this shortly.

Along with tendencies to read and reason in reverse, certain presuppositions about Jews in antiquity greatly affect interpretations of Paul's text. As we recall, Cranfield comes to the conclusion that "though no doubt Paul has especially in mind the sins of the Gentile world," it is the "sin of all men" which is being declared in 1:18–32. Why, then, does he infer that in 2:1 Paul is (primarily) addressing "the typical Jew" instead of any sinful "man" who judges others? Doubtless the answer lies partly in the common assumption that the hypocritical and judgmental character of the interlocutor in 2:1–5 would unmistakably have pertained to Jews. Gathercole, for instance, asserts: "The Jewish credentials of the character addressed in 2:1–16 cannot be dismissed . . . [T]he designation 'the one who judges' is appropriate to a Jew, not because the Jewish people were more judgmental than others but because they took pride in being able to judge, in the sense of *discern*."[94] Whatever the exact difference between being "more judgmental than others" and taking "pride in being able to judge, in the sense of discern," Gathercole's presumption that Paul's interlocutor could only

---

[91] *Boasting* (2002) 204–5 (my emphasis).
[92] It should be noted that even if Paul had added καὶ σύ, that does not necessarily mean that the person addressed in 2:1 is not one of those spoken of in 1:18–32.
[93] See esp. Nygren, *Romans* (1949) 116; Kuss, *Römerbrief* (1957) 1.60–61; Wilckens, *Römer* (1978) 1.123–24 (discussed below). Cf. also Carras, "Romans 2,1–29" (1992) 193; Bell, *No One* (1998) 138–40; Dabourne, *Purpose* (1999) 128–30; Carter, *Paul* (2002) 149–50.
[94] *Boasting* (2002) 198 (his emphasis).

have been Jewish is gravely misguided. To be sure, Jews may have judged—or taken "pride in being able to judge"—the non-Jewish world, and, with some modifications perhaps, Paul was no exception to this, as Romans 1:18–32 testifies.[95] But it is a profound historical distortion to maintain that it would somehow have been self-evident that Paul's interlocutor in Romans 2:1–5 was a Jew, an understanding unseen until Augustine.[96] Stowers correctly objects to such anachronistic notions:

> No evidence exists to show that the character of the hypocritical and arrogant judge was ever applied to Jews until after Paul's time, and then by Christians.... There is absolutely no justification for reading 2:1–5 as Paul's attack on 'the hypocrisy of the Jew.' No one in the first century would have identified the *ho alazôn* [i.e. the pretentious person] with Judaism. That popular interpretation depends upon anachronistically reading later Christian characterizations of Jews as 'hypocritical Pharisees'.... The text simply lacks anything to indicate that the person is a Jew.[97]

Gathercole infers that it is primarily "the Jewishness of 2:1–16" which betrays that Paul's interlocutor must be a Jew. "So," he gathers, "it is no surprise that by the time Paul comes to 2:12–13, he is operating within categories not only that are thoroughly Jewish but also that *could only be Jewish*."[98] In this latter respect, Gathercole is quite right. How could these

---

[95] Cf. esp. Gal 2:15; 1 Thess 4:5a. As Fredriksen notes, "even when addressing Gentiles and in some sense acting as their advocate, [Paul] refers to them, quite unselfconsciously, as 'sinners' (Gal 2:15). Their characteristic social and sexual sins . . . are the varied expression of a more fundamental spiritual error: they worship idols" ("Judaism" [2002] 237). I find it both curious and disappointing how meagerly Donaldson treats Rom 1:18–32 in his extensive study of Paul's convictions about the gentiles (*Paul* [1997]).

[96] And, in fact, only found in his later writings; see Schelkle, *Paulus* (1956) 70–71.

[97] *Rereading* (1994) 13, 101. In an apt critique of Dunn's interpretation (see below), Stowers observes (p. 28): "Paul has been explicit about gentile idolatry only up to 2:1. The picture of the Jew as a hypocritical and arrogant judge would have to be so obvious to ancient readers that they could recognize the sudden, unsignaled shift at 2:1, or else Paul miscalculated and they would have to reread backward from 2:17f., if indeed they understood 2:17 to be a generalization about Jews."

[98] *Boasting* (2002) 198–99 (his emphasis).

"categories" be otherwise than Jewish? The author of the text is a Jew, speaking of matters which are Jewish.[99] Gathercole, however, takes this to mean that it is Paul's interlocutor who could only be Jewish, implying that the person dealt with here is a Jewish "other," thus segregating both Paul and his gentile audience from their Jewish context,[100] a common inclination indeed among interpreters of the letter.

Gathercole's determination of the identity of Paul's interlocutor is mostly dependent upon that of Dunn, who, according to the former, "adduces numerous excellent arguments for a Jewish 'target' in 2:1–16."[101] What is characteristic of Dunn's interpretation of this text, however, is precisely the tendency to distance Paul from the Jewish convictions expressed in it and thus from his own Jewishness. To begin with, Dunn smooths over the difficulties involved in taking the interlocutor as a Jew simply by noting that "διό usually denotes an inference or conclusion drawn from what went before" without much further concern for its function in Romans 2:1. He rightly notes that a "line of argument which accused Jews of idolatry and homosexual practice would be unlikely to commend much support, either from the judgmental Jew or from the God-worshiping Gentile who had previously been attracted to Judaism." But then he strangely asserts: "But the list of 1:29–31 largely consists of vices into which an individual can slide without being fully aware of it. In particular, the last five items are applicable to the sort of attitude among the Pharisees already criticized within the Jesus tradition."[102] Moreover, according to Dunn,

> [Paul's] readers would imagine someone listening to the polemic of 1:18–32 and heartily joining in its condemnation of idolatry, homosexual practice, and the

---

[99] Christianity as "the idea of the third race neither Jewish nor pagan" (Stowers, *Rereading* [1994] 23) is not at issue in Paul's letter.

[100] This understanding is even implied in the very title of Gathercole's work: "Where is Boasting? Early Jewish Soteriology and *Paul's Response* in Romans 1–5."

[101] *Boasting* (2002) 198.

[102] *Romans* (1988) 1.79–80. Dunn refers to Mark 7:9–13 (cf. vv. 21–22) as evidence for Pharisees "already" being "criticized within the Jesus tradition." The last five items in Paul's list are "disobedient to parents" (γονεῦσιν ἀπειθεῖς), "senseless" (ἀσυνέτους), "faithless" (ἀσυνθέτους), "loveless" (ἀστόργους), and "merciless" (ἀνελεήμονας) (trans. Dunn).

rest. . . . Paul's denunciation is abrupt: 'you do the same things'. . . . Paul's attack is aimed most directly at what he sees to be a typically Jewish attitude. . . . In fact we would probably not be far from the mark if we were to conclude that Paul's interlocutor is Paul himself—Paul the unconverted Pharisee, expressing attitudes Paul remembered so well as having been his own![103]

It is striking how many of Dunn's "numerous excellent arguments" for the interlocutor in 2:1–5 being a Jew are sought from allusions to Jewish writings which are critical not of Jews but of gentiles. Dunn repeatedly insists that Paul turns such line of thought "on its head" in order to censure the Jewish interlocutor.[104] But, as we shall see in the next section, it is far more likely that Paul's potential allusions to these texts are meant to bring with them their original context, viz. indictments against non-Jews, and thus support Paul's case against his gentile interlocutor. Furthermore, in his attempt to dissociate the views expressed in 1:18–32 from (the now "converted") Paul, Dunn refers with approval to similar efforts made earlier by Anders Nygren. According to the latter, Paul "merely presents what they [i.e. the Jews] had themselves said. . . . To the Jew, who thinks like that, Paul says, 'The fact that you pass judgment does not make you safe before God'."[105] However, it must be pointed out that there is no sign of Romans 1:18–32 expressing anything but Paul's own convictions. Paul appears to be himself a Jew "who thinks like that."

Interpreters commonly draw a parallel between Paul's address in Romans 2:1 and Nathan's dramatic indictment of David in Second Samuel 12:7 (LXX 2 Kgdms): "You are the man!"[106] While such an analogy may to some

---

[103] *Romans* (1988) 1.89–91. Dunn's reading shows close resemblance with Beker's view that Paul "intends to set a trap for the Jewish auditor" (*Paul* [1980] 79; cf. also Nygren, *Romans* [1949] 113–18). For discussion of and arguments against such interpretations, see Elliott, *Rhetoric* (1990) esp. 173–90.

[104] *Romans* (1988) 1.78–93.

[105] *Romans* (1949) 115–16.

[106] E.g. Sanday and Headlam, *Romans* (1902) 54; Lagrange, *Romains* (1950) 43; Bornkamm, "Gesetz" (1963) 95; Popkes, "Aufbau" (1982) 497; Schmeller, *Paulus* (1987) 282; Dunn, *Romans* (1988) 1.79; Stuhlmacher, *Römer* (1989) 38–40; Hays, *Echoes* (1989) 49; Stowers, *Rereading* (1994) 12; Boyarin, *Jew* (1994) 87; Bell, *No One* (1998) 139.

extent be appropriate, it can be carried too far. This is shown, for instance, by the way in which it is applied by Ulrich Wilckens. Having concluded that διό alludes to 1:18–32 as a whole, but that Paul's interlocutor in 2:1 must nevertheless be a Jew, Wilckens observes that one would actually have expected Paul to say διὸ ἀναπολόγητος εἶ καὶ σύ if he wanted to state that the Jew is "also" without excuse. Wilckens' explanation of this "absence" of καὶ σύ from the text is that Paul intended to surprise his Jewish interlocutor precisely as Nathan surprised David, but a "καὶ σύ würde diesen Überraschungseffekt abschwächen."[107]

The element of surprise in Paul's text should not be overstated. Unlike Nathan, Paul does not turn to his addressee in an entirely unexpected exclamation: "You are the man!" There is at least one significant difference between the two accounts. It is decisive for the exposing effect of Nathan's parable prior to the indictment that the listener, David, is totally unaware of the fact that he himself is being spoken of. Paul, on the other hand, is not telling a cryptic parable in 1:18–32 but alluding to chronicled history, and there is little doubt that his readers would have been aware of the fact that they, as non-Jews, were the subject of this history in which *all* gentiles are said to be under God's wrath. The exposing of the interlocutor has thus already begun in 1:18–32, which suggests that the turn at 2:1 may not be quite as unanticipated and dramatic as often thought. Wilckens' argument is a lucid example of the kind of exegesis called for in order to locate a Jewish interlocutor in 2:1.

This is not to say that there is no element of surprise whatsoever at this point in Paul's discourse. But, while the change of style is certainly abrupt and while Paul appears to portray a somewhat startled interlocutor (see esp. v. 3), it should be noted that 2:1 merely draws a logical conclusion from the preceding: "Therefore (διό) you have no excuse, O man (ὦ ἄνθρωπε), everyone (πᾶς) who judges." What Paul implies is that the interlocutor should have realized already by the reminder in 1:18–32 that he is no better off than the persons depicted there, precisely because he is one of them. Indeed, as if this were not clear enough, Paul continues by referring to his previous words and thus stating the obvious: "for (γάρ) when you judge

---

[107] *Römer* (1978) 1.123–24.

another, you condemn yourself, for (γάρ) you who judge do the same things (τὰ αὐτὰ πράσσεις)." Since Paul provides no further substantiations for his claim that the interlocutor does "the same things," it is only natural to assume that these have already been presented. In other words, the individual addressed condemns himself when he judges others simply because he himself is one of those spoken of in 1:18–32.

In sum, there are many weighty reasons to refute the common view that Paul has a Jewish interlocutor in mind in 2:1. A linear and progressive approach to the text, in which full account is taken of the inferential function of διό, suggests instead that the interlocutor is thought of as belonging to the group of people described in 1:18–32, that is, a gentile.

2.2.2. The Gentile Identity of Paul's Interlocutor in Romans 2:1–5

Not all scholars claim that Paul's interlocutor in 2:1–5 is either a Jew or a gentile. Some hold that Paul is here addressing "mankind" in general.[108] Apart from being based on the assumption that 1:18–32 refers to all humanity, this is thought to be implied by Paul's address "O man" (ὦ ἄνθρωπε) in 2:1. However, as often noted, this form of address typically occurs in writings in which a dialogical style as that of Paul is employed, and should rather be rendered "mister," "sir," "fellow," and the like.[109] Epictetus, in particular, provides us with numerous examples of this kind of expression being used in dialogues. He relates the following incident: "To-day a man (τις) was talking to me about a priesthood of Augustus. I say to him, 'Mister (ἄνθρωπε), drop the matter; you will be spending a great deal to no purpose.'"[110] To a student of his, Epictetus remarks with a touch of irony:

> Suppose someone approaches you when you are going in pale and trembling, and says, 'Why are you trembling, fellow (ἄνθρωπε)? What is the affair that concerns you? Does Caesar inside the palace bestow virtue and vice upon those who

---

[108] E.g. Zahn, *Römer* (1910) 106–7; Barrett, *Romans* (1957) 43–44; Schmidt, *Römer* (1963) 41–42; Segal, *Paul* (1990) 258–59; Winninge, *Sinners* (1995) 282–84; Anderson, *Rhetorical* (1996) 186–89; Engberg-Pedersen, *Paul* (2000) 202.

[109] See esp. Stowers, *Diatribe* (1981) 85–93.

[110] *Diatr.* 1.19.26 (ἄνθρωπε is trans. as "man" in the LCL).

appear before him?' 'Why do you . . . make mock of me and add to my other ills?' 'But yet, philosopher (φιλόσοφε), tell me, why are you trembling? Is not the danger death, or prison, or bodily pain, or exile, or disrepute? Why, what else can it be? Is it a vice at all, or anything that shares in vice? What was it, then, that *you* used to call these things?' 'What have I to do with you, fellow (ἄνθρωπε)? My own evils are enough for me.'[111]

Correspondingly, in Romans 2:1 Paul is not addressing "mankind" in general, but simply using a commonplace expression characteristic of the dialogical style. At the same time, however, it should not be ruled out that by the vocative ἄνθρωπε Paul intends to connect the person addressed with the ἀνθρώπων mentioned in 1:18, which, in turn, supports the conclusion that the interlocutor is precisely one of them. If so, it should be recalled that Paul's words in 1:18 are not related to all humanity but to a particular group of "men," viz. gentiles.[112]

As noted above, it is not the interlocutor's judging per se that provokes Paul's charges against him. Paul seems to be more concerned with the interlocutor's "doing" than "judging," as shown in 2:2 where the act of judging is not even brought up, v. 3 in which Paul does not fail to speak of the interlocutor's doing besides judging, and vv. 5–6 in which doings are clearly under discussion, not to mention the following discourse. In fact, the judgmental character of Paul's own words in 1:18–32 suggests that he may even have approved of such judging (cf. 2:2). Why, then, is this particular person's judging not welcomed? Because he himself falls under the category of people at whom his judging is directed. When he judges the gentiles of 1:18–32 he condemns himself because he is one of them and

---

[111] *Diatr.* 2.19.17–19 (italics original in trans.). See also, in *Diatr.* 1: 1.23; 2.33; 4.9; 17.21; 21.2; 22.20; 25.27; 29.41; in *Diatr.* 2: 1.35; 4.3; 6.17; 7.6; 14.21; 15.3, 7, 18; 16.41; 17.27, 33, 35; 19.16; 20.4, 9, 28; 21.11, 21; 23.5, 37, 42; 24.22; in *Diatr.* 3: 1.22, 30; 5.15; 7.21; 9.6; 12.10; 14.2, 5; 15.9; 17.6; 19.5; 20.4, 5, 16; 21.13; 22.51, 81; 23.23; 24.77, 83; in *Diatr.* 4: 1.134; 4.20; 8.35, 38; 9.6; 13.10.

[112] To maintain, on the other hand, that the adj. πᾶς in 2:1 alludes to πᾶσαν in 1:18 is to stretch the point; so, e.g., Fridrichsen, "Jude" (1922) 187. Whereas πᾶς in 2:1 qualifies the person spoken of in the text, viz. ὁ κρίνων, πᾶσαν in 1:18 qualifies not the persons spoken of but their ἀσέβειαν καὶ ἀδικίαν. Any calculated connection between the adjs. is therefore improbable.

thus guilty of doing the same things. It is this inconsistency which is the focal point of Paul's admonition. His aim is to expose the interlocutor's deceptive behavior and thus his actual position.

That the first person plural οἴδαμεν in v. 2 is employed to introduce a fact which is generally accepted,[113] presumably on scriptural basis, is no doubt correct.[114] It should not be overlooked, however, that v. 2 may also serve as a restatement of the basic contents of 1:18–32, particularly if τὸ κρίμα τοῦ θεοῦ in 2:2 corresponds to ὀργὴ θεοῦ in 1:18. This is likely because God's "judgment" is here clearly meant to be in an unfavorable sense.[115] In 2:1 the interlocutor had been informed of his own self-condemnation. Now he is reminded of the fact that those who do the things described in 1:18–32 are indeed subject to God's condemnation.

Paul follows this up by sarcastically remarking (v. 3): "Do you suppose, fellow (ἄνθρωπε), you who judge those who do such deeds and yet do them yourself, that *you* (σύ) will escape the judgment of God (τὸ κρίμα τοῦ θεοῦ)?" What is implied is that for some reason the interlocutor thinks that he is in a more superior and auspicious position than those whom he judges and that he will therefore be excepted from God's (unfavorable) judgment. The unexpressed answer to Paul's rhetorical question is, of course, that the interlocutor's position is no more advantageous than that of other sinful gentiles.

Dunn calls attention to the "striking parallel" between Paul's words here and *Psalms of Solomon* 15.8: "And those who do lawlessness [i.e. gentile sinners] shall not escape the judgment of the Lord" (καὶ οὐκ ἐκφεύξονται οἱ ποιοῦντες ἀνομίαν τὸ κρίμα κυρίου). According to Dunn, "[t]he attitude that Paul hits out against is just that expressed in *Psalms of Solomon* and in almost the precise words used by Paul."[116] In agreement with

---

[113] Cf. 3:19; 8:22, 28; 1 Cor 8:1, 4; 2 Cor 5:1.

[114] So, e.g., Cranfield, *Romans* (1975) 1.143; Dunn, *Romans* (1988) 1.80, 90. Dunn observes, correctly I think, that "the 'we' who know God's judgment are most obviously those familiar with the Jewish scriptures," but his inference that this would primarily involve a Jewish interlocutor is too rapidly drawn; cf. the discussion above in Ch. 2 sec. 2.2.1.

[115] Cf. esp. 3:8; 1 Cor 11:29, 34; Gal 5:10.

[116] *Romans* (1988) 1.81 (Dunn's trans. of *Pss. Sol.* 15.8).

Dunn, I find the resemblance here indeed striking, but, unlike him, I see no compelling reason to assume that Paul "hits out against" the view expressed in *Psalms of Solomon* 15.8. On the contrary, if anything, the parallel evident here between these texts suggests that their authors both shared the conviction that sinful gentiles would not elude God's judgment.[117] This, I insist, is a more straightforward reading of Paul's text and thus to be preferred. It implies that, instead of being concerned with some sort of twisting of contemporary Jewish convictions about non-Jews, Paul the Jew is reminding his imaginary partner in dialogue that he is no better off than other sinful gentiles. Paul's potential allusion to Jewish texts and traditions in this respect is then meant to be supportive of his case against the gentile interlocutor.[118]

The same goes for Paul's second rhetorical question (v. 4): "Or do you think lightly of the riches of God's kindness (χρηστότητος) and forbearance (ἀνοχῆς) and patience (μακροθυμίας), ignorant of the fact that God's goodness (τὸ χρηστόν) leads you to repentance (εἰς μετάνοιάν σε ἄγει)?" Dunn claims that this text includes "several factors" which "confirm" that Paul's interlocutor is Jewish.[119] These are, however, not easily discerned in his discussion. To be sure, there are some factors here which were prominent in Jewish teaching on salvation, such as the requirement of repentance (μετάνοια). But there is little ground for asserting that "Paul thus seems here to turn one of the Jewish interlocutor's own key beliefs against him." While he is right in stressing the significance of the views expressed in Wisdom of Solomon for the understanding of Paul's words, Dunn's assumption that such views would have been foreign to Paul himself and that he brings them up only for refutation is unfounded: "We will not go far wrong if we assume that it was the attitude expressed particularly in Wisd Sol 15:1–6 which Paul 'heard' being expressed by his Jewish interlocutor and as requiring the strong response of v 4."[120] It is remarkable that Dunn nonetheless admits that in Wisdom of Solomon "repentance [is] seen as

---

[117] Cf. also Sir 16:13a: οὐκ ἐκφεύξεται ἐν ἁρπάγματι ἁμαρτωλός.
[118] Similarly also Elliott, *Rhetoric* (1990) 185–90.
[119] See *Romans* (1988) 1.81–83.
[120] *Romans* (1988) 1.82–83.

something which the Gentiles need to be granted more than Israel," and that Paul's thought with εἰς μετάνοιαν ἄγει is "more of giving opportunity for repentance (as in Wisd Sol 11:23; 12:10 . . .) than of giving repentance itself (as in Wisd Sol 12:19)." Significantly, the latter reference has to do with "repentance for sins" primarily of the Jewish people, while the former two are spoken within the context of God giving the gentiles an opportunity to repent.[121] In light of the close parallels between the indictment of gentiles in Wisdom of Solomon and Paul's own indictment of the same group of people in Romans 1:18–32, it seems reasonable to infer that behind Paul's utterance in 2:4 lies the thought of the opportunity for repentance given by God to gentiles (cf. 12:2).[122] This is also suggested by God's attributes specified in the verse. These were not only envisaged as being enjoyed by the Jewish people,[123] but also by all who were in need of God's kindness, forbearance, and patience.[124] Thus the attributes designate God's love for and rule over the whole world. More importantly for the present discussion, it is a well known characteristic of many Jewish writings from antiquity that God deals differently with the sins of the Jewish people—the regular atonement for which had specifically been provided for—than with the sins of non-Jews, a view which comes to clear expression in Second Maccabees 6:14–15:

> In the case of the other nations (τῶν ἄλλων ἐθνῶν) the Lord waits patiently (ἀναμένει μακροθυμῶν) to punish them until they have reached the full measure of their sins (μέχρι τοῦ καταντήσαντας αὐτοὺς πρὸς ἐκπλήρωσιν ἁμαρτιῶν);

---

[121] Cf. 12:20: "For if you punished with such great care and indulgence the enemies of your servants and those deserving of death, granting them time and opportunity to give up their wickedness. . ." (NRSV).

[122] Cf. also Paul's use of the concept of "repentance" in relation to typical gentile sins in 2 Cor 12:20–21: "I fear that . . . when I come again . . . I may have to mourn over many who previously sinned (προημαρτηκότων) and have not repented (μὴ μετανοησάντων) of the impurity (ἀκαθαρσίᾳ), sexual immorality (πορνείᾳ), and licentiousness (ἀσελγείᾳ) that they have practised." Paul uses the word μετάνοια elsewhere only in 2 Cor 7:9–10, where it has somewhat different connotations.

[123] See, e.g., Ex 34:6–7; Neh 9:17; Joel 2:13; 1 Esd 5:58; Sir 5:4–7; Wis 15:1.

[124] See, e.g., Pss 24:7–8; 85:5; 144:7–9; *Pss. Sol.* 5.12–15.

but he does not deal in this way with us, in order that he may not take vengeance on us afterward when our sins have reached their height. (NRSV)

This seems to be the underlying thought in Romans 2:4, viz. "the case of the other nations."[125] There is no apparent sign of Paul turning this aspect of Jewish belief "on its head." Contrary to common opinion, Paul's choice and use of terminology in these verses point rather clearly to the non-Jewish identity of the interlocutor. Paul's rhetorical questions imply that by his sinful behavior the gentile interlocutor is manifesting his disrespect for the great kindness, forbearance, and patience which God has shown towards gentiles. In fact, at the very closing of the long series of questions and answers in the letter, Paul declares to the imaginary gentile "olive shoot" who, by implication, has been boasting over the Jewish "branches" (11:22): "See then the kindness (χρηστότητα) and the severity of God: severity towards those who have fallen, but God's kindness (χρηστότης) towards you, provided that you continue in that kindness (τῇ χρηστότητι); otherwise you will be cut off as well." Put differently, the gentile grafted on the olive tree should not dare to think lightly of God's kindness towards him, to which he actually has little claim due to his gentile roots.

At this point, Paul sets out to correct the interlocutor's erroneous standpoint by revealing to him the dreadful consequences of his disposition (v. 5): "But by your hardness (σκληρότητα, contrast God's attributes) and unrepentant heart (ἀμετανόητον καρδίαν, cf. 1:21, 24, 28) you are storing up (θησαυρίζεις) wrath (ὀργήν) for yourself on the day of wrath and revealing of God's righteous judgment (ἐν ἡμέρᾳ ὀργῆς καὶ ἀποκαλύψεως δικαιοκρισίας τοῦ θεοῦ)." That Paul's warning comes so close to the view expressed in Second Maccabees about God punishing the gentiles once and for all when they have filled their stores with sins, is probably no coinci-

---

[125] See also the illuminating discussion in Stowers, *Rereading* (1994) 104–7, in which he refers to Sam K. Williams' study of the term ἀνοχή in Rom 3:26 (the only other occurrence of the term in Paul's letters): "Williams has shown that the passage [in 3:25–26a] speaks about God overlooking gentile sin because of his 'restraint' or 'holding back'. . . . God has failed to punish gentiles fully for their sin in the past so that their liability for punishment has accumulated" (p. 105). Similarly also Gärtner, *Areopagus* (1955) 239–40.

dence. Nor is the obvious reference to God's wrath (ὀργὴ θεοῦ, 1:18) against gentile sinners spoken of earlier. Paul's aim here is to make the interlocutor open his eyes to the fact that, contrary to the latter's opinion and pretense, his conduct merely increases his sins along with the accumulation of gentile sins detailed in 1:18–32. When God's sentence is passed he will have no chance whatsoever because God "will render to everyone according to his deeds" (v. 6).

2.2.3. Paul's Gentile Interlocutor and Judgment according to Deeds (2:6–16)

The effect of God's judgment according to deeds (2:6) is listed in vv. 7–16. I have already discussed this text in some detail (see sec. 1 above) and exhibited the way in which it seems to function as subordinate to the preceding discourse in the chapter. That, in turn, suggests that the dialogue with the interlocutor is still in view, which may also explain why the primary focus of the passage remains on gentile conduct. My aim in this section is not to examine every aspect of this difficult text but to consider briefly what its statements may imply with respect to Paul's partner in dialogue.

Paul begins with expounding the consequence of God's judgment according to deeds. It means, on the one hand, that those who "by endurance in doing good " (καθ᾽ ὑπομονὴν ἔργου ἀγαθοῦ) seek for "glory, honor, and incorruption" will be given "eternal life" (ζωὴν αἰώνιον, contrast 1:32) (v. 7). For those, on the other hand, who "out of discord" (ἐξ ἐριθείας)[126] even "disobey the truth" (ἀπειθοῦσι τῇ ἀληθείᾳ, cf. 1:18, 25), being instead "obedient to unrighteousness" (πειθομένοις τῇ ἀδικίᾳ, cf. 1:18, 29), there will be "wrath and anger" (ὀργὴ[ν] καὶ θυμό[ν], cf. 1:18; 2:5)[127] (v. 8). These statements are then iterated in vv. 9–10 in a chiastic manner, specifically highlighting the ἑκάστῳ of v. 6 by adding that God's judgment according to deeds pertains both to Jews and non-Jews; Jews "first" (πρῶτον), to be sure, but others no less (cf. 1:16): There will be "affliction and dis-

---

[126] The meaning of this word is disputed. Cf. 2 Cor 12:20; Gal 5:20; Phil 1:17; 2:3.
[127] The words ὀργὴ καὶ θυμός are surely meant to be in the acc.; cf. ζωὴν αἰώνιον in v. 7.

tress" for those who do "evil things" (τὸ κακόν), whilst for those who do "good things" (τὸ ἀγαθόν) there will be "glory, honor, and peace." In other words, in light of his exposing of the interlocutor's actual doings, Paul now declares that, whatever differences there may be between Jews and non-Jews in other respects (cf. v. 14), both groups will be judged according the same criterion, viz. their deeds. This implies that, although πρῶτον, Jews are not the only ones who are accountable to God but gentiles as well. God shows no partiality in this respect. The maxim of judgment according to deeds pertains to all without exception. What will count at the day of judgment, according to Paul, is whether or not one has truly complied with God's will manifested in the Law: "The doers of the Law (οἱ ποιηταὶ νόμου) will be justified (δικαιωθήσονται)" (v. 13b). Mere "hearers of the Law" (οἱ ἀκροαταὶ νόμου), i.e. those who know what the Law says but do not act accordingly, will not be considered "righteous" (δίκαιοι) (v. 13a). This applies equally to Jews and gentiles.[128] Verse 14, then, is largely hypothetical.[129] That this is the case is indicated by the use of ὅταν (for ὅτε ἄν: "whenever") with the subjunctive. And yet, the example drawn appears to be a potential one as well. Paul insists that, although gentiles do not have the Law "by birth" (φύσει), they may nevertheless act in conformity with the Law (τὰ τοῦ νόμου ποιῶσιν). Indeed, it will become evident on the day of judgment that such gentiles (οἵτινες), i.e. those who act in conformity

---

[128] Differently Dunn, *Romans* (1988) 1.97, 104–5, who takes οἱ ἀκροαταὶ νόμου as a reference to Jews specifically. According to Dunn, here "once again, Paul drives a wedge between the interconnected elements of Jewish self-understanding." "What is attacked, therefore, is the self-confidence of the synagogue attender who faithfully hears the law being read Sabbath by Sabbath and who in consequence counts himself as one of the righteous, one of the chosen people. . ." It must be pointed out, however, that the "synagogue attender" may as well be a gentile adherent to Judaism. Moreover, it is unlikely that Paul intends simply to criticize heedful hearings of synagogue attenders. The contrast between "hearing" (*ergo* knowing) and "doing" appears rather to be aimed at the distinction between hearing without doing, on the one hand, and hearing and doing, on the other. On hearing as prerequisite for doing, cf. Rom 10:14, 17.

[129] For other alternatives, cf. Räisänen, *Paul* (1983) 103–5; Laato, *Paulus* (1991) 100–104.

with the Law, have "the work of the Law" (τὸ ἔργον τοῦ νόμου)[130] inscribed in their hearts (καρδίαις) (vv. 15–16).

What, then, may all this imply for Paul's interlocutor in particular? Obviously, he falls in group with such evildoers as the ones spoken of in vv. 8–9, and like those who sin "in a lawless manner" (ἀνόμως, v. 12a) he will perish accordingly (cf. vv. 2, 3). Whether he is thought of as a "hearer of the Law" (v. 13a) is not evident at this point, but he clearly is no "doer of the Law" (v. 13b; contrast vv. 1 [τὰ αὐτὰ πράσσεις], 3 [καὶ ποιῶν αὐτά]). He does not act in conformity with the Law as do some of his fellow gentiles (v. 14). By contrast, due to his hardness and unrepentant "heart" (καρδίαν) (v. 5), the interlocutor will not be able to show "the work of the Law" to be written on his heart on that day when God, through Christ Jesus, judges the secrets hidden behind his appearance (cf. vv. 15–16).

2.3. Paul's Gentile Interlocutor in Romans 2:17–29

In spite of the often acknowledged difficulties involved in reading Romans 2:17–29 as an indictment of Jews, and despite the fact that Paul does not actually state that the individual addressed in v. 17 *is* a Jew, only that he seeks to be *called* a Jew, no one to my knowledge has approached the problem of identification by questioning the Jewish identity of Paul's interlocutor. Several factors suggest that it may be fruitful to do so.

As we saw in Chapter Three above, epistolary interlocutors tend to remain the same unless otherwise indicated. I have already pointed out that the word Ἰουδαῖος in 2:17 serves poorly as such an indicator. Moreover, I have also argued that Paul's address in v. 17 most likely is a resumption of the one in vv. 1–5, and that the person addressed in vv. 1–5 is a gentile. Hence, the question arises if interpreters have overlooked the possibility that the interlocutor in vv. 17–29 is not a Jew at all, despite the use of the word Ἰουδαῖος in v. 17.

In the following, I intend to challenge the traditional reading of Romans 2:17–29 by arguing that the interlocutor in the passage is thought of not as

---

[130] This phrase is not to be confused with the pl. ἔργα νόμου, cf. sec. 4.2 below.

a (native) Jew but as an individual of gentile origin who wants to call himself a Jew.

2.3.1. A Gentile Who Wants to Call Himself a Jew (2:17a)

In 2:17 Paul continues his direct address to the interlocutor with the words εἰ δὲ σὺ Ἰουδαῖος ἐπονομάζῃ etc. The verb ἐπονομάζω (a *hapax legomenon* in the NT)[131] is here used either in the passive or the middle voice. In the former case, the sense of the verb would be "to be surnamed,"[132] whilst in the latter it would be "to classify oneself by means of a name, title, or attribution,"[133] or even "claim to be."[134] Though it may not be wise to draw too strict boundaries between the two voices in this case,[135] the sense of ἐπονομάζω in Romans 2:17 would probably have been closer to the middle.[136] Thus, Paul's address could be rendered "if you call yourself a Jew,"

---

[131] Cf., however, the variant reading ἐπωνόμασεν (act.) in Luke 6:14 D. In the LXX the verb occurs most often in the Semitic phrase ἐπωνόμασεν τὸ ὄνομα and virtually never in the middle/pass. Apart from references to the LXX, Philo uses the verb only once and then in the act. voice. Josephus, on the other hand, uses it three times in the pass. (*B.J.* 1.118; *A.J.* 2.1 [cf. below]; 4.207).

[132] LSJ s.v. 2. Cf. Josephus, *A.J.* 2.1: Esau "bore the surname of Adom [=Edom]" ("Ἄδωμος γὰρ ἐπωνομάζετο). Cf. also, e.g., Xenophon, *Oec.* 6.17; Polybius 1.29.2; Plutarch, *Tranq. an.* 472B. An interesting example occurs in Justin Martyr's *1 Apol.* 12.9, in which he speaks of Jesus Christ "from whom we have received our name of Christians" (ἀφ᾽ οὗ καὶ τὸ Χριστιανοὶ ἐπονομάζεσθαι ἐσχήκαμεν). We may even compare Josephus, *A.J.* 18.116, where he mentions "John, surnamed the Baptist" (Ἰωάννου τοῦ ἐπικαλουμένου βαπτιστοῦ). For similar uses of the verb ἐπικαλέω, see 1 Macc 2:2; Acts 1:23; 4:36; 10:5, 18, 32; 11:13; 12:12, 25; Heb 11:16. Paul never uses the verb ἐπικαλέω in this sense. For the verb ἐπιλέγω, see John 5:2.

[133] L&N § 33.132.

[134] See Cranfield, *Romans* (1975) 1.163–64.

[135] Cf. BAGD s.v., where the verb in Rom 2:17 is identified as pass. but translated as middle: "pass. σὺ Ἰουδαῖος ἐπονομάζῃ *you call yourself a Jew.*"

[136] See esp. Zahn, *Römer* (1910) 135–36, followed by most commentators (e.g. Kuss, Käsemann, Schlier, Michel, Wilckens, Stuhlmacher, Fitzmyer, Wright). Because the form of the verb does not determine whether it is used in the pass. or middle,

or "if you want to call yourself a Jew," or perhaps even "if you claim to be a Jew."[137]

What is important to note is the fact that Paul does not say that the person addressed *is* a Ἰουδαῖος.[138] He does not say εἰ δὲ σὺ Ἰουδαῖος εἶ, or the like.[139] Rather, the interlocutor in 2:17 is depicted as someone who calls himself, or wants to call himself, a Ἰουδαῖος. This difference was noticed and stressed already by Origen in his commentary on Romans, the earliest of its kind on the letter.[140] Having commented upon Paul's way of addressing divergent *personae* in the letter, Origen remarks: "But now let us see what the Apostle says to him who is called a Jew. First of all it must be observed that he has not said of him, 'But if you are a Jew' (*Iudaeus es*), but rather, 'if you call yourself a Jew' (*Iudaeus cognominaris*). This is because to be a Jew and to be called a Jew are not the same thing (*non idem est esse Iudaeum et cognominari Iudaeum*)."[141] Origen, to be sure, did not question the Jewish identity of the interlocutor, but took this to mean that Paul was

---

the immediate context is decisive. Due to the text's attention to the interlocutor's (false) claims to the aspects described in it, it seems most likely that ἐπονομάζω is here used in the middle voice. It should be noted, however, that a decision to the contrary does not have major consequences for my reading presented below.

[137] Cf. Fitzmyer, *Romans* (1993) 314, who translates: "But suppose you call yourself a Jew."

[138] For general discussion of the term Ἰουδαῖος/*Iudaeus*, see esp. Cohen, *Beginnings* (1999) 25–174 and passim. See also von Rad, Kuhn, and Gutbrod, "Ἰσραήλ" (1965) esp. 359–65, 369–71; Lowe, "'Ιουδαῖοι" (1976); Tomson, "Names" (1986); Kraemer, "Meaning" (1989); van der Horst, *Epitaphs* (1991) 68–72; Harvey, *Israel* (1996); Williams, "Meaning" (1997); Freyne, "Names" (2000).

[139] Cf. Gal 2:14: εἰ σὺ Ἰουδαῖος ὑπάρχων. . ., where the person spoken to is definitely a Jew.

[140] See Gorday, *Principles* (1983) 43–46.

[141] *Comm. Rom.* 2.11.4 (Rufinus). Origen finds resemblance between Paul's words and Rev 2:9: τῶν λεγόντων Ἰουδαίους εἶναι ἑαυτοὺς καὶ οὐκ εἰσὶν ἀλλὰ συναγωγὴ τοῦ σατανᾶ. Cf. 3:9: ἐκ τῆς συναγωγῆς τοῦ σατανᾶ τῶν λεγόντων ἑαυτοὺς Ἰουδαίους εἶναι, καὶ οὐκ εἰσὶν ἀλλὰ ψεύδονται. While the motif of name vs. deed may be present here (see below) it is also quite possible to take these utterances at face value as charges against non-Jews who falsely claim to be Jews. So, e.g., Gaston, "Judaism" (1986) 42–43. Differently Collins, "Insiders" (1985) 204–10.

concerned here with the motif of name versus deed: "In truth the Apostle is saying these things to the one who is a Jew in name but not in deed (*qui nomine, non opere Iudaeus est*)."[142] That is, according to Origen, the Jew in question does not live up to Jewish principles. As observed centuries later by Anton Fridrichsen,[143] and subsequently also by Stowers in particular,[144] Paul may thus have been applying a motif which was frequently used by Hellenistic moralists in their writings and lectures (esp. Epictetus).[145]

However, what these interpreters did not take into account is the possibility argued for in the present study that Paul's interlocutor in 2:1–5 is of a gentile origin *and* that the address to this very person is resumed in 2:17.[146] It is worth noting that none of the texts from the Hellenistic moralists cited by Fridrichsen and Stowers include the verb ἐπονομάζω used by Paul. Instead, λέγω and καλέω are the verbs typically preferred. More pointedly, neither of these scholars considered specifically the use of the name vs. deed motif in a context where the person(s) admonished by a moralist is said to be so-and-so in name only precisely because he or she does not belong to the group of people under discussion.[147] For example, immediately follow-

---

[142] *Comm. Rom.* 2.11.9. Actually, Origen detects three potential addressees here: 1) non-Christ believing Jews (Paul's addressees "in truth" [*verum*]); 2) Christians in name only; 3) Heretics who falsely call themselves Christians (the latter two being Origen's own contemporaries). Cf. Heither, *Origenes* (1990) 1.246 n. 40. On Origen's views of and relation to Jews and Judaism, see de Lange, *Origen* (1976).

[143] "Jude" (1922) 189–92.

[144] *Diatribe* (1981) 100–110; idem, *Rereading* (1994) esp. 144–49.

[145] Cf. also the early Christian application in Ign. *Magn.* 4 (πρέπον οὖν ἐστιν μὴ μόνον καλεῖσθαι Χριστιανούς, ἀλλὰ καὶ εἶναι); *Rom.* 3 (ἵνα μὴ μόνον λέγωμαι Χριστιανὸς ἀλλὰ καὶ εὑρεθῶ).

[146] To be more specific, Origen thought that Paul's address in Rom 2:1–5 was directed at ministers of the church. The works of the other scholars named here are, of course, penned in an entirely different context. Whereas Fridrichsen holds that a Jew is addressed throughout Rom 2, Stowers argues that the interlocutor in 2:1–5 is a gentile but that Paul addresses a Jew in 2:17.

[147] Interestingly, Paul himself uses the cognate verb ὀνομάζω somewhat similarly in 1 Cor 5:11–13 where he writes that if there be "anyone who is called a brother" (τις ἀδελφὸς ὀνομαζόμενος) who nevertheless lives a vicious life, the letter's recipients are not to associate with him but to drive him out of the community. In other

ing the imaginary dialogue cited above (in sec. 2.2.2), Epictetus turns his address directly to the student concerned: "In that you are right. For your own evils (τὰ κακά) *are* enough for you—your baseness (ἀγέννεια), your cowardice (δειλία), the bragging (ἀλαζονεία, cf. Rom 1:30) that you indulged in when you were sitting in the lecture room. Why did you pride yourself upon things that were not your own (τί τοῖς ἀλλοτρίοις ἐκαλλωπίζου)? Why did you call yourself a Stoic (τί Στωικὸν ἔλεγες σεαυτόν)?" While Epictetus' primary intention may be to show that this particular student (and his likes) is less of a Stoic than he claims, what follows suggests that he also has in view the aspect of proper belonging: "Observe yourselves [i.e. the students] thus in your actions and you will find out to what sect (αἱρέσεως) you belong. You will find that most of you are Epicureans, some few Peripatetics, but these without any backbone."[148] In this case, Epictetus may have been using a motif of name vs. deed in order to point out the proper belonging of the individuals in question. In another, well known passage, prior to which he has argued that "deeds that correspond to his true nature (τὰ κατάλληλα ἔργα) strengthen and preserve (αὔξει καὶ σώζει) each particular man," Epictetus asks his partner in dialogue:

> Why do you call yourself (λέγεις σεαυτόν) a Stoic [if you truly are an Epicurean]? Why do you deceive the multitude? Why do you act the part of a Jew, when you are a Greek (τί ὑποκρίνῃ Ἰουδαῖον ὢν Ἕλλην)? Do you not see in what sense men are severally called (λέγεται) Jew, Syrian, or Egyptian? Whenever we see a man playing a double game (ἐπαμφοτερίζοντα), we are in the habit of saying, 'He is not a Jew, he is only acting the part' (οὐκ ἔστιν Ἰουδαῖος, ἀλλ' ὑποκρίνεται). But when he adopts the attitude of mind of the man who has been baptized and has made his choice (τὸ πάθος τὸ τοῦ βεβαμμένου καὶ ᾑρημένου), then he both is a Jew in fact and is also called one (καὶ ἔστι τῷ ὄντι καὶ καλεῖται

---

words, such a "brother" is no better than any sinful outsider and should not be allowed to stay within the group of believers. Cf. the list of typical gentile sins in 6:9–11 which once characterized some of the readers' lives (v. 11).

[148] *Diatr.* 2.19.19–20 (the LCL trans. adds "of the philosophers" to the word "sect" [αἱρέσεως]). Cf. 3.24.40–43 in which Epictetus draws an analogy between falsely calling oneself a Stoic and falsely claiming Roman citizenship.

Ἰουδαῖος). So we also are counterfeit 'baptists' (παραβαπτισταί), ostensibly Jews, but in reality something else (λόγῳ μὲν Ἰουδαῖοι, ἔργῳ δ' ἄλλο τι).[149]

That Epictetus is employing the motif of name vs. deeds seems clear. But it is equally clear that he is also thinking in terms of proper belonging. This is shown by the distinction made between Greeks, Jews, Syrians, and Egyptians, but these can only be ethnic-geographic categories.[150] Moreover, whereas Epictetus' analogy of the man who "acts the part of a Jew" is primarily drawn for the purpose of convincing the audience that one does not become a Stoic without fully conforming to the Stoic way of life, this particular example is not of a Jew who is so in name only, but notably of a non-Jew who may become a Jew by "adopting" a Jewish "attitude of mind."[151]

Inscriptions from the diaspora reveal that Ἰουδαῖος and its Latin equivalent *Iudaeus* were sometimes used as surnames.[152] Thus, commenting on Paul's interlocutor in Romans 2:17, Schlier observes: "Vielleicht kann man es konkret dahin verstehen, daß ihm gesagt wird, er gäbe sich den Beinamen Ἰουδαῖος, so wie in der Diaspora Ἰουδαῖος nicht selten zum Namen gesetzt wird."[153] For most Jews, including Paul,[154] the term would

---

[149] *Diatr.* 2.9.19–21 (the LCL trans. slightly modified; on the textual uncertainty in the passage, see n. 40 ad loc.).

[150] Cf. *Diatr.* 1.11.12; 1.22.4 ("Jews and Syrians and Egyptians and Romans").

[151] Whether Epictetus' reference to baptism may suggest that he actually has Christians in view is beside the point. If so, he seems to equate them with Jews. I find it most likely that he really is speaking of Jews here as he says, but that he either has (mis)taken a Christian rite for a Jewish one or was familiar with Jewish communities in which baptism was considered sufficient for conversion; on the latter possibility, see Stern, *Authors* no. 254; Reynolds and Tannenbaum, *Jews* (1987) 44–45. It is telling that in 4.7.6 Epictetus almost certainly refers to Christians and there he calls them "Galileans." Cf. also the discussion of the passage quoted above in Cohen, *Beginnings* (1999) 60–61.

[152] *CIG* 9916, 9926; *CIJ* 530, 643. Cf. also *CIJ* 680. Some inscriptions show that Ἰουδαῖος/*Iudaeus* could also function as a proper name, e.g. *CIJ* 710, 711.

[153] *Römerbrief* (1977) 82. Needless to say, Schlier envisages the interlocutor as a Jew.

[154] There seems to be no good reason to suppose otherwise. In his discussion of Paul's use of the term Ἰουδαῖος in Rom, Harvey, *Israel* (1996) 77–78, writes: "Nothing

have been perceived as a title of honor, a "theokratische[r] Ehrenname,"[155] often being used in literary contexts in which distinctions were made between Jews and non-Jews. Quite expectedly, this is also the case in Paul's letters, where the term Ἰουδαῖος/-οι typically occurs in contrast to Ἕλλην/-ες or ἔθνη.[156] Ἰουδαῖος, however, did not merely apply to native Jews. From the late second century B.C.E. Jewishness had gradually expanded as a function not only of birth and/or geography but of religion or culture as well,[157] thus enabling people of non-Jewish origin to become members of Jewish communities on certain conditions, i.e. to become Ἰουδαῖοι. It is therefore not surprising to find that sources of various sorts and settings attest that Ἰουδαῖος/*Iudaeus* could be a proper term not only for native Jews but also for proselytes, that is, gentile converts to Judaism. For some people, all adherents to the Jewish way of life could or should be called Ἰουδαῖοι. The following examples illustrate these uses of the term.

We have already seen Epictetus' example of the non-Jew who, when he "adopts the attitude of mind" of a Jew, "both is a Jew in fact and is also called one" (καλεῖται Ἰουδαῖος). I see little reason to doubt that Epictetus is here alluding to instances with which he was acquainted. Even the Jewish historian Josephus does not seem to have difficulties with identifying converts to Judaism as Ἰουδαῖοι. In his report of Hyrcanus' conquest of the Idumeans in the late second century B.C.E., he remarks that Hyrcanus permitted them to stay in their country "so long as they had themselves circumcised and were willing to observe the laws of the Jews." To these condi-

---

Paul says about 'Jews' (or 'Israel') . . . suggests that it has 'played out its role'. It is only 2:17–29 which questions the effect of naming oneself 'a Jew'. . . . Paul, in Romans, does not denigrate 'Jews' or 'Judaism'. His selfperception as 'apostle to Gentiles' means that non-ιουδαῖοι are his focus of attention, but he chooses to address them about their relationship with 'Israel' and the ιουδαῖοι. They have become part of an already existing community and what is left behind is the 'Gentile' lifestyle not the 'Jewish' one."

[155] Fridrichsen, "Jude" (1922) 190.
[156] Rom 1:16; 2:9–10; 3:9, 29; 9:24; 10:12; 1 Cor 1:22–24; 10:32; 12:13; Gal 2:14–15; 3:28. Cf. Col 3:11.
[157] On the history of the word Ἰουδαῖος/*Iudaeus*, see Cohen, *Beginnings* (1999) esp. 69–139.

tions the Idumeans submitted, and thus, Josephus tells, "from that time on they have continued to be Jews (ὥστε εἶναι τὸ λοιπὸν Ἰουδαίους)."[158] Speaking of same events, Ptolemy notes that Jews (or Judeans) and Idumeans differ in that the former are Ἰουδαῖοι "by origin and nature" (ἐξ ἀρχῆς φυσικοί), whereas the latter "were called Jews" (ἐκλήθησαν Ἰουδαῖοι) only after having been subjugated by the Ἰουδαῖοι.[159] Several inscriptions from antiquity give further evidence of people of non-Jewish origin being called Ἰουδαῖοι. This is the case in an inscription from the Jewish catacomb of the Via Nomentana in Rome where a certain Cresces Sinicerius is called *Iudeus proselitus*, and almost certainly also in a catacomb on the Via Appia where an epitaph carries the female name and/or designation [... Ἰου]δέα προσή[λυτος ... θ]εοσεβ(ή)[ς ...].[160] Still more interesting is the famous account in Dio Cassius' work in which he reflects on the term Ἰουδαῖος: "The country has been named (ὠνομάδαται) Judaea, and the people themselves Jews (Ἰουδαῖοι). I do not know how this title (ἐπίκλησις) came to be given them, but it applies also to all the rest of mankind (καὶ ἐπὶ τοὺς ἄλλους ἀνθρώπους), although of alien race (ἀλλοεθνεῖς) who strive for their customs (ὅσοι τὰ νόμιμα αὐτῶν ζηλοῦσι)."[161] According to Dio, then, the "title" Ἰουδαῖος would have applied not only to native Jews or full scale proselytes but to any gentile adherent to Judaism. Such a broad use of the term is indeed not unique, if unusual, and may even be found in rabbinic literature, in which one statement reads: "Anyone who denies idolatry is called a Jew."[162] The following comments by Origen are also telling: "The noun *Ioudaios* is the name not of an *ethnos* but of a choice (in the manner of life). For if there be someone not from the nation of the Jews, a gentile, who accepts the ways of the Jews and be-

---

[158] *A.J.* 13.257–258. For detailed analysis of this passage as well as that of Ptolemy cited below, see Cohen, *Beginnings* (1999) 17–18, 81–82, 110–29. Cf. also *A.J.* 20.38–39.

[159] See Stern, *Authors* no. 146 (date and identity of author unknown).

[160] *CIJ* 68, 202. Cf. also the problematic *CIJ* 21. See further Kraemer, "Meaning" (1989) 50–51; Figueras, "Epigraphic" (1990) 198–200.

[161] *Hist. Rom.* 37.17.1 (the LCL trans. slightly modified).

[162] *b. Meg.* 13a; see Cohen, *Beginnings* (1999) 61.

comes a proselyte, this person would properly be called a *Ioudaios*."[163] Origen, however, did not follow up this insight of his with respect to the identity of Paul's interlocutor in Romans 2:17.

This survey shows that people of gentile origin could on certain conditions be called Ἰουδαῖοι, and so both by Jews and non-Jews. This is not to say that all distinctions between Jews and non-Jews necessarily ceased to exist when the latter became Ἰουδαῖοι. As Shaye J. D. Cohen has pointed out, the ancient sources do not demonstrate unmistakably that proselytes achieved real equality with native Jews. The status of such people in Jewish communities appears instead to have been ambiguous: "In the eyes of outsiders a proselyte or convert was a gentile who became a Jew. But in the eyes of (some?) Jews, a gentile who converted to Judaism became not a Jew but a proselyte—that is, a Jew of a peculiar sort." This is because "[f]or most *Ioudaioi* in antiquity, the ethnic definition was supplemented, not replaced, by the religious definition. Jewishness became an ethno-religious identity." Thus, "gentile converts to Judaism could not attain full equality with the native born because they lacked the blood lineage that was an essential part of the ethnic part of the Jewish self-definition."[164]

Hence, with respect to the data presented above, it is quite possible that Paul's address in Romans 2:17 is aimed, not at a Jew (or any Jew) who is so in name only, but at a gentile who calls himself, or wants to call himself, a Jew, i.e. a person who "acts the part of a Jew" and is thought of either as a proselyte or a potential one. As we shall see, vv. 25–27 in particular suggest the former, but for Paul, it appears, such a person would merely be a circumcised gentile, or a "Jew of a peculiar sort" at the very best.

2.3.2. Jewishness vis-à-vis Gentiles (2:17–20)

Verses 17–20 constitute the protasis of a conditional clause, the form of which is defective since it unexpectedly breaks off at the end of v. 20 with-

---

[163] Cited in Cohen, *Beginnings* (1999) 134.
[164] *Beginnings* (1999) 137, 162, 169. See also pp. 132–33. Cf. Donaldson, "Proselytes" (1990); Feldman, *Jew* (1993) 338–41.

out a formally proper apodosis following.[165] It would probably not be wide of the mark, however, to take vv. 21–22 as functionally equivalent to the apodosis. The relation between these verses and the preceding is, at the same time, being marked as inferential by the conjunction οὖν in v. 21. The protasis comprises five main verbs, all in the present tense, each connected by the conjunction καί (vv. 17–18b). Three participial phrases follow, two of which are in the present tense (vv. 18c, 20c) and one in the perfect tense (vv. 19–20b). This one also differs in that it contains an infinitive construction and is joined by the strong connective τέ. Verses 19–20b may therefore carry special weight in the passage.

Paul opens his address to the interlocutor who wants to call himself a Jew by explaining the meaning of Ἰουδαῖον ἐπονομάζεσθαι. "What the name 'Jew' means Paul shows in vv. 17–20, which describe the religious legacy of the Jew."[166] More specifically, whereas the series καί... καί... καί... καί... in vv. 17–18 defines in basic terms the opening εἰ δὲ σὺ Ἰουδαῖος ἐπονομάζῃ, vv. 19–20 reflect upon the interlocutor's claimed Jewishness vis-à-vis non-Jews.

The verbal phrases in vv. 17–18 do not have negative values, as sometimes assumed. On the contrary, they are used quite positively to specify some fundamental aspects of being a Jew. The first one in the series, ἐπαναπαύῃ νόμῳ, simply means to "rest upon the Law" with no inherent discredit at all.[167] The second phrase, καυχᾶσαι ἐν θεῷ, calls for more attention since it is often taken for granted that the verb καυχάομαι (to "boast") and its cognate nouns καύχημα (a "boast") and καύχησις ("boasting") express something improper per se in Paul's writings.[168] Such assumptions, it should be urged, do not speak for the evidence. This highly favored terminology by Paul receives its value, whether positive or other-

---

[165] On this problem, see Zahn, *Römer* (1910) 135–41; Bornkamm, "Anakoluthe" (1958) 76–78.

[166] Bietenhard, "ὄνομα" (1967) 282.

[167] Cf. 1 Macc. 8:11: "but with their [i.e. the Romans'] friends and those who rely on them (τῶν ἐπαναπαυομένων αὐτοῖς) they have kept friendship" (NRSV: v. 12), positively viewed.

[168] For a survey of the scholarly discussion of "boasting" in the Pauline literature, see Gathercole, *Boasting* (2002) 2–10.

wise, wholly from the context in which it is used.[169] A good example is found in Second Corinthians 5:12 where Paul says to his readers that he is giving them an "opportunity to boast about us" (ἀφορμὴν καυχήματος ὑπὲρ ἡμῶν), so that they may be able to stand up to "those who boast in outward appearance and not in the heart" (τοὺς ἐν προσώπῳ καυχωμένους καὶ μὴ ἐν καρδίᾳ). Whereas the former "boasting" clearly is an apt one, the latter is not. To "boast in God," on the other hand, is always a good thing for Paul, as indicated by the maxim "Let the one who boasts, boast in the Lord" (ὁ καυχώμενος ἐν κυρίῳ καυχάσθω) to which he refers twice (1 Cor 1:31; 2 Cor 10:17).[170] This maxim is well reflected in Romans 5:11 where Paul tells his audience that there is every reason to "boast in God (καυχώμενοι ἐν τῷ θεῷ) through our lord Jesus Christ." Thus, the phrase καυχᾶσαι ἐν θεῷ in 2:17 is by itself scarcely viewed otherwise than positively by Paul. The same goes for the phrases γινώσκεις τὸ θέλημα (τοῦ θεοῦ) and δοκιμάζεις τὰ διαφέροντα in v. 18, the points of which are practically identical, which, in turn, suggests that the following participial phrase, κατηχούμενος ἐκ τοῦ νόμου, relates to both expressions.[171] In other words, both the knowledge of God's will and the determination of vital matters are reached by learning from the Law. The present tense of κατηχούμενος implies that this is an ongoing process.

---

[169] The verb and its cognates occur ca. 54 times in Paul's letters; elsewhere in the NT only 4 times! Paul frequently refers to his own "boasting" of those who have received and accepted his εὐαγγέλιον, a "boasting" which, of course, is entirely appropriate from his point of view (e.g. Rom 15:17; 1 Cor 15:31; 2 Cor 1:14; 7:4; 8:24; 9:2–3; 10:8, 13–17; Phil 2:16; 1 Thess 2:19; contra 1 Cor 9:16?). Occasionally, he also speaks of the "boasting" of his antagonists, which, needless to say, tends to be presented in negative terms (e.g. 2 Cor 11:12–13; Gal 6:13). Cf. also the discussion in Thompson, "Critique" (1986).

[170] A possible reference to Jer 9:23: ἐν τούτῳ καυχάσθω ὁ καυχώμενος συνίειν καὶ γινώσκειν ὅτι ἐγώ εἰμι κύριος. Berkley, *Covenant* (2000) 87–90, 122, proposes that the words καυχᾶσαι, γινώσκεις, and θέλημα in Rom 2:17 all "derive from" Jer 9:23–24. This is difficult to establish with any certainty. Similar vocabulary between these texts does at any rate not warrant Berkley's heavy dependence upon the context of Jer 9:23–24 in his reading of Paul's text.

[171] So also Cranfield, *Romans* (1975) 1.166.

If vv. 17–18 give basic description of what it means to be a Jew, vv. 19–20 focus specifically upon Jewish identity in relation to other nations. In terms of verbal aspect, the significance of this latter focus may be indicated by the use of the perfect participle πέποιθας,[172] which is the only perfect tense used here among a cluster of present tenses. If so, there is a marked emphasis put on the components of this particular clause (vv. 19–20b: πέποιθάς τε σεαυτόν . . . εἶναι . . .) for the passage as a whole.

The expressions employed in the text, all positive designations, allude to well-known traditions concerning Israel's role as a "light to the nations," i.e. her duty to be a guiding and leading figure in the world. A key passage comes from the prophet Isaiah through whom God declares: "I have given you (σε) [i.e. God's chosen "servant"] as a covenant to the people (εἰς διαθήκην γένους), as a light to the nations (εἰς φῶς ἐθνῶν), to open the eyes of the blind (ἀνοῖξαι ὀφθαλμοὺς τυφλῶν), to bring out . . . from the prison those who sit in darkness (ἐν σκότει)" (42:6–7).[173] Such a divinely ordained responsibility would no doubt have been an important part of Jewish identity for many Jews. It seems safe to assume that this was the case for Paul himself who was convinced that God, who had "separated me, even from my mother's womb (ἐκ κοιλίας μητρός μου), and called (καλέσας) me through his grace," was pleased "to reveal his Son in me, that I might preach him among the Gentiles (εὐαγγελίζωμαι αὐτὸν ἐν τοῖς ἔθνεσιν)" (Gal 1:15–16; ASV). We may compare God's calling of Jeremiah: "Before I formed you in the womb (ἐν κοιλίᾳ) I knew you, and before you were born (ἐξελθεῖν ἐκ μήτρας) I consecrated you; I appointed you a prophet to the nations (προφήτην εἰς ἔθνη τέθεικά σε)" (1:5; NRSV), and Isaiah 49 in particular: "The Lord called (ἐκάλεσεν) my name while I was in my mother's womb (ἐκ κοιλίας μητρός μου). . . . And now the Lord says, who formed me in the womb (ἐκ κοιλίας) to be his servant . . . 'I will give you as a covenant to the people (εἰς διαθήκην γένους), as a light to the nations (εἰς φῶς ἐθνῶν), that you may bring salvation to the end of the earth (τοῦ εἶναί σε εἰς σωτηρίαν ἕως ἐσχάτου τῆς γῆς)" (vv. 1, 5–6).

---

[172] See Porter, *Idioms* (1994) 259. For similar phrasing, see 2 Cor 10:7.

[173] Cf., e.g., *1 En.* 105:1; *Sib. Or.* 3.195; Wis 18:4; *T. Benj.* 11.2; *T. Lev.* 14.4; 1QSb 4.27; Philo, *Abr.* 98; Josephus, *C. Ap.* 2.291–295. Cf. also Acts 13:47; 26:23.

That Paul took such a task seriously is beyond question, a task which, we may add, involved him being an ἐθνῶν ἀπόστολος (Rom 11:13), proclaiming the message about God's son, Jesus the Messiah.[174] For Paul, then, many aspects of the portrayal in Romans 2:17–20 would have been essential to his own Jewish identity.

I have stressed above that, when taken separately, the phrases used by Paul in vv. 17–20 do not by themselves have negative values. However, as recognized by many interpreters, Paul's address as a whole in these verses is characterized by a certain sense of irony.[175] This was grasped by Origen, who, we may presume, was well versed in the rhetorical effect of irony: "We need to realize . . . that the Apostle is using irony when he addresses these things to the Jews. For it is impossible to believe that those who truly rest in the law and boast in God and test what is more useful could do the things which are enumerated in this passage [viz. in vv. 21–24]."[176] While Paul's irony comes most explicitly to the fore with v. 21, it may even be detected in the passage under discussion. The basis for the irony is, again, not something inherent in the expressions themselves. Rather, aimed specifically at the interlocutor who wants to call himself a Jew, it is found in his implied claims to the things described. That is, the irony is not that there is something wrong per se with the aspects of Jewish identity listed out in vv. 17–20, but that *this particular person* claims or aims to be all this.

Due to the prominent missionary language in the text, it is possible that the interlocutor is thought of as a Jewish "missionary" or "teacher," a potential competitor of Paul, whose hypocrisy Paul seeks to expose for the audience.[177] However, such a reading would require either that there is a shift

---

[174] Cf. Ch. 1 sec. 3.1.1 above.

[175] For general discussion of irony in Greco-Roman letters, specifically relating to Paul's letter to the Galatians, see Nanos, *Irony* (2002) esp. 32–61.

[176] *Comm. Rom.* 2.11.12.

[177] So, with diverse implications, Goppelt, "Missionar" (1968) 137–39; Stuhlmacher, *Römer* (1989) 47; Stowers, *Rereading* (1994) 143–58. Cf. Watson, *Paul* (1986) 113–15, who thinks that Rom 2 is an attack on the leaders of the Roman Jewish communities. McKnight, *Light* (1991) 105, concludes somewhat ambiguously that an "active Jewish missionary activity" is not made explicit in the language of Rom 2:19–20. He calls these verses "an attack on some form of Judaism [viz.

of interlocutor in v. 17 or that the person addressed in vv. 1–5 is thought of as a Jew, alternatives which I have found to be unlikely. I therefore suggest that the irony detected in vv. 17–20—and conspicuously expressed in the subsequent discourse—may be taken as having its ground in the fact that, in Paul's view, the interlocutor is not a Jew at all. The religious heritage of Israel and her role vis-à-vis gentiles thus underline effectively the irony of the gentile interlocutor's claim or aim of being a Jew. Paul is saying: But if you call yourself a Jew, with all its connotations, having even persuaded yourself (πέποιθάς τε σεαυτόν) that *you* are a guide to the blind, that *you* are a light to those in darkness, that *you* are an instructor of the foolish, that *you* are a teacher of children . . . The trenchant irony of such claims is made explicit in the following verses.

Dunn maintains that in v. 19 Paul chooses the word πέποιθας "rather than 'know' to indicate that this is a conviction which in its present form (as an expression of privileged status) is something to which they [i.e. the Jews] have persuaded themselves rather than something God-given."[178] But to "know" would probably not have been among the options which Paul had in mind in this context. It is more likely that the phrase πέποιθάς τε σεαυτόν is chosen by him because his words are directed at a gentile interlocutor who, ironically enough, has persuaded himself that he has claims to the Jewish heritage described. This also explains why the distinction between Jews and non-Jews shines through almost every thread of the text. Paul's aim is not to undermine Jewish privileges, as presumed by Dunn and others.[179] "Paul does not for a moment reject the specialness of Israel,"[180] as manifested quite clearly in 3:1–3; 9:4–5; 11:11–24. Rather, the distinctive elements are brought to the fore precisely because Paul is engaged in a fictitious dialogue with a gentile who claims or aims to be a Jew, something which Paul rigorously opposes.

Pharisaic] as seen through the eyes of a former Pharisaic Jew" (on Paul's "opponents" here as Pharisees, see p. 153 n. 21).

[178] *Romans* (1988) 1.112.

[179] See esp. Dunn's *Romans* (1988) 1.108–18 and passim. Cf. also, e.g., Käsemann, *Römer* (1974) 64–65; Beker, *Paul* (1980) 78–83; Carras, "Romans 2,1–29" (1992); Barclay, "Paul" (1998) 544–46.

[180] Wright, "Letter" (2002) 446.

Ernst Käsemann suggests that the phrase κατηχούμενος ἐκ τοῦ νόμου in 2:18 refers to "the fixed catechetical traditions of Judaism,"[181] but there is nothing to prevent it from being used of the "catechism" of (potential) proselytes. That such a schooling may be in view is certainly not ruled out by the present tense of κατηχούμενος which implies an ongoing process.[182] Such a process, viz. of learning how to be a Jew, would be appropriately described by the phrase κατηχούμενος ἐκ τοῦ νόμου. Interestingly, Hans Lietzmann once conjectured that in vv. 19–20 Paul may have been quoting from a Jewish writing designed for proselytes: "19 f. machen den Eindruck, als zitiere [Paulus] die Worte einer jüdischen für Proselyten berechneten Schrift. . . . Aus solcher Quelle stammt wohl auch das eigenartige μόρφωσιν τῆς γνώσεως."[183] This suggestion has been endorsed by Schlier, among others: "Dabei wird der νόμος mit einem Wort bezeichnet, das geradezu der Titel einer Proselytenschrift sein könnte: ἡ μόρφωσις τῆς γνώσεως καὶ τῆς ἀληθείας."[184]

As noted above, the participial phrase κατηχούμενος ἐκ τοῦ νόμου is probably connected both to γινώσκεις τὸ θέλημα and δοκιμάζεις τὰ διαφέροντα,[185] expressions which say virtually the same thing. A combination of these occurs in Romans 12:2 where Paul exhorts the gentile readers to "renew" their minds so that they may "determine what is the will of God" (δοκιμάζειν ὑμᾶς τί τὸ θέλημα τοῦ θεοῦ), but, as we saw above (in sec. 2.1.2), Paul's request in 12:1–2 is aimed at urging the audience to transform their lives in absolute contrast to the gentile condition described in 1:18–32. Similarly, Paul's expressions in 2:18 may allude specifically to God's "handing over" of the gentiles to ἀδόκιμον νοῦν, ποιεῖν τὰ μὴ

---

[181] *Römer* (1974) 65: "Spricht der Apostel vom κατηχούμενος, sind die festen katechetischen Überlieferungen des Judentums zu bedenken."

[182] Cf. Gal 6:6 (presumably in relation to the εὐαγγέλιον): κοινωνείτω δὲ ὁ κατηχούμενος τὸν λόγον τῷ κατηχοῦντι ἐν πᾶσιν ἀγαθοῖς. Cf. also 1 Cor 14:19.

[183] *Römer* (1971) 43.

[184] *Römerbrief* (1977) 85. Cf. Michel, *Römer* (1978) 130; Dunn, *Romans* (1988) 1.113.

[185] Cf. Phil 1:9–10 where Paul conveys his wish that the audience may be able to "determine the vital matters" (δοκιμάζειν ὑμᾶς τὰ διαφέροντα) so that they will be "pure and blameless" on the "day of Christ."

καθήκοντα etc. in 1:28–31. If so, the point would be to hint at the paradox involved in the interlocutor's claim of knowing God's will and being able to determine the vital matters in spite of the condition to which he had been "handed over" by God.

"Doing" or "transgressing" the Law clearly is a major theme in 2:17–29. In vv. 17–20 alone, where the interlocutor of vv. 1–5 reappers, Paul mentions the Law three times: The interlocutor claims to "rest upon the Law . . . being instructed by the Law . . . having in the Law the embodiment of knowledge and truth." Here it becomes explicit why the interlocutor believed himself to have a proper basis to "judge" some of his fellow gentiles (v. 1), and why he thought that he would "escape" (v. 3) the judgment of God. Presuming that he would be safe as a "Jew," as a "doer of the Law" by definition, he thought that he was much better off than other sinful gentiles (1:18–32). The interlocutor took for granted that he no longer belonged to the group of people once "handed over" by God to an existence filled with vicious deeds. Paul sweeps away this false belief in the following verses.

2.3.3. A Transgressor of the Law (2:21–24)

With v. 21 Paul's indictment becomes acute: "You, then, who teach others, do you not teach yourself?"[186] The relation to the address in vv. 1–5 is evident. Although the verb διδάσκω is used instead of κρίνω, the basic thought is the same. In vv. 1–5 the interlocutor is charged with inconsistency because he judges others for the very things he does himself, and in v. 21 he is, by implication, censured for telling others how to act without conforming to it himself. This theme of inconsistency is a cardinal theme in the text. As often noted by scholars, the rhetorical question in v. 21a may therefore serve as a heading for the following questions in vv. 21b–22. However, the last one (v. 22b) seems to be exceptional in two respects. First, while the questions in vv. 21–22a focus upon the act of instructing others (διδάσκων, κηρύσσων, λέγων), the one in v. 22b does not. Second, whereas the former questions are built up of clear antitheses (διδάσκων . . .

---

[186] Verses 21–22 are to be taken as rhetorical questions (so most commentators), not statements.

οὐ διδάσκεις, μὴ κλέπτειν κλέπτεις, μὴ μοιχεύειν μοιχεύεις), the antithesis between βδελυσσόμενος τὰ εἴδωλα and ἱεροσυλεῖς is blurred. Indeed, if this question is to correspond strictly with the foregoing, one would rather have expected "You who abhor idols" to have been contrasted with something like "do you practice idolatry?"[187] Thus, whilst the flow of the questions in vv. 21–22 is clearly continuous, there are some notable differences between the first three questions and the fourth one. I will return to this below.

The questions in vv. 21b–22 are chosen by Paul as potential examples of the interlocutor's contradictory conduct. The first two (vv. 21b–22a), those of "stealing" (κλέπτειν) and "committing adultery" (μοιχεύειν), are drawn from the decalogue,[188] both of which will reappear in 13:9 where Paul gives examples of keeping the Law. Why these are specifically chosen here is difficult to say. They may simply be randomly picked out from the decalogue, since violation of any part of the decalogue would, of course, be a serious transgression. On the other hand, it is worth observing that, in addition to Romans 13:9, Paul refers to the vices of stealing and committing adultery also in First Corinthians 6:9–11. There he lists those who will not inherit "the kingdom of God," among whom are "fornicators (πόρνοι), idolaters (εἰδωλολάτραι), adulterers (μοιχοί), effeminate (μαλακοί), male prostitutes (ἀρσενοκοῖται), thieves (κλέπται), covetous persons (πλεονέκται)" and so forth (cf. Rom 1:22–31). Interestingly, Paul states that this is what some of his gentile audience once were (ταῦτά τινες ἦτε). Thus, in Romans 2:21b–22a he may be singling out sins which he considered to be characteristic of the gentile world (cf. the list of gentile sins in Wis 14:24–26 cited above [in sec. 2.1.1]). In any case, the fact that these kinds of acts are specifically spoken against in the decalogue itself underlines the gravity of the interlocutor's implied transgression of the Law.

---

[187] Cf. Bischoff, "Randbemerkungen" (1908) 167: "Wie dem μὴ κλέπτειν das κλέπτειν, dem μὴ μοιχεύειν das μοιχεύειν gegenübersteht, so war zu dem βδελύσσεσθαι τὰ εἴδωλα als Gegensatz etwas wie εἰδωλολατρεῖν zu erwarten." See also Krentz, "Name" (1990) 433; Berkley, *Covenant* (2000) 132–33, 135.

[188] Exod 20:13–14; Deut 5:17, 19.

The third example, "You who abhor idols, are you a temple robber?" (ὁ βδελυσσόμενος τὰ εἴδωλα ἱεροσυλεῖς; v. 22b),[189] has long puzzled scholars, who, needless to say, have taken 2:17–29 to be addressed to a Jew. Don B. Garlington, for instance, declares that this is "[p]erhaps one of the most curious, if not perplexing, passages from the pen of Paul."[190] The reason is, of course, that "robbing temples" was not something which Jews could be or normally were accused of being in habit of doing. Thus, J. Christiaan Beker maintains that Paul "'paganizes' the Jews in Rom. 2:21–29 by indicting them for those cardinal Gentile sins (1:18–32) that the Jews have always abhorred about Gentile life: idolatry ('robbing temples,' v. 21 [sic]), adultery (v. 22), and social vices ('stealing,' v. 21)."[191] E. P. Sanders asks in turn: "Did they all rob temples?" And he continues: "Paul's case for universal sinfulness [i.e. of Jews as well as gentiles], as it is stated in Rom. 1:18–2:29, is not convincing: it is internally inconsistent and it rests on gross exaggeration."[192] Many scholars have endeavored either to locate "empirical evidence" for Jews robbing temples—largely unsuccessfully we may add,[193]

---

[189] The first part, ὁ βδελυσσόμενος τὰ εἴδωλα, alludes to the decalogue (Exod 20:4; Deut 5:8).

[190] *Faith* (1994) 32. Garlington himself reaches the stunning conclusion that "for Paul *the new idol is the Torah!* The 'sacrilege' in question is *Israel's idolatrous attachment to the law itself.* . . . Israel's preference for the law to the exclusion of Christ could for Paul be nothing less than ἱεροσυλεῖν, an act of sacrilege" (pp. 39, 43; emphasis his).

[191] *Paul* (1980) 88.

[192] *Paul* (1983) 125. Cf. Räisänen, *Paul* (1983) 101: "Paul's argument is here simply a piece of propagandist denigration" (referring, it appears, to vv. 21–24).

[193] Gathercole, *Boasting* (2002) 212, strangely asserts: "The charge that Paul has made against the nation that his interlocutor represents [i.e. of "stealing, adultery, and robbery of pagan temples"] is grounded in empirical evidence." Gathercole makes no attempt to inform his readers where this "empirical evidence" may be found. Dunn, *Romans* (1988) 1.114, notes that "we can document at least one case of a Jew in Rome misappropriating funds and gifts intended for the temple," viz. from Josephus, *A.J.* 18.81–84. Dunn, however, rightly doubts the value of this case for the reading of Rom 2:22b. In his interpretation of Deut 7:25–26, Josephus speaks of temple robbery in *A.J.* 4.207, but only to speak against such behavior in gen-

or to provide an allegorical reading appropriate for the context,[194] or to accomodate Paul's words to fit as an accusation of "sacrilege."[195] J. Duncan M. Derrett identifies five "almost contradictory translations" of v. 22b in circulation—and adds the sixth.[196] One scholar notes that Paul's interlocutor is here accused of committing "an act which our old translators rendered as 'sacrilege' (ἱεροσυλεῖς) and which nowadays we do not really know how to translate. (No great loss, perhaps, as we do not have the slightest idea to what action it might refer.)"[197]

These comments testify to the confusion among interpreters in their attempts to make sense of Paul's choice of ἱεροσυλεῖν as a charge against Jews. George P. Carras suggests that "it is best not to take Paul's intent literally since it cannot be said that Jews in general were temple thieves."[198] Several commentators have also settled for a reading in which Paul indicts his Jewish interlocutor for some sort of "sacrilege."[199] And yet, the puzzle remains why Paul would have chosen this particular charge in an indictment of a Jew, since it would have been plain to most people that ἱεροσυλεῖν was far from characteristic of Jewish conduct. In the words of

---

eral; he does not mention any examples of Jews robbing temples. Similarly Philo, *Conf.* 163; *Pss. Sol.* 8:11; *T. Lev.* 14; CD 6.15–17.

[194] Goppelt, "Missionar" (1968) 144–46, rejects the allegorical reading of Origen, which "lebte durch die Jahrhunderte in der Kirche weiter" (Ambrosiaster, Luther, Nygren), only to submit the same sort of reading himself, albeit "nur formal 'allegorisch'." Goppelt sees parallels in Jesus' criticism of "scribes and Pharisees" recorded in Matt 23. Similarly also Wilckens, *Römer* (1978) 1.150–51.

[195] A useful overview of the scholarly discussion may be found in Berkley, *Covenant* (2000) 125–33.

[196] "Abominate" (1994). The translations he lists are divided between: 1) You rob (idols') temples; 2) You are dishonest towards heathen temples; 3) You commit sacrilege; 4) You are indifferent to the rights of God in general; 5) You desecrate holy things in general. Derrett adds the rendering: "You abominate idols (as the written law requires); but do you never profit illegitimately at the expense of an idol's wealth (which the law of conscience forbids)?"

[197] Trocmé, "Jews" (1985) 153.

[198] "Romans 2,1–29" (1992) 201.

[199] E.g. Cranfield, *Romans* (1975) 1.169–70; Schlier, *Römerbrief* (1977) 86; Dunn, *Romans* (1988) 1.114, 117.

C. K. Barrett, "Paul's argument is lost if he is compelled to rely on comparatively unusual events, and it is simply not true that the average Jewish missionary acted in this way."[200] The nature of the problem is even better put by Timothy W. Berkley: "The question is this: how is the interlocutor or someone identified with the interlocutor as a Jew, in Käsemann's words, 'trapped' by accusations that have no application to most individual Jews?"[201] To be exposed as a thief or an adulterer would certainly have been biting for a Jew, but would the charge of ἱεροσυλεῖν have had such an impact? There is every reason to doubt that. Even if taken as a "hyperbolic persuasive device,"[202] or as a reference to occasionally recorded instances of Jewish acts of "sacrilege," such farfetched cases could hardly have served Paul's purpose of exposing the interlocutor. The rhetorical effect would indeed have been none whatsoever. An even likelier outcome is that such an allegation would have sounded ridiculous and thus turned Paul's rhetoric against him.

Berkley insists that "[a]ny hypothesis to account for the charges Paul makes must deal adequately with the legitimacy and universal application of the charges, and the connection of idolatry with temple robbery which Paul implies."[203] This seems to me to be a reasonable demand, although

---

[200] *Romans* (1957) 56 (referring to 2:21–22). Cf. Kuss, *Römerbrief* (1957) 1.87–88.

[201] *Covenant* (2000) 133.

[202] Thurén, *Derhetorizing* (2000) 144. Berkley, *Covenant* (2000) 133, rightly remarks that "[t]here must be some basis upon which these charges can stand, even if Paul is only making a hyperbolic rhetorical point."

[203] *Covenant* (2000) 133. Berkley proposes the solution that Rom 2:21–22 is based on Jer 7:9–11. Paul's charge of ἱεροσυλεῖν then reflects Jeremiah's reference to the temple in Jerusalem as a "den of robbers." While I find Berkley's explanation better than most, it does not answer his own question "why Paul has not charged the Jew of Rom 2:22 with making the temple 'a den of robbers'" (p. 85) instead of accusing him for ἱεροσυλεῖν. I do not find Berkley's argument convincing that "the use of ἱεροσυλεῖν brings the prophet's message into the world with which [Paul's] readers are familiar" (p. 86). How "familiar" would Paul's readers have been with Jewish ἱεροσυλεῖν (cf. pp. 131–33)? How "universal" would such an application have been? Would the charge of ἱεροσυλεῖν have been more effective rhetorically (against a Jewish interlocutor) than an accusation of making the temple itself a "den of robbers"? I doubt that. Moreover, Berkley seems to rely more on the con-

"universal" may be too strong a word. Now, from a Jewish perspective, idolatry is naturally the gentile sin per se, as Paul had already discussed in 1:18–25 where he spoke of the gentiles who exchanged the glory of God for all kinds of despicable images (v. 23) and revered and worshiped the creature instead of the creator (v. 25), and in which he alluded to Jewish traditions in this respect, as the one found in Wisdom of Solomon (see esp. 12:23–14:31 ["For the worship of idols not to be named is the beginning and cause and end of every evil"; 14:27]).[204] To be a Jew is to renounce and denounce all such conduct, or, as Paul puts it, to "abhor idols."

I have already pointed out above that there are some notable differences between Paul's question in v. 22b and those preceding. Unlike the latter, the one in v. 22b does not include the feature of instructing others. Paul simply states: "You who abhor idols," not "You who tell others to abhor idols." Furthermore, the kind of contrasts made in vv. 21–22a becomes less lucid in v. 22b. Many attempts have been made to harmonize Paul's terminology here so that a clear antithesis may emerge. But perhaps Paul did not have such a strict antithesis in view in v. 22b. It is possible that he was not so much concerned with the specific conducts spoken of as with the imaginary individual spoken to and those whom he represented. That is, the contrast implied may primarily be that of identity, a contrast between a person who "abhors idols" and a person who is a "temple robber." Paul would then be saying to his interlocutor: You who claim to abhor idols and thus to be different from other gentiles (i.e. those in 1:18–32), are you a temple robber?

What, then, about the curious ἱεροσυλεῖς? Sources attest that temple robbery was counted among the worst crimes in Greco-Roman antiq-

---

text of Jer 7:9–11 in his reading of Rom 2:21–22 than that of Rom 1–2 itself, an approach which in my view is highly suspect.

[204] See also Wis 14:11: "Therefore there will be a visitation also upon the heathen idols (εἰδώλοις ἐθνῶν), because, though part of what God created, they became an abomination (βδέλυγμα), snares for human souls and a trap for the feet of the foolish" (NRSV). On τὰ εἴδωλα τῶν ἐθνῶν, see further, e.g., 1 Chr 16:26; Pss 113:12; 134:15; Jer 14:22; Tob 14:6; 1 Macc 3:48. On τὰ βδελύγματα τῶν ἐθνῶν, see, e.g., Deut 18:9; 3 Kgdms 14:24; 4 Kgdms 16:3; 21:2; 2 Chr 28:3; 33:2; 36:14; 1 Esd 7:13.

uity.²⁰⁵ Paul's ἱεροσυλεῖς might therefore refer to such crimes in general. However, it seems fair to assume that, in a Jewish context, ἱεροσυλεῖν would first and foremost be associated with the temple in Jerusalem.²⁰⁶ Attempts to plunder the Jerusalem temple—some successful, others not—are often spoken of in Jewish documents from antiquity, attempts which typically are linked with idolatry or idolatrous behavior of some kind.²⁰⁷ As the temple robbers usually were of foreign descent, ἱεροσυλεῖν would no doubt have been counted among the most serious crimes committed by gentiles against the Jewish nation. From a Jewish perspective, then, ἱεροσυλεῖν may have constituted a characteristic gentile sin, an iniquity which would have typified the nation's oppression by other nations.

Hence, as an allusion to historically attested gentile crimes against Jews in an address to a gentile interlocutor, the charge of ἱεροσυλεῖν in Romans 2:22b would have had its "legitimacy" and (reasonably close to) an "universal application," and thus served its rhetorical purpose. Of course, Paul is not saying that every gentile of his time was habitually engaged in plundering the Jerusalem temple, no more than he is accusing every single gentile for committing the sins detailed in 1:18–32. Paul speaks collectively about Jews and gentiles in his letter, and as he in 1:18–32 discussed the collective guilt of gentiles, here he may have the same thought in mind by alluding to well-known Jewish traditions concerning gentile misdeeds against the Jewish nation. Admittedly, I have some doubts about the rhetorical effect of

---

[205] See Schrenk, "ἱερός" (1965) 255–57; Krentz, "Name" (1990) 433–34 n. 22. An interesting case is found in Acts 19:37 where the town clerk in Ephesus defends Paul and his companions with the words: "You have brought these men here who are neither temple robbers (ἱεροσύλους) nor blasphemers (βλασφημοῦντας) of our goddess."

[206] Kuss objects: "Der Gegensatz (εἴδωλα) macht es unmöglich, dabei an den jüdischen Tempel zu denken . . ., es muß sich um heidnische Heiligtümer handeln" (*Römerbrief* [1957] 1.86). But, as I have pointed out above, the antithesis in v. 22b is not as clear as Kuss assumes.

[207] On plunderings of (or attempts to plunder) the Jerusalem temple, and idolatrous behavior in that connection, see, e.g., 1 Macc 1:20–24, 34–40; 6:12; 2 Macc 3:4–40; 5:15–21; 6:1–6; 9:16; 4 Macc 4:1–14; 1 Esd 1:39, 43, 51; Dan 1:2; Josephus, *A.J.* 12.359.

such a charge, but it seems to me that the reading proposed here makes more sense than those in which Paul's target is presumed to be a Jew and in which ἱεροσυλεῖν is thought to refer to Jewish temple robbery or "sacrilege" almost unheard of. This conclusion is anything but discouraged by the immense problems which the traditional approach has faced in reading this "most curious, if not perplexing" text. Paul is not "paganizing" Jews in the passage. Rather, his choice of the charge of ἱεροσυλεῖν suggests that the interlocutor is not a Jew at all. Taken thus, the gentile conversational partner is being confronted along the following lines: You who claim to abhor idols, are you nevertheless guilty of the characteristic gentile misdeed of ἱεροσυλεῖν? Put differently: You who want to call yourself a Jew, do you nonetheless behave as a gentile? Hence, the interlocutor's implied act of ἱεροσυλεῖν exposes his false claim of Jewish identity.

Paul summarizes his indictment in v. 23: "You who boast in the Law, you dishonor God by transgressing the Law." This may also be taken as Paul's fifth rhetorical question, but the following γάρ makes it more likely that v. 23 is a plain statement, "implying that the point of the previous questions cannot be denied."[208] Again, Paul is not asserting that there is something wrong per se with "boasting in the Law," only that this particular individual to whom he is speaking is not consistent with his "boasting." God is not dishonored by a "boasting in the Law," but by the interlocutor's transgression of the Law in spite of his "boasting." Thus, the interlocutor proves to be guilty of the dreadful sin of dishonoring God because, despite his appearance as a Law-abiding Ἰουδαῖος, he violates the Law.

This summary statement is followed up by a scriptural quotation: "For, 'the name of God is blasphemed among the gentiles because of you,' as it is written" (τὸ γὰρ ὄνομα τοῦ θεοῦ δι' ὑμᾶς βλασφημεῖται ἐν τοῖς ἔθνεσιν, καθὼς γέγραπται). The quotation evidently comes from Isaiah 52:5: δι' ὑμᾶς διὰ παντὸς τὸ ὄνομά μου βλασφημεῖται ἐν τοῖς ἔθνεσιν.[209] What scholars have found baffling, however, is the fact that in the text of Isaiah it is not due to something which Israel has committed that God's name is

---

[208] Dunn, *Romans* (1988) 1.115.
[209] That Paul is here relying on the LXX and not the MT is shown by Stanley, *Paul* (1992) 84–86, 256 n. 15.

blasphemed, but because Israel is being oppressed by other nations. In other words, it is because of the oppressing gentiles that God's name is being blasphemed. Thus, the question arises: Why would Paul have chosen an indirect accusation against *gentiles* to proof his case against a *Jewish* interlocutor? No adequate answer to this question has been given by commentators, some of whom suffice to note that Paul is using the scriptural quotation "[i]n freiester Weise,"[210] others that he is "misquoting" the text of Isaiah.[211] Dietrich-Alex Koch, who has studied Paul's citations to scripture, remarks: "Die entscheidende Voraussetzung für die hier vorliegende Verwendung von Jes 52,5c ist allerdings, daß [Paulus] den Textausschnitt völlig aus dem Zusammenhang herauslöst."[212] Richard B. Hays states rather forcefully that Paul's quoting of Isaiah "is not only a low blow but also . . . a stunning misreading of the text."[213] He argues, however, that Paul's "provocative misreading of Isa. 52:5 is only provisional. He knows perfectly well that these chapters of Isaiah are portents of God's grace toward Israel." According to Hays, then,

> [t]he quotation of Isa. 52:5 works metaphorically in Paul's argument only if the reader castigated by the text imaginatively takes on the role of Israel in exile. Yet the reader who assumes that posture cannot then fail to hear also the promises of hope and deliverance that Isaiah speaks to Israel in exile [cf. Rom 11:26–27]. . . . Consequently, to read Paul's citation of Isa. 52:5 as unqualified condemnation of Israel is bad reading, or, more precisely, it is an interpretation possible only on a first reading of the letter.[214]

Hays' assessment that Paul realizes fully that these parts of Isaiah are "portents of God's grace toward Israel" is almost certainly correct. But Hays overlooks the crucial point that Paul's quotation of Isaiah 52:5 is unquestionably used in a context of indictment. This fact cannot be so easily disregarded. It is profoundly unlikely that "the reader castigated by the text"

---

[210] Zahn, *Römer* (1910) 140–41. Cf. Sanday and Headlam, *Romans* (1902) 67.
[211] Harvey, *Israel* (1996) 78.
[212] *Schrift* (1986) 261 n. 5. Cf. Stanley, *Paul* (1992) 85.
[213] *Echoes* (1989) 45. Hays adds that "[t]he marvel is that Paul's misreading has so often met with blithe acceptance by subsequent Christian commentators."
[214] *Echoes* (1989) 46. Hays is followed on this by Wagner, *Heralds* (2002) 178.

simultaneously hears "the promises of hope and deliverance." To Hays' credit, however, it must be noted that he has not attempted to solve the problem by ignoring the relevance of Isaiah 52:5 for Paul's argument nor by bringing in other scriptural texts as proof-texts for Paul.

It has long been a commonplace to hold that in Romans 2:24 Paul mixes Isaiah 52:5 and Ezekiel 36:17–23, the latter of which speaks of Israel's disobedience and profanation of God's name. In his recent "intertextual" study of Romans 2:17–29, Berkley calls Paul's quotation a "complex mixture of reference and citation." According to him, "[t]here is no evidence that Isaiah 52 functions exegetically as a reference for Paul. It serves the separate rhetorical function of a proof-text offering supporting authority for Paul's conclusion, which has its basis in Ezekiel 36."[215] But what more evidence is needed of Isaiah 52 functioning "exegetically" for Paul than Paul's own καθὼς γέγραπται? Isaiah 52 may perhaps function badly as such, but only if it is assumed that it is used within an indictment of Jews. Moreover, if Paul intended to allude to the text of Ezekiel, why did he quote Isaiah so distinctly? Berkley proposes the explanation that "Isa 52:5 provides the concise declarative statement Paul needs in order for the quotation to conform to the form of his indictment, but it does not make Paul's point. Ezek 36:17–23, which lacks the declarative statement which Paul could easily integrate into his indictment, provides the point Paul wishes to make."[216] This explanation seems dubious. Paul would hardly have had difficulties with integrating the text of Ezekiel into his discourse if that was what he intended,[217] or any other text for that matter which contained a similar indictment of Israel, of which there is indeed no lack in Jewish scriptures. He

---

[215] *Covenant* (2000) 137, 139. Cf. also Dunn, *Romans* (1988) 1.115, 118; Wright, "Letter" (2002) 447–48. In addition to Ezek 36, Ito, "Romans 2" (1995) 27, 31–32, brings in Deut 29 as a text on which Paul bases his argument.

[216] *Covenant* (2000) 139–40.

[217] He might, e.g., have said: ἐβεβήλωσαν (γὰρ) τὸ ὄνομά μου τὸ ἅγιον (ἐν τοῖς ἔθνεσιν) (v. 20), or τὸ (γὰρ) ὄνομά μου τὸ ἅγιον ἐβεβήλωσαν οἶκος Ισραηλ ἐν τοῖς ἔθνεσιν (v. 21), or τὸ (γὰρ) ὄνομά μου τὸ ἅγιον ἐβεβηλώσατε ἐν τοῖς ἔθνεσιν (v. 22), or τὸ (γὰρ) ὄνομά μου τὸ μέγα τὸ βεβηλωθὲν ἐν τοῖς ἔθνεσιν ἐβεβηλώσατε ἐν μέσῳ αὐτῶν (v. 23), or anything joined from any of these fit for his purpose.

might even have added such a text to his quotation of Isaiah. Paul, however, neither adds nor quotes any such text, Ezekiel included. It appears rather that Ezekiel 36 has been brought in by interpreters in order to provide the point they wish Paul to make.[218]

Thus, the question remains why Paul chose to refer explicitly to Isaiah 52:5 if he wanted to add a scriptural proof to an indictment of Jews, when he could have cited a number of other texts in which Israel's disobedience was being declared to support such a case. My suggestion is that the context of Romans 2:24 is very different from the context generally assumed, which, in turn, makes Paul's use of Isaiah 52:5 intelligible enough. Paul was not at all concerned with an indictment of Jews, but of a gentile interlocutor. To use Hays' words, the "bad reading" is to read Paul's quotation as a condemnation of Jews, whether qualified or not. It is quite unnecessary to insist that Paul is turning his scriptural quotation upside down. He was probably well aware of the fact that Isaiah 52:5 referred not to the misdeeds of Israel but of other nations, and thus that it could suit his purpose in an indictment of a gentile interlocutor. Hence, Paul's citation of Isaiah is neither a "stunning misreading of the text" nor a "low blow," but a natural application of its basic meaning.

2.3.4. The Value of Circumcision for the Gentile Interlocutor (2:25–29)

Verse 25 is normally taken with what follows. This may speak against the text's structural markers since the conjunction γάρ suggests that this verse goes with and supports the preceding argument. The conjunction οὖν in v. 26 shows furthermore that this verse draws an inference from what precedes, the working out of which extends throughout v. 29. Nevertheless, due to the shared terminology of v. 25 and vv. 26–29, and to the more

---

[218] Cf., e.g., the comments of Tobin, "Controversy" (1993) 311 n. 33: "The wording [of Rom 2:24] is closer to Isa 52:5 . . . but Paul's point in using the quotation seems closer to Ezek 36:20. . . . Only the text of Ezek 36:20 emphasize [sic] the points that the Jews, because of their transgressions of the Law, were forced to leave their own land, and that this departure caused God's name to be dishonored among the Gentiles." Dunn, *Romans* (1988) 1.115, remarks that Ezek 36:17–23 "in effect enables [Paul] to give Isa 52:5 a more accusing note."

general character of Paul's discourse from v. 25 onward, it seems appropriate to analyze and read v. 25 specifically within the context of vv. 26–29. The οὖν in v. 26 seems also to mark an inference drawn mainly from v. 25. On the other hand, due heed must be paid to structural markers put into the text by the writer, and while the function of γάρ in v. 25 may be somewhat ambiguous, it should remind us of the continuity between Paul's argument in vv. 17–24 and vv. 25–29.

Having exposed the interlocutor's inconsistent and godless behavior, Paul informs him that circumcision (περιτομή) is indeed (μέν) of value if he "does the Law." If he, on the other hand (δέ), is a transgressor of the Law his circumcision has become an "uncircumcision" (ἀκροβυστία). Paul has, of course, already shown that the latter pertains to his partner in dialogue. As a marker of Jewish identity and national distinctiveness,[219] the emergence of circumcision as a topic within Paul's discussion of Jewish vis-à-vis non-Jewish identity is anything but surprising. It is widely held that Paul's aim here is to launch an attack on "false confidence" in circumcision as "the mark of [the typical Jew's] religious distinctiveness, the badge of national privilege, the seal of God's covenant favor to Israel his chosen people."[220] This is certainly possible with respect to Paul's isolated remark here. But, seen in a wider perspective, this is probably not what Paul has in mind. Since most of his fellow Jews would have agreed that circumcision as

---

[219] Scholarly discussion of circumcision in ancient Judaism in general, and in relation to Paul's letters in particular, is abundant. With respect to the function of circumcision as a (potential) marker of Jewish identity, see esp. the helpful study of Cohen, *Beginnings* (1999) 39–49, 156–62, 168–74 and passim. Cohen's general assessment is that "[i]n certain times and places circumcision would have functioned as a marker—or the marker—of Jewishness . . ., but not in all times and not in all places" (p. 39). More pointedly for the present study, "in the city of Rome in the first century C.E., certainly in the latter part of the century, circumcision served as a marker of Jewishness" (p. 44).

[220] Dunn, *Romans* (1988) 1.125–26. Kuss, *Römerbrief* (1957) 1.89, states that, according to Paul, circumcision is "der zweite Pfeiler jüdischer Auserwähltheitshybris," the first being the Law.

such entailed no guarantee of salvation,[221] it is not immediately clear at whom Paul's censure would have been aimed. To be sure, Paul's interlocutor is a fictitious person and might therefore represent a Jew who has "false confidence" in his circumcision. But even so, and even if there were Jews who actually had such views, why should Paul want to rebuke them in a letter to a gentile audience? What purpose would that have served for the gentile readers, or for Paul himself? Even if we assume, as most scholars do, that Paul's intended audience was partly Jewish, what would have been the point of attacking Jewish confidence in circumcision, "false" or not? That would seem particularly strange in light of the widely accepted view that one of Paul's main purposes with the letter, if not *the* purpose, was to settle tensions between a "Jewish Christian" minority and a "gentile Christian" majority, as reflected primarily in chapters 14–15, in which the main thrust is not only mutual acceptance but also, according to this theory, that the "gentile Christians" (the strong) are to accept and welcome the "Jewish Christians" (the weak) despite their orientation to a more Jewish way of life. If this is what Paul primarily had in mind when he wrote the letter, would an attack on Jewish confidence in circumcision, whether "false" or otherwise, have served his purpose? Hardly. Dunn writes that "Paul evidently was of the opinion that such a sharp challenge [i.e. 2:25b] was necessary to undermine so central a pillar of Jewish self-understanding and identity."[222] But an attempt to "undermine" the value of circumcision for Jews would seem to be quite at odds with what Paul says about Jewish privileges in 9:4–5 and especially with his definite disapproval of gentile arrogance towards Jews in chapter 11. Paul makes it perfectly clear in 3:1–2 that the benefit of circumcision *for Jews* is "much in every way" (πολὺ κατὰ πάντα τρόπον). When he elsewhere speaks of his own circumcision he does not reject its value; on the contrary, he confirms it (Phil 3:3–5; cf. 2 Cor

---

[221] Cf., e.g., Boyarin, *Jew* (1994) 92–93: "[T]he privilege consists primarily in the guarantee that in the end of days they will be able to repent, and then God will restore Israel to its glory as he had promised to her ancestors [cf. Rom 11] . . . Jewish theology did not provide for justification on the basis of being Jewish alone, although there were some strains that came close to such a view."
[222] *Romans* (1988) 1.121.

11:21b–22). When he, on the other hand, unmistakably refers to circumcision in negative terms it is always related to the question if gentiles are to be circumcised or not (see esp. Gal 5–6). Nowhere does Paul hint at circumcision's invalidation for Jews, except, supposedly, in Romans 2:25–29.

Surely we may wonder if Paul was of the opinion that if Jews transgressed the Law their circumcision would become worthless, but I am not convinced that this is the right question to ask with respect to Paul's words in this passage. This is so because Paul is, in my view, not specifically concerned with circumcision of Jews here. When he subsequently states that the advantage of circumcision for Jews is "much in every way" (3:1–2), he does not add "if they do the Law." Obviously, he is not thinking of its advantage for gentiles as well in 3:1–2. Thus, there is a notable difference between Paul's statements on circumcision in 2:25–29, on the one hand, and 3:1–2, on the other. John M. G. Barclay comments on this difference:

> It is because Paul has finally removed *all* the supports on which his Jewish interlocutor can stand that the questions of 3.1 arise: 'Then what is the advantage of the Jew and of what value is circumcision?' As C. H. Dodd observed, 'The logical answer on the basis of Paul's argument is, "None whatever!"' That Paul does not answer like this, but insists 'Much in every way', is a genuine surprise to the faithful reader of Rom 2.[223]

While the question posed in 3:1 may emerge because the preceding passage includes many potential implications for Jewish identity, Paul's answer in v. 2 does not have to be a "genuine surprise," at least not if circumcision is being spoken of from a different perspective than in 2:25–29.

There is in fact a further aspect of Paul's reference to circumcision in vv. 25–29 which tends to be overlooked by scholars. Circumcision was not only an identity marker for native Jews, but also an initiation rite for converts to Judaism. There were many ways in which gentiles could and did sympathize with Judaism and Jewish communities,[224] but only by circum-

---

[223] "Paul" (1998) 546 (emphasis original). On Dodd's comments, see his *Romans* (1932) 43.
[224] See esp. Cohen, *Beginnings* (1999) 140–74 and passim. Cf. also McKnight, *Light* (1991) 90–101; Feldman, *Jew* (1993) esp. 342–82; Zetterholm, *Formation* (2003) 121–29.

cision could they become proselytes,[225] and, according to many Jews and non-Jews, thus call themselves Ἰουδαῖοι. In an address to a gentile interlocutor who wants to call himself a Jew, and within a letter addressed to (former) gentile adherents to Judaism, Paul's focus on circumcision in vv. 25–29 could well be aimed at this particular aspect of it. Paul would then be countering circumcision of gentiles, which, in turn, explains why the value of circumcision is made suspect in these verses. According to him, God never intended gentiles to be circumcised.

It is worth noting that Paul's language in v. 25 is largely hypothetical. He is speaking in examples. This is shown by his choice of ἐάν with the subjunctive in both conditional clauses. This type of condition (third class) "in distinction to a first class conditional [cf. v. 17], is more tentative and simply projects some action or event for hypothetical consideration."[226] This means that it is not altogether clear at this point whether the interlocutor is thought of as already circumcised or not. In the apodosis of the first clause (v. 25a), Paul merely states in general terms that "circumcision is of value" (περιτομὴ ὠφελεῖ), followed by the hypothetical "if you do the Law" (ἐὰν νόμον πράσσῃς). In the second apodosis (v. 25b), the words "your circumcision" (ἡ περιτομή σου) suggest that the person spoken to is circumcised, but the hypothetical context of the third class conditions nevertheless yields some doubt that he is. This uncertainty is in fact wholly in line with the interlocutor's, as it were, mixed Jewish-gentile identity throughout the chapter. According to Paul, circumcision would indeed (μέν) be of value for the interlocutor, if he should follow the Law. Paul, however, has already shown that this is not the case. Hence, the hypothetical or, better perhaps, exemplifying formulation ἐὰν δὲ παραβάτης νόμου ᾖς gives Paul's address in v. 25 a somewhat more general tone than in the preceding.

---

[225] McEleney argues differently ("Conversion" [1974]), partly supported by Collins, "Symbol" (1985). But see the response of Nolland, "Uncircumcised" (1981). Cf. Donaldson, *Paul* (1997) 58–59; Cohen, *Beginnings* (1999) 158: "[A]s far as is known no Jewish community in antiquity (including Philo's) accepted as members male proselytes who were not circumcised" (cf. p. 219).

[226] Porter, *Idioms* (1994) 262.

At any rate, if the interlocutor is thought of as circumcised, which seems to be the case (cf. v. 27), Paul clearly has some doubts about its worth. He thus portrays this person's confidence in being circumcised as a false one; not because of circumcision itself, but because the individual in question was never meant to benefit from it. This person still belongs to those whom God had punished by "handing them over" to various kinds of vices (1:18–32), those whose existence is still affected by this condition, those whose path to salvation does not lead through circumcision. God had decided otherwise for this group of people. Paul's interlocutor, however, thinks that he is better off than these people are, but his actual conduct exposes his real identity. Even if circumcised, his circumcision would count for nothing; it would indeed be as good as uncircumcision.

Obviously, Paul is not suggesting that circumcision actually becomes an "uncircumcision" (lit. "foreskin"), whether one obeys the Law or not. Rather, what is meant is that on the day of judgment (vv. 5–6) the interlocutor will have no advantage over other sinful gentiles (1:18–32), but will be numbered among those who "do evil things" (v. 9) and sin "in a lawless manner" (v. 12) and will perish accordingly. Instead of being one of the "doers of the Law" who will be justified (v. 13), he is a mere "hearer of the Law" who, despite his instruction from the Law (v. 18), utterly transgresses it and thus his circumcision is as good as worthless. In v. 25, then, Paul issues a warning that to be circumcised will be of no avail for the interlocutor and his likes. God did not design that they should bypass God's judgment of gentiles by becoming Jews. As the subsequent discourse reveals, Paul has a different kind of "circumcision" and a different kind of "doing the Law" in mind for his partner in dialogue.

Paul continues to speak hypothetically in v. 26 by using again the third class conditional clause: "If (ἐάν), then, the uncircumcised (ἡ ἀκροβυστία)[227] keeps the (righteous) requirements of the Law (τὰ δικαιώματα

---

[227] Paul was probably unfamiliar with the adj. ἀκρόβυστος, the use of which is first attested in Ignatius and Aquila; see Cranfield, *Romans* (1975) 1.173. Thus he uses the fem. ἡ ἀκροβυστία to denote a circumcised individual to whom the masc. αὐτοῦ in v. 26b refers.

τοῦ νόμου),²²⁸ will not his uncircumcision be regarded as circumcision?" That the example provided is not just hypothetical but also potential, Paul will show in his subsequent exposition of the εὐαγγέλιον. The relation of v. 26 to the statements made in vv. 14–16 is recognized by most commentators. There Paul gave an analogous, hypothetical example (ὅταν with the subjunctive; v. 14)—a potential one, to be sure—of gentiles who may do what the Law requires (τὰ τοῦ νόμου) although they do not have the Law "by birth." As in this passage, Paul's language in v. 26 is eschatological with the future λογισθήσεται referring to the day of judgment (cf. vv. 5–6, 16). Paul's rhetorical question expects a positive answer (οὐχ): Yes, at the end of times, gentiles may indeed be reckoned by God as circumcised, that is, if they do what the Law requires of them. Hence, gentiles do not have to be circumcised in order to partake of God's covenant with Israel and thus be saved. Indeed, according to Paul, they *should not* undergo circumcision for this purpose.

In v. 27 Paul turns again directly to his interlocutor, stating that the gentiles spoken of in the previous verse, viz. those "physically uncircumcised" (ἡ ἐκ φύσεως ἀκροβυστία)²²⁹ who fulfill the Law,²³⁰ will indeed judge (κρινεῖ) him who transgresses the Law in spite of his circumcision. The καί is probably to be read as adverbial and thus emphatic ("indeed").²³¹ The

---

[228] This phrase must correspond closely to τὸ δικαίωμα τοῦ νόμου in 8:4 (cf. 1:32), despite the difference in grammatical number.

[229] Wright notes that it is "slightly misleading" to refer to the uncircumcision as "physical." Instead, Paul is saying that the uncircumcised are "'naturally' uncircumcised through their Gentile origins" ("Letter" [2002] 448 with n. 73). But, as Wright himself observes, "[a]ll males are 'naturally uncircumcised' in the sense that they are born that way," Jews included. More to the point, would not ἐκ φύσεως be superfluous if Paul simply wanted to speak of "naturally" uncircumcised gentiles? Certainly it would have sufficed for him to say ἡ ἀκροβυστία. Moreover, as the context shows, it is far more likely that he added ἐκ φύσεως precisely because of the contrast made in these verses between "physical" circumcision and non-physical "circumcision."

[230] I take τὸν νόμον τελοῦσα to be equivalent to τὰ δικαιώματα τοῦ νόμου φυλάσσῃ in v. 26.

[231] The question preceding makes the usual connective sense ("and") rather awkward and thus unlikely.

prepositional phrase διὰ γράμματος καὶ περιτομῆς is more difficult. That διά with the genitive is meant to indicate attendant circumstances seems likely,[232] but it is the word γράμμα which causes complications. In relation to the statements of vv. 28–29 the question of what Paul meant by this word has been the subject of a long debate about Paul's understanding of "the letter and the spirit."[233] While earlier interpreters saw in the word a reference to a "literal" (as opposed to "spiritual") understanding of circumcision, usually with a pejorative import, more recently scholars have taken it to refer to "God's commands in written form," or "the law of God in the concrete, written form."[234] According to this view, the phrase διὰ γράμματος καὶ περιτομῆς would then emphasize the possession of God's commandments and circumcision.

The strength of this latter approach is that it takes into consideration the usual sense of the word γράμμα, viz. something written, such as a letter (the character) or a book,[235] and this use is attested elsewhere in Paul's letters.[236] In that case, Paul would probably be alluding to the interlocutor's resting upon (v. 17), learning from (v. 18), and boasting of the Law (v. 23),[237] less likely his "possession" of it. There are, however, at least two

---

[232] So most commentators. Some think that διά is instrumental here, e.g. Dunn, *Romans* (1988) 1.123; Porter, *Idioms* (1994) 149. But it is difficult to see how γράμμα καὶ περιτομή can constitute the means by which the interlocutor transgresses the Law.

[233] See esp. Käsemann, "Spirit" (1971); Westerholm, "Letter" (1984). With respect to potential similarities with Philo's understanding, cf. Boyarin, *Jew* (1994) 78–81, 86–97; and Barclay's response in "Paul" (1998).

[234] Westerholm, "Letter" (1984) 236, 239. Cf. Käsemann, "Spirit" (1971) 143 ("the Mosaic Torah in its written documentation"). Unlike Westerholm, Käsemann is of the opinion that Paul always uses the word in a depreciatory, negative sense. According to Barclay, "Paul" (1998) 553, γράμμα "seems to be shorthand for the Jewish τὰ ἱερὰ γράμματα." He reads the word more broadly as a reference to "the Scriptures as *written* word" (emphasis his).

[235] See LSJ, s.v., who read the word in Rom 2:27 as "the Law of Moses" (III.3).

[236] 2 Cor 3:7; Gal 6:11 (in pl.). What the word means in Rom 7:6 and 2 Cor 3:6 (both in sg.) is much less clear.

[237] As Käsemann notes, the Law "for Paul (as the essential portion and aspect of the Old Testament) is identical with scripture as a whole" ("Spirit" [1971] 143).

weaknesses in this reading. First, if Paul was referring to "God's commands in written form," one would rather have expected him to use the word νόμος instead of γράμμα, especially in light of the preceding discourse, and thus to say διὰ νόμου καὶ περιτομῆς. Second, the immediate context in which Paul uses the word γράμμα appears to be neglected by this reading. From v. 25 onward the main thrust lies in Paul's discussion of circumcision and uncircumcision. A critical point of his is clearly to argue that gentiles need not, and should not, undergo circumcision in order to be justified, and to explain the way in which their "physical uncircumcision" may be reckoned as circumcision. Thus, it is likely that the phrase διὰ γράμματος καὶ περιτομῆς draws attention to "physical" circumcision as opposed to non-physical "circumcision." This is certainly possible if γράμματος καὶ περιτομῆς is read as *hendiadys*.[238] The "written circumcision" would then denote a circumcision in the literal sense, as prescribed by the written Law; not with a negative import, as many earlier interpreters preferred, but simply as a contrast to the "physical uncircumcision." This reading is also supported by Paul's use of γράμμα in v. 29, in which (περιτομὴ ἐν) γράμματι corresponds to ἡ ἐν τῷ φανερῷ ἐν σαρκὶ περιτομή in v. 28, that is, the "visible" circumcision "in (the) flesh." I see no good reason for Paul using γράμμα in two different ways in these verses,[239] a word which he otherwise seldom employs. The contrast made in the text is not between possessing and not possessing. Rather, it is between two kinds of circumcision: one physical and visible, the other non-physical and invisible. Paul's aim is to show that it is only the latter from which his interlocutor may benefit.

In vv. 28–29 Paul supports his argument (γάρ) by drawing attention to the difference between being a Ἰουδαῖος outwardly (ἐν τῷ φανερῷ), visibly and "physically" (ἐν τῷ φανερῷ ἐν σαρκί) circumcised, and being a Ἰουδαῖος inwardly (ἐν τῷ κρυπτῷ), circumcised in heart, not literally (οὐ

---

[238] I.e. a co-ordination of the two words in which γράμμα modifies περιτομή. Cf. χάριν καὶ ἀποστολήν in 1:5 (see above in Ch. 1 sec. 3.1.2).

[239] So Westerholm, "Letter" (1984), for whom γράμμα in v. 27 refers to "the possession of God's commands in written form" (p. 236), whereas the word in v. 29 alludes to those who are "literally circumcised": It denotes "circumcision in a physical, external form."

γράμματι) but "spiritually" (ἐν πνεύματι). Paul focuses still on the contrast between that which is visible and that which is invisible. His point is neither that ethnic Jews are not "true Jews," let alone that "the only true Jew is the Christian,"[240] nor that circumcision has played out its part for Jews. Rather, Paul is using an analogy drawn from a well-known Jewish discourse on the "circumcision of the heart,"[241] the importance of which would hardly have been denied by his fellow Jews, in order to demonstrate that the state of being uncircumcised can and will be reckoned as equal to the one of being circumcised, if those uncircumcised do what the Law requires of them. It is the inward disposition which counts before God, not outward appearance. Paul's argument recalls what he had stated in vv. 15–16 about gentiles having "the work of the Law written on their hearts." The gentile whose heart is circumcised in (the) spirit will be counted as ὁ ἐν τῷ κρυπτῷ Ἰουδαῖος when God judges that which is hidden and invisible (τὰ κρυπτά) through Christ Jesus (v. 16). But the gentile who, like Paul's interlocutor, seeks to be Ἰουδαῖος ἐν τῷ φανερῷ will merely receive praise (ἔπαινος) from men, not from God.

Paul's attempt to provide grounds for the equal value of uncircumcision is not without difficulties, to be sure. That Paul was aware of this, as well as the danger of his argument being (mis)understood as having primarily to do with Jews instead of the salvation of gentiles, is suggested by his immediately following remarks on the advantage of the Jew and his circumcision (3:1–2).

Paul's statement in v. 27 about the interlocutor being "judged" (κρινεῖ) rounds off the chapter. Contrary to his opinion of having grounds for judging his fellow gentiles (vv. 1, 3), it is actually he himself who eventually will be judged by those gentiles who keep the Law without being circumcised. Their uncircumcision will be counted as circumcision because they do

---

[240] Käsemann, "Spirit" (1971) 144. Cf. on p. 146: "The phenomenon of the true Jew ... is eschatologically realized in the Christian who has freed himself from Judaism."

[241] Cf., e.g., Deut 10:16; Jer 4:4; 9:24–25; Ezek 44:7, 9; 1QpHab 11:13; 1QS 5:5; Jub. 1:23; Philo, Migr. 92–93; Spec. 1.304–306; Odes Sol. 11:1–3. Cf. also Jer 38:33 (MT 31:33).

what the Law requires of them (v. 26). Conversely, even if the interlocutor is "literally" circumcised, his circumcision will be counted as nothing (vv. 25, 27) because he is a transgressor of the Law. His fellow gentiles who are not circumcised and yet follow the Law will therefore be saved, while he will not.[242] He will only be praiseworthy among men (v. 29), namely, among those within the Jewish (or "Christian") community who would advocate circumcision of gentiles.[243]

3. The Function of Paul's Interlocutor in Romans 2

As shown in Chapter Three, the literary technique of creating an imaginary interlocutor may be found in all kinds of epistolary settings. As the epistolary medium was generally perceived as a surrogate for oral communication, the dialogical style would have been appropriate to various kinds of epistolary purposes. Not only did the invention of a conversational partner enable the author to respond in advance to potential comments or counter-arguments, but it also served as a device of persuasion by presenting the interlocutor as an object of identification for the audience.

We have already seen that the ways in which Paul makes use of conventional epistolary expressions are clearly meant to establish his "official" status and authority vis-à-vis the gentile audience. He writes as a divinely ordained "apostle to the gentiles," and as such he draws primarily from characteristic official correspondence. While the dialogical style may have given Paul's letter a certain touch of intimacy like that more typically found in private/personal letters, the authoritative framework would have contributed to its didactic character as Paul's proclamation and exposition of

---

[242] Käsemann asserts that Paul is claiming that "the Gentiles will judge the Jews" ("Spirit" [1971] 142). That would be in striking contrast to what Paul states in ch. 11 about Israel's merely temporary disbelief (in Jesus as Messiah), and about the gentiles merely being "grafted on the olive tree."

[243] Cf. Barclay, "Paul" (1998) 549: "Those who are concerned for 'human praise' are those who set much store by their social standing in the Jewish community."

the εὐαγγέλιον, as a "kind of written conversation" between the gentile audience and their apostle.

In functional terms, this would seem to correspond closely to the more or less didactic context of the Greco-Roman "diatribe." Commenting on the intended function of Epictetus' discourses, his student, Arrian, states: "[Epictetus] was clearly aiming at nothing else but to incite the minds of his hearers (τὰς γνώμας τῶν ἀκουόντων) to the best thing.... [L]et those who read [his words] be assured of this, that when Epictetus himself spoke them, the hearer could not help but feel exactly what Epictetus wanted him to feel (ἀνάγκη ἦν τοῦτο πάσχειν τὸν ἀκροώμενον αὐτῶν ὅπερ ἐκεῖνος αὐτὸν παθεῖν ἠβούλετο)."[244] Epictetus, in turn, said of his own teacher, Musonius Rufus, that "he spoke in such a way that each of us as we sat there fancied someone had gone to Rufus and told him of our faults; so effective was his grasp of what men actually do, so vividly did he set before each man's eyes his particular weaknesses (τὰ ἑκάστου κακά)." The didactic method of Musonius Rufus was "diatribal," of course, as was his student's.

Prior to the above words about his mentor, Epictetus had spoken in somewhat ironical terms of the philosopher's lecture as an "invitation" (παράκλησις): "I invite you (παρακαλῶ σε) to come and hear that you are in a bad way, and that you are concerned with anything rather than what you should be concerned with, and that you are ignorant of the good and the evil (ἀγνοεῖς τὰ ἀγαθὰ καὶ τὰ κακά), and are wretched and miserable."[245] Correspondingly, one might say that once an imaginary partner in dialogue is introduced in a letter the audience, instead of merely being passive readers and/or listeners, are summoned to correlate their own views with the interlocutor's and thus to become a living part, so to speak, of the text itself.

The function of Paul's conversational partner in Romans 2 is interwoven with his identity. The interlocutor invented by Paul is a person of gentile origin who fails to recognize that his ethnic roots put him in ranks with the people described in 1:18–32 whose existence is still affected by the divine

---

[244] See Arrian's introductory letter to Lucius Gellius in the LCL ed. of Epictetus' *Diatr.*
[245] *Diatr.* 3.23.28–29.

punishment once imposed upon them. Instead of coming to terms with this state of affairs, he thinks that he can bypass God's own will by becoming a proselyte.

By creating this fictitious individual and discrediting his convictions and conducts, Paul attempts to persuade his gentile audience that the proper path to salvation for them is not through full conversion to Judaism. His target includes everyone among the audience (cf. πᾶς in 2:1) who may reason and act as does the interlocutor. The interlocutor, whose identity as a proselyte (i.e. a circumcised gentile) is sometimes blurred, is singled out as a potential, imaginary representative of the audience.[246] Not only would an identification with such a person be relevant to those who already are proselytes but notably also to those who reflect upon becoming proselytes. Both parties get to know that circumcised gentiles do not have grounds for judging uncircumcised, yet Law-abiding, gentiles as if the former were in a more advantageous position. As a matter of fact, those who remain uncircumcised and do what the Law requires of them are much better off than Paul's interlocutor and his likes.

In this way, the status of proselytes is made suspect. Any proselyte in the audience hears that he should not have undergone circumcision, and any potential proselyte hears that he neither needs nor should undergo circumcision in order to have a chance on the day of judgment. As Dunn writes in his comments on 2:26: "Those who had attended the synagogue as God-worshipers in particular would rejoice at the clear implication of Paul's teaching: that in order to become a full member of the covenant, a full participator in the blessings God had promised to the people of Israel, it was *not* necessary to be circumcised."[247] While Paul would more likely insist that the "God-worshipers" *should not* undergo circumcision for this purpose, Dunn is almost certainly correct in his assessment of the effect of

---

[246] Cf. Stowers, *Diatribe* (1981) 103, 106. Swearingen, "Tongues" (2002) 233, suggests that by using "multiple voices" in Rom "Paul performs his discourses . . . as models for his auditors to emulate in two ways: by following the content of the teaching, and by repeating the teaching as spoken in the letter to other auditors."

[247] *Romans* (1988) 1.126–27 (emphasis his).

Paul's words. Paul's aim is to dissuade such persons from taking the final step to full conversion to Judaism.[248]

Paul's choice of inventing an interlocutor is appropriate to the epistolary situation. The letter constitutes his initial act of proclaiming God's εὐ-αγγέλιον in Rome to an audience largely unknown to him, an audience towards whom Paul's authority as an apostle to the gentiles has not yet been established, but who evidently have already received some knowledge of at least some aspects of the εὐαγγέλιον from someone. The literary technique of creating a conversational partner is effective precisely because the individual addressed is fictitious. That enables Paul to indict him and dispute his views so severely without directly addressing the audience,[249] a mode which might risk the acceptance of his message. Instead, Paul's interlocutor presents an invitation to identification, an invitation that is formed in a way which not only includes proselytes but also—and more importantly—potential ones.

4. Implications for the Subsequent Discourse in Romans

The conclusion reached above on the identity of Paul's interlocutor in Romans 2 has several implications for the following discourse. Here I will confine my discussion to two issues which are of primary significance. First, how does the identity of the interlocutor in chapter 2 as a gentile correspond to the identity of the interlocutor in subsequent dialogical exchanges? Second, does not Paul's statement in 3:9 contradict my conclusion of the identity of the interlocutor in chapter 2? I will begin discussing the second question.

---

[248] Cf. also Gal 5:2–6.
[249] Cf. Stowers' comments on the interlocutor in 2:1–5: "[B]y using the imaginary interlocutor, Paul can criticize any readers who have presumptuous attitudes without directly accusing anyone of anything" (*Rereading* [1994] 103). See also the discussion above in Ch. 3 sec. 1.2.

4.1. The Meaning of the Verb Προητιασάμεθα in Romans 3:9

It has long been held that in 1:18–3:20 Paul seeks to describe the sinfulness of all humanity, first mainly of gentiles (esp. 1:18–32), and then of Jews (esp. chapter 2). The ultimate support for this reading is thought to be found in 3:9 where Paul supposedly states that he has, in his letter, "already charged" (προητιασάμεθα)[250] all for being "under sin," both "Jews and Greeks."

More recently, a number of scholars have criticized the traditional interpretation of 1:18–3:20, pointing out how badly such a charge seems to fit with what Paul has said prior to 3:9.[251] The critique is fully warranted. And yet, the question what Paul meant by the verb προητιασάμεθα has not been sufficiently accounted for.[252] I would suggest that this verb says something quite different from what is usually assumed.

First, it is to be noted that Paul does not use the first person singular, "I have already charged," but the plural, "we have already charged." If the former had been the case, the verb προαιτιάομαι would unquestionably have referred to something which Paul himself had uttered earlier (presumably in his letter), but since he does not do that we cannot be sure that this is what he meant to say. Second, v. 9 is immediately followed by a long series of scriptural quotations introduced by καθὼς γέγραπται (vv. 10–18), and it is these quotations which provide the very proof for Paul's claim that "all are under sin." Now, if Paul's extensive discussion prior to 3:9 had already demonstrated that all are under sin, why would he need such a lengthy list of scriptural quotations to prove exactly that point? In fact, it is first with these citations that the charge of "universal sinfulness" is explicitly announced.

---

[250] Rom 3:9 is the only occurrence of the verb προαιτιάομαι listed in LSJ.
[251] See, e.g., Bassler, *Impartiality* (1982) 154–56; idem, "Impartiality" (1984) 53–57; Snodgrass, "Justification" (1986) 76; Elliott, *Rhetoric* (1990) 105–8, 133–34; Stowers, *Rereading* (1994) 174–84, 192–93, 324–25; Dabourne, *Purpose* (1999) 11–19, 24–26, 47–60.
[252] Cf. Sanders, *Paul* (1983) 123–35; Räisänen, *Paul* (1983) 97–109, who propose the explanation that Paul was simply being inconsistent in his argumentation. Sanders even doubts that Rom 1:18–2:29 was written by Paul.

Seen in this light, it seems to me that the verb προῃτιασάμεθα refers not to what Paul himself had previously said in his letter but to what had previously been stated in the Jewish scriptures about all being under sin (cf. Gal 3:22: συνέκλεισεν ἡ γραφὴ τὰ πάντα ὑπὸ ἁμαρτίαν). This would correspond to Paul's use of the verb προεπηγγείλατο in 1:2 (cf. προεγράφη in 15:4). That he occasionally employs the inclusive first person plural when referring to scripture is attested by λέγομεν γάρ ("for we say") in 4:9. Thus, the words "for we have previously charged" in 3:9 concern not Paul's previous discussion in his letter but charges already made by scripture, examples of which are then given by Paul in the following verses.

If this reading of the verb προῃτιασάμεθα is accepted, the weight of 3:9 for the traditional reading of the prior discourse as Paul's portrayal of the sinfulness of all humanity, "Jews as well as Greeks," is greatly diminished. In other words, Paul's statement in 3:9 does not contradict my conclusion about the identity of Paul's interlocutor in chapter 2.

4.2. Function and Identity of Paul's Interlocutor in the Subsequent Dialogical Exchanges

It goes without saying that the conclusions reached above on the function and identity of Paul's interlocutor in Romans 2 have considerable bearing on the subsequent dialogical exchanges. While questions of function and identity are interrelated, in keeping with the discussion above, the primary focus of this section will be aimed at the latter. I have already suggested that Paul's partner in dialogue remains identical throughout chapters 2–11. As to the question of the identity of Paul's interlocutor subsequent to chapter 4 scholars are divided, but it is widely held that Paul's partner in dialogue in chapters 3–4 is Jewish. I will, therefore, mainly pay attention to these chapters in this section.

As observed in Chapter Three above (in sec. 4), the person who poses the questions in 3:1 is in all likelihood the very interlocutor previously addressed in chapter 2. The dialogical exchange in 3:1–9 does not constitute

Paul's existential "debate . . . with himself,"²⁵³ but is an imaginary dialogue between Paul and his interlocutor.²⁵⁴ Its form is complex, to be sure.²⁵⁵ For instance, the conversation runs from a general third person language (vv. 1–4; excl. the scriptural reference), to uses of the first person plural (v. 5), to be followed by the first person singular (vv. 5, 7), and finally, again, the first person plural (vv. 8–9). However, in light of subsequent dialogical exchanges where the interlocutor normally poses inferential questions and Paul provides the answers, we should expect that 3:1–9 conforms to this relatively uniform procedure. The inclusive first person plural may at the same time be used by Paul in order to widen the scope of potential identification with the interlocutor. A number of factors suggest that Paul's conversational partner here is the one addressed in chapter 2, and that this person is not of Jewish but of gentile origin.

The questions in 3:1 arise not only because of various implications in the previous discourse about Jewish identity but also because the interlocutor has been deprived of his claim of calling himself a Ἰουδαῖος. Thus, the audience may think that Paul is seeking to nullify the advantage of being a (native) Jew and the value of circumcision for Jews. In order to prevent such misconceptions Paul has his interlocutor ask: "What advantage, then, has the Jew? Or what is the value of circumcision?" to which Paul immediately replies: "Much in every way!" As noted above (in sec. 2.3.4), this respond suggests that in 2:17–29 Paul was not specifically concerned with ethnic Jews and their circumcision. Moreover, Paul's following remark indicates that he is speaking to a non-Jewish interlocutor about Jews. He says:

---

253 Dunn, *Romans* (1988) 1.129. Nor does the dialogue tell us much about "the interior emotional state of the writer" (Penna, "Function" [1996] 73).

254 It is striking how frequently scholars speak of Rom 2 being written in the style of the "diatribe" and then proceed to argue that such dialogical exchanges as in 3:1–9 include some sort of Paul's existential converse with himself. If ch. 2 shows similarities with the "diatribe" style (involving uses of fictitious interlocutors), 3:1–9 and parallel dialogues in the letter do so to an even clearer and greater extent.

255 This is well reflected by the divergent ways in which scholars have structured the dialogue; cf., e.g., Stowers, "Dialogue" (1984) 715; Cosgrove, "What" (1987) 93–94; Palmer, "τί οὖν;" (1995) 204–5, 213–14; Penna, "Function" (1996) 72–77; Porter, "Paul" (1997) 576; Vos, "Weaker" (2002) 228–30.

"To begin with, *they* were entrusted (ἐπιστεύθησαν) with the oracles of God (τὰ λόγια τοῦ θεοῦ); what else (τί γάρ)?"[256] That is, instead of saying "we (Jews)" which would have been more natural if he were conversing with a fellow Jew, Paul uses the third person plural "they" of the Jews, thus implying that the interlocutor does not belong to this group of people.[257] Paul's point of Jewish historical priority[258] in v. 2 is furthered by the interlocutor's question in v. 3: "If some (τινες) [Jews] were unfaithful, their unfaithfulness (ἡ ἀπιστία αὐτῶν) will not annul the faithfulness of God (τὴν πίστιν τοῦ θεοῦ), will it?" Paul's answer is definite (v. 4): "By no means (μὴ γένοιτο)!"[259] He will deal with the question of some Jews' ἀπιστία, as well as Jewish "advantage," more thoroughly in chapters 9–11. Significantly, there he speaks to his gentile audience about the Jews in much the same way as in 3:1–3, viz. with the third person plural "they."[260]

With v. 4 the reference shifts, first to "every man" (πᾶς ἄνθρωπος),[261] and then to "us" (v. 5) when the interlocutor asks: "But if *our* unrighteousness (ἡ ἀδικία ἡμῶν) serves to confirm God's righteousness, what shall we say? That God is unrighteous to inflict wrath (τὴν ὀργήν) [on us]?" The allusion to Paul's previous account of God's wrath (ὀργὴ θεοῦ, 1:18; cf. 2:5, 8) against gentile unrighteousness (ἀδικία, 1:18, 29; cf. 2:8) is conspicuous. It implies that the one speaking belongs to the very people whose ἀδικία

---

[256] The γάρ suggests that τί γάρ is to be taken with Paul's response in v. 2. In his *Diatribe* (1981) 133, Stowers observes that "Paul's τί γάρ in 3:3 may be unique."

[257] Paul's own place among different groups of people is more intricate. According to 1 Cor 9:19–23, he has become "all things to all people" (τοῖς πᾶσιν γέγονα πάντα, v. 22).

[258] Cf. Barclay, "Paul" (1998) 555.

[259] It is very difficult to determine who has the role of asking the question in v. 3 and who provides the answer in v. 4. The roles may as well be the reverse of what is proposed above. Even so, the observations made about the interlocutor's identity remain largely unaffected.

[260] E.g. 9:3–5; 10:1–3, 14–15, 18, 19; 11:11–12, 28–31.

[261] The word ἄνθρωπος in 3:4 should not be confused with the voc. ἄνθρωπε in 2:1, 3, the latter of which is a part of the dialogical style (best rendered "fellow," "mister," or the like).

(not ἀπιστία)²⁶² was portrayed in 1:18–32. The question in v. 7 expresses basically the same thought as in v. 5, now more narrowly formulated in the first person singular: "But if the truth of God (ἡ ἀλήθεια τοῦ θεοῦ)²⁶³ abounds in my lie (τῷ ἐμῷ ψεύσματι) to God's glory (δόξαν), why am I still being judged (κρίνομαι) as a sinner (ἁμαρτωλός)?" Again, the reference to 1:18–32 is clear. While the statement in 3:4 may also be in view, the manifold relations with Paul's description of the gentile world cannot be missed. Most explicitly, in 1:25 Paul had told how the gentiles exchanged "the truth of God" (τὴν ἀλήθειαν τοῦ θεοῦ) for a "lie" (τῷ ψεύδει) through their idolatry. A parallel utterance is found in v. 23 which relates how the gentiles exchanged God's "glory" (δόξαν) for all kinds of despicable images. The "truth of God," in turn, points to "the truth" (τὴν ἀλήθειαν) spoken of in 1:18. Moreover, that the interlocutor is being "judged" (κρίνομαι, cf. 2:27) shows that even he, despite his judging of others (2:1, 3), belongs to those who do the things recounted in 1:18–32, and for which they will be subject to God's (unfavorable) judgment (τὸ κρίμα τοῦ θεοῦ, 2:2). He is thus essentially a "sinner" (ἁμαρτωλός), a characteristic Jewish description of gentiles (cf. Gal 2:15: ἐξ ἐθνῶν ἁμαρτωλοί). In chapter 6 in particular Paul will respond more fully to the views expressed by the interlocutor in 3:5–8.²⁶⁴

The questions τί οὖν; προεχόμεθα; and the immediate answer οὐ πάντως in v. 9 (Nestle-Aland, 27th ed.) leave us with tremendous difficulties.²⁶⁵ Apart from textual uncertainties, ambiguities concerning the meaning of the verb προεχόμεθα result in questions which may either be rendered "What then? Are we any better off?" (NRSV) or, conversely, "What then? Are we at any disadvantage?" (NRSV, in n.) These entirely contrasting possibilities greatly diminish the interpretative value of the text. Provided that the text in Nestle-Aland is to be preferred, I find it likely that the verb προεχόμεθα is in the passive, thus yielding the reading: "What then? Are

---

[262] The word ἀπιστία and its cognates do not occur prior to 3:3, and subsequently only in 4:20 (on Abraham) and 11:20, 23 (on Jewish ἀπιστία).
[263] Or "God's truthfulness."
[264] Cf. Paul's responses to the questions posed in 6:1, 15.
[265] See esp. Dahl, "Romans 3.9" (1982); Stowers, *Rereading* (1994) 166–75.

we [gentiles] at a disadvantage?" Such a question would also have been natural in light of the preceding statements. Paul answers in negative terms (οὐ πάντως), explaining (γάρ) that scripture has already declared that "all are under sin," not only gentiles but Jews as well. In other words, although Jews certainly enjoy a historical priority, gentiles are not altogether worse off because it has been attested that both parties are "under (the power of) sin." Most importantly, Paul continues (vv. 21–26), the righteousness of God has now (νυνὶ δέ) been revealed "apart from the Law" (χωρὶς νόμου) through Jesus Christ to "all who believe" (πάντας τοὺς πιστεύοντας), so that gentiles now have a chance to stand before God on the same footing as Jews.

In this light, Paul's interlocutor poses the question (v. 27): "What, then, becomes of [my] boasting (ἡ καύχησις)?" This must refer to his "boasting" of God and the Law in 2:17, 23. Paul replies that it has been "excluded" (ἐξεκλείσθη). The implication is not that any "boasting" of God and the Law is in itself improper, but that this particular individual's "boasting" is wrongly based. The gentile interlocutor's grounds for "boasting" as a Ἰουδαῖος are excluded. According to Paul (v. 28), gentiles can be justified by their "faithfulness" (πίστει), even without doing the "works of the Law" (ἔργων νόμου),[266] by which nothing had in fact been gained (cf. v. 20). Gentiles have received this opportunity because God is not the God of Jews only but of gentiles as well (vv. 29–30).

Again, textual uncertainties make it very difficult to discern the precise content(s) of the interlocutor's question(s) about Abraham in 4:1. In view

---

[266] I cannot discuss this phrase in any detail here. The scholarly discussion is plentiful and opinions differ widely; cf., e.g., Gaston, "Paul" (1979); Moo, "Law" (1983); Dunn, "Noch Einmal" (2002), with further references. See also the brief but helpful discussion in Snodgrass, "Justification" (1986) 84–85. I consider it very unlikely that the phrase (first occurring in 3:20) is equivalent to "doing the Law." Both 3:20 and 3:28 would in that case clearly contradict Paul's earlier statement in 2:13. That ἔργα νόμου may have applied to certain parts of the Law only is suggested by Gal 3:10, in which Paul states that "all who rely on works of the Law (ἐξ ἔργων νόμου) are under a curse," because (γέγραπται γάρ) "cursed is everyone who does not observe everything that is written in the book of the Law" (cf. Deut 27:26). Cf. also Gal 5:3.

of Paul's use of the verb form ἐροῦμεν elsewhere in Romans,[267] it seems likely that the verse includes two questions: τί οὖν ἐροῦμεν; εὑρηκέναι Ἀβραὰμ τὸν προπάτορα ἡμῶν κατὰ σάρκα; (in the sense "What then shall we say? Have we found Abraham to be our forefather according to [the] flesh / by his own human efforts?").[268] In any case, it is telling that within the scope of the dialogue with the interlocutor Paul makes use of Abraham, the "first and prototype proselyte,"[269] to prove his point that one may be justified without being circumcised. It is also significant that the discussion of the interlocutor's (and Abraham's; 4:2) "boasting" is not concluded until chapter 5, in which Paul urges his gentile readership to "boast (καυχώμενοι) in God" not through the Law but "through our lord Jesus Christ" (v. 11; cf. vv. 2–3). In this way, Paul utilizes his imaginary dialogical partner to inform his audience of both the proper and improper basis for *their* "boasting," which implies that the interlocutor was invented precisely so that the gentile readers would identify themselves with him.[270]

Hence, several features of the dialogue strongly suggest that Paul's partner in conversation is precisely the one addressed in chapter 2, and that he is not a Jew but an individual of gentile origin. An identification with such a person would have presented itself as logical, straightforward, and appropriate for the gentile audience. Such an identification would also have continued in the subsequent dialogical exchanges in which Paul's interlocutor and by which Paul's audience is gradually being guided through the letter's

---

[267] Viz. in 3:5; 6:1; 7:7; 9:14, 30 (τί [οὖν] ἐροῦμεν;); 8:31 (τί οὖν ἐροῦμεν πρὸς ταῦτα;). It is never used with the inf. (the form ἐροῦμεν does not occur elsewhere in Paul's letters).
[268] Cf. Ch. 2 sec. 2.2.2 above.
[269] Donaldson, *Paul* (1997) 57.
[270] Cf. Ch. 3 sec. 4 above.

message. Paul's imaginary interlocutor offers thus an invitation to the audience to become, as it were, active participants in a "kind of written conversation" about God's "good news."

Conclusions

In this study I have allowed the larger context and framework of Romans to be of help in the task of determining the function and identity of Paul's interlocutor in chapter 2. The study has proceeded from the whole to the part, namely, from questions of the place and character of the letter in its literary environment, of the relationship between the correspondents, of the identity of the recipients, and of the sender's use of a dialogical style, to the question of Paul's partner in dialogue in Romans 2.

In Chapter One the epistolary structure and setting of Romans was assessed, with the focus specifically aimed at the information provided by these factors about the relationship between the letter's sender and recipients. It was concluded that Paul followed the standard convention in Greco-Roman antiquity of writing letters according to the threefold structure of opening (1:1–7), body (1:8–15:33), and closing (16:1–24). Common epistolary terminology is found in every part of Romans, the rather extensive body included. Paul's choice and employment of such expressions attest a hierarchical relationship between the correspondents, defined by Paul's apostolic commission to proclaim God's "good news" to gentiles and the recipients' subordination to this task of his. Paul's establishment of such a relation was modelled chiefly on characteristic official letter writing. Romans was written within a normative epistolary setting, which means that the subject of the letter arose out of the relationship between the correspondents, and that it was written to a specific, contemporary group of people in the city of Rome. Paul's letter constituted itself his proclamation of the "good news" to this particular audience.

Chapter Two sought to identify Paul's intended audience. It was urged that it is of primary methodological importance to differentiate between the questions of what can be known of "Roman Christianity" at the time when Romans was penned, and what can be known of the particular group of people to whom Paul wrote his letter. The latter question can be answered only by the letter itself, especially since there is virtually no external information available about "Roman Christianity" prior to Paul's letter. Romans itself postulates an audience of non-Jewish origin. Those references to the letter's recipients which the scholarly consensus takes as the most explicit ones, mention a gentile audience only. Such explicit references should, by definition, take precedence over more implicit ones. It was concluded, however, that the latter do not contradict the former. Implicit references neither exclude gentile readers nor necessitate Jewish ones. The particular audience with whom Paul intended to communicate through his letter consisted of people of gentile origin who had been or still were operative within a Jewish community in Rome.

Chapter Three focused upon Paul's invention of an interlocutor in Romans 2–11. Whilst the Greco-Roman "diatribe" is highly significant as a comparative material for the dialogical style in Romans, analogous elements in letters specifically are more helpful for the attempt to identify Paul's interlocutor in the letter. The epistolary genre was widely perceived as a "kind of written conversation" in Greco-Roman antiquity and uses of imaginary partners in conversation are common in this type of literature. Formal and functional features of epistolary interlocutors correspond closely to those of the "diatribe" style. As for the interlocutor's identity, the following norm could be determined. Unless otherwise stated or implied, the interlocutor represents or speaks for the letter's recipient(s) and remains identical throughout the text. It is Paul's very application of such an interlocutor which guides the macrostructure of Romans 2–11 and gives the discourse a progressive character.

Chapter Four included a detailed discussion of Paul's interlocutor in Romans 2 and presented a fresh reading of the chapter. It was concluded that the text in Romans 2:6–16 is a unity the focus of which is still within the scope of Paul's indictment of his interlocutor in 2:1–5, and that the individual addressed in 2:17–29 is the very person addressed earlier in 2:1–5. The somewhat more detailed characterization in 2:17–29 is due to the continuous and progressive flow of the text. When Paul proceeds to indict his interlocutor in 2:17, it is done specifically in light of the information provided in 2:6–16.

Any reading of Romans 2, it was claimed, must attend to the logical connection between 2:1 and 1:18–32, and to the identity of the people spoken of in the latter. The conclusion reached in this study was that 1:18–32 contains a characteristic Jewish polemic against the gentile world, views which are wholly shared by Paul himself. The passage constitutes Paul's reminder not only of the audience's own gentile background but also of the still prevailing gentile condition. The latter recurrently finds expression in Romans through the tension between "once" and "now."

The διό ("therefore") in 2:1, among other factors, indicates that Paul's interlocutor in 2:1–5 belongs to the group of people described in 1:18–32, and that he is thus of a non-Jewish origin. Read linearly, the text does not suggest otherwise. Attempts to identify the interlocutor as a Jew are wrongly based, both methodologically and historically. Several features of Paul's utterances in 2:1–5 confirm that his imaginary partner in conversation is of gentile descent. Paul indicts him for doing the very things for which he judges other gentiles, and for falsely believing that he will nonetheless receive a favorable verdict on the day of judgment.

In 2:17 the indictment of this same individual is resumed. The words εἰ δὲ σὺ Ἰουδαῖος ἐπονομάζῃ etc. do not imply that this person *is* a Jew, only that he wants to *call* himself a Jew. A series of factors suggest in fact that the interlocutor is envisaged not as a (native) Jew but as a person of gentile origin who wants to call himself a Jew. The person is thought of either as a proselyte or a potential one, probably the former. Paul sharply censures this imaginary individual for his pretense and erroneous conduct, and makes his (potential) status as a proselyte highly suspect. According to Paul, gentiles will not be saved through "physical" circumcision. They are not to become converts to Judaism. On the day of judgment they may, on the other hand, be reckoned as circumcised—as "Jews inwardly"—if they undergo a "circumcision of the heart" and do what God's Law requires of them.

Paul's fictitious interlocutor in Romans 2 functions as an object of identification for the gentile recipients. They are meant to correlate their own views with the interlocutor's. Paul aims to dissuade his readers from becoming full scale proselytes through circumcision. Simultaneously, he utters an indirect reproach of those who already are proselytes. The literary technique of creating and indicting an imaginary dialogical partner well fits such a purpose, especially in view of the fact that Paul was addressing an audience largely unknown to him.

The interlocutor engaged in the subsequent dialogical exchanges is most likely the same as the one addressed in Romans 2. Contrary to common opinion, a number of details suggest that the interlocutor in chapters 3–4 in particular is not of Jewish but of gentile origin.

At the very beginning of this study, I referred to the view of one scholar that "something in our usual interpretation of Romans is wrong." These words were uttered some thirty-five years ago. They still hold true. The relationship between Paul and the Roman audience appears to be different from what is usually assumed. The present study suggests that the common opinion that Romans 2 contains Paul's piercing critique of his fellow Jews should be rejected. The individual censured in the chapter is not a Jew, let alone "the typical Jew." Rather, Paul is making use of an imaginary gentile interlocutor in order to persuade his gentile audience that the proper path for them to salvation is not through "physical" circumcision. They are not to become Jews in order to be saved on the day of judgment. Instead, they should seize the chance that is now being offered to them, namely, to be justified through "circumcision of the heart" alone. This message stands at the core of the "good news" preached by Paul to gentiles in Rome.

Bibliography

Abbreviations used in the bibliography and elsewhere in this study follow the list of abbreviations in *The SBL Handbook of Style: For Ancient Near Eastern, Biblical, and Early Christian Studies* (eds. P. H. Alexander et al.; Peabody: Hendrickson, 1999). Abbreviations of the Greek papyri follow the list provided in *Checklist of Editions of Greek and Latin Papyri, Ostraca and Tablets* (eds. J. F. Oates et al.; BASPSup, 7; Atlanta: Scholars Press, [4]1992). In addition, the following abbreviations are used:

Sherk, *RDGE*   Sherk, Robert K., *Roman Documents from the Greek East:* Senatus Consulta *and* Epistulae *to the Age of Augustus* (Baltimore: Johns Hopkins Press, 1969).

Welles, *RCHP*   Welles, C. Bradford, *Royal Correspondence in the Hellenistic Period: A Study in Greek Epigraphy* (New Haven: Yale University Press, 1934).

1. Primary Sources

References to the OT and Apocrypha follow the LXX. Unless otherwise noted, references to the letter's of Cicero follow the LCL ed. and trans. of D. R. Shackleton Bailey. References to the works of Demetrius, Pseudo-Demetrius, Gregory of Nazianzus, Julius Victor, and Pseudo-Libanius follow the texts and trans. in Malherbe, *Ancient Epistolary Theorists*. References to the letters of Diogenes and the Socratics follow the texts and trans. in Malherbe, *The Cynic Epistles*. References to the letters of Aeschines, Artaxerxes, Chio, Isocrates, and Philip follow the texts in *Epistolographi Graeci* (ed. Hercher). Texts (and trans.) of a number of the Greek papyri referred to in this study are found in *Select Papyri* (LCL); Exler, *The Form of the Ancient Greek Letter*; and White, *Light from Ancient Letters*.

Apollonius of Tyana, *Epistles*, in Philostratus, *The Life of Apollonius of Tyana*. Vol. 2 (trans. F. C. Conybeare; LCL; Cambridge: Harvard University Press, 1950).
The Apostolic Fathers (trans. K. Lake; 2 vols.; LCL; Cambridge: Harvard University Press, 1912–13).
Biblia Hebraica Stuttgartensia (eds. K. Elliger and W. Rudolph; Stuttgart: Deutsche Bibelgesellschaft, [5]1997).
Cicero, *Letters to Atticus* (trans. E. O. Winstedt; 3 vols.; LCL; Cambridge: Harvard University Press, 1912–18).
———, *Letters to Atticus* (ed. and trans. D. R. Shackleton Bailey; 4 vols.; LCL; Cambridge: Harvard University Press, 1999).
———, *Letters to Friends* (ed. and trans. D. R. Shackleton Bailey; 3 vols.; LCL; Cambridge: Harvard University Press, 2001).
———, *Letters to Quintus and Brutus* (ed. and trans. D. R. Shackleton Bailey; LCL; Cambridge: Harvard University Press, 2002).
———, *Philippics* (trans. W. C. A. Ker; LCL; Cambridge: Harvard University Press, 1926).
Cornelius Nepos (trans. J. C. Rolfe; LCL; Cambridge: Harvard University Press, 1984).
Corpus Inscriptionum Graecarum (ed. A. Boeckh; 4 vols.; Berlin, 1828–77).
Corpus Inscriptionum Judaicarum (ed. J.-B. Frey; 2 vols.; Rome: Pontifical Institute of Christian Archaeology, 1936–52).
Corpus Papyrorum Judaicarum (eds. V. A. Tcherikover et al.; 3 vols.; Cambridge: Harvard University Press, 1957–1964).
The Dead Sea Scrolls: Study Edition (eds. F. G. Martínez and E. J. C. Tigchelaar; 2 vols.; Leiden: Brill, 1997–98).
Demosthenes, *Funeral Speech, Erotic Essay, Exordio, Letters* (trans. N. W. DeWitt and N. J. DeWitt; LCL; Cambridge: Harvard University Press, 1949).
Dio Cassius, *Roman History* (trans. E. Cary; 9 vols.; LCL; Cambridge: Harvard University Press, 1914–27).
Diogenes Laertius, *Lives of Eminent Philosophers* (trans. R. D. Hicks; 2 vols.; LCL; Cambridge: Harvard University Press, 1925).
Epictetus, *The Discourses as Reported by Arrian, Fragments, Encheiridion* (trans. W. A. Oldfather; 2 vols.; LCL; Cambridge: Harvard University Press, 1925–28).
Epistolographi Graeci (ed. R. Hercher; Paris: Didot, 1873).
Exler, Francis Xavier J., *The Form of the Ancient Greek Letter: A Study in Greek Epistolography* (Washington: Catholic University of America, 1923).
Horace, *Satires, Epistles, Ars Poetica* (trans. H. R. Fairclough; LCL; Cambridge: Harvard University Press, 1929).

Josephus, *Jewish Antiquities* (trans. H. St. J. Thackeray [vols. 1–2], R. Marcus [vols. 2–5], L. H. Feldman [vols. 6–7]; 7 vols.; LCL; Cambridge: Harvard University Press, 1930–65).

———, *The Jewish War* (trans. H. St. J. Thackeray; 2 vols.; LCL; Cambridge: Harvard University Press, 1927).

———, *The Life, Against Apion* (trans. H. St. J. Thackeray; LCL; Cambridge: Harvard University Press, 1926).

Justin Martyr, *Writings of Saint Justin Martyr* (trans. T. B. Falls; FC, 6; Washington: The Catholic University of America Press, 1948).

Malherbe, Abraham J., *The Cynic Epistles: A Study Edition* (SBLSBS, 12; Missoula: Scholars Press, 1977).

———, *Ancient Epistolary Theorists* (SBLSBS, 19; Atlanta: Scholars Press, 1988).

Maximus of Tyre, *Philosophumena – ΔΙΑΛΕΞΕΙΣ* (ed. G. L. Koniaris; Texte und Kommentare, 17; Berlin: de Gruyter, 1995).

Menander Rhetor (eds. and trans. D. A. Russell and N. G. Wilson; Oxford: Clarendon Press, 1981).

Novum Testamentum Graece (Nestle-Aland; Stuttgart: Deutsche Bibelgesellschaft, [27]1993).

The Old Testament Pseudepigrapha (ed. J. H. Charlesworth; 2 vols.; New York: Doubleday, 1983–85).

Origen, *Commentarii in epistulam ad Romanos. Liber primus, liber secundus* (trans. T. Heither; Fontes Christiani; Freiburg: Herder, 1990).

———, *Commentary on the Epistle to the Romans. Books 1–5* (trans. T. P. Scheck; FC, 103; Washington: The Catholic University of America Press, 2001).

Philo (trans. G. H. Whitaker [vols. 1–5], F. H. Colson [vols. 1–10], J. W. Earp [vol. 10], and R. Marcus [suppl. 1–2]; 12 vols.; LCL; Cambridge: Harvard University Press, 1929–62).

Plato, *Timaeus, Critias, Cleitophon, Menexenus, Epistles* (trans. R. G. Bury; LCL; Cambridge: Harvard University Press, 1929).

Pliny, *Letters, Panegyricus* (trans. B. Radice; 2 vols.; LCL; Cambridge: Harvard University Press, 1969).

Plutarch, *Lives* (trans. B. Perrin; 11 vols.; LCL; Cambridge: Harvard University Press, 1914–26).

———, *Moralia* (trans. F. C. Babbitt et al.; 15 vols.; LCL; Cambridge: Harvard University Press, 1927–69).

Polybius, *The Histories* (trans. W. R. Paton; 6 vols.; LCL; Cambridge: Harvard University Press, 1922–27).

Quintilian, *The Orator's Education* (ed. and trans. D. A. Russell; 5 vols.; LCL; Cambridge: Harvard University Press, 2001).

Select Papyri (trans. A. S. Hunt, C. C. Edgar, and D. L. Page; 3 vols.; LCL; Cambridge: Harvard University Press, 1932–41).

Seneca, *Epistles* (trans. R. M. Gummere; 3 vols.; LCL; Cambridge: Harvard University Press, 1917–25).

Septuaginta. Id est Vetus Testamentum graece iuxta LXX interpretes (ed. A. Rahlfs; 2 vols. in 1; Stuttgart: Deutsche Bibelgesellschaft, 1935).

Sherk, Robert K., *Roman Documents from the Greek East:* Senatus Consulta *and* Epistulae *to the Age of Augustus* (Baltimore: Johns Hopkins Press, 1969).

Stern, Menahem, *Greek and Latin Authors on Jews and Judaism* (3 vols.; Jerusalem: The Israel Academy of Sciences and Humanities, 1974–84).

Suetonius, *The Lives of the Caesars, The Lives of Illustrious Men* (trans. J. C. Rolfe; 2 vols.; LCL; Cambridge: Harvard University Press, 1913–14).

Tacitus, *The Annals* (trans. J. Jackson; 3 vols.; LCL; Cambridge: Harvard University Press, 1931–37).

Welles, C. Bradford, *Royal Correspondence in the Hellenistic Period: A Study in Greek Epigraphy* (New Haven: Yale University Press, 1934).

White, John L., *Light from Ancient Letters* (Philadelphia: Fortress, 1986).

Xenophon, *Memorabilia, Oeconomicus* (trans. E. C. Marchant; LCL; Cambridge: Harvard University Press, 1923).

2. Lexica and Tools

Aland, Kurt (ed.), *Vollständige Konkordanz zum griechischen Neuen Testament* (2 vols.; Berlin: de Gruyter, 1983).

Anderson, R. Dean, Jr., *Glossary of Greek Rhetorical Terms Connected to Methods of Argumentation, Figures and Tropes from Anaximenes to Quintilian* (CBET, 24; Leuven: Peeters, 2000).

Bauer, Walter, *Griechisch-deutsches Wörterbuch zu den Schriften des Neuen Testaments und der frühchristlichen Literatur* (eds. K. Aland and B. Aland; Berlin: de Gruyter, ^{6}1988).

Bauer, Walter, William F. Arndt, F. Wilbur Gingrich, and Frederick W. Danker, *A Greek-English Lexicon of the New Testament and Other Early Christian Literature* (Chicago: University of Chicago Press, ^{2}1979).

Blass, F., A. Debrunner, and R. W. Funk, *A Greek Grammar of the New Testament and Other Early Christian Literature* (Chicago: University of Chicago Press, 1961).

Blomqvist, Jerker, *Greek Particles in Hellenistic Prose* (Lund: Gleerup, 1969).

Borgen, Peder, Kåre Fuglseth, and Roald Skarsten, *The Philo Index: A Complete Greek Word Index to the Writings of Philo of Alexandria* (Grand Rapids: Eerdmans, 2000).

Denniston, J. D., *The Greek Particles* (Oxford: Clarendon Press, ²1975).

Hatch, Edwin, and Henry A. Redpath, *A Concordance to the Septuagint and the Other Greek Versions of the Old Testament (Including the Apocryphal Books)* (3 vols.; Oxford: Clarendon Press, 1897–1906).

Lewis, Charlton T, and Charles Short, *A Latin Dictionary* (Oxford: Clarendon, 1879).

Liddell, Henry George, and Robert Scott, *A Greek-English Lexicon. With a Revised Supplement* (rev. and augm. by H. S. Jones with R. McKenzie; Oxford: Clarendon Press, ⁹1996).

Louw, Johannes P., and Eugene A. Nida, *Greek-English Lexicon of the New Testament Based on Semantic Domains* (2 vols.; New York: United Bible Societies, ²1989).

Metzger, Bruce M., *A Textual Commentary on the Greek New Testament: A Companion Volume to the United Bible Societies' Greek New Testament (third edition)* (n.p.: United Bible Societies, [corrected ed.] 1975).

Moule, C. F. D., *An Idiom Book of New Testament Greek* (Cambridge: Cambridge University Press, ²1959).

Moulton, William F., Alfred S. Geden, and Harold K. Moulton (eds.), *A Concordance to the Greek Testament* (Edinburgh: T&T Clark, ⁵1978).

Porter, Stanley E., *Idioms of the Greek New Testament* (Biblical Languages: Greek, 2; Sheffield: Sheffield Academic Press, ²1994).

Rengstorf, Karl Heinrich (ed.), *A Complete Concordance to Flavius Josephus* (4 vols.; Leiden: Brill, 1973–83).

Robertson, A. T., *A Grammar of the Greek New Testament in the Light of Historical Research* (London: Hodder & Stoughton, n.d. [preface dated 1914]).

Thrall, Margaret E., *Greek Particles in the New Testament: Linguistic and Exegetical Studies* (NTTS, 3; Leiden: Brill, 1962).

Turner, Nigel, *A Grammar of New Testament Greek*. Vol. 3. *Syntax* (Edinburgh: T&T Clark, 1963).

——, *A Grammar of New Testament Greek*. Vol. 4. *Style* (Edinburgh: T&T Clark, 1976).

3. Secondary Sources

Achtemeier, Paul J., "'Some Things in Them Hard to Understand': Reflections on an Approach to Paul," *Int* 38 (1984) 254–67.

———, "*Omne verbum sonat*: The New Testament and the Oral Environment of Late Western Antiquity," *JBL* 109 (1990) 3–27.

———, "Unsearchable Judgments and Inscrutable Ways: Reflections on the Discussion of Romans," in E. E. Johnson and D. M. Hay (eds.), *Pauline Theology. Vol. 4. Looking Back, Pressing On* (SBLSymS, 4; Atlanta: Scholars Press, 1997) 3–21.

Alexander, P. S., "Epistolary Literature," in M. E. Stone (ed.), *Jewish Writings of the Second Temple Period: Apocrypha, Pseudepigrapha, Qumran Sectarian Writings, Philo, Josephus* (CRINT, 2; Assen: Van Gorcum, 1984) 579–96.

Althaus, Paul, *Der Brief an die Römer* (NTD, 6; Göttingen: Vandenhoeck & Ruprecht, ⁶1949).

Alvarez Cineira, David, *Die Religionspolitik des Kaisers Claudius und die paulinische Mission* (Herders biblische Studien, 19; Freiburg: Herder, 1999).

Anderson, R. Dean, Jr., *Ancient Rhetorical Theory and Paul* (CBET, 18; Kampen: Pharos, 1996).

Arzt, Peter, "The 'Epistolary Introductory Thanksgiving' in the Papyri and in Paul," *NovT* 36 (1994) 29–46.

Aune, David E., *The New Testament in Its Literary Environment* (LEC, 8; Philadelphia: Westminster Press, 1987).

———, "Romans as a Logos Protreptikos in the Context of Ancient Religious and Philosophical Propaganda," in M. Hengel and U. Heckel (eds.), *Paulus und das antike Judentum* (WUNT, 58; Tübingen: Mohr [Siebeck], 1991) 91–124.

Bahr, Gordon J., "Paul and Letter Writing in the First Century," *CBQ* 28 (1966) 465–77.

Bailey, James L., and Lyle D. Vander Broek, *Literary Forms in the New Testament* (London: SPCK, 1992).

Barclay, John M. G., *Jews in the Mediterranean Diaspora: From Alexander to Trajan (323 BCE–117 CE)* (Edinburgh: T&T Clark, 1996).

———, "Paul and Philo on Circumcision: Romans 2.25–9 in Social and Cultural Context," *NTS* 44 (1998) 536–56.

Barrett, C. K., *A Commentary on the Epistle to the Romans* (BNTC; London: Adam & Charles Black, 1957).

Bartsch, Hans-Werner, "Die historische Situation des Römerbriefes," *CV* 8 (1965) 199–208.

Bassler, Jouette M., *Divine Impartiality: Paul and a Theological Axiom* (SBLDS, 59; Chico: Scholars Press, 1982).

———, "Divine Impartiality in Paul's Letter to the Romans," *NovT* 26 (1984) 43–58.

———, "Centering the Argument: A Response to Andrew T. Lincoln," in Hay and Johnson (eds.), *Pauline Theology*, 160–68.

Bauckham, Richard, "Pseudo-Apostolic Letters," *JBL* 107 (1988) 469–94.

Baur, Ferdinand Christian, "Über Zweck und Veranlassung des Römerbriefs und die damit zusammenhängenden Verhältnisse der römischen Gemeinde," *Tübinger Zeitschrift für Theologie* 3 (1836) 59–178.

———, *Paulus, der Apostel Jesu Christi: Sein Leben und Wirken, seine Briefe und seine Lehre* (Stuttgart: Becher & Müller, 1845).

Becker, Jürgen, *Paulus: Der Apostel der Völker* (Tübingen: Mohr [Siebeck], ²1992).

Beker, J. Christiaan, *Paul the Apostle: The Triumph of God in Life and Thought* (Philadelphia: Fortress, 1980).

Bell, Richard H., *No One Seeks for God: An Exegetical and Theological Study of Romans 1.18–3.20* (WUNT, 106; Tübingen: Mohr Siebeck, 1998).

Benko, Stephen, "The Edict of Claudius of A.D. 49 and the Instigator Chrestus," *TZ* 25 (1969) 406–18.

———, "Pagan Criticism of Christianity During the First Two Centuries A.D.," in *ANRW* 2.23.2 (1980) 1055–1118.

Berger, Klaus, "Apostelbrief und apostolische Rede: Zum Formular frühchristlicher Briefe," *ZNW* 65 (1974) 190–231.

———, "Hellenistische Gattungen im Neuen Testament," in *ANRW* 2.25.2 (1984) 1031–1432, 1831–85.

Bergmeier, Roland, "Das Gesetz im Römerbrief," in *Das Gesetz im Römerbrief und andere Studien zum Neuen Testament* (WUNT, 121; Tübingen: Mohr Siebeck, 2000) 31–102.

Berkley, Timothy W., *From a Broken Covenant to Circumcision of the Heart: Pauline Intertextual Exegesis in Romans 2:17–29* (SBLDS, 175; Atlanta: Society of Biblical Literature, 2000).

Betz, Hans Dieter, "Christianity as Religion: Paul's Attempt at Definition in Romans," *JR* 71 (1991) 315–44.

Bickermann, E., "Bellum Antiochicum," *Hermes* 67 (1932) 47–76.

Bietenhard, Hans, "ὄνομα κτλ.," in *TDNT* 5 (1967) 242–83.

Bischoff, A., "Exegetische Randbemerkungen," *ZNW* 9 (1908) 166–72.

Bjerkelund, Carl J., *Parakalô: Form, Funktion und Sinn der parakalô-Sätze in den paulinischen Briefen* (Oslo: Universitetsforlaget, 1967).

Blumenfeld, Bruno, *The Political Paul: Justice, Democracy and Kingship in a Hellenistic Framework* (JSNTSup, 210; Sheffield: Sheffield Academic Press, 2001).

Boers, Hendrikus, "The Problem of Jews and Gentiles in the Macro-Structure of Romans," *SEÅ* 47 (1982) 184–96.

———, *The Justification of the Gentiles: Paul's Letters to the Galatians and Romans* (Peabody: Hendrickson, 1994).

Bonhöffer, Adolf, *Epiktet und das Neue Testament* (Religionsgeschichtliche Versuche und Vorarbeiten, 10; Giessen: Töpelmann, 1911).

Bornkamm, Günther, "Gesetz und Natur: Röm 2,14–16," in *Studien zu Antike und Urchristentum: Gesammelte Aufsätze II* (BEvT, 28; München: Kaiser, ²1963) 93–118.

———, "Die Offenbarung des Zornes Gottes: Röm 1–3," in *Das Ende des Gesetzes: Paulusstudien. Gesammelte Aufsätze I* (BEvT, 16; München: Kaiser, ⁵1966) 9–33.

———, "Paulinische Anakoluthe," in *Das Ende des Gesetzes: Paulusstudien. Gesammelte Aufsätze I* (BEvT, 16; München: Kaiser, ⁵1966) 76–92.

Botermann, Helga, *Das Judenedikt des Kaisers Claudius: Römischer Staat und Christiani im 1. Jahrhundert* (Hermes, 71; Stuttgart: Franz Steiner, 1996).

Boyarin, Daniel, *A Radical Jew: Paul and the Politics of Identity* (Berkeley: University of California Press, 1994).

Brändle, Rudolf, and Ekkehard W. Stegemann, "The Formation of the First 'Christian Congregations' in Rome in the Context of the Jewish Congregations," in Donfried and Richardson (eds.), *Judaism and Christianity*, 117–27.

Brawley, Robert L., "Multivocality in Romans 4," in C. Grenholm and D. Patte (eds.), *Reading Israel in Romans: Legitimacy and Plausibility of Divergent Interpretations* (Romans Through History and Cultures Series, 1; Harrisburg: Trinity Press, 2000) 74–95.

Brown, Michael Joseph, "Paul's Use of Δοῦλος Χριστοῦ Ἰησοῦ in Romans 1:1," *JBL* 120 (2001) 723–37.

Brown, Raymond E., "Not Jewish Christianity and Gentile Christianity but Types of Jewish/Gentile Christianity," *CBQ* 45 (1983) 74–79.

———, "Further Reflections on the Origins of the Church of Rome," in R. T. Fortna and B. R. Gaventa (eds.), *The Conversation Continues: Studies in Paul and John. In Honor of J. Louis Martyn* (Nashville: Abingdon, 1990) 98–115.

———, and John P. Meier, *Antioch and Rome: New Testament Cradles of Catholic Christianity* (New York: Paulist Press, 1983).

Bruce, F. F., "The Romans Debate—Continued," in Donfried (ed.), *Romans Debate* [1981–82], 175–94.

———, "Travel and Communication (NT World)," in *ABD* 6 (1992) 648–53.

Bryan, Christopher, *A Preface to Romans: Notes on the Epistle in Its Literary and Cultural Setting* (Oxford: Oxford University Press, 2000).

Bultmann, Rudolf, *Der Stil der paulinischen Predigt und die kynisch-stoische Diatribe* (FRLANT, 13; Göttingen: Vandenhoeck & Ruprecht, 1910).

———, "Glossen im Römerbrief," *TLZ* 72 (1947) 197–202.

Burkitt, F. C., "The Punctuation of New Testament Manuscripts," *JTS* 29 (1927–28) 397–98.

Buss, Martin J., "Principles for Morphological Criticism: With Special Reference to Letter Form," in R. A. Spencer (ed.), *Orientation by Disorientation: Studies in Lit-*

erary Criticism and Biblical Literary Criticism (Pittsburgh: Pickwick, 1980) 71–86.

Bussmann, Claus, *Themen der paulinischen Missionspredigt auf dem Hintergrund der spätjüdisch-hellenistischen Missionsliteratur* (Bern: Lang, 1971).

Byrne, Brendan, "'Rather Boldly' (Rom 15,15): Paul's Prophetic Bid to Win the Allegiance of the Christians in Rome," *Bib* 74 (1993) 83–96.

Byrskog, Samuel, "Co-Senders, Co-Authors and Paul's Use of the First Person Plural," *ZNW* 87 (1996) 230–50.

———, "Epistolography, Rhetoric and Letter Prescript: Romans 1.1–7 as a Test Case," *JSNT* 65 (1997) 27–46.

Callow, Kathleen, "The Disappearing Δέ in 1 Corinthians," in D. A. Black (ed.), *Linguistics and New Testament Interpretation: Essays on Discourse Analysis* (Nashville: Broadman, 1992) 183–93.

Campbell, Douglas A., *The Rhetoric of Righteousness in Romans 3.21–26* (JSNTSup, 65; Sheffield: JSOT Press, 1992).

———, "Towards a New, Rhetorically Assisted Reading of Romans 3.27–4.25," in S. E. Porter and D. L. Stamps (eds.), *Rhetorical Criticism and the Bible* (JSNTSup, 195; Sheffield: Sheffield Academic Press, 2002) 355–402.

Campbell, William S., "Romans III as a Key to the Structure and Thought of the Letter," *NovT* 23 (1981) 22–40.

———, *Paul's Gospel in an Intercultural Context: Jew and Gentile in the Letter to the Romans* (Studies in the Intercultural History of Christianity, 69; Frankfurt: Peter Lang, 1992).

Cancik, Hildegard, *Untersuchungen zu Senecas Epistulae morales* (Spudasmata, 18; Hildesheim: Georg Olms Verlagsbuchhandlung, 1967).

Capelle, W., and H. I. Marrou, "Diatribe," in *RAC* 3 (1957) 990–1009.

Caragounis, Chrys C., "From Obscurity to Prominence: The Development of the Roman Church between Romans and *1 Clement*," in Donfried and Richardson (eds.), *Judaism and Christianity*, 245–79.

Carras, George P., "Romans 2,1–29: A Dialogue on Jewish Ideals," *Bib* 73 (1992) 183–207.

Carson, D. A., *Exegetical Fallacies* (Grand Rapids: Baker, 1984).

Carter, T. L., *Paul and the Power of Sin: Redefining 'Beyond the Pale'* (SNTSMS, 115; Cambridge: Cambridge University Press, 2002).

Chae, Daniel Jong-Sang, *Paul as Apostle to the Gentiles: His Apostolic Self-Awareness and Its Influence on the Soteriological Argument in Romans* (Paternoster Biblical and Theological Monographs; Carlisle: Paternoster, 1997).

Chesnut, Glenn F., "Eusebius, Augustine, Orosius, and the Later Patristic and Medieval Christian Historians," in H. W. Attridge and G. Hata (eds.), *Eusebius, Christianity, and Judaism* (StPB, 42; Leiden: Brill, 1992) 687–713.

Classen, Carl Joachim, "Paulus und die antike Rhetorik," *ZNW* 82 (1991) 1–33.

———, *Rhetorical Criticism of the New Testament* (WUNT, 128; Tübingen: Mohr Siebeck, 2000).

Cohen, Shaye J. D., *The Beginnings of Jewishness: Boundaries, Varieties, Uncertainties* (Hellenistic Culture and Society, 31; Berkeley: University of California Press, 1999).

Collins, Adela Yarbro, "Insiders and Outsiders in the Book of Revelation and Its Social Context," in Neusner and Frerichs (eds.), *"To See Ourselves,"* 187–218.

Collins, John J., "A Symbol of Otherness: Circumcision and Salvation in the First Century," in Neusner and Frerichs (eds.), *"To See Ourselves,"* 163–86.

Cosgrove, Charles H., "What If Some Have Not Believed? The Occasion and Thrust of Romans 3.1–8," *ZNW* 78 (1987) 90–105.

———, *Elusive Israel: The Puzzle of Election in Romans* (Louisville: Westminster John Knox, 1997).

Cotton, Hannah M., "Greek and Latin Epistolary Formulae: Some Light on Cicero's Letter Writing," *AJP* 105 (1984) 409–25.

Crafton, Jeffrey A., "Paul's Rhetorical Vision and the Purpose of Romans: Toward a New Understanding," *NovT* 32 (1990) 317–39.

Cranfield, C. E. B., *A Critical and Exegetical Commentary on the Epistle to the Romans* (2 vols.; ICC; Edinburgh: T&T Clark, 1975–79).

———, "Changes of Person and Number in Paul's Epistles," in M. D. Hooker and S. G. Wilson (eds.), *Paul and Paulinism: Essays in Honour of C. K. Barrett* (London: SPCK, 1982) 280–89.

Dabourne, Wendy, *Purpose and Cause in Pauline Exegesis: Romans 1.16–4.25 and a New Approach to the Letters* (SNTSMS, 104; Cambridge: Cambridge University Press, 1999).

Dahl, Nils A., "Letter," in *IDBSup* (1976) 538–41.

———, "Paul: A Sketch," in *Studies in Paul: Theology for the Early Christian Mission* (Minneapolis: Augsburg Publishing House, 1977) 1–21.

———, "The Missionary Theology in the Epistle to the Romans," in *Studies in Paul: Theology for the Early Christian Mission* (Minneapolis: Augsburg Publishing House, 1977) 70–94.

———, "Romans 3.9: Text and Meaning," in M. D. Hooker and S. G. Wilson (eds.), *Paul and Paulinism: Essays in Honour of C. K. Barrett* (London: SPCK, 1982) 184–204.

———, "Paul's Letter to the Galatians: Epistolary Genre, Content, and Structure," in Nanos (ed.), *Galatians Debate*, 117–42.
Davies, Glenn N., *Faith and Obedience in Romans: A Study in Romans 1–4* (JSNTSup, 39; Sheffield: JSOT Press, 1990).
Deissmann, Adolf, *Licht vom Osten: Das Neue Testament und die neuentdeckten Texte der hellenistisch-römischen Welt* (Tübingen: Mohr [Siebeck], [4]1923).
Derrett, J. Duncan M., "'You Abominate False Gods; But Do You Rob Shrines?' (Rom 2.22b)," *NTS* 40 (1994) 558–71.
Dodd, Brian, *Paul's Paradigmatic 'I': Personal Example as Literary Strategy* (JSNTSup, 177; Sheffield: Sheffield Academic Press, 1999).
Dodd, C. H., *The Epistle of Paul to the Romans* (MNTC; London: Hodder & Stoughton, 1932).
Donaldson, Terence L., "Proselytes or 'Righteous Gentiles'? The Status of Gentiles in Eschatological Pilgrimage Patterns of Thought," *JSP* 7 (1990) 3–27.
———, *Paul and the Gentiles: Remapping the Apostle's Convictional World* (Minneapolis: Fortress, 1997).
Donfried, Karl P., "A Short Note on Romans 16," in idem (ed.), *Romans Debate* [1970], 44–52.
———, "False Presuppositions in the Study of Romans," in idem (ed.), *Romans Debate* [1974], 102–25.
———, "Introduction 1977: The Nature and Scope of the Romans Debate," in idem (ed.), *Romans Debate*, xli–xlvii.
——— (ed.), *The Romans Debate: Revised and Expanded Edition* (Edinburgh: T&T Clark, 1991).
———, and Peter Richardson (eds.), *Judaism and Christianity in First-Century Rome* (Grand Rapids: Eerdmans, 1998).
———, and Johannes Beutler (eds.), *The Thessalonians Debate: Methodological Discord or Methodological Synthesis?* (Grand Rapids: Eerdmans, 2000).
Dormeyer, Detlev, *The New Testament among the Writings of Antiquity* (Biblical Seminar, 55; Sheffield: Sheffield Academic Press, 1998).
Doty, William G., "The Classification of Epistolary Literature," *CBQ* 31 (1969) 183–99.
———, *Letters in Primitive Christianity* (GBS; Philadelphia: Fortress, 1973).
Drane, John W., "Why Did Paul Write Romans?" in D. A. Hagner and M. J. Harris (eds.), *Pauline Studies: Essays Presented to Professor F. F. Bruce on His 70th Birthday* (Exeter: Paternoster, 1980) 208–27.
Dunn, James D. G., "Paul's Epistle to the Romans: An Analysis of Structure and Argument," in *ANRW* 2.25.4 (1987) 2842–90.
———, *Romans* (2 vols.; WBC, 38; Dallas: Word Books, 1988).

———, *The Theology of Paul the Apostle* (Grand Rapids: Eerdmans, 1998).
———, "Noch Einmal 'Works of the Law': The Dialogue Continues," in I. Dunderberg, C. Tuckett, and K. Syreeni (eds.), *Fair Play: Diversity and Conflicts in Early Christianity: Essays in Honour of Heikki Räisänen* (NovTSup, 103; Leiden: Brill, 2002) 273–90.
———, "What Makes a Good Exposition? *The Expository Times* Lecture, June 2002," *ExpTim* 114 (2003) 147–57.
Dziatzko, Carl, "Brief," in PW 3 (1897) 836–43.
Eckstein, Hans-Joachim, "'Denn Gottes Zorn wird vom Himmel her offenbar werden': Exegetische Erwägungen zu Röm 1.18," *ZNW* 78 (1987) 74–89.
Elliott, J. K., "The Language and Style of the Concluding Doxology to the Epistle to the Romans," *ZNW* 72 (1981) 124–30.
Elliott, Neil, *The Rhetoric of Romans: Argumentative Constraint and Strategy and Paul's Dialogue with Judaism* (JSNTSup, 45; Sheffield: JSOT Press, 1990).
———, *Liberating Paul: The Justice of God and the Politics of the Apostle* (Sheffield: Sheffield Academic Press, 1995).
Engberg-Pedersen, Troels, *Paul and the Stoics* (Edinburgh: T&T Clark, 2000).
Epp, Eldon Jay, "New Testament Papyrus Manuscripts and Letter Carrying in Greco-Roman Times," in B. A. Pearson (ed.), *The Future of Early Christianity: Essays in Honor of Helmut Koester* (Minneapolis: Fortress, 1991) 35–56.
Erbes, K., "Zeit und Ziel der Grüße Röm 16,3–15 und der Mitteilungen 2 Tim 4,9–21," *ZNW* 10 (1909) 128–47, 195–218.
Eriksson, Anders, *Traditions as Rhetorical Proof: Pauline Argumentation in 1 Corinthians* (ConBNT, 29; Stockholm: Almqvist & Wiksell, 1998).
———, Thomas H. Olbricht, and Walter Übelacker (eds.), *Rhetorical Argumentation in Biblical Texts: Essays from the Lund 2000 Conference* (Emory Studies in Early Christianity, 8; Harrisburg: Trinity Press, 2002).
Fahy, Thomas, "St. Paul's Romans were Jewish Converts," *ITQ* 26 (1959) 182–91.
Feldman, Louis H., *Jew and Gentile in the Ancient World: Attitudes and Interactions From Alexander to Justinian* (Princeton: Princeton University Press, 1993).
Figueras, Pau, "Epigraphic Evidence for Proselytism in Ancient Judaism," *Imm* 24/25 (1990) 194–206.
Finsterbusch, Karin, *Die Thora als Lebensweisung für Heidenchristen: Studien zur Bedeutung der Thora für die paulinische Ethik* (SUNT, 20; Göttingen: Vandenhoeck & Ruprecht, 1996).
Fischer, James A., "Pauline Literary Forms and Thought Patterns," *CBQ* 39 (1977) 209–23.
Fitzmyer, Joseph A., "Some Notes on Aramaic Epistolography," *JBL* 93 (1974) 201–25.

———, *Romans: A New Translation with Introduction and Commentary* (AB, 33; New York: Doubleday, 1993).

Flückiger, Felix, "Zur Unterscheidung von Heiden und Juden in Röm. 1,18–2,3," *TZ* 10 (1954) 154–58.

Fraikin, Daniel, "The Rhetorical Function of the Jews in Romans," in P. Richardson with D. Granskou (eds.), *Anti-Judaism in Early Christianity*. Vol. 1. *Paul and the Gospels* (ESCJ, 2; Waterloo: Wilfrid Laurier University Press, 1986) 91–105.

Fredriksen, Paula, "Judaism, the Circumcision of Gentiles, and Apocalyptic Hope: Another Look at Galatians 1 and 2," in Nanos (ed.), *Galatians Debate*, 235–60.

Frend, W. H. C., *Martyrdom and Persecution in the Early Church: A Study of a Conflict from the Maccabees to Donatus* (Oxford: Basil Blackwell, 1965).

Freyne, Sean, "Behind the Names: Samaritans, *Ioudaioi*, Galileans," in S. G. Wilson and M. Desjardins (eds.), *Text and Artifact in the Religions of Mediterranean Antiquity: Essays in Honour of Peter Richardson* (ESCJ, 9; Waterloo: Wilfrid Laurier University Press, 2000) 389–401.

Fridrichsen, Anton, "Der wahre Jude und sein Lob: Röm. 2,28f.," in *Exegetical Writings: A Selection* (WUNT, 76; Tübingen: Mohr [Siebeck], 1994 [1922]) 186–94.

Funk, Robert W., "The Apostolic *Parousia*: Form and Significance," in W. R. Farmer, C. F. D. Moule, and R. R. Niebuhr (eds.), *Christian History and Interpretation: Studies Presented to John Knox* (Cambridge: Cambridge University Press, 1967) 249–68.

Furnish, Victor Paul, *Theology and Ethics in Paul* (Nashville: Abingdon, 1968).

Gager, John G., *Reinventing Paul* (New York: Oxford University Press, 2000).

Gamble, Harry, "The Redaction of the Pauline Letters and the Formation of the Pauline Corpus," *JBL* 94 (1975) 403–18.

———, *The Textual History of the Letter to the Romans: A Study in Textual and Literary Criticism* (SD, 42; Grand Rapids: Eerdmans, 1977).

———, *Books and Readers in the Early Church: A History of Early Christian Texts* (New Haven: Yale University Press, 1995).

Garlington, Don B., *Faith, Obedience, and Perseverance: Aspects of Paul's Letter to the Romans* (WUNT, 79; Tübingen: Mohr [Siebeck], 1994).

Gärtner, Bertil, *The Areopagus Speech and Natural Revelation* (ASNU, 21; Lund: Gleerup, 1955).

Gaston, Lloyd, "Paul and the Torah," in A. T. Davies (ed.), *Antisemitism and the Foundations of Christianity* (New York: Paulist Press, 1979) 48–71.

———, "Judaism of the Uncircumcised in Ignatius and Related Writers," in S. G. Wilson (ed.), *Anti-Judaism in Early Christianity*. Vol. 2. *Separation and Polemic* (ESCJ, 2; Waterloo: Wilfrid Laurier University Press, 1986) 33–44.

———, "Reading the Text and Digging the Past: The First Audience of Romans," in S. G. Wilson and M. Desjardins (eds.), *Text and Artifact in the Religions of Mediterranean Antiquity: Essays in Honour of Peter Richardson* (ESCJ, 9; Waterloo: Wilfrid Laurier University Press, 2000) 35–44.

———, "Romans in Context: The Conversation Revisited," in J. C. Anderson, P. Sellew, and C. Setzer (eds.), *Pauline Conversations in Context: Essays in Honor of Calvin J. Roetzel* (JSNTSup, 221; Sheffield: Sheffield Academic Press, 2002) 125–41.

Gathercole, Simon J., *Where is Boasting? Early Jewish Soteriology and Paul's Response in Romans 1–5* (Grand Rapids: Eerdmans, 2002).

———, "A Law unto Themselves: The Gentiles in Romans 2.14–15 Revisited," *JSNT* 85 (2002) 27–49.

Geytenbeek, A. C. van, *Musonius Rufus and Greek Diatribe* (Wijsgerige Texten en Studies, 8; Assen: Van Gorcum, ^{2}1963).

Gilliard, Frank D., "More Silent Reading in Antiquity: *Non omne verbum sonabat*," *JBL* 112 (1993) 689–96.

Glad, Clarence E., *Paul and Philodemus: Adaptability in Epicurean and Early Christian Psychagogy* (NovTSup, 81; Leiden: Brill, 1995).

Goppelt, Leonhard, "Der Missionar des Gesetzes: Zu Röm. 2,21 f.," in *Christologie und Ethik: Aufsätze zum Neuen Testament* (Göttingen: Vandenhoeck & Ruprecht, 1968) 137–46.

Gorday, Peter, *Principles of Patristic Exegesis: Romans 9–11 in Origen, John Chrysostom, and Augustine* (Studies in the Bible and Early Christianity, 4; New York: Mellen, 1983).

Görgemanns, Herwig, "Epistolographie," in *DNP* 3 (1997) 1166–69.

———, and Michaela Zelzer, "Epistel," in *DNP* 3 (1997) 1161–66.

Grabner-Haider, Anton, *Paraklese und Eschatologie bei Paulus: Mensch und Welt im Anspruch der Zukunft Gottes* (NTAbh, NF, 4; Münster: Aschendorff, 1968).

Grobel, Kendrick, "A Chiastic Retribution-Formula in Romans 2," in E. Dinkler (ed.), *Zeit und Geschichte: Dankesgabe an Rudolf Bultmann zum 80. Geburtstag* (Tübingen: Mohr [Siebeck], 1964) 255–61.

Gruen, Erich S., *Diaspora: Jews amidst Greeks and Romans* (Cambridge: Harvard University Press, 2002).

Guerra, Anthony J., *Romans and the Apologetic Tradition: The Purpose, Genre and Audience of Paul's Letter* (SNTSMS, 81; Cambridge: Cambridge University Press, 1995).

Güting, Eberhard W., and David L. Mealand, *Asyndeton in Paul: A Text-Critical and Statistical Enquiry into Pauline Style* (Studies in the Bible and Early Christianity, 39; Lewiston: Mellen, 1998).

Haacker, Klaus, "Der Römerbrief als Friedensmemorandum," *NTS* 36 (1990) 25–41.
Hansen, G. Walter, "A Paradigm of the Apocalypse: The Gospel in the Light of Epistolary Analysis," in Jervis and Richardson (eds.), *Gospel in Paul*, 194–209.
Hartmann, K., "Arrian und Epiktet," *NJahrb* 15 (1905) 248–75.
Harvey, Graham, *The True Israel: Uses of the Names Jew, Hebrew and Israel in Ancient Jewish and Early Christian Literature* (AGJU, 35; Leiden: Brill, 1996).
Harvey, John D., *Listening to the Text: Oral Patterning in Paul's Letters* (ETS Studies, 1; Grand Rapids: Baker, 1998).
Hay, David M., and E. Elizabeth Johnson (eds.), *Pauline Theology*. Vol. 3. *Romans* (Minneapolis: Fortress, 1995).
Hays, Richard B., "'Have We Found Abraham to be Our Forefather According to the Flesh?' A Reconsideration of Rom 4:1," *NovT* 27 (1985) 76–98.
——, *Echoes of Scripture in the Letters of Paul* (New Haven: Yale University Press, 1989).
Heckel, Ulrich, "Das Bild der Heiden und die Identität der Christen bei Paulus," in R. Feldmeier and U. Heckel (eds.), *Die Heiden: Juden, Christen und das Problem des Fremden* (WUNT, 70; Tübingen: Mohr [Siebeck], 1994) 269–96.
Hedner-Zetterholm, Karin, "The Jewish Communities of Ancient Rome," in B. Olsson, D. Mitternacht, and O. Brandt (eds.), *The Synagogue of Ancient Ostia and the Jews of Rome: Interdisciplinary Studies* (Stockholm: Paul Åström, 2001) 131–40.
Hellholm, David, "Amplificatio in the Macro-Structure of Romans," in Porter and Olbricht (eds.), *Rhetoric and the New Testament*, 123–51.
Hirsch, E. D., Jr., *Validity in Interpretation* (New Haven: Yale University Press, 1967).
Holmberg, Bengt, *Paul and Power: The Structure of Authority in the Primitive Church as Reflected in the Pauline Epistles* (ConBNT, 11; Lund: Gleerup, 1978).
Holmstrand, Jonas, *Markers and Meaning in Paul: An Analysis of 1 Thessalonians, Philippians and Galatians* (ConBNT, 28; Stockholm: Almqvist & Wiksell, 1997).
Hooker, M. D., "Adam in Romans 1," *NTS* 6 (1959–60) 297–306.
Horst, Pieter W. van der, *Ancient Jewish Epitaphs: An Introductory Survey of a Millennium of Jewish Funerary Epigraphy (300 BCE–700 CE)* (Kampen: Pharos, 1991).
Ito, Akio, "Romans 2: A Deuteronomistic Reading," *JSNT* 59 (1995) 21–37.
Jeffers, James S., *Conflict at Rome: Social Order and Hierarchy in Early Christianity* (Minneapolis: Fortress, 1991).
Jeremias, Joachim, "Zu Rm 1,22–32," *ZNW* 45 (1954) 119–21.
——, "Chiasmus in den Paulusbriefen," *ZNW* 49 (1958) 145–56.
Jervell, Jacob, "The Letter to Jerusalem," in Donfried (ed.), *Romans Debate* [1971], 53–64.

Jervis, L. Ann, *The Purpose of Romans: A Comparative Letter Structure Investigation* (JSNTSup, 55; Sheffield: JSOT Press, 1991).

———, and Peter Richardson (eds.), *Gospel in Paul: Studies on Corinthians, Galatians and Romans for Richard N. Longenecker* (JSNTSup, 108; Sheffield: Sheffield Academic Press, 1994).

Jewett, Robert, "Romans as an Ambassadorial Letter," *Int* 36 (1982) 5–20.

———, "Following the Argument of Romans," in Donfried (ed.), *Romans Debate*, 265–77.

———, "Ecumenical Theology for the Sake of Mission: Romans 1:1–17 + 15:14–16:24," in Hay and Johnson (eds.), *Pauline Theology*, 89–108.

Judge, E. A., "Judaism and the Rise of Christianity: A Roman Perspective," *TynBul* 45 (1994) 355–68.

Jüngel, Eberhard, "Ein paulinischer Chiasmus: Zum Verständnis der Vorstellung vom Gericht nach den Werken in Röm 2,2–11," in *Unterwegs zur Sache: Theologische Bemerkungen* (BEvT, 61; München: Kaiser, 1972) 173–78.

Karris, Robert J., "Romans 14:1–15:13 and the Occasion of Romans," in Donfried (ed.), *Romans Debate* [1974], 65–84.

Käsemann, Ernst, "The Spirit and the Letter," in *Perspectives on Paul* (NTL; London: SCM, 1971), 138–66.

———, *An die Römer* (HNT, 8a; Tübingen: Mohr [Siebeck], ³1974).

Kaye, B. N., "'To the Romans and Others' Revisited," *NovT* 18 (1976) 37–77.

Kaylor, R. David, *Paul's Covenant Community: Jew and Gentile in Romans* (Atlanta: John Knox, 1988).

Keck, Leander E., "Searchable Judgments and Scrutable Ways: A Response to Paul J. Achtemeier," in E. E. Johnson and D. M. Hay (eds.), *Pauline Theology*. Vol. 4. *Looking Back, Pressing On* (SBLSymS, 4; Atlanta: Scholars Press, 1997) 22–32.

———, "*Pathos* in Romans? Mostly Preliminary Remarks," in T. H. Olbricht and J. L. Sumney (eds.), *Paul and Pathos* (SBLSymS, 16; Atlanta: Society of Biblical Literature, 2001) 71–96.

Kennedy, George A., *New Testament Interpretation through Rhetorical Criticism* (SR; Chapel Hill: University of North Carolina Press, 1984).

———, "Historical Survey of Rhetoric," in Porter (ed.), *Handbook of Classical Rhetoric*, 3-41.

———, "The Genres of Rhetoric," in Porter (ed.), *Handbook of Classical Rhetoric*, 43-50.

Kern, Philip, *Rhetoric and Galatians: Assessing an Approach to Paul's Epistle* (SNTSMS, 101; Cambridge: Cambridge University Press, 1998).

Kettunen, Markku, *Der Abfassungszweck des Römerbriefes* (AASF, 18; Helsinki: Suomalainen Tiedeakatemia, 1979).

Keyes, Clinton W., "The Greek Letter of Introduction," *AJP* 56 (1935) 28–44.

Klauck, Hans-Josef, *Die antike Briefliteratur und das Neue Testament: Ein Lehr- und Arbeitsbuch* (UTB, 2022; Paderborn: Schöningh, 1998).

Klein, Günter, "Paul's Purpose in Writing the Epistle to the Romans," in Donfried (ed.), *Romans Debate* [1969], 29–43.

———, "Romans, Letter to the," in *IDBSup* (1976) 752–54.

Klostermann, E., "Die adäquate Vergeltung in Rm 1,22–31," *ZNW* 32 (1933) 1–6.

Knox, John, "The Epistle to the Romans: Introduction and Exegesis," in *IB* 9 (1954) 353–668.

———, "A Note on the text of Romans," *NTS* 2 (1955–56) 191–93.

Koch, Dietrich-Alex, *Die Schrift als Zeuge des Evangeliums: Untersuchungen zur Verwendung und zum Verständnis der Schrift bei Paulus* (BHT, 69; Tübingen: Mohr [Siebeck], 1986).

Koskenniemi, Heikki, *Studien zur Idee und Phraseologie des griechischen Briefes bis 400 n. Chr.* (AASF, B 102.2; Helsinki: Akateeminen Kirjakauppa, 1956).

Köster, Helmut, *Einführung in das Neue Testament im Rahmen der Religionsgeschichte und Kulturgeschichte der hellenistischen und römischen Zeit* (Berlin: de Gruyter, 1980).

———, "Writings and the Spirit: Authority and Politics in Ancient Christianity," *HTR* 84 (1991) 353–72.

Kraemer, Ross S., "On the Meaning of the term 'Jew' in Greco-Roman Inscriptions," *HTR* 82 (1989) 35–53.

Krentz, Edgar, "The Name of God in Disrepute: Romans 2:17–29 [22–23]," *CurTM* 17 (1990) 429–39.

Krieger, Norbert, "Zum Römerbrief," *NovT* 3 (1959) 146–48.

Kümmel, Werner Georg, *Römer 7 und das Bild des Menschen im Neuen Testament: Zwei Studien* (TB, 53; München: Kaiser, 1974).

———, *Einleitung in das Neue Testament* (Heidelberg: Quelle & Meyer, ^{21}1983).

Kuss, Otto, *Der Römerbrief übersetzt und erklärt* (3 vols.; Regensburg: Pustet, 1957–78).

Laato, Timo, *Paulus und das Judentum: Anthropologische Erwägungen* (Åbo: Åbo Academy Press, 1991).

Lagrange, M.-J., *Saint Paul: Épître aux Romains* (EBib; Paris: Gabalda, ^{6}1950).

Lambrecht, Jan, "Syntactical and Logical Remarks on Romans 15:8–9a," *NovT* 42 (2000) 257–61.

Lampe, Peter, *Die stadtrömischen Christen in den ersten beiden Jahrhunderten* (WUNT, 2.18; Tübingen: Mohr [Siebeck], 1987).

———, "The Roman Christians of Romans 16," in Donfried (ed.), *Romans Debate*, 216–30.

Lane, William L., "Social Perspectives on Roman Christianity during the Formative Years from Nero to Nerva: Romans, Hebrews, *1 Clement*," in Donfried and Richardson (eds.), *Judaism and Christianity*, 196–244.

Lange, N. R. M. de, *Origen and the Jews: Studies in Jewish-Christian Relations in Third-Century Palestine* (University of Cambridge Oriental Publications, 25; Cambridge: Cambridge University Press, 1976).

Lausberg, Heinrich, *Handbuch der literarischen Rhetorik: Eine Grundlegung der Literaturwissenschaft* (München: Max Hueber Verlag, 1960).

Levens, Robert G. C., Peta G. Fowler, and Don P. Fowler, "Letters, Latin," in *OCD* (^{3}1996) 847–48.

Levinsohn, Stephen H., "Some Constraints on Discourse Development in the Pastoral Epistles," in S. E. Porter and J. T. Reed (eds.), *Discourse Analysis and the New Testament: Approaches and Results* (JSNTSup, 170; Sheffield: Sheffield Academic Press, 1999) 316–33.

Levison, John R., *Portraits of Adam in Early Judaism: From Sirach to 2 Baruch* (JSPSup, 1; Sheffield: JSOT Press, 1988).

Lietzmann, Hans, *Einführung in die Textgeschichte der Paulusbriefe an die Römer* (HNT, 8; Tübingen: Mohr [Siebeck], ^{5}1971).

Lindenberger, James M., *Ancient Aramaic and Hebrew Letters* (SBLWAW, 4; Atlanta: Scholars Press, 1994).

Llewelyn, Stephen Robert, "Sending Letters in the Ancient World: Paul and the Philippians," *TynBul* 46 (1995) 337–56.

Longenecker, Bruce W., *Eschatology and the Covenant: A Comparison of 4 Ezra and Romans 1–11* (JSNTSup, 57; Sheffield: JSOT Press, 1991).

Louw, Johannes P., *A Semantic Discourse Analysis of Romans* (2 vols.; Pretoria: University of Pretoria, 1979).

Lowe, Malcolm, "Who Were the Ἰουδαῖοι?" *NovT* 18 (1976) 101–30.

Lüdemann, Gerd, *Paulus, der Heidenapostel I: Studien zur Chronologie* (FRLANT, 123; Göttingen: Vandenhoeck & Ruprecht, 1980).

Malherbe, Abraham J., "Μὴ γένοιτο in the Diatribe and Paul," *HTR* 73 (1980) 231–40.

———, *Moral Exhortation: A Greco-Roman Sourcebook* (LEC, 4; Philadelphia: Westminster Press, 1986).

———, "Hellenistic Moralists and the New Testament," in *ANRW* 2.26.1 (1992) 267–333.

Marcus, Joel, "The Circumcision and the Uncircumcision in Rome," *NTS* 35 (1989) 67–81.

Marxsen, Willi, *Einleitung in das Neue Testament: Eine Einführung in ihre Probleme* (Gütersloh: Mohn, 1963).

Mason, Steve, "Paul, Classical Anti-Judaism, and Romans," in J. Neusner (ed.), *Approaches to Ancient Judaism: New Series*. Vol. 4. *Religious and Theological Studies* (South Florida Studies in the History of Judaism, 81; Atlanta: Scholars Press, 1993) 141–80.

———, "'For I am Not Ashamed of the Gospel' (Rom. 1.16): The Gospel and the First Readers of Romans," in Jervis and Richardson (eds.), *Gospel in Paul*, 254–87.

McEleney, Neil J., "Conversion, Circumcision and the Law," *NTS* 20 (1974) 319–41.

McKnight, Scot, *A Light Among the Gentiles: Jewish Missionary Activity in the Second Temple Period* (Minneapolis: Fortress, 1991).

Meecham, Henry G., *Light from Ancient Letters: Private Correspondence in the Non-Literary Papyri of Oxyrhynchus of the First Four Centuries, and Its Bearing on New Testament Language and Thought* (London: George Allen & Unwin, 1923).

Meeks, Wayne A., *The First Urban Christians: The Social World of the Apostle Paul* (New Haven: Yale University Press, 1983).

———, "Judgment and the Brother: Romans 14:1–15:13," in G. F. Hawthorne with O. Betz (eds.), *Tradition and Interpretation in the New Testament: Essays in Honor of E. Earle Ellis for His 60th Birthday* (Grand Rapids: Eerdmans, 1987) 290–300.

Michel, Otto, *Der Brief an die Römer* (KEK, 4; Göttingen: Vandenhoeck & Ruprecht, [14]1978).

Miller, James C., "The Romans Debate: 1991–2001," *CurBS* 9 (2001) 306–49.

Minear, Paul S., *The Obedience of Faith: The Purposes of Paul in the Epistle to the Romans* (SBT, 19; London: SCM, 1971).

Mitchell, Margaret M., "Concerning περὶ δέ in 1 Corinthians," *NovT* 31 (1989) 229–56.

———, "New Testament Envoys in the Context of Greco-Roman Diplomatic and Epistolary Conventions: The Example of Timothy and Titus," *JBL* 111 (1992) 641–62.

Mitternacht, Dieter, *Forum für Sprachlose: Eine kommunikationspsychologische und epistolär-rhetorische Untersuchung des Galaterbriefs* (ConBNT, 30; Stockholm: Almqvist & Wiksell, 1999).

———, "Foolish Galatians?—A Recipient-Oriented Assessment of Paul's Letter," in Nanos (ed.), *Galatians Debate*, 408–33.

———, "Current Views on the Synagogue of Ostia Antica and the Jews of Rome and Ostia," in B. Olsson and M. Zetterholm (eds.), *The Ancient Synagogue From Its Origins Until 200 C.E.: Papers Presented at an International Conference at Lund University, October 14–17, 2001* (ConBNT, 39; Stockholm: Almqvist & Wiksell, 2003) 521–71.

Moiser, Jeremy, "Rethinking Romans 12–15," *NTS* 36 (1990) 571–82.

Moo, Douglas J., "'Law,' 'Works of the Law,' and Legalism in Paul," *WTJ* 45 (1983) 73–100.
Mosley, D. J., *Envoys and Diplomacy in Ancient Greece* (Historia, Einzelschriften 22; Wiesbaden: Steiner, 1973).
Müller, Markus, *Vom Schluß zum Ganzen: Zur Bedeutung des paulinischen Briefkorpusabschlusses* (FRLANT, 172; Göttingen: Vandenhoeck & Ruprecht, 1997).
Müller, W. G., "Brief," in *Historisches Wörterbuch der Rhetorik* 2 (Tübingen: Niemeyer, 1994) 60–76.
Mullins, Terence Y., "Petition as a Literary Form," *NovT* 5 (1962) 46–54.
———, "Disclosure: A Literary Form in the New Testament," *NovT* 7 (1964) 44–50.
———, "Greeting as a New Testament Form," *JBL* 87 (1968) 418–26.
———, "Formulas in New Testament Epistles," *JBL* 91 (1972) 380–90.
———, "Visit Talk in New Testament Letters," *CBQ* 35 (1973) 350–58.
Munck, Johannes, *Paul and the Salvation of Mankind* (London: SCM, 1959).
Murphy-O'Connor, Jerome, *Paul the Letter Writer: His World, His Options, His Skills* (GNS, 41; Collegeville: Liturgical Press, 1995).
———, *Paul: A Critical Life* (Oxford: Clarendon Press, 1996).
Myers, Charles D., Jr., "Romans, Epistle to the," in *ABD* 5 (1992) 816–30.
Nanos, Mark D., *The Mystery of Romans: The Jewish Context of Paul's Letter* (Minneapolis: Fortress, 1996).
———, "The Jewish Context of the Gentile Audience Addressed in Paul's Letter to the Romans," *CBQ* 61 (1999) 283–304.
———, *The Irony of Galatians: Paul's Letter in First-Century Context* (Minneapolis: Fortress, 2002).
——— (ed.), *The Galatians Debate: Contemporary Issues in Rhetorical and Historical Interpretation* (Peabody: Hendrickson, 2002).
Neumann, Hans, and Peter L. Schmidt, "Brief," in *DNP* 2 (1997) 771–75.
Neusner, Jacob, and Ernest S. Frerichs (eds.), *"To See Ourselves as Others See Us": Christians, Jews, "Others" in Late Antiquity* (Chico: Scholars Press, 1985).
Niebuhr, Karl-Wilhelm, *Heidenapostel aus Israel: Die jüdische Identität des Paulus nach ihrer Darstellung in seinen Briefen* (WUNT, 62; Tübingen: Mohr [Siebeck], 1992).
Nolland, John, "Uncircumcised Proselytes?" *JSJ* 12 (1981) 173–94.
Nygren, Anders, *Commentary on Romans* (Philadelphia: Muhlenberg, 1949).
O'Brien, Peter T., *Introductory Thanksgivings in the Letters of Paul* (NovTSup, 49; Leiden: Brill, 1977).
———, "Letters, Letter Forms," in G. F. Hawthorne, R. P. Martin, and D. G. Reid (eds.), *Dictionary of Paul and His Letters* (Downers Grove: InterVarsity Press, 1993) 550–53.

Ollrog, Wolf-Henning, "Die Abfassungsverhältnisse von Röm 16," in D. Lührmann and G. Strecker (eds.), *Kirche: Festschrift für Günther Bornkamm zum 75. Geburtstag* (Tübingen: Mohr [Siebeck], 1980) 221–44.

Olson, Stanley N., "Pauline Expressions of Confidence in His Addressees," *CBQ* 47 (1985) 282–95.

Olsson, Birger, "Rom 1:3f enligt Paulus," *SEÅ* 37–38 (1972–73) 255–73.

Ortkemper, Franz-Josef, *Leben aus dem Glauben: Christliche Grundhaltungen nach Römer 12–13* (NTAbh, NF, 14; Münster: Aschendorff, 1980).

Palmer, Micheal W., "τί οὖν The Inferential Question in Paul's Letter to the Romans with a Proposed Reading of Romans 4.1," in S. E. Porter and D. A. Carson (eds.), *Discourse Analysis and Other Topics in Biblical Greek* (JSNTSup, 113; Sheffield: Sheffield Academic Press, 1995) 200–218.

Pardee, Dennis, "An Overview of Ancient Hebrew Epistolography," *JBL* 97 (1978) 321–46.

Pearson, Brook W. R., and Stanley E. Porter, "The Genres of the New Testament," in S. E. Porter (ed.), *Handbook to Exegesis of the New Testament* (NTTS, 25; Leiden: Brill, 1997) 131–65.

Pedersen, Sigfred, "Theologische Überlegungen zur Isagogik des Römerbriefes," *ZNW* 76 (1985) 47–67.

Penna, Romano, "Les Juifs à Rome au temps de l'Apôtre Paul," *NTS* 28 (1982) 321–47.

———, "The Structural Function of 3:1–8 in the Letter to the Romans," in *Paul the Apostle: A Theological and Exegetical Study.* Vol. 1. *Jew and Greek Alike* (Collegeville: Liturgical Press, 1996) 60–89.

Pfitzner, Victor C., *Paul and the Agon Motif: Traditional Athletic Imagery in the Pauline Literature* (NovTSup, 16; Leiden: Brill, 1967).

Pohlenz, Max, "Paulus und die Stoa," *ZNW* 42 (1949) 69–104.

Popkes, Wiard, "Zum Aufbau und Charakter von Römer 1. 18–32," *NTS* 28 (1982) 490–501.

———, *Paränese und Neues Testament* (SBS, 168; Stuttgart: Verlag Katholisches Bibelwerke, 1996).

Porter, Calvin L., "Romans 1.18–32: Its Role in the Developing Argument," *NTS* 40 (1994) 210–28.

Porter, Stanley E., "The Theoretical Justification for Application of Rhetorical Categories to Pauline Epistolary Literature," in idem and Olbricht (eds.), *Rhetoric and the New Testament*, 100–122.

———, "The Argument of Romans 5: Can a Rhetorical Question Make a Difference?" in *Studies in the Greek New Testament: Theory and Practice* (Studies in Biblical Greek, 6; New York: Peter Lang, 1996) 213–38.

——— (ed.), *Handbook of Classical Rhetoric in the Hellenistic Period 330 B.C.–A.D. 400* (Leiden: Brill, 1997).
———, "Paul of Tarsus and His Letters," in idem (ed.), *Handbook of Classical Rhetoric*, 533–85.
———, "Paul as Epistolographer *and* Rhetorician?," in idem and D. L. Stamps (eds.), *The Rhetorical Interpretation of Scripture: Essays from the 1996 Malibu Conference* (JSNTSup, 180; Sheffield: Sheffield Academic Press, 1999) 222–48.
———, "Diatribe," in C. A. Evans and S. E. Porter (eds.), *Dictionary of New Testament Background* (Downers Grove: InterVarsity Press, 2000) 296–98.
———, "The Rhetorical Scribe: Textual Variants in Romans and Their Possible Rhetorical Purpose," in idem and D. L. Stamps (eds.), *Rhetorical Criticism and the Bible* (JSNTSup, 195; Sheffield: Sheffield Academic Press, 2002) 403–19.
———, and Thomas H. Olbricht (eds.), *Rhetoric and the New Testament: Essays from the 1992 Heidelberg Conference* (JSNTSup, 90; Sheffield: JSOT Press, 1993).
Poster, Carol, "The Economy of Letter Writing in Graeco-Roman Antiquity," in Eriksson, Olbricht, and Übelacker (eds.), *Rhetorical Argumentation*, 112–24.
Purcell, Nicholas, "Postal service," in *OCD* (³1996) 1233–34.
Rad, Gerhard von, Karl Georg Kuhn, and Walter Gutbrod, "Ἰσραὴλ κτλ.," in *TDNT* 3 (1965) 356–91.
Räisänen, Heikki, *Paul and the Law* (WUNT, 29; Tübingen: Mohr [Siebeck], 1983).
Reasoner, Mark, *The Strong and the Weak: Romans 14.1–15.13 in Context* (SNTSMS, 103; Cambridge: Cambridge University Press, 1999).
Reed, Jeffrey T., "Using Ancient Rhetorical Categories to Interpret Paul's Letters: A Question of Genre," in Porter and Olbricht (eds.), *Rhetoric and the New Testament*, 292–324.
———, "Are Paul's Thanksgivings Epistolary?" *JSNT* 61 (1996) 87–99.
———, *A Discourse Analysis of Philippians: Method and Rhetoric in the Debate over Literary Integrity* (JSNTSup, 136; Sheffield: Sheffield Academic Press, 1997).
———, "The Epistle," in Porter (ed.), *Handbook of Classical Rhetoric*, 171–93.
Reichert, Angelika, *Der Römerbrief als Gratwanderung: Eine Untersuchung zur Abfassungsproblematik* (FRLANT, 194; Göttingen: Vandenhoeck & Ruprecht, 2001).
Reiser, Marius, *Sprache und literarische Formen des Neuen Testaments: Eine Einführung* (UTP, 2197; Paderborn: Schöningh, 2001).
Reynolds, Joyce, and Robert Tannenbaum, *Jews and God-Fearers at Aphrodisias: Greek Inscriptions with Commentary* (Cambridge Philological Society Suppl. Vol. 12; Cambridge: Cambridge Philological Society, 1987).
Richards, E. Randolph, *The Secretary in the Letters of Paul* (WUNT, 2.42; Tübingen: Mohr [Siebeck], 1991).

Richardson, Peter, "Augustan-Era Synagogues in Rome," in Donfried and Richardson (eds.), *Judaism and Christianity*, 17–29.

Riesner, Rainer, *Die Frühzeit des Apostels Paulus: Studien zur Chronologie, Missionsstrategie und Theologie* (WUNT, 71; Tübingen: Mohr [Siebeck], 1994).

Roberts, J. H., "Pauline Transitions to the Letter Body," in A. Vanhoye (ed.), *L'Apôtre Paul. Personnalité, style et conception du ministère* (Leuven: University Press—Peeters, 1986) 93–99.

Roller, Otto, *Das Formular der paulinischen Briefe: Ein Beitrag zur Lehre vom antiken Briefe* (BWANT, 4.6; Stuttgart: Kohlhammer, 1933).

Roosen, A., "Le genre littéraire de l'Epître aux Romains," in TU 87 [=SE 2] (1964) 465–71.

Rowe, Galen O., "Style," in Porter (ed.), *Handbook of Classical Rhetoric*, 121-57.

Russell, D. A., *Criticism in Antiquity* (Classical Life and Letters; London: Duckworth, 1981).

Rutgers, Leonard Victor, *The Hidden Heritage of Diaspora Judaism* (Leuven: Peeters, ²1998).

———, "Roman Policy toward the Jews: Expulsions from the City of Rome during the First Century C.E.," in Donfried and Richardson (eds.), *Judaism and Christianity*, 93–116.

Saake, Helmut, "Echtheitskritische Überlegungen zur Interpolationshypothese von Römer ii.16," *NTS* 19 (1972–73) 486–89.

Salles, Catherine, "L'épistolographie hellénistique et romaine," in J. Schlosser (ed.), *Paul de Tarse. Congrès de l'ACFEB (Strasbourg, 1995)* (LD, 165; Paris: Cerf, 1996) 79–97.

Sampley, J. Paul, "Romans in a Different Light: A Response to Robert Jewett," in Hay and Johnson (eds.), *Pauline Theology*, 109–29.

———, "The Weak and the Strong: Paul's Careful and Crafty Rhetorical Strategy in Romans 14:1–15:13," in L. M. White and O. L. Yarbrough (eds.), *The Social World of the First Christians: Essays in Honor of Wayne A. Meeks* (Minneapolis: Fortress, 1995) 40–52.

Sanday, William, and Arthur C. Headlam, *A Critical and Exegetical Commentary on the Epistle to the Romans* (ICC; Edinburgh: T&T Clark, ⁵1902).

Sanders, E. P., *Paul, the Law, and the Jewish People* (Philadelphia: Fortress, 1983).

Sanders, Jack T., "The Transition from Opening Epistolary Thanksgiving to Body in the Letters of the Pauline Corpus," *JBL* 81 (1962) 348–62.

———, *Schismatics, Sectarians, Dissidents, Deviants: The First One Hundred Years of Jewish-Christian Relations* (Valley Forge: Trinity Press, 1993).

Sandnes, Karl Olav, *Paul—One of the Prophets? A Contribution to the Apostle's Self-Understanding* (WUNT, 2.43; Tübingen: Mohr [Siebeck], 1991).

Sass, Gerhard, "Zur Bedeutung von δοῦλος bei Paulus," *ZNW* 40 (1941) 24–32.
Schelkle, Karl Hermann, *Paulus Lehrer der Väter: Die altkirchliche Auslegung von Römer 1–11* (Düsseldorf: Patmos, 1956).
Schlatter, Adolf von, *Gottes Gerechtigkeit: Ein Kommentar zum Römerbrief* (Stuttgart: Calmer Verlag, ²1952).
Schlier, Heinrich, "Von den Heiden.—Röm. 1,18–32," in *Die Zeit der Kirche: Exegetische Aufsätze und Vorträge* (Freiburg: Herder, ⁴1966) 29–37.
———, "Von den Juden.—Röm. 2,1–29," in *Die Zeit der Kirche: Exegetische Aufsätze und Vorträge* (Freiburg: Herder, ⁴1966) 38–47.
———, *Der Römerbrief* (HTKNT, 6; Freiburg: Herder, 1977).
Schmeller, Thomas, *Paulus und die „Diatribe": Eine vergleichende Stilinterpretation* (NTAbh, NF, 19; Münster: Aschendorff, 1987).
Schmidt, Hans Wilhelm, *Der Brief des Paulus an die Römer* (THKNT, 6; Berlin: Evangelische Verlagsanstalt, 1963).
Schmidt, Peter L., "Epistolographie," in *KlPauly* 2 (1967) 324–27.
Schmithals, Walter, "Die Irrlehrer von Röm. 16,17–20," in *Paulus und die Gnostiker: Untersuchungen zu den kleinen Paulusbriefen* (TF, 35; Hamburg: Reich, 1965) 159–73.
———, *Der Römerbrief als historisches Problem* (SNT, 9; Gütersloh: Mohn, 1975).
Schneider, J., "Brief," in *RAC* 2 (1954) 564–85.
Schnider, Franz, and Werner Stenger, *Studien zum neutestamentlichen Briefformular* (NTTS, 11; Leiden: Brill, 1987).
Schrenk, Gottlob, "ἱερός κτλ.," in *TDNT* 3 (1965) 221–83.
Schubert, Paul, "Form and Function of the Pauline Letters," *JR* 19 (1939) 365–77.
———, *Form and Function of the Pauline Thanksgivings* (BZNW, 20; Berlin: Töpelmann, 1939).
Schulz, Siegfried, "Die Anklage in Röm. 1,18–32," *TZ* 14 (1958) 161–73.
Scott, James M., *Adoption as Sons of God: An Exegetical Investigation into the Background of ΥΙΟΘΕΣΙΑ in the Pauline Corpus* (WUNT, 2.48; Tübingen: Mohr [Siebeck], 1992).
———, *Paul and the Nations: The Old Testament and Jewish Background of Paul's Mission to the Nations with Special Reference to the Destination of Galatians* (WUNT, 84; Tübingen: Mohr [Siebeck], 1995).
Scroggs, Robin, "Paul as Rhetorician: Two Homilies in Romans 1–11," in R. Hamerton-Kelly and R. Scroggs (eds.), *Jews, Greeks and Christians: Religious Cultures in Late Antiquity. Essays in Honor of William David Davies* (SJLA, 21; Leiden: Brill, 1976) 271–98.
Segal, Alan F., *Paul the Convert: The Apostolate and Apostasy of Saul the Pharisee* (New Haven: Yale University Press, 1990).

Sevenster, J. N., *Paul and Seneca* (NovTSup, 4; Leiden: Brill, 1961).
Siegert, Folker, *Argumentation bei Paulus gezeigt an Röm 9–11* (WUNT, 34; Tübingen: Mohr [Siebeck], 1985).
Slingerland, Dixon, "Chrestus: Christus?" in A. J. Avery-Peck (ed.), *New Perspectives on Ancient Judaism*. Vol. 4. *The Literature of Early Rabbinic Judaism: Issues in Talmudic Redaction and Interpretation* (Lanham: University Press of America, 1989) 133–44.
——, "Suetonius *Claudius* 25.4, Acts 18, and Paulus Orosius' *Historiarum adversum paganos libri VII*: Dating the Claudian Expulsion(s) of Roman Jews," *JQR* 83 (1992) 127–44.
Smallwood, E. Mary, *The Jews under Roman Rule: From Pompey to Diocletian. A Study in Political Relations* (SJLA, 20; Leiden: Brill, ²1981).
Smiga, George, "Romans 12:1–2 and 15:30–32 and the Occasion of the Letter to the Romans," *CBQ* 53 (1991) 257–73.
Snodgrass, Klyne R., "Justification by Grace—To the Doers: An Analysis of the Place of Romans 2 in the Theology of Paul," *NTS* 32 (1986) 72–93.
Spicq, Ceslas, "εὐνοέω κτλ.," *Notes de lexicographie néo-testamentaire* (3 vols.; OBO, 22; Göttingen: Vandenhoeck & Ruprecht, 1978–82) 3.316–21.
——, "προθυμία κτλ.," *Notes de lexicographie néo-testamentaire* (3 vols.; OBO, 22; Göttingen: Vandenhoeck & Ruprecht, 1978–82) 2.746–51.
Stamps, Dennis L., "Rhetorical Criticism of the New Testament: Ancient and Modern Evaluations of Argumentation," in S. E. Porter and D. Tombs (eds.), *Approaches to New Testament Study* (JSNTSup, 120; Sheffield: Sheffield Academic Press, 1995) 129–69.
Stanley, Christopher D., *Paul and the Language of Scripture: Citation Technique in the Pauline Epistles and Contemporary Literature* (SNTSMS, 69; Cambridge: Cambridge University Press, 1992).
Stendahl, Krister, *Final Account: Paul's Letter to the Romans* (Minneapolis: Fortress, 1995).
Stirewalt, M. Luther, Jr., "Paul's Evaluation of Letter-Writing," in J. M. Myers et al. (eds.), *Search the Scriptures: New Testament Studies in Honor of Raymond T. Stamm* (Gettysburg Theological Studies, 3; Leiden: Brill, 1969) 179–96.
——, "The Form and Function of the Greek Letter-Essay," in Donfried (ed.), *Romans Debate* [1977], 147–71.
——, *Studies in Ancient Greek Epistolography* (SBLRBS, 27; Atlanta: Scholars Press, 1993).
——, *Paul, the Letter Writer* (Grand Rapids: Eerdmans, 2003).
Stowers, Stanley K., *The Diatribe and Paul's Letter to the Romans* (SBLDS, 57; Chico: Scholars Press, 1981).

———, "Paul's Dialogue with a Fellow Jew in Romans 3:1–9," *CBQ* 46 (1984) 707–22.

———, *Letter Writing in Greco-Roman Antiquity* (LEC, 5; Philadelphia: Westminster Press, 1986).

———, "Social Typification and the Classification of Ancient Letters," in J. Neusner et al. (eds.), *The Social World of Formative Christianity and Judaism: Essays in Tribute to Howard Clark Kee* (Philadelphia: Fortress, 1988) 78–90.

———, "The Diatribe," in D. E. Aune (ed.), *Greco-Roman Literature and the New Testament: Selected Forms and Genres* (SBLSBS, 21; Atlanta: Scholars Press, 1988) 71–83.

———, Review of Thomas Schmeller, *Paulus und die „Diatribe": Eine vergleichende Stilinterpretation*, *JBL* 108 (1989) 538–42.

———, "'Ἐκ πίστεως and διὰ τῆς πίστεως in Romans 3:30," *JBL* 108 (1989) 665–74.

———, "Paul on the Use and Abuse of Reason," in D. L. Balch, E. Ferguson, and W. A. Meeks (eds.), *Greeks, Romans, and Christians: Essays in Honor of Abraham J. Malherbe* (Minneapolis: Fortress, 1990) 253–86.

———, "Greek and Latin Letters," in *ABD* 4 (1992) 290–93.

———, *A Rereading of Romans: Justice, Jews, and Gentiles* (New Haven: Yale University Press, 1994).

Stuhlmacher, Peter, "The Purpose of Romans," in Donfried (ed.), *Romans Debate* [1986], 231–42.

———, *Der Brief an die Römer* (NTD, 6; Göttingen: Vandenhoeck & Ruprecht, [14]1989).

Suhl, Alfred, "Der konkrete Anlaß des Römerbriefes," *Kairos* 13 (1971) 119–30.

Swearingen, C. Jan, "The Tongues of Men: Understanding Greek Rhetorical Sources for Paul's Letters to the Romans and 1 Corinthians," in Eriksson, Olbricht, and Übelacker (eds.), *Rhetorical Argumentation*, 232–42.

Sykutris, Ioannes, "Epistolographie," in PWSup 5 (1931) 185–220.

Taatz, Irene, *Frühjüdische Briefe: Die paulinishcen Briefe im Rahmen der offiziellen religiösen Briefe des Frühjudentums* (NTOA, 16; Freiburg, Schweiz: Universitätsverlag, 1991).

Tellbe, Mikael, *Paul between Synagogue and State: Christians, Jews, and Civic Authorities in 1 Thessalonians, Romans, and Philippians* (ConBNT, 34; Stockholm: Almqvist & Wiksell, 2001).

Theobald, Michael, "Warum schrieb Paulus den Römerbrief?" in *Studien zum Römerbrief* (WUNT, 136; Tübingen: Mohr Siebeck, 2001 [1983]) 2–14.

———, "Zorn Gottes: Ein nicht zu vernachlässigender Aspekt der Theologie des Römerbriefs," in *Studien zum Römerbrief* (WUNT, 136; Tübingen: Mohr Siebeck, 2001) 68–100.

Thompson, Richard W., "Paul's Double Critique of Jewish Boasting: A Study of Rom 3,27 in Its Context," *Bib* 67 (1986) 520–31.

Thorsteinsson, Runar M., "Paul's Missionary Duty Towards Gentiles in Rome: A Note on the Punctuation and Syntax of Rom 1.13–15," *NTS* 48 (2002) 531–47.

Thraede, Klaus, *Grundzüge griechisch-römischer Brieftopik* (München: Beck, 1970).

Thurén, Lauri, *Derhetorizing Paul: A Dynamic Perspective on Pauline Theology and the Law* (WUNT, 124; Tübingen: Mohr Siebeck, 2000).

Tobin, Thomas H., "Controversy and Continuity in Romans 1:18–3:20," *CBQ* 55 (1993) 298–318.

Toit, A. B. du, "Persuasion in Romans 1:1–17," *BZ* 33 (1989) 192–209.

Tomson, Peter J., "The Names Israel and Jew in Ancient Judaism and in the New Testament I," *Bijdr* 47 (1986) 120–40.

———, *Paul and the Jewish Law: Halakha in the Letters of the Apostle to the Gentiles* (CRINT, sec. 3: Jewish Traditions in Early Christian Literature, 1; Assen: Van Gorcum, 1990).

Trapp, Michael B., "Letters, Greek," in *OCD* (^{3}1996) 846–47.

———, "Philosophical Sermons: The 'Dialexeis' of Maximus of Tyre," in *ANRW* 2.34.3 (1997) 1945–76.

Trobisch, David, *Die Entstehung der Paulusbriefsammlung: Studien zu den Anfängen christlicher Publizistik* (NTOA, 10; Freiburg, Schweiz: Universitätsverlag, 1989).

Trocmé, Etienne, "The Jews as Seen by Paul and Luke," in Neusner and Frerichs (eds.), *"To See Ourselves,"* 145–61.

Vielhauer, Philipp, *Geschichte der urchristlichen Literatur: Einleitung in das Neue Testament, die Apokryphen und die Apostolischen Väter* (Berlin: de Gruyter, 1975).

Vos, Johan S., "'To Make the Weaker Argument Defeat the Stronger': Sophistical Argumentation in Paul's Letter to the Romans," in Eriksson, Olbricht, and Übelacker (eds.), *Rhetorical Argumentation*, 217–31.

Wagner, J. Ross, "The Christ, Servant of Jew and Gentile: A Fresh Approach to Romans 15:8–9," *JBL* 116 (1997) 473–85.

———, *Heralds of the Good News: Isaiah and Paul 'In Concert' in the Letter to the Romans* (NovTSup, 101; Leiden: Brill, 2002).

Walser, Georg, "The Greek of the Jews in Ancient Rome," in B. Olsson, D. Mitternacht, and O. Brandt (eds.), *The Synagogue of Ancient Ostia and the Jews of Rome: Interdisciplinary Studies* (Stockholm: Paul Åström, 2001) 145–50.

Walters, James C., *Ethnic Issues in Paul's Letter to the Romans: Changing Self-Definitions in Earliest Roman Christianity* (Valley Forge: Trinity Press, 1993).

———, "Romans, Jews, and Christians: The Impact of the Romans on Jewish/Christian Relations in First-Century Rome," in Donfried and Richardson (eds.), *Judaism and Christianity*, 175–95.

Watson, Francis, *Paul, Judaism and the Gentiles: A Sociological Approach* (SNTSMS, 56; Cambridge: Cambridge University Press, 1986).

Wedderburn, A. J. M., "Adam in Paul's Letter to the Romans," in E. A. Livingstone (ed.), *Studia Biblica 1978: Papers on Paul and Other New Testament Authors* (3 vols.; Sheffield: JSOT Press, 1979–80) 3.413–30.

———, *The Reasons for Romans* (Edinburgh: T&T Clark, 1988).

Weima, Jeffrey A. D., *Neglected Endings: The Significance of the Pauline Letter Closings* (JSNTSup, 101; Sheffield: JSOT Press, 1994).

———, "Preaching the Gospel in Rome: A Study of the Epistolary Framework of Romans," in Jervis and Richardson (eds.), *Gospel in Paul*, 337–66.

———, "Epistolary Theory," in C. A. Evans and S. E. Porter (eds.), *Dictionary of New Testament Background* (Downers Grove: InterVarsity Press, 2000) 327–30.

Weiss, Bernhard, *Der Brief an die Römer* (KEK, 4; Göttingen: Vandenhoeck & Ruprecht, ^{9}1899).

Wessel, B., "Captatio benevolentiae," in *Historisches Wörterbuch der Rhetorik* 2 (Tübingen: Niemeyer, 1994) 121–23.

Westerholm, Stephen, "Letter and Spirit: The Foundation of Pauline *Ethics*," *NTS* 30 (1984) 229–48.

White, John L., "Introductory Formulae in the Body of the Pauline Letter," *JBL* 90 (1971) 91–97.

———, "The Ancient Epistolography Group in Retrospect," *Semeia* 22 (1981) 1–14.

———, "The Greek Documentary Letter Tradition Third Century B.C.E to Third Century C.E," *Semeia* 22 (1981) 89–106.

———, "Saint Paul and the Apostolic Letter Tradition," *CBQ* 45 (1983) 433–44.

———, "New Testament Epistolary Literature in the Framework of Ancient Epistolography," in *ANRW* 2.25.2 (1984) 1730–56.

———, "Ancient Greek Letters," in D. E. Aune (ed.), *Greco-Roman Literature and the New Testament: Selected Forms and Genres* (SBLSBS, 21; Atlanta: Scholars Press, 1988) 85–105.

———, "Apostolic Mission and Apostolic Message: Congruence in Paul's Epistolary Rhetoric, Structure and Imagery," in B. H. McLean (ed.), *Origins and Method: Towards a New Understanding of Judaism and Christianity. Essays in Honour of John C. Hurd* (JSNTSup, 86; Sheffield: JSOT Press, 1993) 145–61.

———, *The Apostle of God: Paul and the Promise of Abraham* (Peabody: Hendrickson, 1999).

Whitsett, Christopher G., "Son of God, Seed of David: Paul's Messianic Exegesis in Romans [1]:3–4," *JBL* 119 (2000) 661–81.
Wiefel, Wolfgang, "The Jewish Community in Ancient Rome and the Origins of Roman Christianity," in Donfried (ed.), *Romans Debate* [1970], 85–101.
Wilckens, Ulrich, *Der Brief an die Römer* (3 vols.; EKKNT, 6; Zürich: Benziger, 1978–82).
Williams, Margaret H., "The Structure of Roman Jewry Re-Considered: Were the Synagogues of Ancient Rome Entirely Homogenous?" *ZPE* 104 (1994) 129–41.
——, "The Meaning and Function of *Ioudaios* in Graeco-Roman Inscriptions," *ZPE* 116 (1997) 249–62.
Williams, Philip R., "Paul's Purpose in Writing Romans," *BSac* 128 (1971) 62–67.
Winninge, Mikael, *Sinners and the Righteous: A Comparative Study of the Psalms of Solomon and Paul's Letters* (ConBNT, 26; Stockholm: Almqvist & Wiksell, 1995).
Wright, N. T., "Romans and the Theology of Paul," in Hay and Johnson (eds.), *Pauline Theology*, 30–67.
——, "The Law in Romans 2," in J. D. G. Dunn (ed.), *Paul and the Mosaic Law* (WUNT, 89; Tübingen: Mohr [Siebeck], 1996) 131–50.
——, "The Letter to the Romans: Introduction, Commentary, and Reflections," in *NIB* 10 (2002) 395–770.
Wuellner, Wilhelm, "Paul's Rhetoric of Argumentation in Romans: An Alternative to the Donfried-Karris Debate over Romans," in Donfried (ed.), *Romans Debate* [1976], 128–46.
——, "Arrangement," in Porter (ed.), *Handbook of Classical Rhetoric*, 51–87.
Yinger, Kent L., *Paul, Judaism, and Judgment According to Deeds* (SNTSMS, 105; Cambridge: Cambridge University Press, 1999).
Zahn, Theodor, *Der Brief des Paulus an die Römer* (KNT, 6; Leipzig: Deichert, 1910).
Zetterholm, Magnus, *The Formation of Christianity in Antioch: A Social-Scientific Approach to the Separation Between Judaism and Christianity* (London: Routledge, 2003).
Ziesler, John, *Paul's Letter to the Romans* (TPINTC; London: SCM, 1989).

Index of Names

A
Achtemeier, P. J., 13, 36, 41, 89, 96, 163
Aeschines, 62, 75
Alciphron, 75
Alexander, P. S., 18, 71
Althaus, P., 88
Alvarez Cineira, D., 88, 92-93
Anderson, R. D., 14-18, 44, 46, 73, 124, 141, 147, 181-82, 188
Antiochus II, 50
Apollonius of Tyana, 49, 62, 136
Arrian, 124, 129, 232
Artaxerxes, 42
Artemon, 16, 131
Arzt, P., 27-29, 45
Aune, D. E., 7-8, 13, 16, 19-21, 24, 30, 57, 70-72, 79, 147

B
Bahr, G. J., 63
Bailey, J. L., 7, 136
Barclay, J. M. G., 95-96, 209, 224, 228, 231, 238
Barrett, C. K., 4, 88, 179, 188, 215
Bartsch, H.-W., 88
Bassler, J. M., 156-58, 169, 235
Bauckham, R., 21, 71, 82
Baur, F. C., 88
Becker, J., 88, 92
Beker, J. C., 88, 105, 115, 174, 186, 209, 213
Bell, R. H., 183, 186
Benko, S., 93, 95
Berger, K., 25, 30, 53, 70-71, 125
Bergmeier, R., 163
Berkley, T. W., 206, 212-15, 220
Betz, H. D., 176
Bickermann, E., 50
Bietenhard, H., 205
Bion, 124
Bischoff, A., 212
Bjerkelund, C. J., 47-52, 66, 68

Blumenfeld, B., 33
Boers, H., 88, 119, 146
Bonhöffer, A., 126
Bornkamm, G., 127, 155, 158, 167, 186, 205
Botermann, H., 93-95
Boyarin, D., 1, 186, 223, 228
Brändle, R., 88, 92
Brawley, R. L., 89
Brown, M. J., 33
Brown, R. E., 88, 90, 92
Bruce, F. F., 61, 88, 92
Bryan, C., 52, 105, 171
Bultmann, R., 125-26, 155, 178
Burkitt, F. C., 154
Buss, M. J., 6-7, 74
Bussmann, C., 167
Byrne, B., 58
Byrskog, S., 31, 117

C
Callow, K., 163
Campbell, D. A., 88, 115, 118, 147

Campbell, W. S., 88, 147
Cancik, H., 134
Capelle, W., 125
Caragounis, C. C., 44, 88, 92
Carras, G. P., 3, 156, 183, 209, 214
Carson, D. A., 164
Carter, T. L., 88, 92-93, 183
Chae, D. J.-S., 88,
Chesnut, G. F., 94
Chio, 62
Cicero, 8, 17, 47, 59-62, 72, 131-144
Classen, C. J., 14-18, 71
Claudius, 4, 20, 92-96, 99, 101
Cohen, S. J. D., 90, 96, 198, 201-4, 222, 225
Collins, A. Y., 198
Collins, J. J., 225
Cornelius Nepos, 134
Cosgrove, C. H., 89, 237
Cotton, H. M., 61
Crafton, J. A., 92
Cranfield, C. E. B., 4, 61, 88-89, 93, 104-8, 117, 162, 169, 170-71, 177-83, 190, 197, 206, 214, 226
Crates, 75

D
Dabourne, W., 6, 14, 88, 92, 108, 181, 183, 235
Dahl, N. A., 8, 38, 54, 71, 74, 84, 108, 239
Davies, G. N., 35, 156,
Deissmann, A., 39, 73, 133
Demetrius, 16, 18, 131
Demosthenes, 14-15, 39, 42, 49
Derrett, J. D. M., 214
Dio Cassius, 94, 203
Dio Chrysostom, 125
Dio of Prusa, 124, 126
Diogenes, 16, 75, 131, 135, 140
Dodd, B., 175
Dodd, C. H., 3, 88, 224
Donaldson, T. L., 89, 184, 204, 225, 241
Donfried, K. P., 17, 66, 78-79, 91-92, 97, 124
Dormeyer, D., 40
Doty, W. G., 7, 16, 24-27, 41, 71, 73, 78,
Drane, J. W., 88, 927
Dunn, J. D. G., 3-6, 25, 35-36, 40-41, 55, 61, 69, 78, 88, 93, 97, 106, 157, 159, 161-62, 171-75, 184-86, 190, 191, 195, 209-210, 213-14, 218, 220-23, 228, 233, 237, 240
Dziatzko, C., 71, 73

E
Eckstein, H.-J., 173
Elliott, J. K., 61
Elliott, N., 4, 34, 41, 44, 70, 89, 92, 113, 147, 157, 159, 161, 163, 165, 186, 191, 235
Engberg-Pedersen, T., 89, 100, 147-48, 156, 188
Epictetus, 124, 126, 129, 144, 188, 199-202, 232
Epicurus, 76, 79- 81
Epp, E. J., 61
Erbes, K., 67
Eriksson, A., 14
Euripides, 75
Exler, F. X. J., 18-21, 32, 37-38, 64, 72

F
Fahy, T., 88
Feldman, L. H., 204, 224
Figueras, P., 203
Finsterbusch, K., 163

Fischer, J. A., 156
Fitzmyer, J. A., 18, 41, 61, 66, 68, 77-78, 88, 93, 110, 147, 157, 159, 178, 181, 197-198
Flückiger, F., 178
Fraikin, D., 89, 100
Fredriksen, P., 184
Frend, W. H. C., 93
Freyne, S., 198
Fridrichsen, A., 178, 189, 199, 202
Funk, R. W., 56-57
Furnish, V. P., 53

G
Gager, J. G., 89, 147
Gamble, H., 7, 22, 59, 60-68, 73, 83-84, 92
Garlington, D. B., 171, 213
Gärtner, B., 193
Gaston, L., 89, 96, 162, 198, 240
Gathercole, S. J., 163, 182-85, 205, 213
Geytenbeek, A. C. van, 129
Gilliard, F. D., 13
Glad, C. E., 97
Goppelt, L., 208, 214
Gorday, P., 198
Görgemanns, H., 71
Grabner-Haider, A., 52

Gregory of Nazianzus, 132
Grobel, K., 154, 260
Gruen, E. S., 93, 96, 260
Guerra, A. J., 70, 88, 90, 105, 115
Güting, E. W., 110, 154

H
Haacker, K., 70, 92
Hansen, G. W., 54
Hartmann, K., 129
Harvey, G., 198, 201, 219
Harvey, J. D., 154
Hays, R. B., 35-36, 114, 118, 153, 186, 219, 221
Headlam, A. C., 65, 69, 88, 110, 178, 186, 219
Heckel, U., 105
Hedner-Zetterholm, K., 95
Hellholm, D., 40
Heraclitus, 75
Hirsch, E. D., 6
Holmberg, B., 34
Holmstrand, J., 41, 154
Hooker, M. D., 171
Horace, 62
Horst, P. W. van der, 198

I
Ignatius, 31, 199, 226
Isocrates, 62
Ito, Akio, 220

J
Jeffers, J. S., 88, 92
Jeremias, J., 154, 172
Jervell, J., 77, 113
Jervis, L. A., 41, 56, 59, 65, 88, 91, 108, 112
Jewett, R., 33, 40, 55, 67, 70
Josephus, 21, 33, 38, 42, 48-49, 79, 94-95, 197, 202, 207, 213, 217
Judge, E. A., 93
Julius Victor, 15, 19, 132, 144
Jüngel, E., 154
Justin Martyr, 197

K
Karris, R. J., 97
Käsemann, E., 41, 44, 61, 88, 112, 177, 197, 209-10, 215, 228, 230-31
Kaye, B. N., 55
Kaylor, R. D., 88
Keck, L. E., 13, 89, 96
Kennedy, G. A., 13, 15, 16, 44, 182

Kern, P., 14
Kettunen, M., 88
Keyes, C. W., 61
Klauck, H.-J., 14, 20, 61, 71, 79
Klein, G., 89, 108
Klostermann, E., 172
Knox, J., 57, 66, 69
Koch, D.-A., 219
Koskenniemi, H., 19-20, 24, 28, 37, 45, 57, 63, 72, 82, 131
Köster, H., 70, 73, 84
Kraemer, R. S., 198, 203
Krentz, E., 212, 217
Krieger, N., 88
Kuhn, K. G., 198
Kümmel, W. G., 92, 99, 113, 175
Kuss, O., 167, 178, 183, 197, 215, 217, 222

L
Laato, T., 195
Lagrange, M.-J., 88, 186
Lambrecht, J., 119
Lampe, P., 30, 44, 65-66, 88, 93
Lane, W. L., 88, 92
Lange, N. R. M. de, 199
Lausberg, H., 141

Levens, R. G. C., 71
Levinsohn, S. H., 154, 163
Levison, J. R., 171
Lietzmann, H., 61, 65, 69, 177, 210
Lindenberger, J. M., 18
Llewelyn, S. R., 61
Longenecker, B. W., 171
Louw, J. P., 154, 179
Lowe, M., 198
Lüdemann, G., 93

M
Malherbe, A. J., 15-18, 26, 76, 125, 129-31
Marcus, J., 90-92
Marrou, H. I., 125
Marxsen, W., 92
Mason, S., 88, 100-4, 107, 109
Maximus of Tyre, 124-26, 144
McEleney, N. J., 225
McKnight, S., 4, 208, 224
Mealand, D. L., 110, 154
Meecham, H. G., 20, 42, 72
Meeks, W. A., 65, 97
Menander Rhetor, 49
Metzger, B. M., 60-61, 118

Michel, O., 88, 93, 110, 177, 197, 210
Miller, J. C., 79, 91
Minear, P. S., 88, 92, 97
Mitchell, M. M., 39, 50, 58
Mitternacht, D., 14, 28, 50, 54, 73, 93
Moiser, J., 92
Moo, D. J., 240
Mosley, D. J., 50
Müller, M., 14, 22, 61, 98
Müller, W. G., 71
Mullins, T. Y., 1, 23, 28, 42, 48, 56-57, 63, 98
Munck, J., 89
Murphy-O'Connor, J., 14, 30, 95-96
Musonius Rufus, 124, 126, 129, 232
Myers, C. D., Jr., 88

N
Nanos, M. D., 14, 70, 89, 96, 100, 108, 113, 208
Nero, 95, 101
Neumann, H., 71
Nida, E. A., 179
Niebuhr, K.-W., 88, 111
Nolland, J., 225

Index of Names

Nygren, A., 183, 186, 214

O
Ollrog, W.-H., 66-69
Olson, S. N., 54-55
Olsson, B., 55
Origen, 198-99, 203, 208, 214
Ortkemper, F.-J., 52

P
Palmer, M. W., 118
Pardee, D., 18, 267
Paulus Orosius, 94
Pearson, B. W. R., 7, 73
Pedersen, S., 108
Penna, R., 95
Pfitzner, V. C., 59
Phalaris, 75
Philip of Macedonia, 49
Philo, 49, 126, 167, 197, 207, 214, 225, 228, 230
Plato, 62, 76, 135
Pliny, 15, 47, 62, 95, 133-142
Plutarch, 79, 81, 124, 126, 129, 134, 139-42, 197
Pohlenz, M., 155
Polybius, 197
Polycarpus, 62

Popkes, W., 26, 167, 171, 173, 186
Porter, C. L., 172
Porter, S. E., 7, 14, 30, 70, 73, 124, 154, 164, 207, 225, 228, 237
Poster, C., 63
Pseudo-Demetrius, 18, 50, 61, 71
Pseudo-Libanius, 18, 19, 49, 61, 71, 132
Ptolemy, 48
Purcell, N., 61
Pythagoras, 75

Q
Quintilian, 134

R
Rad, G. von, 198
Räisänen, H., 161, 195, 213, 235
Reasoner, M., 92, 98
Reed, J. T., 6, 10, 14, 17-20, 24, 28-29, 32, 36, 42, 47-48, 57, 59, 154
Reichert, A., 87, 89, 91, 96-97, 102, 107, 109, 176
Reiser, M., 7, 125
Reynolds, J., 201
Richards, E. R., 62-63, 73

Richardson, P., 96
Riesner, R., 93
Roberts, J. H., 29-41
Roller, O., 18-20, 32
Roosen, A., 70
Rowe, G. O., 14, 142
Russell, D. A., 14
Rutgers, L. V., 93, 96

S
Saake, H., 155
Salles, C., 71
Sampley, J. P., 67, 97
Sanday, W., 65, 69, 88, 110, 178, 186, 219
Sanders, E. P., 2-3, 88, 116, 213, 235
Sanders, J. T., 29, 41-42, 88
Sandnes, K. O., 34
Sass, G., 33
Schelkle, K. H., 184
Schlatter, A. von, 105
Schlier, H., 88, 93, 167, 178-79, 197, 201, 210, 214
Schmeller, T., 124-30, 156, 172, 186
Schmidt, H. W., 88, 188
Schmidt, P. L., 71
Schmithals, W., 61, 67, 97, 113, 156
Schneider, J., 13, 71

Schnider, F., 19, 25, 28-29, 33, 41, 56
Schrenk, G., 217
Schubert, P., 9, 27-29, 84
Schulz, S., 167
Scott, J. M., 35, 105, 108
Scroggs, R., 113
Segal, A. F., 1, 188
Seneca, 16, 19-20, 47, 73, 124-26, 129-31, 134-45
Sevenster, J. N., 135
Shackleton Bailey, D. R., 136
Sherk, R. K., 21, 33, 42, 49
Siegert, F., 110
Slingerland, D., 93-94
Smallwood, E. M., 93
Smiga, G., 53
Snodgrass, K. R., 1, 153-54, 163, 235, 240
Socratics, 62, 75
Spicq, C., 50
Stamps, D. L., 14
Stanley, C. D., 2, 14, 36, 54, 114, 116, 126, 162, 218, 219
Stegemann, . W., 88, 92,
Stendahl, K., 89

Stenger, W., 19, 25, 28-29, 33, 41, 56,
Stern, M., 201, 203
Stirewalt, M. L., Jr., 9, 16, 19-20, 39, 61, 72-83, 142
Stowers, S. K., 2-5, 14-18, 24, 61, 65, 70-73, 81, 87, 89, 97, 100, 110, 116, 118, 124-29, 140-48, 162, 167, 171, 181, 184-88, 193, 199, 208, 233-39
Stuhlmacher, P., 88, 92, 110, 186, 197, 208
Suetonius, 93-96, 134
Suhl, A., 89
Swearingen, C. J., 233
Sykutris, I., 71

T
Taatz, I., 24-25
Tacitus, 95, 101, 133
Tannenbaum, R., 201
Teles, 124, 126
Tellbe, M., 96, 100
Theobald, M., 88, 92, 166, 173
Thompson, R. W., 206
Thorsteinsson, R. M., 43, 44, 106
Thraede, K., 16, 18, 73, 82, 131

Thrall, M. E., 154
Thurén, L., 215
Tobin, T. H., 156, 221
Toit, A. B. Du, 14, 30, 41, 56
Tomson, P. J., 89, 92, 198
Trapp, M. B., 71, 124
Trobisch, D., 61
Trocmé, E., 214
Turner, N., 35, 154

V
Vander Broek, L. D., 7
Vielhauer, P., 88
Vos, J. S., 237

W
Wagner, J. R., 89, 96, 119, 219
Walters, J. C., 88, 92
Watson, F., 1, 88-92, 97, 103-9, 208
Wedderburn, A. J. M., 47, 79, 88, 92, 108, 171
Weima, J. A. D., 14, 18, 22, 27, 34, 41, 44, 56-65, 69, 74, 98
Weiss, B., 88, 178
Welles, C. B., 21, 48-51, 82
Wessel, B., 30
Westerholm, S., 228-29

Index of Names

White, J. L., 8, 13, 16-25, 29-32, 37, 41, 42, 47-48, 54, 56, 64, 71-74, 82, 125, 133, 145
Whitsett, C. G., 35, 89, 120
Wiefel, W., 88, 92, 93
Wilckens, U., 4, 41, 44, 88, 93, 118, 178, 183, 187, 197, 214
Williams, M. H., 96, 198
Williams, P. R., 88, 193
Winninge, M., 188
Wright, N. T., 1, 2, 3, 88, 92-93, 155-56, 163, 181, 197, 209, 220, 227
Wuellner, W., 14, 40, 70

X
Xenophon, 197

Y
Yinger, K. L., 156

Z
Zahn, T., 88, 110, 178, 188, 197, 205, 219
Zelzer, M., 71
Zetterholm, M., 224
Ziesler, J., 93

CONIECTANEA BIBLICA
NEW TESTAMENT SERIES

Present editors: Birger Olsson (Lund) and Kari Syreeni (Uppsala)

1. *Hartman, L.*: Prophecy Interpreted: The Formation of Some Jewish Apocalyptic Texts and of the Eschatological Discourse Mark 13 par. 1966.
2. *Gerhardsson, B.*: The Testing of God's Son (Matt 4:1–11 & Par): An Analysis of an Early Christian Midrash.
   Fasc. 1 (chapters 1–4). 1966.
   Fasc. 2 in preparation.
3. *Kieffer, R.*: Au delà des recensions? L'évolution de la tradition textuelle dans Jean VI, 52–71. 1968.
4. *Kieffer, R.*: Essais de méthodologie néo-testamentaire. 1972.
5. *Forkman, C.*: The Limits of the Religious Community: Expulsion from the Religious Community within the Qumran Sect, within Rabbinic Judaism, and within Primitive Christianity. 1972.
6. *Olsson, B.*: Structure and Meaning in the Fourth Gospel: A Text-Linguistic Analysis of John 2:1–11 and 4:1–42. 1974.
7. *Cavallin, H. C. C.*: Life After Death: Paul's Argument for the Resurrection of the Dead in 1 Cor 15.
   Part 1. An Enquiry into the Jewish Background. 1974.
   Part 2 in preparation.
8. *Caragounis, C.*: The Ephesian *Mysterion*: Meaning and Content. 1977.
9. *Fornberg, T.*: An Early Church in a Pluralistic Society: A Study of 2 Peter. 1977.
10. *Westerholm, S.*: Jesus and Scribal Authority. 1978.
11. *Holmberg, B.*: Paul and Power: The Structure of Authority in the Primitive Church as Reflected in the Pauline Epistles. 1978.
12. *Hartman, L.*: Asking for a Meaning: A Study of 1 Enoch 1–5. 1979.
13. *Hellholm, D.*: Das Visionenbuch des Hermas als Apokalypse: Formgeschichtliche und texttheoretische Studien zu einer literarischen Gattung.
    Band 1. Methodologische Vorüberlegungen und makrostrukturelle Textanalyse. 1980.
    Band 2. Gattungsbestimmung und Interpretation. In preparation.
14. *Franck, E.*: Revelation Taught: The Paraclete in the Gospel of John. 1985.
15. *Gerhardsson, B.*: The Gospel Tradition. 1986.
16. *Johansson, B. C.*: To All the Brethren: A Text-Linguistic and Rhetorical Approach to 1 Thessalonians. 1987.
17. *Enermalm-Ogawa, A.*: Un langage de prière juif en grec. Le témoignage des deux premiers livres des Maccabées. 1987.
18. *Hartman, L., and B. Olsson* (eds.): Aspects on the Johannine Literature: Papers Presented at a Conference of Scandinavian New Testament Exegetes at Uppsala, June 16-19, 1986. 1987.
19. *Strandenaes, T.*: Principles of Chinese Bible Translation as Expressed in Five Selected Versions of the New Testament and Exemplified by Mt 5:1–12 and Col 1. 1987.
20. *Portefaix, L.*: Sisters Rejoice: Paul's Letter to the Philippians and Luke-Acts as Seen by First Century Philippian Women. 1988.

21. *Übelacker, W. G.*: Der Hebräerbrief als Appell.
   1. Untersuchungen zu *exordium*, *narratio* und *postscriptum* (Hebr 1–2 und 13,22–25). 1989.
   2. Untersuchungen zu *argumentatio* und *peroratio* (3,1–13,21). In preparation.
22. *Ulfgard, H.*: Feast and Future: Revelation 7:9–17 and the Feast of Tabernacles. 1989.
23. *Christofferson, O.*: The Earnest Expectation of the Creature: The Flood-Tradition as Matrix of Romans 8:18–27. 1990.
24. *Byrskog, S.*: Jesus the Only Teacher: Didactic Authority and Transmission in Ancient Israel, Ancient Judaism and the Matthean Community. 1994.
25. *Lövestam, E.*: Jesus and 'This Generation': A New Testament Study. 1995.
26. *Winninge, M.*: Sinners and the Righteous: A Comparative Study of the Psalms of Solomon and Paul's Letters. 1995.
27. *Chow, S.*: The Sign of Jonah Reconsidered: A Study of Its Meaning in the Gospel Traditions. 1995.
28. *Holmstrand, J.*: Markers and Meaning in Paul: An Analysis of 1 Thessalonians, Philippians and Galatians. 1997.
29. *Eriksson, A.*: Traditions as Rhetorical Proof: Pauline Argumentation in 1 Corinthians. 1998.
30. *Mitternacht, D.*: Forum für Sprachlose: Eine kommunikationspsychologische und epistolär-rhetorische Untersuchung des Galaterbriefs. 1999.
31. *Hillert, S.*: Limited and Universal Salvation: A Text-Oriented and Hermeneutical Study of Two Perspectives in Paul. 2000.
32. *Svartvik, J.*: Mark and Mission: Mk 7:1–23 in Its Narrative and Historical Contexts. 2000.
33. *Starr, J. M.*: Sharers in Divine Nature: 2 Peter 1:4 in Its Hellenistic Context. 2000.
34. *Tellbe, M.*: Paul between Synagogue and State: Christians, Jews, and Civic Authorities in 1 Thessalonians, Romans, and Philippians. 2001.
35. *Larsson, T.*: God in the Fourth Gospel: A Hermeneutical Study of the History of Interpretations. 2001.
36. *Gerdmar, A.*: Rethinking the Judaism – Hellenism Dichotomy: A Historiographical Case Study of Second Peter and Jude. 2001.
37. *Runesson, A.*: The Origins of the Synagogue: A Socio-Historical Study. 2001.
38. *Kazen, Th.*: Jesus and Purity Halakhah: Was Jesus Indifferent to Impurity? 2002.
39. *Olsson, B., and M. Zetterholm* (eds.): The Ancient Synagogue From Its Origins until 200 C.E.: Papers Presented at an International Conference at Lund University, October 14–17, 2001. 2003.
40. *Thorsteinsson, R. M.*: Paul's Interlocutor in Romans 2: Function and Identity in the Context of Ancient Epistolography. 2003.

Distributed by:
Almqvist & Wiksell International
P.O. Box 7634
SE-103 94 STOCKHOLM
SWEDEN
Phone: +46 8 613 61 00
Fax: +46 8 24 25 43
E-mail: order@city.akademibokhandeln.se